BRASS BANDS
OF THE SALVATION ARMY

– their mission and music

STREETS PUBLISHERS
ENGLAND SG5 4AF

In Dedication

To the Men and Women I have had the privilege of leading
in the Salvation Army Student Fellowship Brass Band
of Asbury College and Asbury Theological Seminary

BRASS BANDS

BANDS

OF THE

SALVATION ARMY

Their Mission and Music
Volume One

Ronald W. Holz
Foreword by Ray Steadman-Allen

First published in 2006 by
Streets Publishers,
'Richmond', Poplar Drive, Stotfold, Hitchin, Herts. SG5 4AF
England

Copyright © 2006 Streets Publishers

ISBN: 978-0-9551988-4-7

Designed and Printed in England by
Streets Printers, Royston Road, Baldock, Herts SG7 6NW

Captions:

Above, New York Staff Band, January 1899, Bandmaster
Charles Anderson (second row, fourth from right).

Page i, The Fry Family

Page iii, Bandmaster Harry Appleby and
the Household Troops Band

CONTENTS

Foreword   Ray Steadman-Allen

Author's Preface

Acknowledgements

Introduction

Volume IA:
SA Bands and Their Early History, 1878-1939   Ronald W. Holz

Volume IB:
Regional and National Essays

Volume IC:
Assessing the Present and Projecting the Future   Ronald W. Holz

Projected Contents for
Brass Bands of The Salvation Army
Volume II
Musical Study (Ronald W. Holz)

Introduction

List of Musical Examples for Volume II

List of Illustrations – Facsimiles, Tables, and Appendices, Volumes I and II

List of Current Salvation Army Brass Band Publishers

Salvation Army Brass Band Music Tables

Selected and Annotated Discography

Bibliography for Volumes I and II

Index of Names and Musical Organizations, Volume II

FOREWORD

Lieut-Colonel (Dr) Ray Steadman-Allen
D.Mus, FTCL, FTCM, ARSM, FNCM, FCSM, FGMS.

I am delighted to be asked to write this foreword to Dr. Holz' valuable book. Ronald Holz comes from a legendary family in the Salvationist musical tradition. His father, onetime music director of the SA musical forces of the Eastern USA, was a pace setter; his innovative style influenced post World War II renewals and developments in a unique way. He was also encouraging to me at a difficult turning point. However, these introductory lines relate to the prodigious research work of the author and compiler of this symposium, who has been kind enough to acknowledge my own delving into SA history; this has been something of an obsession which has been an important element in my own doctorate. But from this book I have gathered a wealth of new and interesting material, even of what has occurred in my own country, so thorough have been Dr Holz' interviews and his securing of local documentation.

William Booth, founder of The Salvation Army, once declared *People seem to think I have said* 'I will have an Army and captains, and bands of music,' *but these things were not in my mind.* Of course not! Most Army innovations have evolved rather than have been planned on the drawing board. Those early-day bandsmen, some of them illiterate, could have had no idea of the international escalation of their music making, though with the eye of faith and brimming enthusiasm William Pearson wrote in 1882:

> *With a thousand bands and a thousand drums*
> *We will praise Lord in bright happy homes.*

They were unsophisticated days. *Blow and believe!* was often the watchword. But there were sensitive souls conditioned by quiet Victorian churches and chapels, who complained of the big drum perhaps understandably! Holz shares with us 'outside' criticisms of the unmusicality of the infant bands. It is important to an understanding of the use of Army music to be clear that aesthetic and cultural concerns were (and are) secondary. The intention was to make people take notice and listen to a gospel message.

Booth did not want performance as an end in itself, which in principle still pertains depending on the context. Even the most top-flight concerts are expected to contain an invocation and scripture reading. Beginnings were primitive, with street marching being aided by such instruments as violins, bells and huntsmen's horns; but as brass bands became established there were soon signs of improvement. With an enviably large and growing body of musicians it was inevitable that some of the more talented would seek and find lucrative returns, and an unquantifiable number of professionals have been, and are, usually happy to pay tribute to initial training and opportunities afforded by the movement.

At a mature age I have pleasantly conjured up personal memories of many former 'greats' mentioned in these pages. Bramwell Coles, as my first departmental head in the International Music Editorial Department, instructed me in the techniques of editorial practice and it was a thrill to handle manuscripts and documents by men like Slater and Hawkes.

I have a memory, well over fifty years ago, of playing on the piano to Arthur Goldsmith a newish band suite of mine, *The Bethlehem Story*. Even earlier, as a teenage office boy to General Evangeline Booth, I would listen with my peers outside the Staff Band room during lunchtime rehearsals. Perhaps the singling out of individuals is invidious, but Eric Ball and Erik Leidzén were giants who set levels of craftsmanship and commitment that leave one humbled. For these are all flesh and blood people who have left a heritage to be prized.

This leads me to add that there is an unsentimental but rich fellowship of SA band people with a consistent admission: once a bandsman, always a bandsman. Going further, to mention in parenthesis, that the term 'bandsman' does not signify gender though some prefer 'bandswoman.' By and large, and until comparatively recently, the British brass band world has been a somewhat male prerogative and the same has been true of SA bands except in wartime or in smaller bands. A healthier attitude now prevails but it was quite a barricade to be stormed. It does not seem to have been nearly as great a problem in the USA or European countries as it was in Great Britain and her Commonwealth nations where the SA flourished.

Reference is made more than once to administrative controls and regulations. Though regrettably these have too often been enforced insensitively, the first 'rules' were a sensible means of unification; their expansion was usually the result of experience and the foibles of human nature. As far as Britain is concerned the strong pull of the contest field and 'crack' bands could create tests of loyalty. One has the feeling that the establishment was occasionally just a little insecure, though I believe we have been right to avoid the competition element, aid to development though it can be. At the end of the day, because the Salvationist bandsman is, or claims to be, a Christian, the factor of motivation is fundamental. The 1915 Commission of Inquiry in London was a sincere exercise to discover thinking at all levels in order to produce policies that could keep first purposes in view whilst giving musicians their heads (well, almost!)

It is difficult to refer to the influence adverse criticism has had without introducing a somewhat discordant note. Balanced reviewing and the sharing of diverse views are, of course, a healthy part of evolution and development. Encouragement supports motivation and the sharp word, if truthful, can have its antiseptic value. Salvation Army musicians do not expect the reception of all they do to be sweetness and light. Human nature doesn't work that way. Newspaper editors are prone to feed the fires of controversy in the quest for sales figures.

The Army's in-house publications have regrettably sometimes indulged the cold-water-anti-band-brigade, which has, I believe, been an active means of discouragement. I once made an official representation about "pillorying people to peddle papers"! But I readily concede that there have been the many whose sympathetic pens have revealed understanding of and insights into the tremendous resource of a ministry of music and the commitments of its participants.

The heyday of brass banding in the SA saw an awesome aggregation of manpower, with families attached. One hopes that the negative, if well meaning, approaches of those in authority who minimize banding will realize the personnel losses beyond bandsmen themselves which are almost invariably the accompaniment to the disappearing band. Fortunately some aware areas have developed programs which are bearing fruit.

It is a curious phenomenon, in light of those who are unable to put any value on bands or to handle this resource, that in newly-opened areas (Russia, for example), there is a strong desire to have uniforms, a flag, and a brass band!

One last word on composing and arranging. The brass band has its obvious strengths but also its technical limitations. Range is but one. What I see as a remarkable phenomenon has been the steady stream of creative activity in which new voices appear within the movement, taking up old themes, and somehow finding in their problem-solving a stimulus to fresh expression. I must confess that in my own writing I have found this aspect enjoyable, and if what the Salvationist does and shares has not that element something has gone wrong.

I am glad to be introducing this book but I am also glad indeed that there is now such a book to be introduced. I know of only five official composer biographies and two or three books reviewing the historical progress of Salvationist music and musicians. There has, however, been a good deal of supplementary documentation, mainly in the form of personal-memoir articles and booklets produced by local band historians, generally for centenary and celebration occasions. The material gathered in these pages provides fascinating reading and leaves one with even greater admiration for the trailblazers and their deeds depicted within. The work goes on.

Many names are recorded in this book. We do not forget that what we read is but representative of innumerable unknowns who have laboured, often without much technique, but a ready willingness to be part of something bigger than themselves.

Lieut-Colonel (Dr.) *Ray Steadman-Allen* has been a guiding and leading figure in Salvation Army brass band culture for over 50 years. As one of its finest composers, he is considered by many to be the most gifted, prolific, and forward-looking talent within 20th-century SA music (and into the 21st!).

Over 200 instrumental and choral works of his have been printed by the SA, and with significant and major works still remaining in manuscript. As a long-standing editor and staff member, and later Editor-in-chief (1967-80) of the

*Lieut-Colonel
Dr. Ray Steadman-Allen*

International Music Editorial Department (London), his influence and contribution borders on the incalculable.

He has travelled all across the world as a guest conductor, performer, clinician, and speaker. Many consider him one of the most articulate spokesmen for the SA and especially for its music, both in extensive writings and in his public appearances. A mark of this came with his assignment to write an article on Salvation Army music for the new edition of the *Grove's Dictionary of Music and Musicians*. He is the author of a textbook *Colour and Texture in the Brass Band Score*.

In retirement he has maintained an active role as an arranger and composer, and he has been commissioned a whole series of test-pieces for the brass band contesting scene, including *The Beacons*, *Chorale*, *Seascapes*, and *Hymn at Sunrise*. He gained his B.Mus. degree at Durham University and is a Doctor in Music. With an FTCL (and Phillips Prize) he holds several honorary fellowships, is President of the National College of Music, and a vice president of the Brass Band Conductors' Association.

AUTHOR'S PREFACE

To understand a history, know about the historian. As the principal writer in this book on the mission and music of Salvation Army [SA] bands, I took on the task while continuing to be an active member of the SA, a Salvationist. I have been a commissioned bandmaster continuously since I was 16 years old, serving at the corps (Hartford Citadel, CT, 1965–1975), divisional (Divisional Music Director, Western Pennsylvania, and Massachusetts Division, 1975–1981), and national level (SASF Brass Band of Asbury College, 1981 to the present).

My father, the late Commissioner Richard E. Holz (1914–1986), was an important figure in SA music history within both the American and the international SA. I cannot remember a time in my life when I was not fully involved in some kind of SA music making. My doctoral dissertation examined in detailed manner aspects of SA band repertoire, and I have written three books that also dealt with aspects this subject. My travels have taken in a good portion of the Army world, and I have experienced nearly every kind of SA band activity. I seem to have taken on the role for the past 25 years of a chronicler and evaluator of SA music, whether in books, magazine articles, book and compact disc reviews, or compact disc booklets written for a wide range of brass bands.

Yet, who can claim to have a complete grasp of such a vast topic? I would be the first to admit that the more I learn, the more I find that I have only begun the task. This is why I am particularly honoured that Ray Steadman-Allen graciously consented to write the Foreword, for he has been our most gifted, innovative, and knowledgeable contributor to SA music, in the broadest sense of that category, within the last 60 years.

As the new millennium approached and I wrestled with shaping this book, I felt that Salvationists needed to take time to carefully review their musical past and think clearly and imaginatively about the future of SA musical ministry. I also thought that a resource was needed from which anyone interested in SA brass bands and their music could carry out further study. I hope these two volumes can provide some guidance in those pursuits.

Balancing the objective pursuit of the scholar with that of the committed 'soldier' has produced a fertile tension during the creative process that brought this book into being. My colleagues who joined me in this task, who became vulnerable enough to write essays they knew could only scratch the surface of their topic, shared this same experience. Caring for our denomination does not mean we cannot bring critical thought to bear upon it. This study is in no way an "Army" endeavor, it had no official sanction nor censure, though SA personnel have been generous in their support of the effort and in supplying data.

I am trained as a historical musicologist, not as a theologian. A theology of SA music is only beginning to emerge, and I make no claim to expertise in that area. That is not to say I have not enjoyed tackling a number of challenging issues where SA music and musical practice interact with the SA's theological traditions. The noun 'mission' has been placed first in the subtitle of this book because without their sacred 'mission' SA brass bands and their music could border on cultural absurdity.

The remarkable development of the musical skill of SA musicians and the sacred brass repertoire by SA composers and arrangers over a 128-year period must be examined within the context of the SA's role within the Christian church. My hope is that I have been able to strike that balance between mission and music within these admittedly limited pages.

June, 2006

About the Author: Ronald W. Holz, Ph.D., holds the rank of Professor of Music Literature and Instrumental Music at Asbury College, a 4-year Christian liberal-arts university located in central Kentucky. He and his wife, Dr. Beatrice Holz, joined the faculty there in 1981. At the college he has served as Chairman of the Division of Fine Arts from 1985–1991 and now coordinates the chamber music, composition/arranging, and music history curricula. Dr. Holz is the conductor of the Lexington Brass Band, the Salvation Army Student Fellowship Brass Band of Asbury College, and the Asbury College Orchestra. He is a noted music historian,

conductor, lecturer, and clinician, particularly in the fields of brass band and wind music. He has written several books in the area of band history, including *Erik Leidzén: Band Arranger and Composer* and a history of the New York Staff Band - *Heralds of Victory*. His graduate training in historical musicology was completed at the Cincinnati College-Conservatory of Music and the University of Connecticut. He has served two consecutive terms as President of the North American Brass Band Association [NABBA]. In addition, he held the position of Contest Controller in NABBA for a period of ten years. He edited NABBA's quarterly journal from 1992 to 1996, and for 11 years (1991–2002) wrote the compact disc and book review sections of the *Brass Band Bridge*, a task he took up again in 2005. He frequently writes liner notes for brass band compact discs by some of the world's finest brass bands, and contributes articles on a regular basis to a range of brass periodicals.

ACKNOWLEDGEMENTS

So many people have contributed to this extended project that I fear I am liable to have left individuals out who have had significant impact on its production, its content, or on the author's ideas and perspective. For the large majority not mentioned, for those who have provided much to me, I humbly ask their forgiveness and thank them for all they have done in helping me.

First and foremost, I thank the principal contributors to the book, including Warren Baas, John Cleary, W.L. (Wally) Court, and Torgny Hanson. They risked much in trying to distill into a very small space the great stories of SA bands in their region.

Each of these writers could equally have listed individuals who assisted them, like former Melbourne Staff Bandmaster Colin Woods, who graciously handed off the Australia chapter to John Cleary. Closely attached to this list would be Fred Creighton, (Toronto, Ontario) without whose excellent databases of SA publications this project would have been infinitely more difficult, if not impossible. His contribution to the *Brass Band Music Table* in Volume II and in a variety of other research questions has been invaluable.

Colonels Brindley Boon and Ray Steadman-Allen have provided me with invaluable help, encouragement, supportive data, and moral support. They provided the excellent, initial models of and vision for SA music history that I have hopefully carried on with integrity. Both of them loaned priceless materials and research that they had undertaken themselves, but had not yet used in print.

Asbury College has lent support to this book in the form of half-year sabbaticals in the spring of 1995 and 2003, and a further research grant in the spring of 1999. I am particularly grateful to Dr. Ray Whiteman, Provost, and the Faculty Development Committee. In addition, the Asbury College Library Staff has been most cooperative and helpful. One faculty colleague, Dr. Edward McKinley, noted SA historian, has always been generous with things he has found that he felt would be of benefit in my own work.

During three visits to the United Kingdom [1995, 1999, 2003], a host of individuals contributed to my research or provided me with much needed hospitality:

SA British Territory:
Music Ministries Unit Staff, including Trevor Davis, Stephen Cobb, Len Ballantine, Richard Phillips, Andrew Blyth, and Peter Ayling; SP&S, Ltd., including Lt. Colonel Michael Williams and Trevor Caffull; Heritage Centre, including Major Jenty Fairbanks and Gordon Taylor;

Salford University:
Dr. Roy Newsome, Dr. Peter Graham, Dr. David King; Dr. Newsome's help with the Mortimer Centre materials deserves special notice.

The Archives of Wright & Round, Gloucester:
Roger Thompson and Rachel Jones

Archives of the *British Bandsman*:
Peter Wilson, former editor, and staff.

Friends:
who helped me at various times during my visits: Geoffrey and Violet Brand, Peter and Janey Graham, Melvin James, Alan Jenkins and Robert Mulholland (*Brass Band World*), Bram and Margaret Gay, Geoff and Barbara Goldspink, Philip and Keitha Needham, Ray and Joy Steadman-Allen, John and Audrey Stubbings, The Thompson family of Castleford Corps; Phil Wall, David Wooton.

Most of the existing SA Territorial Music Departments contributed materials and surveys during the early stages of my work; specific individuals in this data-gathering phase are cited in Chapter 1. The five North American territorial music departments and archive centers have born the brunt of my many questions and requests for information or music:

Canada and Bermuda Territory:
Music Department--Brian Burditt and Len Ballantine; Heritage Centre and Archives--Fred Creighton

USA Central Territory:
Archives--Jan Odel, Flor Mofat; Music Department--William Himes, Peggy Thomas, Janey Mardis

USA Eastern Territory:
Music Department--Ronald Waiksnoris, Thomas Scheibner, Aaron Vanderweele, Kevin Norbury; Heritage Museum—Kathleen Bearcroft; Individuals--Lt. Colonel Thomas Mack, Michael Orfitelli, Major Richard Munn

USA Southern Territory:
Music Department--Richard Holz, Evelyn Pulkin

USA Western Territory:
Archives--Francis Dingman; Music Department—Ivor Bosanko and James Anderson; Individuals--Lambert Bittinger, Bob Doctor, Bill Gordon

I am grateful to Paul Bierley, noted Sousa scholar, for particular help and inspiration in a variety of matters.

John Street, Director of Egon Publishers, had the courage to go through with this project, so he deserves significant praise for bringing this work to fruition. In the production phase special credit must go to Egon editor, Wendy Hiles, music typesetter (Volume II) Simon Birkett, and technical support specialist Dave Watson of Streets Printers.

The support of SP&S, Ltd. (Trevor Caffull, Director) and USA music and trade secretaries in the initial marketing and promotion of the book is greatly appreciated, without which support this project would not have been completed.

Finally, three members of my immediate family have continually given me support throughout the eleven year period in which this book took shape and I make special mention of their contribution to the project: my wife, Beatrice; my son, Byron, and my brother, Dr. Richard Holz.

INTRODUCTION

Limits and Scope of the Study

My hope for this book is that it can serve as the starting point for anyone interested in Salvation Army bands and their music. This could include the scholar who wishes to pursue detailed research in the subject, the practicing Salvationist musician seeking a better understanding of their calling, or the general reader for whom the subject is of some interest. I can make no claim to providing a comprehensive study, but I hope that these two volumes[†] will provide the means for a better knowledge of this impressive, on-going sub-culture of Protestant church music.

Homage must be paid at this point to the past achievements of Brindley Boon, in particular his seminal history of SA bands, *Play the Music, Play*, and Ray Steadman-Allen, in his series of articles, *The Evolution of Salvation Army Music*. Both men, after the publication of these works in 1965, continued to provide large amounts of thoughtful writing and study concerning Army bands, their history, and their music. It is their foundational work that made this present volume possible.

Within the last 25 years various books dealing with the British-style brass band and its repertoire have contained single chapters about SA bands, including studies in Geoffrey and Violet Brand's *Brass Bands in the 20th Century*, Arthur R. Taylor's two comprehensive studies, and Cyril Bainbridge's *Brass Triumphant*. Alf Hailstone's social history of brass bands, *The British Bandsman Centenary Book*, was written in such a way that SA bands are tied into that history on a consistent basis. All of these works have been helpful to me in placing SA music within the context of the larger brass band scene.

A recent study of SA bands, their music, and their history has come from British musicologist Trevor Herbert in an excellent, concise chapter on SA bands, "God's Perfect Minstrels," within the larger volume *The British Brass Band: A Social History* (Oxford University Press, 2000). I have been grateful to have had access to his expert overview, especially from outside the denomination, for not a great deal of detailed, critical or scholarly literature has been written about SA bands and music since Steadman-Allen's and Boon's works mentioned above.

The exception to this has come in the form of several recent, and notable histories of specific SA bands, including Brindley Boon on the International Staff Band and my own work on The New York Staff Band. (See Bibliography, Volume II). SA periodicals that are primarily concerned with its music and musical mission, however, have abounded since the late 19th century and provide vast amounts of material that the scholar or student can spend a lifetime studying.

I did not feel it necessary to retell the entire history of The Salvation Army, or its forerunner from 1865 to 1878, The Christian Mission. Endnotes for each chapter and bibliography should point the keen reader to sources that would aid in that interest. Various summary Tables and Chronologies should also be of benefit in that regard.

Primary source documents are provided whenever possible. The sheer quantity of general information written about SA music and musicians from its earliest days to the present makes it imperative that this book presents a concentrated distillation of the important issues and events that have shaped SA musical culture. The quotations provided at the head of each chapter have been chosen to reveal an underlying philosophy, perhaps even a theology, of SA music that, while never officially made systematic, can still be seen to be the driving ideas behind current efforts. The emphasis on quotations from William Booth, the SA's founder, is intentional. It will reveal him to be both autocrat and visionary, one who gradually became more and more convinced of the power of band music for the extension of the Army's evangelical mission.

A great deal of the documentation and commentary is found in early SA propaganda-like periodicals. While the SA did not dwell on its defeats, there is enough balance available in personal writings, and in the outside band press to put matters in a better perspective. Reinterpreting the past can be a dangerous endeavour.

The two primary emphases in this study, the mission and music of SA brass bands, have been placed in both an historical context and in terms of the current and future relevance of each within the worldwide SA as it faces new challenges of the 21st century. Volume I divides into three basic parts. Volume I(A) provides a broad introduction to SA bands and music published for them, followed by two chapters that trace historical developments within the first six decades (1878–1939). The scope is broad, and not intended to be comprehensive. The Chronological Table of Important Events in SA Music and Music Publications 1878–2004 allows the reader an encapsulation of that discussion, as well as a summary of later developments in the 'modern', or post-World-War II era. Salvationists may find Chapter 1, *Function and Organisational Structure*, rather elementary, yet they may also find a review of this material helpful despite what may be to them rather obvious facts.

Volume I(B) offers six individual essays on the history and current state of brass bands within selected regions of the Army's worldwide work. No doubt other countries or regions might have been included. After all, the SA has work within 111 countries (SA 2005 *Yearbook*) and uses 175 languages in that work. A very good portion of this world wide SA contains some kind of brass band activity.

The end result of trying to discuss every aspect of SA banding would have exceeded our production limits and may have only served up redundant patterns. A bias towards the English-speaking territories is apparent, and perhaps unavoidable. The one chapter on Sweden shows how rich and needful further study in other Army territories can be, even if language and cultural barriers are somewhat constraining.

In Volume I(C) I hoped to bring various world wide concerns, challenges, and hopes for the future into focus so that the reader would not be hearing the same stories over and over again from the various writers without some kind of final synthesis. With the postponement of these volumes' release, an Epilogue was able to be added in which the 2000 International Congress in Atlanta, GA, is studied as a time capsule. Here we can view what is current and officially sanctioned SA musical practice, including that of several excellent brass bands.

My colleagues who joined me in this task did so by taking the risk that they would probably offend many in their region because space and length limitations meant many individuals, bands, and events would be left out. Please do not hold them accountable; they have achieved much within very narrow limits. For every bandmaster or band they or I mention, there are a dozen that must be left out! Likewise, the book is not entirely gender sensitive, terms like bandsman or bandsmen being used, rather than band member, particularly as these were the terms of historical use. The whole issue of the gradual inclusion of females into SA bands is one that could not be given justice within these pages, and will have to await a future, and much needed, study. John Cleary does supply in his chapter on Australia a representative starting point for such work.

Volume II (to be published at a later date) takes the form of more technical study of SA band instrumentation, scoring, repertoire, and supportive documents. The repertoire study is divided into three broad categories in four chapters according to function and style: 1) the short attention-getting piece, ranging from marches to festival arrangements; 2) more reflective music designed for use in worship and evangelism; 3) large-scale concert or 'festival" works. The pieces selected are representative only, and are not necessarily chosen as the finest of their kind. Indeed, one could have discussed the development of SA brass repertoire by using only a handful of composers, but I rather chose to highlight as many of the leading figures in the modern era as possible. The discussion does make reference to many works, though specific analysis had to be restricted to a limited number of pieces.

Within this musical study of the post World War II era I have tried to relate the development of the musical repertoire to the general history of the bands themselves within that same time period.

Analysis in and of itself provides no real insight. What theoretical study has been included was designed to show more than technical means chosen and problems solved. By showing the formal aspects of SA band music we gain an understanding of the motivation behind the arrangers, as well as an appreciation of how their craft aided in communicating the intended spiritual message of the Christian Gospel. Such analysis should also aid the developing music leader in their preparation and interpretation of this music. I have relied on material from my doctoral dissertation and other writings in recent years, but hopefully revised in an appropriate way for these final chapters. The privilege of writing CD notes for some of the world's finest brass bands has aided me as well, and I make no apology in using some of my material from those booklets.

The reader may complain that the broad historical overview in Volume I only covers SA band history up until World War II. Discussion in some of the regional chapters helps overcome that gap, as do the chapters in Volume II on musical repertoire since 1940. By World War II nearly every aspect of SA banding activity and musical form had made at least a beginning appearance and a pattern for further development and expansion set.

Definitions

While The Salvation Army is one of the most recognized 'charitable, faith-based' organizations, the general public rarely has a clear idea of exactly how the denomination explains itself. The international mission statement of the SA is unequivocal in that regard:

> *The Salvation Army, an international movement, is an evangelical part of the universal Christian Church. Its message is based on the Bible. Its ministry is motivated by love of God. Its mission is to preach the gospel of*

Jesus Christ and meet human needs in his name without discrimination.[1]

The brass bands of the SA have been formed primarily to help spread the biblical message of salvation from sin through the redemptive power and grace of Jesus Christ. How these bands went and still go about assisting in this mission is explained in more detail in Chapter 1, *Function and Organizational Structure*.

A Salvation Army band has been traditionally defined as *a company of not fewer than four Salvationists who work together, in accordance with orders and regulations, to further the purposes of The Salvation Army by means of instrumental music.*[2] While all sorts of instrumental combinations have thrived within that broad definition, brass and percussion ensembles formed using the instrumentation of the British-style brass band are the focus of this study. Similarly, while the SA has sponsored many kinds of instrumental groups under the broad title of 'bands' (in early days everything from drum-and-fife bands to concertina bands or, at present, 'contemporary praise-and-worship' groups), this study is restricted to this same brass band tradition and the music published for such combinations. These range from band journals requiring as few as four players to the full *Festival Series*.

Just what is 'Salvation Army' music has been open to question from time to time. Steadman-Allen wrestled with this at the outset of his *Evolution* series: *In a sense there is no such thing as Army music recognizable by definition: it is rather a matter of spirit and association...[it is] a kind of folk music shaped by functional trend and enriched by personal characteristic.*[3] That was written in 1965. A generation later, a Salvationist who is a trained historical musicologist can more arbitrarily assert that Salvation Army band music is music written almost exclusively by members of the SA and published by the SA for its brass bands for the furtherance of the Army's mission. The category is more utilitarian, and yet does embrace a significant body of music numbering well over 7,000 individual items. No doubt what has been composed for SA bands can be placed in many different cubbyholes, just like the sacred music of J.S. Bach can be examined as being German, Baroque, Protestant, Lutheran, according to the convenience of the scholar. What is impressive to note is that the vast majority of band compositions in this repertoire have been and are still being written by members of the SA for the specific use of its bands.

The further you go in SA music history the more the tune and song sources of this band music become more exclusively 'Army.' Pinning down what is different about SA hymnody or song from any other Protestant denomination of the same period can be a daunting task that is beyond the scope of this study.

Recent developments are beginning to cloud this issue of, 'what is SA band music?'. The sale of SA brass music to bands outside the denomination, and, at least in some SA territories, the relaxing of regulations that kept SA bands from playing music other than that published by the SA, contribute to that lack of clarity. This becomes more apparent when you realize that SA music publishing departments are now releasing music designed specifically for brass band contests as well as music with a more secular slant, though there seems to be an effort to keep a vaguely sacred aspect to the effort.[4]

Chapter 1 provides working definitions for many SA terms that will recur frequently in the book, from types of bands to aspects of the Army's quasi-military structure. The extensive bibliography and tables of music and publishers provided in Volume II should point the interested reader to sources that specialize in other aspects of SA structure, history, and mission.

From an historiographic perspective, the author prefers to use the date of the publication of a work, when the work became generally available, as the more important, rather than when the work may have been composed or played in manuscript by one band. Where the latter is of more than passing significance, this is pointed out either in the body of the text or in an endnote.

This study was first completed by December 1999. In essence, therefore, we ended our work with the turn of the Millennium. Since that date the manuscript has gone through several revisions whilst awaiting publication. Each writer has made a diligent effort to bring their portion as up-to-date as possible (as of June 2006), bearing in mind that the writing of a history, especially recent history, is never complete. We ask our readers to give us the benefit of the doubt concerning new data that may not have been available to us.

Notes

1. *The Salvation Army Yearbook* 1998, iii.

2. SA *O&R*, 1961, p. 5.

3. Ray Steadman-Allen, "Evolution of Salvation Army Music" [*Evolution*], *The Musician* (UK), June 19, 1965, p. 390.

4. The 1999 release of Joseph Turrin's *Hymn for Diana* (the late Princess of Wales) by the Eastern Territory USA would be representative of such a 'borderline' work. Mr. Turrin is a good friend of the SA, but not a member. His work is certainly reflective and moving, but it is not directly connected to the evangelical mission of SA bands.

† *Brass Bands of The Salvation Army, Volume 2* is due to be published at a later date.

Chapter 1

FUNCTION AND ORGANISATIONAL STRUCTURE

Ronald W. Holz

As to our Brass Bands, The Founder was keen and wise enough to perceive their value as revealed by facts. Although he did not personally gain much pleasure or help from them in his meetings. He never used a Brass Band in his meetings but to accompany singing, although in the latter part of his life he permitted them to play while audiences assembled, but then only from a list of pieces made out by the Music Dept. at his request, of Salvation music such as would be in place in a Sunday night's meeting. Richard Slater, from an unpublished manuscript, *The History of Salvation Army Music, Part II: Instrumental Music,* p22.

Types of Bands and Membership in a Salvation Army Band

The most typical and most numerous Salvation Army brass band is found at the local worship centre level, what for years has been called the Corps, later Corps Community centre, and more recently in some portions of the world, Community Worship and Service centre. In the earliest days of corps growth these centres were numbered according to the order in which they started, thus New York

1, Oslo 3. Soon, larger corps received more exalted status by being labelled a citadel, temple, or even tabernacle: Montreal Citadel Corps Band, Cleveland Temple Corps Band, Hollywood Tabernacle Corps Band. Most corps developed not only adult, or Senior bands, but also youth, or Junior bands. Membership is derived from local senior or junior soldiers, lay people who have been 'sworn in' as saved or regenerate participants in the mission of the corps. Officers, ordained clergy, may also participate.

In recent years more flexibility is being allowed in some territories so that musicians attracted to the Army, but who are not yet soldiers, may still participate in musical ministry for a stipulated period of time while they are deciding upon a full-time commitment to such Christian service.

The most recent editions of various territorial *Orders and Regulations* [*O&R*] still list somewhat exacting criteria for SA musicians, the most important one being that they are enrolled as soldiers within The Salvation Army. This means that they are in full support of the sacred mission and doctrine of the SA, acknowledging this in a number of regular behaviours, including the wearing of uniform. Participation within a divisional, territorial, or staff band (See below) usually requires active status in a local corps band, along with an endorsement by the corps commanding officer and corps bandmaster.

Participation on the corps level has always been a volunteer, altruistic endeavour. SA musicians, with the exception of professional music directors at the divisional or territorial level, receive no payment for their services. Indeed, they are required to support their band via a modest donation of band dues. Even the leadership is held to this standard. In the USA and a few other territories several community worship centres have recently begun to hire a director of music who oversees and administers the music ministry at the local level. At the moment, such a professional position is the rare exception, rather than the rule throughout the international SA.

Bands are administered via a series of guidelines and broad principles laid down in *O&R* issued at the territorial level, or in the case of the USA, for instance, shared nationally by all four territories. These documents delineate the chain of command within a corps, how soldiers become band members, and how leadership is chosen.

The various duties of band officers are spelled out in some detail. Thus, the corps commanding officer, the ordained pastor of the corps appointed by headquarters, 'commissions' the leadership, the bandmaster or principal local officer, and, upon recommendation of the bandmaster as to their musical and spiritual fitness, individual band members.

Bands may organise themselves by establishing a band board made up of commissioned local officers as follows: Bandmaster, Deputy Bandmaster (assistant leader), Band Sergeant (chaplain), Secretary (correspondence and finance), Librarian, Quartermaster (equipment), and Colour Sergeant (in charge of flags). Of course, only larger ensembles would have boards of this size or complexity. These local officers are held to an even higher standard of conduct, as detailed in *Orders and Regulations for Local Officers* that a territory or region maintains.

Above the corps or local level, the SA forms bands at the divisional, and, in some locations, the territorial level. Later in this chapter more attention is given to the full administrative structure of SA music.

At this point it is important to note that the Divisional Commander, the leading officer (clergy) within a division, frequently forms divisional bands (senior or youth). These are structured to assist evangelistic efforts and division-wide gatherings within the region as well as fund-raising and public relations activities.

Equally important, they provide a fellowship opportunity for corps musicians who rarely have the chance to play in larger, more proficient groups. For example, when the author was a professional Divisional Music Director in the Massachusetts Division (USA East), he directed three area senior bands and a divisional youth band within that state: Western Massachusetts Regional Band, Merrimack Valley Brass (Northeast of Boston), Southeast Regional Band and the Massachusetts Youth Band.

From the very beginning of SA bands, ensembles have

been formed at the headquarters level, usually territorial headquarters, for the purpose of providing an outstanding model that local bands could emulate, as well as providing that region with effective support for fund-raising, evangelical, and promotional endeavours. In the process, many members of these 'staff' bands took on local leadership at the corps level, as they were receiving the best musical training available at the time. The term Staff Band used to refer to a group made up of officers and soldiers who actually worked at the headquarters in a wide variety of positions.

In recent years these Staff Bands are more likely to be a composite grouping of area corps band members of outstanding skill who have the time and energy to pursue further musical work beyond their corps involvement. Being an employee or appointed officer is no longer a criteria for membership.

Currently, the active Staff Bands are as follows: Amsterdam Staff Band (Netherlands), Canadian Staff Band (Toronto, THQ), Chicago Staff Band (USA Central), German Staff Band (Cologne, THQ), International Staff Band (London, THQ), Melbourne Staff Band (Australia Southern), New York Staff Band (USA East), and the Japan Staff Band.

In addition, territorial bands are frequently formed for special occasions, or on an intermittent basis. The most recently successful example would be the Southern Territorial Band, which meets on average three to four times a year for concentrated campaigns and which draws its membership from outstanding musicians from every division within the Southern Territory, USA.

Beyond the basic three-tiered system of corps–division–territory, bands have been formed at nearly every conceivable centre of SA activity. Wherever the SA had a work, it could form a band: orphanages, prisons, boys' clubs, hospitals, boy scout troops, Adult Rehabilitation centres (formerly called Men's or Women's Social Service centres). Bands were even formed within special departments at the headquarters level. Several famous examples included Salvationist Publishing & Supplies Band (London) and the Rosehill Band (London), the latter a spin-off band formed in

The International Staff Band of The Salvation Army (Bandmaster Stephen Cobb).

The New York Staff Band (Bandmaster Ronald Waiksnoris).

*The Canadian Staff Band.
(Bandmaster Kevin Hayward),
December 2005.*

The Chicago Staff Band (Bandmaster William Himes).

The Melbourne Staff Band, Australia, playing in the grounds of Buckingham Palace.

The Amsterdam Staff Band (Bandmaster Howard Evans).

The German Staff Band (Bandmaster Heinrich Schmidt).

The Japan Staff Band (Bandmaster Hajime Suzuki).

connection with an Army-based insurance firm's band, The Salvation Army Assurance Society Band, as well as certain members of The International Staff Band. Sometimes they were organised by gender—women's bands, boys' bands, girls' bands. Recently, Fellowship Bands, or Reservist Bands, are becoming popular, bands which are formed by older, frequently retired, band members who still have a desire to make good music.

What do SA Bands do and why?

Three primary functions for SA bands continue to be emphasised by formal *Orders and Regulations* by which bands are administered:

1) *Attracting people to the meetings. In this case the brass band has great advantages. Out of doors, it can readily operate in any part of the district, and its pleasing strains, reaching farther than the human voice or than most other instruments, will draw many within earshot of the Army's message, and often lead to their salvation.*

2) *Accompanying the singing, and thereby helping and enriching it.*

3) *Conveying, by association of ideas, salvation messages direct to the hearts of the hearers. This is likely to take place when tunes or selections are wisely chosen...*[1]

In a typical SA worship service the brass band serves not only by accompanying congregational singing but also by presenting musical items of relevance to the sermon topic or general worship emphasis.[2] SA worship services in which bands participate can be divided into three principal categories:

1) The Open-Air: The sole purpose of this meeting is evangelical outreach. The meeting is held outside the worship centre—or corps—usually on the street corner, in a shopping mall, or at a housing project. By this means, the organisation takes its 'portable organ' (the band) and the Gospel to the unconverted. Bands frequently divide into smaller ensembles to carry on

more informal evangelism and outreach in the form of visitation to nursing homes, prisons, even to sick members of the corps, neighbourhood, or community.

2) The Sunday Services: These are divided into two main categories: the morning service, traditionally called the Holiness Meeting, designed primarily for Christian believers, especially the soldiers (lay members) of the corps, and the evening service, traditionally called the Salvation Meeting, designed primarily to reach unbelievers who may have been attracted inside the corps hall as a result of an Open-Air Meeting. An additional and less frequent type, called a Praise Meeting, often combines qualities of both Holiness and Salvation Meetings, as well as a few aspects of Music Festivals. Praise Meetings may take place either on Sunday (usually in the afternoon) or on a weekday evening.[3]

3) The Music Festival: While primarily evangelical and sacred in nature, the Festival allows music groups in a corps further opportunities for musical performance. Festival is the SA term for concert.

Bands also assist the organisation with fund-raising activities as well as public relations efforts. Such activities do not directly fall within the above-listed categories. SA bands have additionally played significant roles in civic and patriotic events within their communities, the SA always seeing these, however, as an additional opportunity for ministry.

The SA has maintained throughout its history a careful control over the use of music in its worship services and concerts, primarily through (until recently) a stringent policy that restricted the use of band music to that which was published by the organisation according to the guidelines set by the Army's administration.

An understanding not only of Army worship forms and practices but also of the Army's publishing and administrative policies is basic to an understanding of the history of SA bands, as well as the development of musical forms by composers of this denomination within the 20th century. It is not surprising to find that such an autocratic and militaristic institution has placed restrictions on the musical styles and forms it finds useful as adjuncts to corporate worship.

Unaffected until recently by the whims of outside music publishers or quickly changing church music styles during this century, the SA has, in spite and perhaps because of these very restrictions, developed a rich, artistically and spiritually consistent repertoire for its brass bands. That achievement can be considered one of the major achievements within Protestant instrumental music of the last two centuries.

Congregational Singing

As one of the primary responsibilities of SA bands is to accompany congregational singing, it is not surprising, therefore, to find that the Army's hymn and song literature is the basis of all its instrumental music. All SA brass music does make reference in the course of development to a hymn or song text through complete or partial quote of a melody associated with that text. Only classical transcriptions and certain rarities in the *Festival Series* are exceptions from this policy.

The first twenty years of published band music in the SA, 1883–1902, consisted solely of hymn tunes, Gospel songs, and transcriptions of vocal works from the organisation's principal vocal publications, primarily *The Musical Salvationist* [MS]. This was a direct order of the Army's founder, General William Booth. It was intended to limit musical performance to those items with a clear message, or textual basis. SA music is, therefore, referential music, music that refers the listener beyond the notes to spiritual ideas and concepts.

The current English language *Song Book of The Salvation Army* (1987; Revised edition) contains 962 songs and 251 choruses, words only, the exception being in the American-Canadian edition which contains a *Supplement* with 30 songs with music, 2 with text only.[4] This *Song Book* functions in English-speaking countries as the official congregational hymnal. The brass band accompaniments for these texts are printed in the *Band Tune Book,* which is divided into two spiral bound books containing 871 tunes; book 1, 1–500; book 2, 501–871, plus in the North American edition the *American-Canadian Supplement* containing 30 additional tunes. The keyboard edition, *The Salvation Army Tune Book* contains the music for the same 871 tunes as the *Band Tune Book*, plus music for the 251 choruses. The congregation usually sees only words. To a Salvationist, therefore, a 'song', generally speaking, refers to the text only and the term 'hymn tune' refers to the melody associated with a particular song. Each entry in the congregational *Song Book* will cite several different melodies or hymn tunes to which the song may be sung, an important fact to be remembered when discussing instrumental forms based on these melodies.

The *Song Book* has had and continues to have a vibrant history of growth and change. The first official full-size congregational song book, entitled *Salvation Army Songs*, was printed in 1899 along with the release of a companion instrumental tune book entitled *Band Music No. 1.* [See Chapter 2 for congregational song publications that pre-date this effort].

Three further editions of these primary sources have been issued in this century, the first 1928-31, the second, in 1953 (with supplementary *Tune Books* released in 1963 and 1978), and the third in 1987. The International Music Council (see below, this chapter) had on its agenda for the past few years the matter of once again revising the *Song Book*, and a new edition can probably be expected by the second decade of the 21st century.

In between editions of a *Song Book*, new congregational songs are released intermittently in such periodicals as *The War Cry*, the choral journal *Sing to the Lord* (formerly *The Musical Salvationist*), or gleaned from a host of other outside Christian publishers.

The fast-changing nature of Salvationist worship, as it embraces many contemporary 'praise-and-worship' songs and choruses, has led several territories to supply effective brass band accompaniment series. The most notable of these are the *Hallelujah Choruses* produced by the Norridge Citadel Band, USA Central, and the United

Kingdom's series of *Scripture-based Songs*.[5] New hymn tunes have also been introduced within the *General Series* or *Triumph Series* band journals. The vitality of this hymn tune repertoire, which gives a band access to over 1000 hymn tunes for the accompanying of congregational singing, each playable by 4 or more brass players, has been one of the inner strengths of the Army's band music. While a majority of tunes are derived from standard Western church repertoire or Gospel song tradition, with each successive edition, a larger number of them are the original work of composers and poets who are or have been members of the SA.

Open-Air and Indoor Worship Services

As the SA enters the 21st century its modes of worship are undergoing significant, even radical change. Within the past 20 years Open-Airs have become rare in many parts of the SA world. The traditional bifurcation between Holiness and Salvation Meetings is also becoming blurred, or changed, with many corps having to adjust their times for and styles of worship in ways that can still attract people to the Army hall.

In order to understand, however, the broad history of SA banding discussed later in this book, a more detailed look at the traditional types of services in which bands have been called upon to participate is essential.

William Booth began his Christian movement, or mission, in 1865 in an effort to reach the unconverted and the socially outcast within Victorian England. Booth's message stressed 'Redemption for all through Jesus Christ'. His meetings avoided liturgical forms, and mainly followed the shape of the Wesleyan style song-service:

> Song, Testimony/Scripture, Reading, Prayer, Song, Testimony/Scripture, Song/Collection, Vocal Solo, Bible Address, Invitation/Invitational Song, Dismissal/Benediction.

Those traditional church sacraments which were part of early Army meetings were eventually discontinued. The Open-Air meeting served to attract outsiders to the two main indoor services on Sunday, and, in early eras, on

Typical Open-Air scene with SA Band and children; Hull East (UK) Corps Band, 1960s.

multiple weeknights. Neither the Open-Air, the freest of SA services in which the band essentially makes loud, entertaining sounds in order to attract attention and maintain interest, nor the indoor services followed any organisational plan at first. This is somewhat the case even in present-day meetings, except that certain practices have now, after six generations, become fixed in the generally non-liturgical 'liturgy' or format of Army meetings.

General Frederick Coutts (General 1963–1969) explained this unstructured approach to worship in an essay on SA meetings. *No one is more free to be led of the Spirit than he who is responsible for conducting a Salvation Army meeting. There is no liturgy which he must follow (In Good Company*, p133). Officers are cautioned to pursue careful coordination of any music and song with the general tenor of the service. For years, however, the only basic requirements for an Army meeting, aspects that should, or must be present, were a prayer, a bible reading, personal testimony, congregational singing, and a Bible address. (*Orders and Regulations for SA Officers*, Part 2, Chapter 3, p45).

Years ago, Fred Brown once gave a clear, official clarification of the difference between the two principal

Sunday worship services in his book *The Salvationist at Worship:*

The morning gathering [Holiness Meeting], *primarily for Salvationists and adherents (though it is still a public meeting), could be called a holy community service. Not that the people who attend preen themselves with a 'holier than thou' look upon their faces, but their motive is the worship of God and the sincere wish to learn more of scriptural holiness. They assemble, not because they imagine themselves righteous, but because they want to offer to Almighty God the sacrifice of their love and thanksgiving.*

The night meeting [Salvation Meeting] *is for the proclamation of salvation to the unconverted, nothing more and certainly nothing less. Self-evidently the two meetings should be completely different in character: broadly speaking, one is for saints, the other for sinners; one devotional (even sacramental), the other evangelical; one deepens faith, the other seeks to communicate it; one is for the offering of worship to God; the other for the offering by the same worshippers of Christ to the people.*[6]

The brass band participates in the Open-Air, Salvation Meeting, and intermittent Praise Meetings not only by accompanying the singing but also by providing separate instrumental musical items of a direct, familiar nature to aid in the corporate worship.

In the Holiness Meeting of the not too distant past, if the band was permitted to participate other than in a prelude and by accompanying the songs, the music chosen was usually of a more devotional, meditative, and thought-provoking nature. More recently, many territories have provided broader guidelines in their *O&R* allowing for fuller participation by music sections in the Sunday AM service.[7]

Illustrations 1 and 2 [Appearing at the end of this chapter] provide outlines of two sample meetings held on the same day in the Atlanta (Georgia, USA) Temple Corps, November 23, 1980 during a special anniversary weekend at that centre. Despite the special nature of the day, the order of service exhibited in these examples would be standard, with few exceptions, to almost any Army worship meeting. The band provided prelude music, accompanied the songs, and offered one individual item during the service.

In this particular case, in the Holiness Meeting the band provided a hymn tune arrangement *St Columba*, arranged by Keith Griffin (GS 1621), associated with a textual paraphrase of the 23rd Psalm. In the Salvation Meeting the band played a hymn tune arrangement by Kenneth Elloway of the well-known church hymn *Now Thank We All Our God* (GS 1537–1), appropriate both for the season of the year and the celebration at the corps.

Notable in the Salvation Meeting are the personal 'testimonies' by members of the congregation and, in this particular instance, a public ceremony – almost a 'sacrament' – the enrollment of junior and senior soldiers into the ranks of the SA.

Many corps do not print weekly bulletins, for economic reasons, pointing out the necessity of clear communication during these services between the officer (clergy) or local officers (bandmaster, songster leader, etc.) and the congregation. It is the responsibility of the bandmaster to refer the congregation to the *Song Book* number of a text under portrayal in the band piece prior to its presentation.

One cannot assume anymore that people know the words, or the tunes! Meeting repertoire might range from sprightly marches and short, up-tempo song arrangements, selections (works incorporating two or more hymns related in subject matter), and hymn meditations/arrangements (using one tune associated with one text), to name the principal forms.

The Music Festival

In addition to providing music for specific worship or evangelical outreach, Army bands are given the opportunity for performance within the format of the music festival. This is the Army's compromise between the sacred and the secular, between entertainment and proselytising. Various kinds of music may be included in a festival, from the most advanced, lengthy works of either original or classic origin to simple vocal and instrumental solos. For many years the only restrictions that applied were:

1. Each festival must include, in addition to music, an opening congregational song, an invocation, a scripture reading, a brief 'Salvation' address, and a benediction.

2. All music performed must be published by The Salvation Army or, in the case of 'outside' material, must receive the prior sanction of the appropriate branch of Army administration.

3. Each festival must include vocal music to ensure the communication of words, even though the festival may be intended to feature the band alone.

4. No deviations are allowed from the approved, printed programme [No encores!].[8]

Illustrations 3 through 7 contain various festival programmes representing a century of such events within the SA. Illustration 3 is a reprinted list of items performed by the combined Regent Hall and Wood Green Corps [UK]

The International Staff Band of The Salvation Army takes centre stage at a Music Festival in The Royal Albert Hall, London.

Bands, December 15, 1898. The variety of items is remarkable, though the programme exhibits a careful use of Army vocal and instrumental music, even in the second massive programme.

Illustration 4 cites an earlier programme, dated August 5, 1898, from the Brass Band Holiday at the Alexandra Palace with over 500 band members participating. Illustration 5 lists a programme, one of three, used by the New York Staff Band during a May 27–June 2, 1937 tour of New York, Pennsylvania, and Ontario. Included are more sophisticated items available by this time for bands, such as lengthy meditations, festival marches, instrumental solo features, and vocal items.

The target audience of a festival greatly affects the type of programme that is formed. Illustration 6 is from an evangelical Brass and Vocal Festival presented by the Cambridge Citadel (Massachusetts, USA) Band and Songsters as part of the City of Boston's First Night Celebrations, December 31, 1978. In this festival the musical items, particularly those of the band, reflect hymn material generally recognisable at that time by the average American citizen.

Finally, Illustration 7, the Gala Concert presented by the Chicago Staff Band at the 1999 conference of the North American Brass Band Association Championships. This list shows that while recent practice allows for greater flexibility, including the performance of test pieces – *Purcell Variations* (though from the pen of a Salvationist!) and demanding secular concert material – the Ellerby *Tuba Concerto* played by a leading non-Salvationist musician, most of the essentials are still there. The band sang at least one item and scripture was read (though not shown in the programme). Bandmaster William Himes shaped a programme that catered to the needs of the special audience, while still sending forth a Christian message.

Festivals are given all kinds of formats, styles, themes, etc., from composers' festivals to holiday concerts. The activity allows for advanced musical expression coupled with a continued affirmation of the movement's evangelical goals. The participants broaden their musical education by the widened range of the repertoire, which can include large numbers of classical transcriptions or adaptations, both vocal and instrumental. There is no attempt to compete with professional or 'outside' musical performances, although the proficiency of several SA ensembles can place them on a par with all but the very finest professional groups.

Music Publishing

The decade of the 1990s can already be viewed as one of the most important periods in the history of SA music publishing. In 1991 the international SA emerged from over 100 years of isolation and decided to allow the sale of all its music, particularly band music, to bands outside the organisation.

Some vocal music released by International Headquarters [IHQ] had already been available to the general public and other territories that were producing band music had already been marketing their journals beyond the Army.

The new policy established in principle what had been essentially the *modus operandi* for decades, for each territory was told to monitor the sale and marketing of band music at 'territorial discretion'. Significantly, however, in many territories SA bands were still not allowed to use the music of outside publishers nor even SA band music from outside that territory.

Fast on the heels of this monumental and controversial decision came the reorganisation of the British Territory (1992). Within the next few years the formerly named International Music Editorial Department [IMED] became part of the Territorial Music Department of the United Kingdom Territory (with the Republic of Ireland). While the title "International" had been in use for nearly a century, whether officially or otherwise, the return to a territorial command clarified the fact that this department had always seen itself as primarily serving the bands of the United Kingdom (still approximately 70% of their target market).

By 1999 this department was renamed the Music Ministries Unit, within which the music editorial work is undertaken [See Chapter 4 for a more extensive discussion of this new administrative structure].

A truly International Music Council was established in October, 1991 for the purpose of coordinating world wide efforts in SA music, though it was not directly concerned with specific publishing efforts. The Council recommended to the General broad based policy issues and advised the administration concerning such issues as international copyright law/performing rights, *Song Book* revision, revisions of various *Orders and Regulations*, and sought to provide a general coordination for musical ministries and publications world-wide.[9]

The Chief of the Staff at IHQ appointed the membership of the council. He tried to ensure that there was always a broad international representation, including territorial music secretaries, corps officers, corps bandmasters/songster leaders, and SA officer administration, such as the managing director of Salvationist Publishing and Supplies and the head of the UK Music Ministries Unit. The council met at IHQ twice a year.

The initial 'Terms of Reference' under which the International Music Council worked detailed four areas in which the council, and, by extension, all SA musicians should *apply the standard of the Army's mission to the Army's music:*

> **Outreach** *by examining ways Army music could be used to reach and attract those outside the Army.*
>
> **Worship** *by promoting music for congregational use, including accompaniment, and for sectional selections which convey spiritual truths in and of themselves.*
>
> **Evangelism** *by recognising the primacy of soul-saving music and exploiting the mobility of bands indoors and out.*
>
> **Fellowship** *by recognising the potential for creative fellowship in the inclusive and diverse nature of music making.*

Early in 2000 a decision was made at International Headquarters to disband three International Councils:

Literary Council; Music Council; and Communications Council. In the words of Commissioner Verna Skinner, General John Gowans had decided that the councils had served their useful, short-term purpose. The International Resources Department at IHQ was to retain the coordinating function previously handled by these councils.

However, the Music Council was soon replaced by the International Music Forum, which first met on July 2–4, 2001 directly following the UK Territory's annual Bandmasters' and Songster Leaders' Councils. This body was expanded to include 50–60 participants, allowing for even greater, worldwide diversity. Every territory was encouraged to send a representative, their appointed music director or equivalent and those territories with greater financial resources were asked to fund delegates from those that could not fund a representative.

Then Chief of the Staff, John Larsson placed the basic idea of international cooperation and pooling of resources in the following perspective:

> *The General's intent in confirming this gathering is to give opportunity to envision the way in which Salvation Army music and musicians should support its mission in a new millennium. The Forum will therefore focus on a worldview and project a wide perception of the part in which all creative ministries play in our mission strategies.*

> [Information and quote shared with the author by Dr. Richard E. Holz]

In a further effort to coordinate international efforts in music and the arts Colonels Robert and Gweneth Redhead assumed in June 2003 the positions of General's Representatives for the Development of Music and other Creative Arts for Evangelism and Worship. While an IHQ appointment, they directed their work from Toronto, Canada.

By December 1997 the new cooperative effort had led to the production of the *International Catalog of Salvation Army Music Publications,* the first such venture in the history of the SA. This significant event and tool has transformed the working relationships between territorial publishing efforts as well as assisted in the first world-wide marketing effort for SA music both within and beyond the organisation. The handsome, multicolored booklet is now augmented by the insertion of an annual Price List Order Form as well as a compact disc Music Series Sampler containing representative excerpts from a wide range of publications.

Symbolic of this new cooperation has been the excellent trade booth manned annually by the combined efforts of the four American territorial music and trade departments and, on some years, SP&S, Ltd., starting with the December 1997 Midwest International Band and Orchestra Clinic in Chicago, Illinois.

In 2006 brass band music is published on a regular basis for SA bands in the following territories: United Kingdom, Canada, USA East, USA Central, USA South. This would include regular journals offered for sale on subscription schemes, individual brass band pieces, educational/tutorial methods, solo and small ensemble music, and music for the accompanying of congregational singing.

Several other territories release band music on an occasional basis, including Australia, Norway and Sweden. Table 1 of Volume II lists current SA band publishers, while the Salvation Army Brass Band Music Table (Volume II) contains a listing of nearly every brass band publication series released by the SA in the last 120 years.

Each territory that maintains active music publishing usually establishes some kind of council or board that assists the territorial music director [TMD, or Territorial Music Secretary, TMS] and his staff in the decision-making process of which items to publish. The SA has usually relied upon the volunteer contributions of its composers and arrangers, supplemented by the assigned work given to the music staff of a particular department. The review board is usually guided by either a grading form (See Illustration 8 for the form used by the USA East in reviewing its band publications) or some other set of criteria.

In the 1971 (Revised edition) *Minutes Outlining Responsibilities and Membership of a Territorial Music Board (Council)* from *Orders and Regulations for*

Territorial Commanders and Chief Secretaries we learn that each member of that broadly representative group was required to grade the 'edited manuscript'. While each territory now might choose different wording or grading scales, the essential criteria are selected to not only maintain musical quality, but also to ensure its suitability for the Army's mission, attractiveness to 'the man on the street', and usefulness in evangelical outreach or corps worship:

Manuscripts shall be graded as poor, mediocre, acceptable, excellent, or exceptional, on each of the following points: a) Soul-saving appeal; b) How practical is the music in relation to the capacity of the territory's musicians; c) suitability to corps congregations; d) eloquence of music to attract outsiders other than church-goers; e) Standard of music:

> *1 melodic and rhythmic content.*
> *2 harmonic (also contrapuntal).*
> *3 instrumentation (contrast, interest, colour, balance).*
> *4 shading, dynamics, effects.*

f) Special merit:

> *1 unusually eloquent.*
> *2 original.*
> *3 worth frequent hearing.*[10]

Naturally, the editor and/or the TMD control to a great degree what goes before such a board. Therefore, each department must have a clearly worked out philosophy behind its publishing - why and for whom they release their music. This would hopefully ensure that 'territorial discretion' is more than a licence to do whatever is of aesthetic interest to a small elite group of musicians.

The meetings of the International Music Council and International Music Forum, supplemented by such coordinated efforts as yearly regional meetings, such as that of the five territorial music secretaries in North America, are helping to gradually shape an intelligent rationale for the various brass band journals each territory produces.

Administrative and Educational Support Structures

SA bands can be provided with administrative support and educational training programmes on both the territorial and the divisional level, depending on financial resources. Within the United States most divisions have either professional divisional music directors [DMD] (and several have an assistant DMD or more) or officers given charge of music within the division as part of their memorandum of appointment.

In other territories wherein bands flourish there is more likely to be just a department at the territorial level (See Chapters 4–8 for further details). The United Kingdom long maintained a system of the honorary Divisional Bandmasters, who would assist the National Secretary for Bands and Songsters in his efforts. While the modern era of the DMD began in the US in the decade of the 1970s (see Chapter 9), as early as the 1890s soldiers had been hired to oversee regional and divisional music programmes. (The most famous of these being Erik Leidzén, who in the 1920s–30s served as a professional music director for the Scandinavian Department, New England Province, and finally, the New York Metropolitan Division.)

The territorial music secretary/director position used to be an exclusively officer-held appointment. By the late 1970s this had begun to change so that now, in North America and the UK, 5 of the 6 TMDs are soldiers hired in professional appointments and the pattern is being repeated across the Army world.

A Divisional Music Director generally finds his/her work divided into six broad categories:

1) Maintaining, directing, scheduling, and administering any Division-wide, or regional musical ensembles (bands, songsters, timbrel brigades, mime-troupes, musicals for Youth Councils, etc.).

2) Working directly with corps groups within the division, via direct visitation, assisting with inventory, training programmes, running and observing rehearsals, etc.

3) Running summer music camps/schools, and perhaps more extended summer music conservatories.

4) Offering divisional or regional training programmes during the regular year, such as area band schools, leadership training workshops, music councils, music competitions, etc.

5) Maintaining resource files (music and educational materials) for use by musicians within the division and maintaining a direct communication link to musicians within the division via efforts like newsletters and bulletins, whether in print, website, or by email.

6) Coordinating the division-wide music calendar for the Divisional Commander and assisting in various public-relations efforts at both the DHQ and corps level as assigned by their direct superior.

The DMD, while essentially working autonomously, does relate directly to the Territorial Music Director, who can serve as an advocate and supporter for the DMD's programmes in addition to the normal cooperative ways in which the divisional and territorial programmes interact.[11]

Territorial Music Departments shape their work around the specific needs of their constituents, only part of whom would be SA bands. As an example of a comprehensive, modern programme, a survey report received by the author from the USA South Territorial Music Department in

"Trombones to the Fore" at the 1999 Territorial School of Music, UK.

October 1994 is summarised below, with personnel updated to the Fall of 2002. This summary is representative of similar reports received from the following territorial music departments, spring of 1994: Australia East (Carolyn Everett); Australia South (Noel Jones); Canada/Bermuda (Brian Burditt); Norway/Iceland/The Faroes (Eiliv Herikstad); United Kingdom (Trevor Davis); USA Central (William Himes); USA East (Ronald Waiksnoris).[12]

USA Southern Territorial Music and Music Education Department consists of Dr. Richard E. Holz, Territorial Music and Music Education Secretary and bandmaster of the Southern Territorial Band; Major Michael McDonald, Assistant to the TMS; Robert Snelson, Territorial Music Education Director; Jude Gotrich, Territorial Gospel Arts Director; James Curnow, Territorial Music Editor; Evelyn Pulkin, Department Secretary; Marty Mikles, Department Clerk; William McNeiland, Music Education Consultant (Seasonal position); Captain Stan Colbert, an officer serving in the Carolinas Division, was serving at that time as conductor of the Territorial Songsters.

The work of the department focuses on three overlapping areas: 1) Music Education; 2) Music Publications; 3) Promotion and Supervision of Music Programmes. A Territorial Music Council (music publications, recordings, music performance) and a Territorial Music Committee (music and music education programming), a group that includes all current DMDs in the territory, aid the Music Department in this work.

Music education programmes include, but are not restricted to, the following: 1) the annual Territorial Music Institute; 2) the TMI Adult Music Leadership Seminar; 3) Territorial Music Leaders Councils/Music Councils (held in 1984, 1989, 1994, 1997, 2001); 4) Local Officers Training School (L.O.T.S.) music leadership courses; 5) Music courses at the College for Officers Training (CFOT); 5) Divisional Music Conservatories; 6) Divisional music institutes, camps, and councils.

Beginning in 1987 the Southern Territory Music Department has developed a range of instrumental and vocal music publications and now is the second largest publisher of music in the international Salvation Army.

Their publications for bands include the *American Instrumental Ensemble Series* [*AIES*] and the *American Instrumental Solo Series*. (They also offer a wide range of vocal/choral music). In addition to music publications, the department supervises and approves all divisional and corps recordings and provides copyright protection for all Southern Territory music publications.

In the area of promotion and supervision, the department supervises and encourages divisional music directors and provides assistance in the recruitment and training of all full-time DMDs. Promotional activities include the planning and conducting of annual international SA performing tours including, within the decade of the 1990s, such model brass groups as the International Staff Band, Enfield Corps Band, Hendon Corps Band, London Corps Band, Ontario and many others.

Also included in the area of promotion (and modelling) are the USA Southern Territorial Band and Songsters and the Territorial Band Sextet. The department has published on a quarterly basis the *Southern Musician*, a music leaders' bulletin, and regularly submits articles to the *Southern Spirit* (territorial newspaper) and the national *War Cry*. Richard Holz, Robert Snelson, Michael McDonald, Jude Gotrich, and William McNeiland provide regular field service at the divisional and corps level (divisional music conservatories and camps, corps music weekends, etc.). Monitoring adherence to *Orders and Regulations for SA Music Organisations in the USA* and to the USA Copyright Law also falls in their province.

Such a short summary cannot really do complete justice to all that would be done in such a department, with the same kind of list duplicated with regional differences throughout the Army world where a territorial department exists. Chapter 4 includes a similar overview of the UK Territory's Musical Ministries Unit, and so comparisons can be made with the above example.

Ways in which bands are being better and better served through comprehensive and strategic planning comes via the establishment of the Music Secretaries Committee, a national committee in the USA that submits minutes and recommendations to the USA Commissioners Conference.

In this way, the somewhat parochial 'territorial discretion' model is at least in this region of the world, becoming more enlightened, especially when combined with the efforts of the International Music Council and its successor, the International Music Forum. A remarkable administrative network now serves SA bands.

Notes

1. *Orders and Regulations for Bands and Songster Brigades* (London: SP&S, 1977), p6. This wording is retained nearly verbatim in the 1998 edition *Sing and Make Music: Orders and Regulations for Music Organisations in the USA* (Alexandria, VA: The Salvation Army, 1999), 2. The change from 'bands and songster brigades' to 'Music Organisations' in the title of *Orders and Regulations* is significant.

2. During the Sunday morning service bands in some territories were, until very recently, still restricted to accompanying the opening song, possibly a prelude item, or at most, all the congregational singing. See Chapter 2-3 for details concerning the gradual inclusion of bands within indoor worship.

3. Recent patterns in SA worship are defying these traditional alignments. See Chapter 10 for further discussion.

4. While the English editions of the *Songbook* and *Tune Book* are used widely, several territories in non-English speaking nations, have developed their own song and band tune books.

5. *Hallelujah Choruses*, designed for four or more players (SATB voicing) also provides parts for traditional rhythm section. *Scripture-based Songs* is scored for *Triumph Series*-sized bands. In 2003, the UK Territory released an additional band accompaniment series entitled *Magnify*, which contains an additional 75 contemporary-style accompaniments for congregational singing.

6. Fred Brown, *The Salvationist at Worship* (London: SP&S, 1950), pp69–70. Not much official information exists regarding early Open-Air meetings, though ample eye-witness accounts abound. See, however, one official, anonymous article of instruction entitled 'The Importance of Music to the Open-Air', *The Field Officer* (June, 1908), p231.

7. Until very recently in the UK or British Territory bands did not play in the Holiness Meeting after accompanying the initial song, the exception being special weekends focused on the local or a visiting band's ministry. This has now been changed, as reflected in the new UK Territory's *Regulations and Guidelines for Musicians*, the new name for the old *O&R*. In America this order

was rescinded with the 1972 edition of the *O&R*, although American bands had begun to offer additional music on a regular basis in Holiness Meetings no later than directly following World War II.

8. See, for example, *Orders and Regulations for Bands and Songster Brigades* (London: SP&S, 1977 edition), Chapter IV, p57.

9. The Minutes of the International Music Council for November 10, 1998 show that the group dealt with such issues as: International Music Publications Catalogue; Revision of the *Song Book of The Salvation Army*; Revision of *Orders and Regulations for Bands and Songsters*; Mandatory establishment of Territorial/Command Music Departments; Music Copyright and Royalties on Salvation Army Music; Christian Copyright Licensing, Incorporated CCLI; Current music publication projects and future projects; International Millennial Congress and Music Leadership Training session during the event; Discussion of Tonic-Solfa edition for *Songs For Joy*; French translation music book; Individual reports by each member.

10. I served as a member of the USA East Territorial Music Board, 1977-80. At that time the board met quarterly, assisted by *ad hoc* committees. Occasional needs between sessions were met by individual review and grading sent by mail through the offices of the TMD. Works that were accepted for publication had to receive high averages and considerable personal recommendation from the various musical, editorial, and literary 'experts' who served on this board.

11. In the Spring of 1999 I taught an independent study seminar at Asbury College for students interested in the DMD position. One of the projects undertaken by the class was a comprehensive survey concerning the position of the DMD. This was sent to every division within North America, the results received by August, 1999. Initial evaluation of responses confirms the basic six-part division of labour presented but also points to a remarkably diverse number of programmes. See also an unpublished, but excellent paper about the DMD job: Harold Burgmayer (Pendel Division, USA East), *Keeping the Divisional Music Director's Workload in Balance: Surviving the Madness.*

12. This four-page survey requested the person completing it to respond in four general areas: 1) Overview of activities the department undertakes in its administration of SA banding, including any networking with efforts on the divisional and corps level; 2) Listing of any current brass publication efforts and future plans; 3) How brass music is secured and approved for publication or how manuscript brass music is monitored and approved; 4) Personal reflections on future of both SA brass music and the ministry of SA brass bands.

Illustration 1: Holiness Meeting;
Atlanta Temple Corps, November 23, 1980; 11:00 AM.

Preliminary Music by Temple Band and Songsters
Call to Worship (Psalm 47:8; 48:14)
Opening Congregational Song *Jehovah Is Our Strength*
Prayer Chorus and Pastor's Prayer
Scripture Reading (2nd Corinthians. 4: 1–18)
Congregational Song *The People of God*
Announcements and Offering
Band Hymn Tune Arrangement *St. Columba* (Keith Griffin)
Congregational Chorus *Praise Him With Melody*
Songster Selection *Not Unto Us, O Lord* (Charles Skinner)
Message: *In the Beginning, God* [Major Edward Laity]
Closing Congregational Song *Praise to the Lord*
Congregational Benediction *O Father Let Thy Love Remain*

Illustration 2: Salvation Meeting,
Atlanta Temple Corps, November 23, 1980; 7:00 PM.

Preliminary Music by Temple Band and Songsters
Singspiration using Choruses of the Past and
   Two Selected Testimonies
Congregational Song *Lord of Intrepid Soldiers*
Prayer of Thanksgiving
Enrollment of Junior and Senior Soldiers
Scripture and Testimony
Songster Selection *Jesus, I My Cross Have Taken* (Lloyd Scott)
Announcements and Offering
Band Hymn Tune Arrangement *Now Thank We All Our God*
   (Ken Elloway)
Male Chorus Selection [unidentified]
Message: *Coming Home or Home Coming?*
Closing Congregational Song *Now Thank We All Our God*
Benediction

Illustration 3: Report of Combined Music Festival Programme;
Regent Hall and Wood Green Corps bands, December 15, 1898;
Musical Salvationist [MS], XIII (1898-99), 83.

It will be of interest to many Army Bands to see the specimen
programme of one or two of the first-class London Bands for an
up-to-date Musical Festival. We give therefore, the programme

of the latest Festivals by the Regent Hall and Wood Green
Bands.

1. Band, BJ 357
2. Solo, *The Army of our Saviour,* MS, (Nov.1898)
3. Cornet Duet, *My Burden at the Feet,* MS, (Vol IV, 26).
4. Baritone Solo, *The Friendship of Jesus*, BJ 353, and *Over Life's Ocean*, BJ 310
5. Band, BJ 359
6. Solo, *Death's Rolling Tide*, MS (March, 1898)
7. Quartette, *The Sufferings of Jesus*, BJ 361
8. The Band, BJ 361
9. Bombardon Solo, *The Pilot*, BJ 319; *The Storm and the Reaching of the Port*, BJ 337
10. Piano Duet, *Salvation from Sin*, BJ 22; *Proud to be a Soldier*, BJ 270
11. Songsters, *Salvation*, MS (March, 1896)
12. Cornet Solo, *Questions at Bethlehem*, BJ 330
13. Band, BJ 356
14. Vocal Quartette, *But the Story is True?* (MS (Nov. 1898)
15. Band, BJ 32
16. Solo, *Scenes from a Prodigal's Life*, MS (May, 1897)

...The programme is, it will be noticed, a very long one, made
up of Army material throughout, and most distinctly it is a
programme of an up-to-date character, showing the progressive
and all-alive status of our music comrades at the old Rink. The
CHRISTMAS JOURNAL has evidently proved of much
attraction to the Regent Hall Band, for it figures largely in the
above Programme...

**Illustration 4: Brass Band Holiday Festival, Alexandra Palace,
Massed Bands, August 5, 1898.
As reported in the *Musical Salvationist,*
XIII (1898-99), 33.**

The following is a list of the pieces of the Band Festival, which
was also quite up-to-date and well chosen:

1. BJ 208. *Sagina*. Selected Bands with singing
2. BJ 264. *Glory to God*. All Bands

3. BJ 197. *The Sinner's Prayer*. Woolwich Band

4. BJ 281. *Medley with 'Ernan'*. IHQ Band

5. BJ 211. *Bithynia and Weber*. Chalk Farm Band

6. BJ 231. *Roll Over Me*. All Bands

7. BJ 206. *Tried, Faithful, and Precious*. Poplar Band

8. BJ 286. *My God the Spring*. Regent Hall Band

9. BJ 270. *A Charge to Keep*. All Bands, then singing with Basses accomp.

10. BJ 287. *Grace Enough*. IHQ Band

11. BJ 284. *How goes the War?* and *The Call of Jesus*. Great Western Hall Band

12. BJ 251. *The Absent Guest*. IHQ Band

13. BJ 142. *Ere the Sun Goes Down*. Varied with singing

14. BJ 270. *Proud to be a Soldier* and *Dear Jesus is the One*. All Bands

About 500 London Bandsmen took part, and the playing was an evident sign of the great progress our London bands are making. The I.H.Q. Band was beautifully in tune and smart in its general playing. The Great Western Hall Band played with remarkable spirit and lightness. For close observance of expression marks and ease in performance, the Regent Hall Band won great praise. Other Bands deserve recognition, but space is too limited to do justice to this most successful Festival.

Illustration 5: New York Staff Band Tour Festival, Programme B; May 27–June 2, 1937.

Fanfare – Opening Song – Prayer

March *Army of God* (Emil Soderstrom)

Selection *The Saviour's Name* (Erik Leidzén)

Male Chorus *God's Voice* (Words by Gilliard to Sibelius' tune *Finlandia*)

Cornet Solo *Lover of the Lord* (William Parkins/arr. Erik Leidzén) William Parkins, Soloist

Selection *Missionary* (William Slater)

Euphonium Solo *Lift Up the Banner On High* (James Merritt) Harold Jackson, Soloist

Bible Reading

Intermission

Cornet Quartet *The Trumpeters* (Erik Leidzén)

William Parkins, Paul Carlson, Fred Farrar,
William Wrieden
Vocal Solo *Rose of Sharon* Frank Fowler, Soloist
Meditation *Home, Sweet Home* (Erik Leidzén)
Trombone Solo *Unfathomed Love* (Frederick Hawkes)
Kenneth R. Ayres, Soloist
Male Chorus *Onward to Battle* (Erik Leidzén)
Cornet Duet *Always Cheerful* (Albert Jakeway)
Fred Farrar and William Wrieden, Soloists
March *Brooklyn Citadel* (William Bearchell)
Benediction

Illustration 6: First Night, City of Boston, December 31, 1978; Cambridge Citadel Band and Songsters.

[The programme listed three different options per musical offering, only the first is shown here. The short programme was played multiple times that evening.]

Festive March For Band: *Hillcrest* (Bruce Broughton)
Congregational Song: *America the Beautiful*
Song Arrangement for Band: *This Is My Father's World*
(Stephen Bulla)
Congregational Song: *O God Our Help In Ages Past*
Choral Selections: *Tell All the People* (Howard Davies);
Our Glorious King (Wilfred Heaton)
Congregational Song: *Amazing Grace*
Solo Selection: *The Old Rugged Cross* (arr. Leidzén),
Trombone Soloist Thomas Scheibner
Meditation by the Divisional Commander,
Major Wallace C. Conrath
Congregational Song: *Onward Christian Soldiers*
Benediction
Band Postlude: *How Great Thou Art* (James Curnow)

Salvation Army officers are available for spiritual counselling following the programme.

We sincerely hope you enjoyed our programme. In lieu of an admission fee, your offering or donation will be gratefully received in our red kettle as you exit.

Coffee is available at our Canteen on the Columbus Avenue side of the building and at other locations within the downtown area.

Illustration 7: North American Brass Band Association annual conference, Gala Concert by the Chicago Staff Band, Pheasant Run Resort, St. Charles, IL, April 24, 1999.

March *Hillcrest* (Bruce Broughton)

Gaudete! (Kevin Norbury)

Caprice for Cornet and Brass Band (William Himes),
   Randy Cox, soloist

Band Choral Selection *Through My Saviour's Merit*
   (Leslie Condon)

Deep River (William Broughton)

Purcell Variations (Kenneth Downie)

[Presentation of Awards]

Concertante, Movement 1 (Stephen Bulla)

Concerto for Tuba and Brass Band (Martin Ellerby),
   guest soloist Stephen Sykes

[Encore: *Czardas* (Monti/Sykes]

American Civil War Fantasy (Jerry Bilik/William Himes)

Illustration 8: Instrumental Grading Form, Territorial Music Council of the Eastern Territory, USA.

♫ Instrumental Grading Form ♫
Territorial Music Council of the Eastern Territory USA

Title _____   Date _____

Type _____   Usage of Song _____

Elements of Grading: An average grade of four is required for consideration of publication. An element marked "No Evaluation" will not be used in averaging the scores.

Utility and/or Purpose of the Music	Exceptional (6)	Excellent (5)	Acceptable (4)	Mediocre (3)	Poor (2)	Failure (1)	No Evaluation
How practical is this music in relation to the capacity of our groups?							
Suitability to Salvation Army Corps audiences?							
Suitability to "man in the street" (recognition and association of themes and quality of music to captivate listeners)							
Evangelical Appeal							

Standard of Music	Exceptional (6)	Excellent (5)	Acceptable (4)	Mediocre (3)	Poor (2)	Failure (1)	No Evaluation
Melodic and Rhythmic Content							
Harmonic Interest (also contrapuntal)							
Instrumentation (contrast, interest, color, balance shading, dynamics, effects (in character with other elements))							
Special merit (is the music unusually eloquent? Original? Would you like to hear often?)							

Comments: _____   Individual Average _____

_____

_____   Signature _____

Chapter 2

A SHORT HISTORY OF SALVATION ARMY BANDS AND THEIR MUSIC
Part I (1878–1904)

Ronald W. Holz

...you must be careful not to over-estimate its importance [SA band music] *or come into bondage to it. Music, in itself, has neither a moral nor a religious character. This can only be imparted to it by the thoughts or feelings of the soul when under its power. That is to say, if music is to have any holy, any Divine influence on the hearts of those who listen, it must be associated with holy feelings and with Divine thoughts. It is this that makes good singing more important to us than the grandest music the Band can play, unless accompanied by the singing of words calculated to carry home its appeal to our hearts.* General William Booth, from an article in the form of an interview: 'All About the Local Officer', Chapter 4, 'Singing'. *The Local Officer* (III, 8) March, 1900, p. 181–182.

Prologue

Salvation Army bands did not develop in isolation. Their rapid growth and deployment in the first decade of their existence (1878–1888) were possible because of the musical and cultural climate in which the Army itself emerged. Bands had been a major feature of British life for many decades before the Army first flew its flag. Church bands, Temperance bands, and the semi-military bands of the Volunteer movement (after 1859) were to prove the models for SA bands, as well as sources from which early SA bands derived help and support. Using bands in the aid of church work, in the form of parades and public demonstrations, was commonplace by the late 1870s.

The difference between SA bands and other bands of the period came from the manner in which the bands interacted with the public. No one objected to a band playing in a Sunday School parade, or for a Temperance Rally, or for a village Whitsun Wakes church service – these were all undertaken within established social guidelines and expectations. SA bands would be radical, confrontational, and would challenge accepted practice, blaring forth their

The Fry family quartet comprised the first Salvation Army Band, with two cornets, a valve trombone and a euphonium.

fervent evangelical message in a manner that would cause, initially, controversy, violent opposition and general public disapproval. In addition, within a few short years, a true isolation was imposed via internal autocratic control of SA bands and their music.[1]

The formation of the first official SA brass ensemble in 1878 underscores the cultural and religious forces at work in the early days of the SA. Well before this date Charles William Fry (1837–1882) of Salisbury played first cornet in the First Wiltshire Volunteer Rifle Corps Band, a typical band of the 1859–1880 period. In addition, *he formed a Brass Band connection with the* [Wesleyan Methodist] *chapel to which he was attached* [to] *assist at the Sunday School treats and demonstrations as well as to aid local religious and philanthropic efforts.*[2]

Fry's church instrumentalists had also functioned in worship services in the tradition of the west gallery bands so lovingly portrayed in the works of Thomas Hardy.

Like Hardy's group in *Under the Greenwood Tree* Fry's band was soon banished out of the chapel when the harmonium took over, played by Charles' oldest son, Fred, at the early age of eight, while the father still led the singers and the congregation.[3]

In the spring and summer of 1878 members of William Booth's Christian Mission (founded in 1865) began services in the city of Salisbury.

They soon attracted the support of the, by then, master builder and itinerant preacher, Charles Fry, who along with his three sons, supported the outdoor efforts of the missioners, providing both an attraction and further help in crowd control.

Fred William Fry, in a letter dated February 20, 1928, told how they were first referred to as 'Mary Sayers' Angels', after the leader of the mission, and dressed in white tunics and trousers during the summer of 1878. The group was made up of two cornets, a valve trombone, and a euphonium, with the entire group capable of doubling as a string quartet.

By autumn 1878 the Christian Mission had been renamed The Salvation Army and the work in Salisbury was under the direction of Captain Arthur Watts. The use of brass music as an aid in overt evangelism was proving effective and soon caught the attention of General William Booth, who soon used the Fry family band in his campaigns throughout the country. This small quartet provided the impetus and official sanction for the use of brass bands by early Salvationists. Nothing could be more natural. Brindley Boon has summarised it quite neatly:

> *...Little wonder that the idea caught on with Salvationists! Brass banding was a medium they understood. How natural that it should become the basic unit of musical forces of an organisation which exits to meet the needs of 'the man on the street...'* [4]

William Booth, the Christian Mission, and Music

William Booth saw music as a means to an end. Christian music should attract people and speak the message of salvation to their hearts.

Plaque at Salisbury Cathedral commemorating the 'Centenary Promotion to Glory of Charles William Fry'.

To Booth, instrumental music in and of itself had no moral force. The spiritual power of the associated texts and ideas, regardless of tunes chosen (the contrast ranged from mid-century revivalist hymns to tavern-room ballads made into *contrafacta* in the spirit of Martin Luther or perhaps the Wesleys), made all the difference.

Booth's approach to music was direct, simple, and practical. He advocated music that was attractive, carried a solid message, and, in the process avoided the 'dangers' of sophisticated church music making. At the same time that the Church of England had been removing its gallery bands, getting rid of secular tune use, reforming its choir schools, and generally refining itself, non-conformist groups, especially Booth's Christian Mission, embraced what Glen Horridge has rightfully called...*in effect a combination of religion and entertainment,* a worship style soon to be reviled as *services* [that] *are frequently a travesty of musical hall entertainment.*[5]

Beginning in 1865, William Booth's East London Christian Mission used musical tactics that would become inseparable from the idea of a 'Salvation Army', particularly with the additional use of brass bands 13 years later. Writing in his journal in the fall of 1865 Booth described his pioneer work and the role of music, then exclusively vocal, in it:

> *Evening* [Service], *from half past five to seven. Mile-end road; excellent service. Hundreds appeared to listen with undivided attention. The Word was with power. Every sentence seemed to penetrate the hearts of the listening throng. We then formed a procession and sang down White-chapel Road to the Room* [a rented 'Dancing Room']. *We had an efficient band of singers and as we passed along the spacious and crowded thoroughfare, singing 'We're bound for the land of the pure and the holy', the people ran from every side. From the adjacent gin palaces the drinkers came forth to hear and see; some in mockery joined our ranks, some laughed and sneered, some were angry, the great majority looked on in wonder, while others turned and accompanied us, as on we went, changing our song to 'There is a Fountain filled with Blood', and then to 'with a turning from sin, let repentance begin'.*

It was a scene to be repeated over and over again, one that would have even more attractive power and disruptive force with the addition of a marching brass band.

Booth's Christian Mission, as it was called by September, 1869, grew large enough by the early 1870s for Booth and his wife, Catherine, to compile several hymnbooks: *The Christian Mission Hymnbook, Hymns for Special Services, The Penny Revival Hymn Book, and The Children's Mission Hymn Book.* In 1876 *The Christian Mission Hymn Book* contained 531 standard hymns, spirituals, and songs set to popular and national tunes, a combination that would be the main sources of SA band music for two decades.[6]

William Booth was suspicious of organised music groups and even solo singing, despite his later effective use of both. While he would soon allow bands to flourish in outdoor evangelism, he only begrudgingly allowed them any role whatsoever in indoor services (see quote at head of Chapter 1). As for choirs, he did not allow the formation of songster brigades, the SA designation for adult choirs, in Army corps until 1898!

He gave mixed signals, however, as he constantly used 'musical specials' wherever he travelled. Several of his own children were gifted performers and song writers, particularly Ballington and Herbert. In reality, music became Booth's best help, despite his continual reservations about the potential evils of music that was not carefully controlled.

Booth's ambivalence might be traced to trouble with a trained choir in his first ministerial appointments, though we do not have direct evidence of this. While he always supported hearty congregational singing, he did not approve of people gaining prominence in a fellowship merely because of their music skill. This is something to be born in mind when one considers how he suppressed individuality and recognition, other than for members of his own immediate family, in early music publications. It would be decades before Army band scores identified arrangers and composers, and even later for names to appear on the instrumental parts! (See later discussions in this chapter, as well as Chapter 3).

In 1877, as 'General Superintendent' of the Christian Mission, Booth once delivered a remarkable address on 'Good Singing' that contained the essence of his practical approach to music, as well as his fears about structured musical groups. This 'philosophy' would provide the context in which he would control all SA band and choral activity:

> [I have] *ever found choirs to be possessed of three devils, awkward, ugly and impossible to cast out. They are the quarrelling devil, the dressing devil, and the*

*courting devil, and the last is the worst of the three...
Merely professional music is always a curse and
should you ever find a choir in connection with any
hall in this mission, I give you my authority to take a
besom [broom] and sweep it out. Promising that you do
so as lovingly as possible. You must sing good tunes.
Let it be a good tune to begin with. I don't care much
whether you call it secular or sacred. I rather enjoy
robbing the devil of his choicest tunes, and, after his
subjects themselves, music is about the best commodity
he possesses. It is like taking the enemy's guns and
turning them against him. However, come whence it
may, let us have a real tune, that is, a melody with
some distinct air in it, that one can take hold of, which
people can learn, nay, which makes them learn it,
which takes hold of them and goes humming in the
mind until they have mastered it. That is the sort of
tune to help you; it will preach to you, and bring you
believers and converts.*[7]

When the Fry ensemble met, and exceeded, Booth's
expectations, he soon convinced them to enter the SA full
time. By 1879 bands were emerging all over the country,
with Booth's son, Herbert, forming one in Manchester by
March, 1879, and the first official local corps band
functioning publicly in Consett, County Durham, by
December of the same year. Booth's priority was soul
saving, whatever the means. Musical ensembles, whatever
his personal reactions, should be mustered in Salvation
warfare.

His first 'Order for Bands' from *The War Cry*, early 1880
(Reproduced in Appendix 1 at the end of this chapter)
captured Booth's obsession with practical results,
regardless of the long-range consequences. The whirlwind
of musical activity this endorsed and unleashed was
unprecedented. Notice that it did not directly encourage
brass bands, *per se*. Booth immediately needed an
organisational staff to administer the groups and to publish
music for them.

His 'Second General Order for Brass Bands' of February
24, 1881 (Also Appendix 1) – the title carefully chosen now

to highlight the preferred combination – established the first regulations, primarily to do with authority (no democracy!), membership requirements, and ownership of equipment. A preliminary attempt to control *what* was played as 'Salvation music' was broadly drawn, at best, as the SA had not published any music yet for its bands. The bands were using music from 'outside' band publishers or arranging themselves for each unique combination. Booth's staff was still two steps behind his enthusiastic followers. Improvisation reigned.[8]

By Their Bootstraps or With Help?

An account of the origin of the corps band at Whitechapel, dictated by the first bandmaster, John B. Agar, in 1934, shows the humble start of most SA bands and underscores the point that outside help was essential in the early going:

> [Band origination] *Immediately after the holding of the Council of War in 1879 but before his sister Rachel was married to Captain Ebden this places the date at the end of July or beginning of August 1879–, Captain Payne bought at Halliday's* [Whitechapel Rd] *(Mr. Agar says the shop is still there) two cornets and several other instruments. The two cornets were given to the then brother Ted Whatmore* [later Commissioner] *and himself. The same evening that these instruments were bought Captain Payne bought four concertinas, the idea being to form a concertina band which could play in the meantime until the bandsmen learnt to play their brass instruments.*
>
> *Later eight instruments were bought from a pawnbroker's shop. They were in very poor shape. This would be several days or even weeks later. He said that Captain first asked* [him] *whether he would play a cornet if he got one for him. Mr. Agar agreed. The idea struck Captain Payne of forming a band. At that time the congregations were good and the Whitechapel Station had plenty of money.*
>
> *They advertised for a bandmaster capable of instructing learners. In response to this advertisement a man came to whom they paid 7/6d. for tuition one*

evening of the week. They did not continue doing this for long. They then appointed their own bandmaster, Mr. Agur himself holding this position for a time, although he states Frank Spooner was their leading cornet player.

He said that the visit of the 'Fry' family to Whitechapel had a good deal to do with the idea of their starting a band. He confirmed what Commissioner Whatmore had told me about their using the ordinary four part tune book [piano] for music, and added 'Saints of God' to the tunes that they at first tackled.[9]

Vic Elstow's recent history of the Wellingborough SA Band also confirms the importance of the Fry ensemble in providing the spark that got this band going in 1879:

...Francis Ireson was so impressed by their talent [Fry band] that he decided to form a Brass Band at the Wellingborough Corps. He collected a few instruments together and acquired the services of Mr. William Ward, Bandmaster of the Band of the First Battalion I and K Companies, Northamptonshire Rifle Volunteers. Bandmaster Ward wrote manuscript band parts and taught the group of Salvationists the rudiments of Brass Banding. For these services, each man paid him sixpence per week. The music came mostly from 'Wright and Round Brass Band Journal' there being very little Salvation Army music published at that time.[10]

SA bands needed help getting started and fortunately found many friends, or at least sympathetic professionals, to help them pull themselves up by their own bootstraps. Here is a selective series of examples of how British SA bands interacted with the larger musical, and especially banding, community in the early going, either in terms of direct teaching of the bands or via new SA soldiers with musical training:[11]

1. First Staff Bandmaster Harry Appleby: Trained as a musician in the Essex Rifles Regimental Band

(Colchester), then a military staff band; professional brass musician with Black Star Minstrels before conversion.

2. Bandmaster Samuel Webber: Before joining SA, Bandmaster of the Inniskinning Dragoon Guards; formed the Household Troops Band 2 at London HQ.

3. Arthur Goldsmith, member of early music department: At age 10, joins Invicta Military Band associated with Bath Chapel in Poplar, East London. Invicta and local SA corps band frequently exchange and work together; Goldsmith 'loaned' to corps from Invicta one day, becomes soldier and by age 15 is bandmaster at the corps. Hired at IHQ by December 1888.

4. Cambridge Heath Band had a 'teacher' named Mr. Faux, who later became bandmaster; bandsmen encouraged to attend Besses-O-the-Barn Band concerts. (*British Bandsman,* March 19, 1904, p57).

5. Derby II Band (Central): Received early training from George Walker, deputy bandmaster of the Derby Volunteer Band, who soon became a soldier and then led the corps band for 38 years. (Derby Corps Centennial Program, 1982).

6. Newcastle City 'Temple' Corps received instruments as a gift from a Scottish draper, purchased from a Mr. Tom Woods, a famous contesting conductor of those days who taught the [corps] candidates for Bandsmanship their scales and how to manipulate their instruments. ('A Tynside Jubilee', *Bandsman and Songster* (UK), November 23, 1932, p390).

7. Bandmaster William Boyd of Paisley Corps Band was a former drum-major with the 93rd Sutherland Highlanders.

8. After the visit of the Consett SA Band, the South Shields Corps Band is formed in 1881, with Robert Dennison, a well-known contesting conductor, agreeing to instruct them. The band is totally illiterate, and Dennison first teaches them their tunes via hand signs; later the entire band learns both to read and write English, as well read musical

notation. (South Shields Corps Anniversary Program, 1878–1978).

9. Richard Slater, 'father of SA music', trained by a Higgins and Sidney Jones, former military bandsman, and, according to Slater, a good player on the violin, harp, and instruments of the military band. Before his conversion Slater joins the Royal Albert Hall Amateur Orchestral Society as a violinist.

10. In 1883 the Culceth Temperance Band gave their entire set of instruments to the Manchester 2 Corps, having purchased a new set for themselves. (*War Cry*, December 1883).

11. The Chalk Farm Band of nine newly converted soldiers first trained in the home of a Mr. Foulkes, *a bandmaster in the Volunteers.* Band soon has a Guards-trained drum major; shortly later Walter Reynolds of the London County Council teaches and helps young bandmaster Punchard. (*Story of the Chalk Farm Band, 1882–1932*, p4).

12. The first bandmaster of the SA band in Penicuik, Scotland, a Mr. Lumsden, was a student of J. Ord Hume.

Such accounts can be duplicated many times in the histories of early SA bands. Yet what is more remarkable is the fact that many other bands received very little help, and essentially, did it on their own, much in the tradition of amateur music making in Great Britain. The initial results were not always encouraging, with the band press being very negative rather than supportive, as seen in a column entitled *The Salvation Army Brass Bands* that appeared on December 1, 1882 of the *Brass Band News*:

> *Whatever good objects the leaders of this movement may have in view, music is clearly not included in the category. What is meant by music in this case is something approaching to decent harmony, and this does not exist, or at least in very, very rare and exceptional cases among Salvation Army Brass Bands. The mistake lays in supposing that enthusiasm goes to*

make up for lack of knowledge, practice, and musical experience, a clear erronerous [sic] view, which is as incompatible with reason as it is unworthy of any show of respect.

The organisers of the movement appear to think that the only difficulty in the forming of a band is the purchase of the instruments; the idea of any sort of capacity, practice, a study to manipulate them, never seems to enter the question at all, Thus the instruments are bought, and the efforts to play before the gamut is known, simply provoke ridicule and contempt all round, which is to say least, is a painful witness. Tone and tune is invariably unknown, and as for balance of parts or harmony, such a thing is as foreign as it can well be.

As a set-off against this idiosyncrasy, we are told that it is for 'a good cause', and enthusiasm should make up for what is otherwise lacking, This sort of argument is unworthy of the slightest claim to the meanest understanding, and only serves to show the estimation the leaders of the movement hold the understanding of their followers...[12]

Growth figures – Spiritual element

In 1878 the newly named Salvation Army had 31 established 'corps' and opened 26 more that same year. 47 were added in 1879, to a total of 104. The SA grew at a phenomenal rate within the first 5 years, totalling 519 corps by 1883, with Higbie estimating perhaps 400 of those 519 with a band of some kind.

Horridge has pointed out that the main growth was in towns with populations exceeding 10,000, showing that of 304 such towns, 203 had corps. The greatest strength seemed to be in the industrial north, the old industrial southwest, London, and South Wales; mining and coastal villages also figured in this upsurge. Most of these areas would be regions in which brass banding would be a highly attractive and already established part of the musical and cultural scene. Agricultural areas did not usually support large corps growth. While the number of corps continued to grow after 1883, Horridge states that the numbers did so at a slower rate. From 1883–1905 the net gain was 705 more corps, though 95 were lost in the same period, bringing the total within the time frame of this chapter to 1,116 corps, a remarkable number by any account. Most of them had, by the International Congress of 1904, some form of a brass band! Accurate statistics are few and far between in this early period, but a report prepared by William Booth at the time of the 1904 International Congress listed the number of bandsmen world-wide in 1894 as 12,440 and by 1904, at 17,099. This is an increase of 4,659 in ten years.[13]

Richard Slater would claim in 1896 that there were 15,000 bandsmen in all parts of the world, the majority no doubt still to be found in Great Britain. His *Brief History of SA Bands*, in which he made this claim, named the Northwich Corps Band as the Army's first, after the Fry Ensemble. This led to controversy, and soon Slater carried out an investigation on the origins of SA bands in the United Kingdom.

He formulated a *Table of 50 of the Earliest Bands of The Salvation Army*, most of which was reprinted in various guise in *Musical Salvationist* articles. The table shows that he could account for 50 'regular' bands by early 1884. This contrasts with the vast number of 400 in Bigbie's estimation sited above, which would have included many very small ensembles or bands in the process of formation. Slater also showed that 27 of these 50 were formed as a result of the visit of the Fry, or 'First Army Band'.

The years 1881–1882 seemed particularly meaningful to Slater. It was in these years that so many of the finest Army corps bands were started, including (in chronological order) Hull (Icehouse), Carlisle (Citadel), Portsmouth, Leeds 1, Bristol, Exeter, South Shields, Gloucester, Regent Hall, Clapton, Chalk Farm, Castleford, Derby, Upper Norwood, Kettering, and Sunderland (Monkwearmouth). The honours for the first three went to Consett (December, 1879), Northwich (March, 1880), and Nottingham 1, later called William Booth Memorial Hall (March, 1880).[14]

Two series of articles that ran in the *Local Officer* within the period 1897–1902 (one on bands, one on band-masters) provide a great deal of information about these representative bands. Appendix 5 contains a list of each of these, one of the most remarkable sources for information on early SA bands and their leaders.[15] Each article could include a current photo, names of leaders, names of members, their assigned instrumentation, origin, occupations of the members, even data concerning how long each was 'saved' and how long they had served as bandsmen.

In reading these fascinating accounts, I was struck by the obvious sincerity of the reports, the emphasis on the spiritual aspect of band work, and also by the fact that by this time many members were coming into bands as a result of the establishment of junior bands.

Time after time these success stories show that the early Army bands became well organised, disciplined ensembles primarily to spread the Gospel message, and that these bands were the heart of most corps work. The corps became the centre of their lives, with bands frequently on call for an average of two or more weeknights for Open-Air outreach, an evening for band practice, Saturday night Open-Air and indoor service, with Sunday being the climactic, and busiest of the days.

Bands of this period also took weekends away at other corps, boosting the morale of other struggling concerns, or encouraging other bands via shared fellowship. While it would be the intent of the editor of such a magazine to stress the Army's spiritual work, the balance struck between profiling the musical success of these groups and the solid endorsements by local corps officers and divisional officers point beyond mere propaganda.

Not surprisingly, the area of the country and local economy greatly influenced the profiles of these bands. In the 28-piece Trealaw Corps Band (South Wales) of 1903 every member but two, a boy still in school (listed as 'scholar') and a British Army pensioner serving as colour-sergeant, worked in the mining industry of the town. 20 were designated as miners, the other related occupations listed as engine driver, hauler, pointsman, coker, quarryman, and lamp boy. Five were listed as having been saved as a 'junior' and having come into the band through its training program.

As was rather typical in these days, the commissioned

bandmaster, W. H. Thomas, played first-chair cornet, while the band was conducted by Band-Instructor P. J. Prior, reforred to as Brother Prior. The band listed could also show the band had a commissioned band secretary, band-sergeant, colour sergeant, and, as was not uncommon, two other important corps local officers, the corps secretary and treasurer. Bands were the heart of many Army corps.

One profile of a small village band, rare in this series, showed a related sociological profile, with 14 members of the 16-piece Farcet Corps Band of 1903 (from the Cambridge area) listed as brickmakers, the other two being a farm labourer and a SA Assurance Agent.

By this time the SA was running many different commercial ventures, so it is not surprising to find in many bandsmen employed in SA firms, whether publishing, instrument manufacturing, uniform/clothing industry, or some of its financial corporations.

The large 36-piece Luton 2 Corps Band of 1902 included the manager of the SA Bonnet Factory and at least five others working in the same firm, including straw hat blockers and packers. The variety of jobs held by the majority demonstrates that the pattern of drawing Salvationists from among the labouring class and lower middle-class trades held true in this band (and most others profiled in this series). Jobs held by members of the 1902 Luton 2 Band included plasterer, moulder, labourer, brass finisher, railway porters, shoemaker, house decorator, coal carman, fitter, builder, trainee in a draftsman's office, baker, fitter, turner, and one still in school!

The Barrow-in-Furness Band of industrial Lancashire had 18 of its 44 members in 1902 trained in the junior band. Many of these bandsmen, young and old, were employed in heavy industry as steel workers, steel dresser, steel smelter, boiler maker, steel contractor, machine tenter, and blastfurnace men, while others in this seaside town served as shipwrights, ship plater, and even a fishmonger.

The short history included on the band indicates that, in the earliest days of the band, other members of the corps were opposed to the formation of the band. The band broke up for a time when local authorities forbade street marching, yet by the Coronation of King Edward VII the band was being requested to play civic functions, and being paid 'handsomely' for it.

This pattern of early opposition, frequently violent in nature, followed by a respectful embracing by the community was duplicated all across Great Britain (See below for further observations on this gradual gaining of respectability). Saved Salvationists became not only good evangelists, but, through sheer hard work, fine musicians, and, eventually, solid citizens within their community.

Opposition to the Army's work grew as a direct result of its aggressive outdoor evangelism, in which bands, of course, had the major role. While church processions and outdoor rallies with brass bands were indeed commonplace throughout the land by the time the SA got started, the manner, times, and places chosen by the SA challenged social conventions. Marching to and from the Open-Air on the Sabbath, and direct confrontation with taverns, pubs, and 'gin palaces', brought about serious legal challenges, physical abuse, and imprisonment.

At first the SA sought means to control their troops, requiring via a 'General Order' of June 1882, that bands avoid marching past places of worship or doing so in silence. Many local ordinances throughout the kingdom were enacted specifically to stop the Army processions and Army bands playing on Sundays.

In 1885 the city of Eastbourne passed the Eastbourne Town Improvement Act which forbade processions with music, an indirect attack on Army practices, one intended to keep the Army out of the town. By 1891 the SA decided to challenge the act by launching their Open-Air programs via a newly established corps band. There were serious disturbances and riots within the town that led to national attention and outrage.

By 1892 the Salvationists had won the right to march the streets of the town with music. Another colourful account, that at Whitchurch in 1889, tells of a wise, shrewd, and daring mobilisation of SA bands and supporters that changed public opinion, and soon the law, in the Army's favour. Headquarters brought a large procession of approximately 2500 soldiers and 12 bands, the 12 bandmasters of whom were promptly arrested and convicted. The Queen's Bench case of July 1,1890 was decided in favour of the SA.

As in the persecution of the early Christian church, such opposition only made for martyrs, and a gradual turn of the general public in support of the Army's work. SA bands did pay a heavy toll, but they would also reap the largest benefits in the form of steadfast support by headquarters in every area of SA banding – from music, to equipment – and above all, in a carefully undertaken educational program that would bring about an educated leadership pool. As a result, bands were strengthened and improved whereby they became no longer objects of derision, but of admiration and social acceptance.[16]

Educating and Training a Musical Army

In 1882 William Booth had appointed Fred Fry to begin producing brass arrangements for SA bands (see below). The establishment in October, 1883 of the first official Music Department, (later to be called the International Music Editorial Department or IMED), brought about the beginning of not only the first successful publication of instrumental and vocal music, but the start of a focused program of music education.

The department was placed under the broad supervision of Booth's able son, Herbert, but with Richard Slater taking charge of the actual running of the department, in which Slater was assisted by Fred Fry and Harry Hill. In Slater, Booth had a natural pedagogue, a man eager to teach and help the development of musicians within the young movement.

The first educational tool published for bands by the department was a sheet of scales, in 1887. This was followed up in July, 1890 with the release of a *Band Tutor*, the first one for cornet, those for other instruments printed in the next few years.

Up until that time Army bands used what materials they could find, most frequently Henry Round's *Brass Band Primer or First Instructions for Brass Bands*, which contained scales, fingering/positioning charts, several hymns, simple dances, and practical performance hints. What is also likely is that they relied on the manuscript exercises provided by the large number of band instructors hired by Army corps in order to get their groups 'jump-started'.[17]

While their primary efforts centred on much needed practical music for bands and vocal soloists/vocal parties, Slater was to use the pages of the *Musical Salvationist* to educate his musicians. The *Musical Salvationist* began in May 1886; it was primarily a periodical containing new vocal music, mostly new songs, choruses, and vocal solos.

The cover of The Musical Salvationist, September 1903.

"THE DICTIONARY OF MUSIC" WAS COMMENCED IN JULY, 1902.

Make Sure of Getting each Number from that Issue.

Copyright]   [ALL RIGHTS RESERVED.

THE

MUSICAL SALVATIONIST

A MONTHLY MAGAZINE FOR SONGSTERS BANDSMEN AND THE HOME CIRCLE

PRICE 3D

Part III. SEPT., 1903. Vol. XVIII.

CONTENTS.

	PAGE
Jesus Only	25
Dear Lord of Calvary	26
They'll Never be Remembered	27
Wash and be Clean	28
Speak, Lord, Again	29
Now I am Glad and Free	30
Stand to Arms	30
Oh, List While I Sing	32
Vital Spark	34

Printed and Published monthly by WILFRED LEVICK SIMPSON, at THE SALVATION ARMY PUBLISHING DEPARTMENT 79 & 81 FORTESS ROAD, LONDON, N.W.

But it also would contain articles on various musical subjects (theoretical, performance practice, choices of literature, organisational issues), notes for bandmasters about the latest band journals, 'chats' for bandsmen on a variety of spiritual and musical topics as well as instrumental solos and pieces for instrumental ensembles.

With the success of the magazine *The Local Officer* (starting 1897; later the *Bandsman and Songster*, and eventually the *Musician*), such articles gradually moved out of the vocal publication and notes on band music began to be placed within the full band scores.

Appendix 4 contains a partial list of the kinds of detailed articles written by Slater and his new associate, Frederick Hawkes, that were printed in the *Musical Salvationist*. These men had a pronounced pedagogical streak, which would pay great dividends. Their lay music leaders became highly skilled and knowledgeable, one of the most remarkable aspects of SA music in its first generation.[18] Slater and Hawkes continued this trend in the form of a series of books or extended tutors, several of which appeared first in serialised form in publications like the *Musical Salvationist*, the *Bandsman and Songster*, or the *Young Soldier*:

> **Richard Slater:** *Pianoforte Tutor* (1904); *First Lessons in Music* (1906); *First Lessons in Harmony* (1906); *The Salvation Army Dictionary of Music* (1908); *Studies in Modulation* (1928).

> **Frederick Hawkes:** *Studies in Band Training* (1905); *The Slide Trombone* (1910); *Musical Calligraphy* (1924); *Studies in Time and Tempo: A Handbook for Conductors* (1936).

Richard Slater's 150-page, tightly packed *Dictionary* not only included the expected definitions of musical terms and explanations of theoretical concepts, but also contained valuable information on various aspects of Salvation Army musical life. As compiled by Slater *to meet the needs of Bandsmen and Songsters* its importance at the time, and as an important historical document, can not be overstated.

Printed literature about music and music making was soon supplemented by gatherings of musicians, the first being the December 10, 1899 Bandsmen's Councils, a day aimed as much at spiritual renewal as at musical improvement. Four years later, on January 17–18, 1903 the first Bandmaster and Songster Leaders' Councils were held, thereby setting a pattern that has continued to the present day.

At this same event one year later, Bramwell Booth (Chief of the Staff) announced the intention to institute examinations for determining proficiency of music leaders. Courses of study were in place by 1905 (See Chapter 3).

The other means of teaching was by example, something proved overwhelmingly successful with the Fry quartet. The Household Troops Band formed in 1887 was to have the greatest impact both within Great Britain and in North America in stirring up interest in excellent band service:

> [HTB] *was organised for continuous musical work so that its members volunteered for this kind of field labour as the ordinary candidate does for Field operations. The first notice about the Band in which suitable Army musicians were asked to offer themselves, appeared in the War Cry dated the 12th of March, 1887. Those who offered and were found suitable were called up to the Congress Hall the following May. The first tour was one in the Black Country and it commenced in June; and on the late Queen's Jubilee Day the Band was at Birmingham, its playing winning the highest praises from the crowds of that city. In February, 1888, the band went to Ireland, and later in the year, in October, it left England for a tour of Canada and the United States, gaining by its music that public attention of those countries as had never been done before by any other Army means.*[19]

While not yet called a staff band, this group set the pattern for such bands world-wide, providing outstanding training to the members, who would then take their experience either to local corps as music leaders, or as officers who had caught the vision for effective musical ministry. The impact of the Household Troops Band on the first official staff band, what is now called the New York Staff Band, that formed the same year, June 1887, cannot be overemphasised.[20]

While the first official International Staff Band was directed by Fred William Fry when established in 1891, several years before that date William Booth appointed 'Staff Captain' Harry Appleby in 1887 *to have oversight of all the staff bands*. These included the Household Troops Band 1 (1887–1893), the Household Troops Band 2 (initially under BM Samuel Webber), formed while HTB1 was on tour in America, and a Headquarters' Junior Staff Band, a group commissioned under Webber at the welcome home meeting for the HTB1 band in April, 1889. Caleb Burgess took over HTB2 and soon the Junior Staff Band was merged with this group.

Staff Bands were formed at four centres of operation in a very short time, all of them under the administration of Appleby: 1) Home Office (National Headquarters); 2) Trade Headquarters; 3) International Headquarters; and 4) Social Wing.[21]

Harry Appleby, one of the most colourful of early army musicians, was converted in 1882 at the 'Rink' corps in Colchester while in the city for a guest appearance with the

The Household Troops Band, with BM Harry Appleby playing his cornet in the foreground, on a break from arduous duty! c.1889.

local town band. Trained as a professional musician in the Essex Rifles from age 10 and by age 14 as a cornetist in a military staff band, Appleby had become an outstanding soloist. He divided his time between the military service with the regiment (intermittent) and professional playing with such groups as the Black Star Minstrels. Major Thomas Blandy, the SA Divisional Officer in that area, introduced Appleby to William Booth, requesting that the musician serve on his staff.

After military discharge, Appleby worked for 18 months for Blandy organising and supervising bands of the Eastern Division, thus being perhaps the first 'Divisional Music Director' in the history of SA music.

In May–June 1885, Herbert Booth enlisted him for the 'Great Kent March' by the first of many 'Life Guards' of that era. In this case Appleby was involved with a group of 125 men 'cadets' and a band of 25 who took on an evangelistic campaign that sowed the organisational seeds for the establishment of the more permanent travelling group, the Household Troops Band. [See Slater *Dictionary of Music* entry on this group] Appleby's military training paid dividends, as relayed in two diaries of HTB members that survive from this era, that of Edwin Cork and William Nicholson.

On day 157 of the Canada/USA Tour Nicholson related that they spent the afternoon at practice…*former military man that he is, with true military discipline he drilled us to his heart's content.* Edwin Cork's diary covers a five-year period in which he calculated he had travelled in that period *30,000 miles by water, railway, and foot* in the HTB. This highly efficient, model group soon had the honour of being the first SA band to play 'solo' at a national event.

On July 15, 1890, they were the chief musical attraction at the first Crystal Palace rally, a day that saw Fred Fry playing the large organ there, Slater leading a large 'string band', and Appleby, in his role as leader of all staff bands, directing a large massed band.[22]

By 1891 Appleby was no longer leading the Household Troops, but took over the leadership of the Home Office Band and continued his supervisory work of all staff bands until 1894. In July of that year at the Second International

Congress at the Crystal Palace, Appleby's march with trio, *A Great Salvation*, later referred to as *Appleby's March*, was performed, much to the disliking of General William Booth, who *threatened to sack him if he wrote more of the like*. Though published perhaps with modifications in the *Band Journal* (GS 213), it was not allowed to become a model.

Ever an innovator, Appleby had played an earlier role in 1885 by getting the first 'bass solo' march approved, having Herbert Booth audition it for his father. The work was *Roused from My Slumber*, GS 33, an excerpt drawn from Donizetti's opera, *Lucia di Lammermoor* and can thus be considered the first classical transcription for SA bands.

Known not only for bringing British military discipline of the highest order into SA banding, he was also known for his great improvisational skill on the E Flat Soprano Cornet. This 'skill' was a factor in many early SA band performances, though the abuses by less proficient musicians soon led to the banning of such practices. He retired from active service by the early 1900s, but did see further service as corps bandmaster at Southend.

The pattern set by Herbert Booth and Harry Appleby in providing a model, touring band of the finest musical and spiritual condition is the one followed to this day. That initial success continues to support the rationale behind all band 'tours' intended to help spread the Gospel as well as build, renew, or encourage local musicians in the areas visited.[23]

What Music did the Early Bands Play?

Early SA bands gained their music from three principal sources prior to the establishment of the IMED and before the 1885 General Order forbidding the use of non-SA music.

This included the following: 1) manuscript arrangements made by their band instructors or bandmasters, usually 'arrangements' or transpositions of keyboard tune books of hymns and songs; 2) at least one publication by an 'outside' publisher prepared especially for SA bands; 3) brass band music of a sacred nature already being published by various firms.

Prior to the start of SA bands, brass band publishers in Great Britain had been providing for quite some time music suitable for occasions of sacred intent. There would have been a considerable market, bearing in mind the large numbers of church bands, missions bands, temperance bands, to say nothing of the involvement of other bands in church functions.

The principal publishers to whom early SA bands could have turned to for music included: 1) in the London area, Hawkes, J. R. Lafleur & Son, R. Smith (started in Hull 1857, moved to London, 1878), and R. de Lacy; 2) in Hull, T.A. Haigh; 3) in Manchester, J Frost & Son, and 4) in Liverpool, Wright & Round.

At the 1903 Bandmaster and Songster Leaders' Councils then Chief of the Staff Bramwell Booth, when discussing the history of the gradual emancipation of SA band literature from severe restrictions, acknowledged in an off-hand way these sources of early band music for SA bands... *Then came all kinds of music* [printed or written music before the Army had its own publications], *with Introductions, Links, and so on. Some from Liverpool, some from Hull, and some from Hell!*[24] No doubt the better of the early SA bands would have risen to the challenge of such pieces as Linter's *Sacred Fantasia: Reminiscences of Moody and Sankey*, a lengthy, rhapsodic medley of ten songs advertised in the October 1st, 1882 issue of the *Brass Band News* as part of the Wright & Round subscription for 1882.

What was more likely to see use were the many hymn tune and carol sheets that many of these publishers released during this period. The Christmas issue of the *Liverpool Brass Band and Military Journal* (Wright & Round) for 1881 included the following seven items more suitable for developing bands: *Hail, Smiling Morn* (Spofforth), *A Virgin Unspotted* (arr. H. Round), *Work for Jesus* (Sankey), *Washed in the Blood* (Cookman), *The Angel's Song* (arr. Linter), *The Invitation* (Bliss), and *Hosanna* (H. Round).

Hymns sheets, transcriptions of sacred and classical choral anthems, and marches suitable for church processions had been available for a number of years. J. R. Lafleur's *Second Series of 'Inseparables' Book* (see *Brass Band News*, July 1st 1882) contained 'religious music, glees, andantes, etc.', with such favourites as shortened versions of the *Kyrie, Gloria, Credo* from Mozart's *12th Mass*, an evocative work called *Church Call* (W. Jones), and the sufficiently vague *Andante Religioso* (Reyloff). Many publishers put together such 'Sacred Series' sets of bound books not for SA bands, who were only beginning to be noticed, but for all types of brass bands who continued to be involved in various kinds of semi-religious events.

By mid-1882, when Fred Fry's early penny-card sheets for SA bands proved a failure (see below), the SA turned to a relatively new London publisher, R. de Lacy, of Brixton, southwest London. De Lacy produced in late 1882–early 1883, a band tune book of 44 tunes, 34 of which were taken from the 1880 publication, *Salvation Army Music*.[25]

More interesting for the history of SA band music were some of the sacred marches printed at this time. By 1884, for example, Wright & Round had available pieces that seem to anticipate, in many details, the experimental works Slater would begin publishing in 1902.

The 'Sacred Quick March' *What a Friend We Have in Jesus* by Linter contained four distinct sections in traditional march format. The first three are in the tonic, and the fourth, or Trio, in the subdominant key, with the option for a *da capo* repeat.

The march begins with a 16-measure first strain made up of original material of very moderate demands. C. C. Converse's relatively new gospel song is then sounded in its entirety. A typical 'Bass Solo' strain of 30 measures completes the first portion. The Trio is only 16 measures long, and is not repeated; the tune strongly resembles the syncopated chorus *Oh, Remember, O Remember, Jesus dying on the Tree*. This, in itself, would be the kind of model piece that a Slater or Hawkes would have been familiar with.

The general form and reference, if not musical substance, must have made an impression on the SA music department, and was certainly the type of item quickly grasped by SA bands. T. A. Wright's Sacred Quick March *The Cross of Jesus/The Lifeboat* (Wright & Round Journal No. 139) was another type, the march medley, available by no later than 1881. Indeed, one of John Philip Sousa's earliest marches fell into this category, *The Revival March*, written in 1876, which also featured a popular gospel song of the day, *In the Sweet By and By*. (By the 1890s, this march had its title expanded into *The Great Revival March and Salvation Army Rally*, in recognition of the growing awareness of SA activities and SA bands in America at the time.)

The first music the SA printed for its bands came out in July 1882, a series of 13 single card sets that contained usually 7–8 tunes per card, primarily to accompany congregational singing. Selling for sixpence a copy, Set No. 1 included the following tunes: 1. *Fire away*; 2. *O, the voice*; 3. *Lift Up the Banner*; 4. *Land beyond the blue*; 5. *Are you ready*; 6. *Now I can read my title*; 7. *We shall sing*; 8. *We're traveling home*.

Fred Fry was working by himself under extremely poor conditions (especially with equipment). SA bands did not embrace the end result. This led, in turn, to the extraordinary loss at that time of over 100 pounds sterling. Richard Slater admitted that the cards failed to meet the wishes of bands on both technical (part-writing) and interest level, the 'outside' music (published or manuscript) was still better.[26]

In October 1883 Booth established an expanded music department under the leadership of Richard Slater, but under the supervision of Herbert Booth, whose influence in the development of early SA bands deserves more attention. Slater was joined by Fred Fry, and Bandmaster Henry Hill, a police sergeant from Hull, formerly with the Hull Police Band (his corps was Hull 2), who was asked to resign his police work, and come to the music department, as well as lead the Clapton Congress Hall Corps Band!

By November, 1884 they had produced the first band tune book for accompanying singing, *Band Music for The Salvation Army*, a revised (in part-writing and scoring) and expanded version of Fry's sixpenny cards. It contained 88 tunes, numbered consecutively, and arranged for 14 instrumental parts.

Earlier that summer (August, 1884) they launched the *Band Journal*, then issued monthly, a series that would go through successive name changes—*Ordinary Series, General Series*—and is still being produced. BJ, or GS 1 contained three songs: *Steadily Marching On; I Will Follow Thee, My Saviour; Never To Come Back Any More.* Within less than a year, armed with only a half dozen issues of the *General Series*, plus the 88-tune *Band Music*, General Booth ordered in the May 27, 1885 *War Cry* that *from this date no Band will be allowed to play from any music excepting The Salvation Army General Band Journal, the Journals published by us from time to time, and other music issued by HQ. Quicksteps and Introductions are strictly prohibited.*

That this order created difficulties would be a gross understatement. By this edict Booth was to gain absolute autocratic control (he was indeed "a committee of one," his son Bramwell frequently sharing *My father was really less an organizer than a legislator; he was a whole legistlature in himself*) He laid down the law in every detail, thinking of everything. He left others to organise the administration of his bands' music and enforce an incredibly limited repertoire.

Oddly enough, for years this music was sold beyond the SA. Slater once stated in a profile of his department (*Musical Salvationist* XIII, 1898–99, pp35–36) that *Our Band music is extensively used among mission bands in all directions, and we have heard that some of our Christmas number have been utilised by a Volunteer band for their Christmas music.* Respectability, indeed!

However, Booth's decision, first with music, and then with equipment and instruments, would cause a century-long rift in the British brass band culture worldwide.

In the brass press of the 1890s General Booth was frequently taken to task for these decisions, something that reached fever pitch in the attack levelled on him by Algernon Rose in *Talks With Bandsmen* (1896).[27]

For Booth, such a decision would allow him to keep his troops focused on the main task, evangelism, by ensuring the music was always tied to a message. He would lose bands, as acknowledged grudgingly in various official accounts (usually by such nice metaphors as 'cloudy, dark skies', which eventually clear), but he held fast to his principles.[28] Most likely his sons, with the help of Slater, gradually convinced him to loosen the reins. This initial

THE READING 1 S.A. CITADEL BAND (1892)

An 1892 photograph of the Reading 1 Citadel Band, taken from the corps centenary booklet.

'circling of the wagons' was a complicated decision, one taken in light of a host of problems facing Booth at the time both within his emerging band culture and within his movement as a whole. Trevor Herbert points out that we must bear in mind several factors when evaluating Booths' decision:

> *The growth of independent, semi-professional brass bands, the controversies that surrounded the relationship between bands and the volunteer forces, and, perhaps, the independence of temperance bands from their original purpose, caused Booth to take steps that ensured that Salvationist bands would be discrete from the brass band movement for more than a hundred years.*[29]

By this time, Booth had seemingly caught up with his enthusiastic banding movement, the improvisational days were over, and, though he always left the details to others, he had indeed set the future course of SA bands with his indelible stamp.[30]

Musical Form and Practice in Early SA Band Music

The majority of *Band Journal* numbers from 1884–1901 consisted of 2 or 3 tunes per band part page. This music was drawn from the following sources: 1) Simple, one-strophe settings of well-known hymn tunes/gospel songs; 2) popular songs or classical airs to which Salvationists had written new texts (*contrafacta*); 3) transcriptions of new songs printed in the *Musical Salvationist*.

The individual items for a band journal 'page' were usually linked in subject, though sometimes not. Many of them were transcriptions of vocal items appearing in the *Musical Salvationist*, which began publication in 1886.

A typical single *Band Journal* item from this period would be GS 210, No.2., *Are You Washed?* The full band states the verse of this famous war song ('Have you been to Jesus for the cleansing power?') at *mf* volume. The first statement of the chorus, without the dotted rhythm pick-up of later versions, is marked *forte*, and the euphonium adds a few decorative runs. The chorus is then repeated *fortissimo* by the entire low end of the band (baritones on down), accompanied by typical fanfare figures in the cornets, horns, and clarinets (See in Volume II the Chapter *Scoring and Instrumentation*).

General Booth soon allowed the successive playing of *Band Journal* tunes while bands were on the march, thus forming a type of march medley or selection in the 'string of pearls' variety.

In his *Analysis of the Brass Band Journal* for 1900, Nos. 383–386, Slater clarified, on the eve of significant changes in SA music, basic types and functions in SA brass music. Score notes such as this first appeared in the *Musical Salvationist*, then the *Local Officer*, and eventually on the covers of the *Band Journals* themselves:

> *Music for Army Bands is such as to form three classes of pieces, viz., 1) Tunes intended for congregational singing, 2) Marches, and 3) Pieces for stationary*

playing, as for use when the collection is being taken, or when the Band is called upon to exercise its power of musical attraction.

In that above-mentioned issue of June 1900 (GS 383–386) there were eleven pieces contained within the four journal numbers. These were grouped in units of songs that could be played together as a medley; or each tune could be played separately.

GS 383 (containing three tunes in 4/4 time, all marked at the same metronome marking, crotchet = 112), for example, could be played as a 'March', as Slater referred to it in the quote above. The first, *Hampshire*, is in A Flat, the second, *Our King*, in E Flat, and the final, climactic tune, *We March to Victory*, returns to A Flat. The middle tune is

Early Full Band Score, Band Journal 253, June 1894; 'The History of The Army'. Produced by a lithographic hand-written process.

a transcription of one of Slater's best songs, a tune that Leidzén would use for the entire Trio of his famous march *In the King's Service*, GS 1213 (first published in the *Svensk Festmusik* No. 189, as *Nattan Flytt*).

In June, 1894, the entire *Band Journal* Nos. 253–256 was given the broad programmatic title 'The History of the Army', and contained ten 'chapters', using 10 tunes or songs:

> [BJ 253] No. 1. *The General* (4/4, allegro mod., D Flat major) No. 2. *Mile End Waste* (4/4, andante con espress., F major) [BJ 254] No. 3. *The Army Converts and Soldiers* (6/8, allegretto, B Flat major) No. 4. *The Officers* (4/4, allegro mod., D Flat major) [BJ 255] No. 5. *The Army's Aim* (4/4, allegro mod., G Flat major) No. 6. *Rows and Riots* (4/4 allegro con spirito, D Flat major) No. 7. *The War Cry and Army Literature* (4/4, allegro mod., F major) No. 8. *The Social Wing* (6/8, andante con espress., A Flat major) [BJ 256] No. 9. *The Junior Soldiers War* (6/8, allegretto mod., F Major) No. 10. *The Army Music* (4/4, Vivace, D Flat Major)

Most likely this piece could only be attempted in its entirety at a festival. There are no links between songs, though like in BJ 210, there are repeated choruses with modified scoring and part writing.

Other medleys taking up just one Band Journal number came shortly after, among the first being *Hallelujah* (GS 281, May 1895), *Indian Medley* 1 (GS 309, May 1896), and *Let Me Hear You Tell It Over* (GS 331, March 1897). BJ 351 was announced in a *Musical Salvationist* advertisement, Autumn, 1898, as *a brilliant Medley...suitable for marching as well as other purposes... This medley was played by the INTERNATIONAL STAFF BAND as one of their special pieces at the great day of the Anniversary of the Army at the Alexandria Palace, on July 18th, and all the most important Bands have the medley already in view.*[31]

SA bands were desperate for quality music. The Army itself was encouraging more and more musical skill and discipline, and was even consciously fostering an informal sense of competition, or at least a sense of tiered levels among its bands.

Slater and his staff faced pressures that exerted a strong pull toward a musical evolution in the SA band journal. Music leaders desired music with a challenge to keep their enthusiasm fresh. More accomplished players demanded music of a quality high enough to offset the constant attraction of 'outside' and contesting bands. Even non-musicians were demanding more sophisticated worship services, with the possible addition of musical meditations to inspire them in Christian growth. The SA was becoming as beset as any denomination emerging from its first generation.

On September 4, 1901, the Music Board submitted a memorandum to William Booth requesting certain changes in music publication policy. The resultant decisions gave the IMED further latitude, subject to the General's direct approval, for changes in instrumentation, arrangement, and compositional style. Band music might be allowed to contain original material for which no words had been composed or intended. Members of the IMED were put to work immediately providing sample works that would serve as models for future contributions.

With this decision came the very carefully monitored development of a band literature which could be considered uniquely Salvation Army. Three major precedents were set at this time which have continued to serve as guidelines for SA instrumental composition: 1) An evangelical message was to remain the primary motivation behind all SA band music; 2) Standard instrumentation was adopted for SA bands along exclusively brass band guidelines (See Volume II, Chapter *Instrumentation and Scoring*); 3) members of IMED would provide model pieces to serve as examples for contributors from outside the department.

Three types of 'original' compositions were soon launched, basic forms that still occupy the largest portion of SA brass music: the march, the meditation, and the selection.

The first published piece for SA bands labelled a 'selection' was entitled *Old Song Memories*, and it was released in December 1901 as a free supplement to *Band*

Journal 407–410. Without journal number, the work was in all but name a long medley of 11 songs. Only one slight link, via a two-measure solo cornet 'cadenza' (slow falling scale) between the fourth and fifth tune, separates it from other medleys that preceded it. However, the scoring called for solos by the First Horn, First Cornet, Solo Euphonium, and First Trombone, a new innovation. The band parts, printed on two pages back-to-back, carried the rubric 'A Selection for Festival Use', the kind of order that would appear regularly when the SA launched the *Festival Series* in 1921. One of the amusing aspects of this item appears on the First Trombone part, where just prior to his exposed solo, the player is instructed in Italian *Volti subito* – 'turn quickly'!

Several months later in GS 418 the first true episode between two tunes was inserted, which linked 418, No. 1, *Comrades, arouse to the call*, with 418, No. 2, *Onward Christian Soldiers*.

A special note concerning this daring innovation was printed in the June, 1902, *Local Officer* (p. 421) under the bold heading *ATTENTION! BANDMASTERS AND BANDSMEN!*: *A special connecting Episode following the Bass Solo of the first [tune] prepares the way for the second tune. The Episode is six bars in length, and by a series of transitions it carries us over to the second tune, providing additional interest to the music by linking the two tunes on the sheet as parts of one whole.*

Slater considered his *Songs of Scotland* selection, released several months after *Old Song Memories*, GS 428–429, as the true first selection, having an introduction preceding eleven songs, though with very short links between several of them.

The archetypal meditation, a SA band composition based on one previously composed hymn or song, was published in the March 1902 *Band Journal*, GS 412, No. 2. Entitled *Jesus, Hope of Souls Repentant*, it was based on Slater's own vocal piece, a kind of chorale in the unusual key of B Major provided with a somewhat elaborate piano accompaniment, first published in the *Musical Salvationist* (XVI, p84). It is the first SA composition for band in which the composer attempts to portray the separate verses of a song through instrumental means. Slater described his piece as *...a fourfold arrangement...so that the whole gives, as it were, a different setting of the four verses of the song, the aim being to bring out different aspects and moods of the same piece.*[32]

The band arrangement contains four statements of the chorale differing mainly in orchestration and in detail of melodic accompanying figures. The 'running bass', seen in the keyboard part of the vocal version is used only for the final statement of the chorale in the brass arrangement; this device became standard, and, later, abused, in Army meditations.

The effect of the whole arrangement is similar to that of an organ improvisation upon a given chorale, with the changing verses of the text evoking variations by the performer upon the tune. Slater's simple form had its basis in variation principle, setting the tone for all later subjective meditations, the Salvationist composer's 'testimony' in music.

Slater's second, more successful experiment in song illustration was entitled *Lead Kindly Light: A Festival Arrangement* (GS 436, 1902). This was based on the tune *Sandon* to which were sung the familiar words by Cardinal John Henry Newman, these having been incorporated into the 1899 *Songbook*.

The subtitle made it clear that the preferred function for this music was in concert only. Technically demanding, the work was the subject of controversy because of the florid solo cornet obbligato (thought by some to be a pretext for egoistic showmanship) which accompanied the third presentation of the tune, as well as a solo scored for the First Baritone. The proportions of the work were also greater than in *Jesus Hope of Souls*. After a lengthy introduction in the tonic minor, with chromatic 'wanderings' perhaps intended as a musical depiction of the 'encircling gloom' from verse one, Slater presents four varied orchestrations of the principal tune. These are linked by short episodes, in a quicker tempo, between all but the third and fourth statement of the tune.

There is a gradual building of dynamic level and a thickening of texture throughout, with the final statement (verse four) accompanied by the characteristic 'running' bass.[33] Self-conscious and stilted as these early Slater works may seem to us now, they were the harbingers of all advanced music developed within the SA.

Three 'specimens', as the composer Slater called them, of the new SA march were released in 1902. The first, *The Morning Hymn March* (GS 411, March 1902) used the *Morning Hymn* tune as its Trio, but was otherwise fully original. *Our Battalions* (GS 415, June, 1902), was described by Slater as being made up of two well-known melodies (*Come and Join Our Army, the Army of the Lord*, and the title hymn tune), adapted with intros, links, and episodes.

The Festival March (GS 422, September, 1902) was fully original, but Slater did not consider it successful, hoping to have done a better job giving it *in sound an Army stamp*. (See George Bernard Shaw's comments on early Army marches, Chapter 3). Both *Our Battalions* and *Evening Hymn March* (both expansions and improvements on Slater's first effort) also contain final endings, to be played after the *da capo* has been taken.

Hawkes' *Spanish Chant March* (GS 427, January, 1903) was a better example of how the Army could write marches within Booth's restraints, but also in line with contemporary march styles. The introduction sounds in a fiery F minor and is based on several simple, but clear motivic ideas that unite the first part of the march.

Slater had also used short rhythmic figures in this way, but the results seem cluttered, busy, and the part writing rather thick at times, the whole giving a rather laboured, strained feel, though with each succeeding effort Slater improved. His colleague may not have been as good a song writer as Slater, but he could write a better march. Hawkes' form is an economic compression of many military marches of the day:

> *Part 1:* Introduction (8 bars [measures]) and Letter A (10 bars) in F Minor; Letter B (8 bars) episode beginning in A Flat but modulating back to the tonic minor; Letter C (8 bars), a repeat of A, except ending in A Flat; Letter D (10 bars), bass solo with trumpeting, A Flat major [No sections repeated]

Trio: 3-bar link into D Flat major; Letter E (24 bars) presenting the tune in augmented, chorale fashion, soft dynamic; Letter F (8 bars) gradually more animated episode modulating back to A Flat; *Maestoso* (final 10 bars), tune played in normal rhythm, *fortissimo*, accompanied by running bass. [D.C. indicated, even though the resolved tonic of Part 1 has been regained]

Slater and Hawkes worked as a dynamic team in supplying the vast bulk of journal arrangements at this critical point in SA music.

By 1902 other names began to be seen, if not on the scores or band parts, but on the official departmental copies of the score, with the name of the composer or arranger written in, usually in Slater's pen. At the top of the score to GS 407, No. 3, *Warriors Arise*, Slater has written in pen *arr. by Bandmaster Pursglove. The Swedish March*, GS 419 is marked *Major Otto Lundahl, arr. Lt. Col. R. Slater*,

The cover of the Band Journal Score, 403 - 406, 1901.
Right: First page of the score.

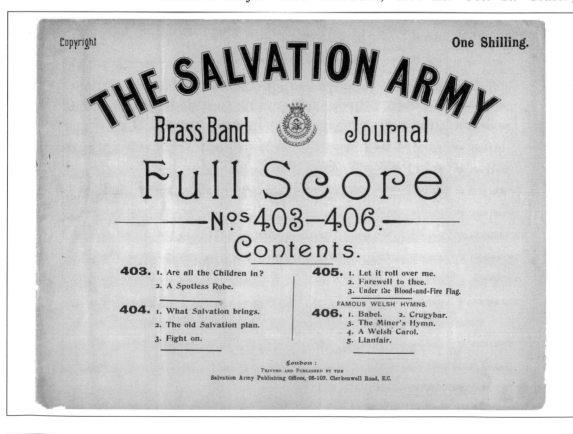

Lundahl having been the first head of the SA music department in Sweden.

Klaus Östby's *Norwegian March* appeared in August, 1903 (GS 443, No. 3), yet Ostby himself had penned the first truly original SA march, *Kabelvåg*, way back in 1891–92, though not published until decades later [See Chapter 6 for Lundahl and Östby].

The music of classical composers provided Slater with a deep resource for much of his vocal music, and, as a result of transcription, early band music (See Donizetti reference above).

Medleys of classical shorts, or 'gems from' type selection appeared a few years later with *Thoughts From the Great Masters No. 1* [September, 1907; GS 546]. It contained excerpts from Beethoven, Mozart, Meyerbeer, and Mendelssohn arranged by Slater.

The first two complete, purely instrumental transcriptions appeared in the *Special Funeral Number of the Band Journal*, October 1903: No. 1 *Dead March in 'Saul'*

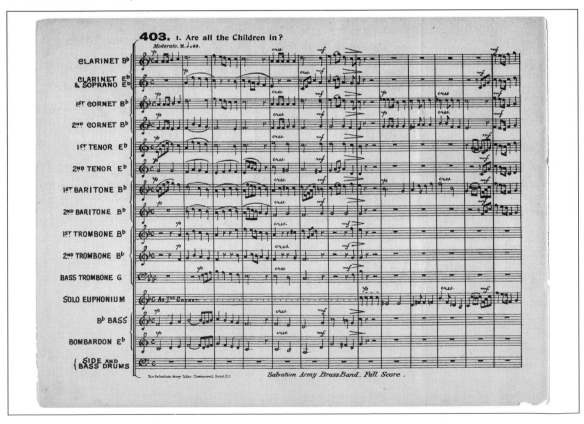

(Handel); and No. 2 *Funeral March* (from Mendelssohn's *Songs Without Words*). It seems that Hawkes scored the Handel march, according to a notation written in ink on the department's printed score that still exists. The issue also contained the transcription of a Victorian choral favourite, Harwood's setting of Pope's *The Vital Spark*, which had appeared in the September, 1903 *Musical Salvationist* (p34).

The team of Slater and Hawkes shared the arranging tasks for the May, 1904 *Band Journal* (GS 459–462) designed for the upcoming International Congress that summer at which SA bands were to come of age and gain acceptance, even a measure of respectability. The four items were actually conservative in nature, the two marches being as much medleys as the two selections: GS 459 *The Army March* (arr. Slater, 7 tunes); GS 460 *The Army Flag Selection* (arr. Hawkes, 6 tunes); GS 461 *The Praise March* (arr. Hawkes, 5 tunes); GS 462 *Crown Him Selection* (arr. Slater, 5 tunes).

While Slater's experiments of 1901–1903 pointed towards future developments, these four works summarised an era.

Respectability, or At Least Tolerance

SA bands reached their first peak at the International Congress of 1904. Over 200 bands took part in aspects of the celebration that ran from June 24th to July 14th.

At that time the offices of the *British Bandsman* were right across the street from one of the centres of activity, Congress Hall.

The huge demonstrations at the Crystal Palace and on the Strand were within easy striking distance. The editor reported with amazement and envy that 7,000 bandsmen, with instruments worth over £100,000 were attending the Congress. Repeating a figure he had heard of 17,000 current bandsmen within the Army, he even speculated *if only each bought a copy of the British Bandsman!* Actually many were buying it (without permission, it might be noted), with the slow trickle of coverage of SA band activity commencing in the late 1890s gaining in volume and frequency within the first few years of the century.

Hailstone has summarised the impact of SA bandsmen taking an interest in the brass press this way: *One effect of the influx of SA readers was a swing towards a more learned type of article, often by contributors with the academic qualifications of Mus, Bac, and F.R.C.O...outside bands lapped up the activities of these SA bands and were overawed by their discipline and dedication.*[34]

The first positive comments about SA bands in the British band press appeared in the *Brass Band News*, August 1, 1895 under the Luton District report: *The Salvation Army Band* [Luton 2] *have also played for several school treats. They are in many cases preferred to any other band in the town, for they play really well, as well as conduct themselves well, which goes a long way.*

Several years (June 1, 1897) later in the same magazine, this time under the Bristol District report, some ambivalent praise was given: *Heard the No. 1 SA Band playing the other Sunday. Not at all a bad band. Several of the other six or seven SA bands would do well to copy.*

An early gathering of corps soldiery; corps officer, small band and timbrelists; possibly Worcester, MA, USA, late 1880s.
The Officer, with folded arms is Richard E. Holz 1, (later Commissioner).

The Chalk Farm Band was briefly profiled in the December 20, 1899 *British Bandsman*, readers being told that the band was sporting a new set of instruments at £354, including a quartet of saxophones. The anonymous author also shared that ...*some of the bands belonging to the SA have wonderfully improved in a musical sense during the past few years, and none more so than that presided over by Mr. A.W. Punchard in the neighbourhood of Chalk Farm.*

Tensions continued between the brass band industry (publishers and instrument manufacturers, who usually controlled magazines like *Brass Band News* or *British Bandsman*) and the SA, though this did not stop the occasional advertisement of SA products in the pages of these journals, from band lamps to SA-made musical instruments.

Despite the apparent good will, one could read between the lines. Sentences such as the following told of the continuing exasperation felt by having no access to the huge but closed market that SA bands represented: *The playing was of an unusually high order and was, of course, confined to the SA Journal* (May 12, 1901 *British Bandsman* report on Regent Hall and Wood Green Corps Bands' festival).[35]

Still, a rapprochement of sorts was underway, as seen in the reports coming out of the *British Bandsman's* coverage of the International Congress. Appendix 2 includes the entire article from the July 9, 1904 issue. This provides perhaps a more objective view of the proceedings and bands, including several international units that had come for the event, staff bands from Canada, Germany, Norway, New York, Sweden, and even a representative group from the island of Bermuda.

In addition to describing the style of several bands, we learn that the London County Council had become so impressed with SA bands that it was now allowing them to play at the Villiers Street section of the Victoria Embankment Gardens. SA bands had indeed arrived! Also, the New York Staff Band and perhaps others did not seem constrained by *Orders and Regulations*, providing items more suited to a Sousa concert.[36]

The climactic July 5th Festival at the Crystal Palace contained 13 hours of band and songster music and drew a

Blackpool and Derby 2 Bands take part in the 1904 Festival.

crowd reported to be over 100,000. In its article entitled 'Ceaseless Music', (July 18, 1904, p395) the *British Bandsman* gave special praise to three corps bands heard on the grounds – Blackpool, Worthing, and Southend.

The author listed nearly every one of approximately 100 bands that participated, either on the grounds, in the Grand Review march, or in the Massed festivals directed by Staff Bandmaster George Mitchell, including those given by the combined bands of the ISB, Chalk Farm, Congress Hall, Penge, and Highgate Corps.

The writer's insight into what had been wrought by SA bands within 25 years stands as an appropriate summary of this first era in SA banding:

> *It seems scarcely possible that this huge gathering was the outcome of a movement which a very few years since had to pass through a time of ridicule and abuse which would have killed ninety-nine out of every hundred other undertakings no matter how high their ambition or sincere their principles. The Salvation Army believes in music, and good playing is now more common in their bands than what the poor and*

excruciating noises used to be. Commissioner [Alex] Nicol ...assured us that the band playing of The Salvation Army is only in its infancy, and that the Staff were fully alive to the great impetus which good band playing gave to their work, both social and religious.

One final factor must be borne in mind at this stage of SA band history. While the main events in the development of SA bands and music seemed to be all focused in Great Britain, the 1904 International Congress provided an excellent opportunity for international exchange of ideas and styles.

Many regions of the Army world were developing successful bands programs, some modelled on Great Britain (notice the thinly veiled bias in the press accounts), some on their own wind and brass traditions. The Congress bands were but a symbolic representation of the health and energy of the SA band movement.

Notes

1. Taylor, *Brass Bands*, pp14–21. Elgar Howarth discusses three main sources of 19th-century banding, *What a Performance*, pp15-16/23 27. Please also note the following related observations by Russell and Elliot in *The Brass Band Movement: The village church band to some degree had kept music alive in the remote rural districts and now the chapels in the manufacturing districts, as rallying points, began to do the same with bands at the end of the Napoleonic wars. One of the earliest records of the Stalybridge Band is of their first public engagement in the procession and foundation-stone-laying ceremony of Chapel Street Sunday Schools on 24th June, 1815, a few days after the Battle of Waterloo* (p65). *A remarkable number of bands were initially founded in connection with Sunday schools, missions, and various kinds of religious institutes, though few of them remained long attached to their sources of origin* (p124). See page 133ff regarding Volunteer Bands.

2. Richard Slater, typescript article entitled the *Origins of SA Bands*, p5. SA International Heritage Centre, London.

3. See Boon, *Play the Music Play*, Chapter 1 for a more detailed story of the Fry family. See also K. H. Macdermott. *The Old Church Gallery Minstrels: An Account of the Church Bands and Singers in England from About 1600 to 1860*, (London: SPCK, 1948) and Florence Emily Hardy, *The Early Life of Thomas*

Hardy, 1840–1891 (New York: Macmillan, 1928), 13–17. For a broad overview of the subject: E.D. Mackerness, *A Social History of English Music* (Greenwich, CT: Greenwood Press, 1954), , pp121–125,164–169,190–195.

4. *Play the Music Play*, [PMP] p4.

5. Higbie, *William Booth* Volume I, 407–408.Horridge, *Origins*, 90, and 113, the later from a Wesleyan attack on the SA in 1882! See Mackerness, 193, on this purification of church music.

6. Joy Steadman-Allen, *Notes on the use and Development of Salvation Army Music*, part of unpublished thesis Trent Park College, University of London, 1970. See also, Ray Steadman-Allen, *Evolution* series.

7. *Christian Mission Magazine*; Chadwick points out that SA bands would replace the 'old hallelujah bands' of many such missions. O. Chadwick, *The Victorian Church*, Part II. London: 1970, p291. The Christian Missioners used music whenever they could, using solo brass instruments by 1877 (Sanders, *History of SA*, Vol. 1, pp211–212) and even musical services, including one as part of the finale for the August 3–8, 1878 War Congress; *Christian Mission Magazine*, Sept 1878, p250–252. Murdoch explains that early CM indoor meetings combined American revivalism with English music-hall entertainment, with 'sing-song', 'free-and-easy' styles dominating. Murdoch, *Origins*, pp62–63.

8. Richard Slater once wrote concerning the early travels of the Fry band that *the foundations were laid for scores of Army bands because of the direct illustration the Band gave of what could be done in the Army by the use of Brass instruments*. Slater, *Origins*, p21. There is some confusion concerning the exact premiere of the Fry family band. Gordon Taylor, International Heritage Centre, London, has pointed out that Arthur Watts' account on pages 67–75 of *Lion Hearts: Memoirs of the Christian Mission* [c 1930] differs with that of Fry, whereby they started playing for Mary Sayer, who preceded Watts at Salisbury. Both remembrances, of course, are much after the fact, so the account still needs further clarification. I was pleased during a visit to Salisbury Cathedral to accidentally find a plaque honouring the first SA bandmaster on the outside wall of the cathedral facing the cloister walk.

9. Interview with Mr. John B. Agar, November 11, 1934, p4. Typescript transcription in Whitechapel Corps file, International Heritage Centre, London.

10. Vic Elstow, *A Century of Brass: A History of the Wellingborough SA Band*, (Privately published, 1990), p10.

11. In this list, unless otherwise noted, the information was provided by Brindley Boon, from two unpublished chapters, 'Harry

Appleby', and 'Personality Parade', not used in his book *ISB*. Similar patterns can be found in the United States and other countries.

12. The article goes on with even more scathing criticism directed at the music presented at a SA rally in Liverpool the author witnessed.

13. Horridge gleans his initial figures from the 1878 *Christian Mission Magazine* through to the *Army's Pocket Book* of 1884, pp38–40,60. Booth's figures from *The Open Door Before The Salvation Army: Our Present Position*, (London: SP&S,1904), p20.

14. 3-page typescript *Table of 50 of the Earliest Bands of The Salvation Army*, prepared by Richard Slater. International Heritage Centre, London. For a report of a 'Hallelujah Brass Band' under Ballington Booth's command, functioning as early as March 23, 1879, in the Manchester area (Chorlton-on-Medlock) see Glenn K. Horridge, "Invading Manchester: Responses to The Salvation Army 1878–1900", *Manchester Region History Review*, pp19,22. The same author provides some information on early Welsh SA bands in "The Salvation Army in Wales: 1878–1900", *The Journal of Welsh Ecclesiastical History* (Vol 6, 1989), pp51–70.

15. The earliest band profiles listed in Appendix 5 did not give detailed lists of band membership, occupation, but usually did include a short history and overview of current work. Most articles contained pictures of the band or bandmaster.

16. A comprehensive overview of SA band involvement in the most violent opposition would be the official accounts provided by Arch Wiggins, in *The History of the SA*, Vol 4: 1886–1904, especially 245ff.; See Martin Smith, *The Whitechurch Salvation Army Disturbances*, 1881-1890 (Whitechurch: Whitechurch Local Historical Society, 1990), and an account of the famous Eastbourne riots of 1891–1892 in Charles King's pamphlet *Marching With Music* (Eastbourne: Privately published, 1963), which provides the first-hand account of a then 16-year old bandsman, Walter Guy. More recent, scholarly, coverage is given in Horridge, *Origins*, 110–111, and 198–207, the latter dealing with problems in Honiton, *where several of the musical instruments of the Army were smashed and kicked about the streets*, not an uncommon experience wherever the Army was opposed.

17. This primer was advertised as early as February 1, 1882, *Brass Band News (BBN)*. Henry Round, of Wright & Round, Liverpool, then printed an article in the March 1, 1882 issue of *BBN*, one of the few of its kind in that era, *How I Teach a Newly-raised Brass Band*.

18. In comparison to the majority of articles printed in the *BBN* and *British Bandsman [BB]* of this era these articles are indeed detailed. Each page is jammed in small print, single spaced, with all kinds of helpful data, philosophy, exhortation, and general practical advice.

19. Richard Slater, entry on Household Troops Band, *SA Dictionary of Music*, p52. Frederick Hawkes related that appointment to the band meant that the members were officially regarded as *Lieutenants, or officers, in training, and that as their term of service would finish Commandant Herbert Booth, who had appointed them, would transfer them to 'field work' as officers.* See Hawkes' "Reminiscences of Early-Day Fighting," *The Officers' Review*, XVI, No. 6 Nov-Dec 1947, p367.

20. See Holz, *Heralds of Victory*, pp5–7, for an account of the impact of the HTB visit to America.

21. From the unpublished Chapter *Harry Appleby* by Brindley Boon. In recent years there have been several studies of Army staff bands as they reached their centenary year, included those on the ISB, New York Staff Band, and Melbourne Staff Band. See Bibliography. Boon's unpublished chapter, 'Personality Parade', contained a note on Staff Bandsman George Holmes, who recounted playing in a HQ 'Boys Band' under Adjutant Abraham Story as early as 1883, having been hired in January 1881. The Household Troops Band has been resurrected several times, most recently as 2002, when the group undertook a North American tour under the leadership of Major John Mott. Membership is drawn from across the UK.

22. Nicholson handwritten diary and Edwin Cook, *My Travels in the Household Troops Band*, April 1887–1892. International Heritage Centre London.

23. Parts of 'Appleby's March' were later featured in Albert Jakeway's *General Series* march from 1941, *Old Campaigners*; Erik Leidzén provided a type of reconstruction in the *American Band Journal* version called *The Veteran's March*, intended by Leidzén as a tribute to this great pioneer. See Steadman-Allen, *Evolution*, June 19, 1965, p390, on the first classical transcription, which George Bernard Shaw refers to in his play *Major Barbara*. Steadman-Allen points out that it is odd that Slater, who claimed to have done the transcription, identified the piece as by Bellini. He also points out the first printed 'bass solo' came out in GS 18, *Soldiers Song*, which predates the Donizetti adaptation.

24. Parenthetical comment by Richard Slater, quoted by him in 'The First Bandmasters' Council', *Bandsman and Songster*, September 18, 1926, p290. For a more detailed account of mid-to-late 19th-century brass band publishers, see Chapter 5 of Roy

Newsome, *Brass Roots: A Hundred Years of Brass Bands and Their Music, 1836–1936*, Aldershot: Ashgate, 1998). Newsome does not discuss SA music.

25. The October 28, 1983 issue of *The Musician* was designed as a souvenir issue celebrating the centenary (1883–1983) of the IMED. Various articles in the issue trace early efforts, but see in particular Ray Steadman-Allen's *Publishing Music for The Salvation Army*, pp702–704, as well as Ray Bowes's overview of the department in 1983. Wright & Round produced nearly a half-dozen collected bound sets of its *Sacred Series, Set 1 and 4* of which were used by the New York Staff Band into the late 1920s (Parts in the author's possession; see Chapter 3 for further discussion). While Set 4 was published after the General Order restricting SA bands, several of the pieces within the set had been released separately well within the time frame when such music could be used: *Set 1—Wright&Rounds Sacred Series of Popular Band Books (57 separate hymns, carols, anthems, etc); Set 4—Twenty-Four Celebrated Sacred Marches Arranged for Brass (& Military) Bands.*

26. The 100 pounds figure related by Slater in his unpublished history as well as Hawkes in 'Early Reminiscences'. This would have been a somewhat staggering amount in that time.

27. While the SA has tried on different occasions to explain Booth's action as a result of agreements with British publishers, the ultimate verdict is that the publishers would have gladly supplied music. Booth really wanted total control. However, Steadman-Allen has related to me that one active variable at this time was the desire of some publishers to ask that SA music not be sold to 'outside' bands, particularly if Booth was to continue his own embargo against 'outside' music being played by SA bands. Both Steadman-Allen, whose source was Frederick Hawkes, and Bram Gay, whose source was Eric Ball, shared with me that Booth reached this agreement with a band publisher/instrument manufacturer—the firm now called Boosey & Hawkes—who was not only a significant donor to the SA cause, but also tied up with the SA's St. Albans instrument factory in some Byzantine way. The documentation is thin or nonexistent, unfortunately. Rose's rambling attack in *Talks With Bandsmen*, pp250–258, is typical of several in this period. One must bear the chronology in mind. Booth first restricts SA bands by 1885 to SA publications while still selling the same to outside bands as late 1899. It is only in 1900–1910 era that things get tense with non-SA publishers, because the SA finally begins producing music that could be of much wider interest and SA bands emerge from obscurity with units capable of playing most of the finest brass band music. It must have been within the first five years of the

new century, 1900–1905, that Booth reached this gentlemen's agreement.

28. The *BBN* and *BB* contain citations throughout this period of bands coming in and out of the SA for a variety of reasons, musical resources being only one of the issues.

29. Trevor Herbert, *Making of a Movement*, in *The Brass Band Movement in the 19th and 20th Centuries*, p47. Arthur Taylor, who in his excellent history of the brass band movement, declared that SA bands *are not and have never been a part of the mainstream of the brass band movement* (*Brass Bands*, p92). He also asserted that the Army's main influence on brass bands *is and always has been, through people who leave the ranks and bring their talents, as instrumentalists,, conductors, composers, or arrangers in 'civilian bands'*, p136. While the issue is more complex than that, the interaction of these two subcultures still needs comprehensive study – for all practical purposes Booth's decision did indeed bring this about.

30. Concerning losses at this time, Herbert states: *The steps taken to separate Salvationist brass bands from the brass band movement were remarkably successful. However, from the late 19th century there was considerable involvement of individual Salvationist players in contesting bands.* Herbert, *Making of a Movement 48–49*. From Slater's unpublished history *many bands lost, but Army strong enough to survive* p62.

31. A typical thematic grouping within one number of a *Band Journal* set at this time would be that of BJ 388, September 1900, three songs about harvest: *Come Ye Thankful People Come* (4/4, moderato, A Flat major), *The Harvest Past* (3/4, Andante, D Flat major), and *What Shall the Harvest Be?* (6/8, allegretto, D Flat) (p62).

32. Richard Slater, *The New Band Journal for March*, 411–414, *The Local Officer* (February, 1902), p260. Steadman-Allen has pointed out to me that William Booth could also be ahead of his advisers in terms of his vision to SA bands and their music. One wonders what might have happened if Herbert and Ballington Booth, the two most talented Booth offspring, had stayed within the Army fold and continued to advise their father on musical matters.

33. Frederick Hawkes, (as quoted by Boon, *PMP*, p150) considered this work a precursor of the form soon termed meditation, while others thought it more like an *air varié*, or variation, which, of course, in many ways meditation-style works do follow. See the author's doctoral dissertation for a comprehensive study of the form. Steadman-Allen has pointed out that there is a possible link between these early Slater arrangements and similar hymn arrangements in the repertoire of 'outside' bands. (*Evolution*

series, *Musician* (UK) October 11, 1965, p. 495). Roy Newsome has shared with me *air variés* that began to be released by Wright & Round in 1894, some of which would be based on hymn tunes, demonstrating many stylistic similarities to early SA works, including those running bass finales. Two early ones by Linter (probably a nom-de-plume for H. Round) I have seen are *Adeste Fidelis* (1895) and *Hanover* (1896). Establishing a direct correlation and chronology is an elusive task.

34. Hailstone, *British Bandman Centenary*, p47. In the Sept. 10, 1901 issue (p. 168), the editor of the *BB* requested that the 'leading bands' of the SA write in reports on a regular basis. He followed this with an unsigned letter to the editor that gave a fair and flattering overview of the best SA bands in Great Britain, including the ISB, Regent Hall, Bristol I, South Shields, Luton II, Derby II, Chalk Farm, and Wood Green.

35. IHQ Trade Department ran an advertisement starting in November, 1903, *BBN* for its SA Band Lamp. While they couldn't sell their music by this time, they certainly attempted to sell other items. The ad ran for at least 3 months that season. Likewise 'Triumph' instruments from the SA Campfield Works were advertised in the *BB*, Spring of 1902.

36. At the NYSB's Embankment appearance the cornet soloist featured in a non-Army variation solo [See Appendix 2] was John Allan, later SA Chief of the Staff, who as a young cornetist played in the famous American Band of Providence, RI (See also Chapter 9, USA).

Appendix 1: First Two Orders for Salvation Army Bands
General Booth's Order for Bands [1]; *War Cry, March 27, 1880*

MUSICAL INSTRUMENTS
By the General
Psalm xcviii, 6. – 'With trumpets and sound of cornet make', etc.
Psalm cl.4. – 'Praise Him with the timbrel', etc.
Isaiah xxxviii.20 – 'The Lord was ready to save me; therefore we will sing my songs to the stringed instruments'.

Whereas, during the late Welsh and Cornish Councils, and before that time at Plymouth, Nottingham and elsewhere, we have proved the great utility of musical instruments in attracting crowds to our open-air and indoor services, we do here express our desire that as many of our Officers and Soldiers generally, *male or female*, as have the ability for so doing, learn to play on some suitable instrument. And as in many instances the obtaining of an instrument is a difficulty, we shall be glad if any friends who may have such instruments lying idlo will consecrate them to this service, and send them to Headquarters. This includes violins, bass viols, concertinas, cornets or any brass instruments, drums or anything else that will make a pleasant sound for the Lord.

Headquarters, 272 Whitechapel Road, London, E

General Order [2] for Brass Bands; War Cry, February 24, 1881

In order to prevent misunderstanding, and to secure the harmonious working of the Brass Bands with various Corps to which they are attached, the following Regulations are to be strictly observed:

1. No one will be admitted or retained as a member of the Band who is not a member of the Army.
2. All instruments in every Band are to be the property of The Salvation Army, no matter by whom they may be purchased, or through whom they may be represented. The words 'Salvation Army brass band', followed by a number of the corps, must be marked on every instrument. In no case are instruments to be used to play anything but Salvation music; or in any but Salvation Army service.
3. In the event of any member of the Band resigning his position as such, he will leave his instrument behind him.
4. In no case will any Committee be allowed in connection with any Band.
5. In every case the Captain of the Corps to which the band is attached shall direct the movements of the Band and shall appoint the Bandmaster.
6. In no case will any band, or member of any band, be allowed to go into debt, either for instruments, or anything else, connected with the band.
7. In no case is the practice of the band, or any member of the band to interfere with the meetings of the corps.
8. It is strongly recommended that in cases where a treasurer or secretary is required by a band, the treasurer or secretary of the corps to which it is attached shall act in that capacity.
9. Any band that may have been, or may have formed, which does not carry out this order will not be recognised as a

Overleaf: The Salvation Army International Congress, July 1904. General William Booth, (front right) listens to one of the largest brass bands ever assembled.

Salvation Army band, and must not in future be allowed to take part in any operations of the Army.

10. Any band failing to carry out this order will at once be disbanded.

By order of the General, W. Bramwell Booth, Chief of the Staff; 24 February, 1881.

Appendix 2: Article entitled 'A Gigantic Musical Festival' (*British Bandsman*, July 9, 1904, p384)

Preparations have been made during the last few months for what will probably have proved to be the largest continuous band festival ever held in this country. We refer to The Salvation Army International Congress. A special building has been erected which holds about 6,000 people, and throughout each day bands of all nationalities are to be heard in the neighbourhood of the Strand heading processions of enthusiastic Salvationists. The bands which have come under our notice are as follows:

1. The Swedish, in their peculiar uniform. It is a small band, of unusual instrumentation, and rather soft in tone.
2. The Norwegian, of similar formation, but rather more boisterous in tone.
3. The French, with a pleasing reed combination, including saxophones.
4. The German, a rather vigorous body of brass bandsmen.
5. The Bermuda Band, of coloured men, who are hard-working and with the best intentions, but overblow, and are consequently out of tune. They would play far better if one of their number conducted.
6. The Canadian Staff, a most genial set of fellows. The band numbers about 26, and has a very clean and neat tone.
7. The New York Staff, a large reed band combination, who obtain remarkable effects, but are decidedly Yankee in their style.

Several of these bands use instruments with rotary action, and the Canadians used Koenig horns instead of saxhorns. The English bands which have taken part during last week were the Headquarters Staff, Chalk Farm, Penge, Wood Green, and Regent Hall.

For the first time since the L.C.C. [London City Council] undertook to foster band playing in the parks, the SA bands were permitted to perform on the Villiers Street bandstand from 1 to 2 each day The Staff Band were there on June 27, 29, 30; the Canadians on June 28th, and the American Staff on July 1st. One or two of the programmes were decidedly secular, the American band contributing a cornet air varie of 'Old Folks at Home' and a clarionet [sic] solo. On June 23rd a special band festival was held in the Congress Hall, when all the bands mentioned took part.

The massing of the English bands was very well carried out, under the conductorship of Lieut. Co. Mitchell; and the foreign and colonial bands contributed separate pieces. This gave an excellent opportunity for comparisons, and we must say that they were all favourable to the English, the nearest to whom, in our opinion, being the Canadians, who played in a very neat and clean style.

The foreign bands have a great deal of room for improvement. The Headquarters Staff Band is a very strong band, and although their ensemble at times was not so good as could be wished, they reflect great credit on Mr. Mitchell as a conductor. The festival included choir singing by contingents from Denmark, Switzerland, Bermuda, Germany, Norway, American Southern States, and the Staff Songsters.

The 'General' gave a very interesting address on the music of The Salvation Army, and the meeting concluded with a massed band performance of the march 'Jesus is my Saviour' [GS 443, 3]. On Tuesday (5th) about 200 bands visited the Crystal Palace.

Their [sic] is no doubt that the SA have profited by the process of the great Crystal Palace Contests, and have adopted the plan of massed performances conceived and carried out by Mr. J. Henry Iles, the Contest Director.

Appendix 3: Summary Report of the 1916 Commission of Inquiry and Historical Compliance with Recommendations

The following listing cites, in italics, the *Summary of Report* from the 1916 *Report of Commission of Inquiry into Matters Relating to Salvation Army Music*, dated March 23, 1916, followed by this author's annotations indicating when such a recommendation was acted upon.

1. *Fresh edition of the Band Tune Book*. Completed by 1928.

2. *Tunes pitched too high in present edition* [1899 Tune Book] *to be lowered and issued in current Band Journals*. Gradually corrected over the next forty years in the General Series and various Tune Book editions, but not fully until the latest edition [1986–88]. Slater reported that many of the 1928 arrangements were merely reprints of the old 1899 edition, even when the pitch, according to members of his department, was considered too high. The IMED was not given final authority in this matter during the 1928 revision!

3. *Fresh edition of the Song Book and S.A. Tune Book* [Keyboard edition], *with additions & emendations*. Completed 1930 and 1933 respectively.

4. *Increase supply of suitable music for Sunday night and other Salvation services*. New song and hymn tune arrangement forms, as well as shortened selections, aid in the increase of such material within the next 25 years.

5. *The leader of the meeting to be responsible for the selection for the music to be played and sung at his services*. A matter that continues to be stressed in Officer Training Colleges, but still not always complied with in many corps.

6. *The publication of a Music Book consisting of songs selected from back volumes of the Musical Salvationist*. First *Gems for Songsters* released in the 1920s. Eight collected volumes published to date.

7. *Rearrangement of future Band Journals so as to provide music suitable for the various grades of bands*. Second Series, later called *Triumph Series*, begun for smaller bands, 1921; *Festival Series*, for larger, more advanced groups, begun in 1923.

8. *Occasional arrangements of Band Selections to provide for a verse or chorus being sung by a Band group with Instrumental accompaniment*. Such pieces offered regularly in the *General Series* of the 1930s and 40s.

9. *Episodes and elaboration of parts for particular instruments deprecated. Music Board to exercise censorship*. Use of florid counter-melodies persisted for many years; while the nature of technical display changed (fewer and fewer cadenzas, etc.), technique is only further encouraged. The aesthetic changed by the late 1930s.

10. *Band Marches to revert to the older type of arrangement, with a definite religious theme.* Compromise reached, allowing for freedom of expression but demanding at least one clear tune reference.

11. *Minute to C.O.'s and D.C.'s and Training College Authorities respecting strict adherence to Regulations re music.* Released immediately in 1917.

12. *List of approved copyright songs to be published in Bandsman & Songster or War Cry.* Regularly released in these periodicals.

13. *Special paragraph on the same matter* [Copyright issues] *to be inserted in the Orders and Regulations for Field Officers.* Added to the next revision of this *O&R*.

14. *Encouragement of original song composition.* Continued by efforts of IMED through articles, competitions, etc.

15. *Publication of Solo and Chorus Books.* Various vocal solo publications published in the 1920s and 30s; *Chorus Book* released in 1946.

16. *Provide supply of suitable music for Y.P. Singing Companies and Children's Drills.* Collections for children's voices released regularly starting in the 1930s.

17. *Safeguards against breaches of Regulations governing Musical Festivals.* Establishment of National Bands Department in 1921 aided in the enforcement of this, but 'abuses' continue for many years, especially overseas.

18. *Festivals by Outside Choirs.* Administered by Bands Department.

19–22.

More direct soul-saving work for Bands and Brigades; Songster Brigades as a fighting force; Social and fraternal spirit of band life; Closer relationships between C.O.'s and Bandmasters and Songster Leaders. Each of these four concerns continued to be addressed in educational articles, Music Councils, etc., over the next few decades. They are issues that seem to always need attention within the SA.

Appendix 4: Representative list of articles by Richard Slater and Frederick Hawkes, *Musical Salvationist*, 1895–1901

Volume X: 1895–96
Anonymous, *A Table Showing the Strength and Formation of Some of the Best Known Army Bands and the Present Time.* p47.

Richard Slater, *The Songs of Commandant H. Booth*, pp70–72.
Frederick Hawkes, *How to Conduct a Band Practice*, pp83–84.
Frederick Hawkes, *The Bandsmen's Page: Phrasing*, p107.
Richard Slater, *Famous Bands of the SA, 1: The International Headquarters Band*, pp119–120.
Richard Slater, *Famous Bands 2: The International Trade Band*, pp131–132.

Volume XI: 1896–97
Richard Slater, *A Brief History of Salvation Army Bands*, pp59–60.

Volume XII: 1897–98
Richard Slater, *On the Choices of Pieces from the B.J.* [Band Journal] *and Their Correct Rendering*, pp47–48,60.
Frederick Hawkes, *The Bandmaster's Notebook* [Variety of topics, from Sunday service issues, to practice planning, correcting mistakes, recording keeping, and accompanying of congregational singing], pp119–120.

Volume XIII: 1898–99
Richard Slater, *The Salvation Army Musical Department*, pp35–36,47–48.
Frederick Hawkes, *The Disposition of Bands* [instrumentation], pp59–60.
Richard Slater, *A Band's Temptations*, p71.
Richard Slater, *The Music of The Salvation Army*, pp131,144.

Volume XV: 1900–1901
Frederick Hawkes, *Salvation Army Band Music: Its Character and Uses*, p155.
Richard Slater, *On Form in Music*, pp160–161.

Appendix 5: Bandmaster and Band profile articles in the *Local Officer* magazine. 1897–1906

The Bandmaster profiles, sometimes with photo:

BM MacDonald, Londonderry (Aug. 1897, p24); BM Hayton, Carlisle II (Sept. 1897, p56); BM E. Hill, Southport (Oct. 1897, p88); BM Bowers, Regent Hall (Nov. 1897, p121); BM Burgess, Clapton Congress Hall (Dec. 1897, p153); BM Kelly,

Sunderland 5 (Jan. 1898, p185); BM Punchard, Chalk Farm
(Sept, 1898, pp52–53); BM Lowery Halcrow, South Shields
(Oct. 1898, p84); BM William Steel, Swansea 1 (June, 1899,
p377), BM Kichenside, Highgate (Feb. 1900, pp262–263); BM
Foster, 'OK' Divisional Band (Feb, 1900, p268); Provincial BM
L. Halcrow, Northern Province (March, 1900, p308); BM
William Morris Brand, South Tottenham (March 1901,
pp305–306); BM Sydney Cox, Exeter (April 1901, pp343–344);
BM Froeden, Karlstad Sweden (May, 1902, pp370–371).

The Band profiles for the same period, 1897–1902:
Volume I (1897–98) Folkestone (Aug. pp22–23); Holloway 1
(Sept. pp54–55); Southall (Oct., pp86–87); Chalk Farm (Nov.
pp118–119); Woolwich (Dec. pp150–151); Exeter (Jan.
pp182–183); Kristiana 3, Norway (Feb. pp214–215);
Sunderland 1 (March. pp246–247); Shadwell Slums (April.
pp278–279); Blaina, Wales (May. pp308–309); Hamilton 1,
Bermuda (June. pp342–343); Kilmarnock, Scotland (July.
pp374–375)

Volume II (1898–99) IHQ Staff Band (Aug. p–21–23); Dunedin,
New Zealand (Sept. pp54–55); Port Elizabeth 1, South Africa
(Oct. pp86–87); Tyne Dock (Nov. pp118–119); Ramsgate (Dec.
pp150–151); Canadian HQ Staff Band (Feb. pp211–213);
Worthing (March. pp252–253); South Shields 1 (April.
pp289–291); Albany, Australia, Cycle Brigade Band (May.
pp330–332); Clapton Congress Hall (June. pp368–370)

Volume III (1899–1900) Reading 2 (Aug. pp12–13); Ipswich 1
(Sept. pp50–51); Grecian (Oct. pp90–91); South Tottenham
(Nov. pp131–133); Bedford 1 (Dec. pp170–172); Manchester 8
(Feb. pp254–265); Coventry (March. pp304–307); Watford
(April. pp344–346); Hemel Hempstead (May. pp380–381);
Hamilton, Scotland (July. pp466–467)

Volume IV (1900–1901) Wood Green (Aug. pp22–24); Lowestoft
1 (Sept. pp64–65); Chartham, Kent (Oct. pp104–105);
Pontycymmer, Wales (Nov. pp144–145); Blyth, England (Dec.
pp184–185); Launceston, Tasmania (Jan. pp226–228);
Woolston (Feb. pp268–269); German-Swiss Officers Band
(April. pp347–349); Grantham (May. pp386–387); Plymouth 1
(June. pp430–431); Weston-super-Mare (July. pp463–465)

Volume V (1901–1902) Edmonton (Aug. pp26–27); Liverpool 1 (Sept. pp59–61); Lavenham (Oct. pp104–106); Grays (Nov. pp144–146); New Brampton (Dec. pp176–178); Derby 3 (Jan. pp217–219); Evesham (Feb. pp249–251); Cape Town 1, South Africa, and Swedish Staff Band (March. pp294–297); St. Peter Port, Guernsey (April. pp336–338); Luton 2 (May. pp375–378); St. Helier, Jersey (June. pp434–435); Abertillery (July. pp453–455); Green Street, Kent (July. pp453–455).

Series continued intermittently for several more years, including in *Volume VI:* Barrow-in-Furness (Nov. 1902 p136); *Volume VII:* Manchester 15 (Feb. 1904, p247); *Volume VIII:* Consett (Jan. 1905, p495), Chelmsford (Jan. 1906, p18), Chippenham (May. 1906, p176), and Paisley (November. 1906, p416).

Chapter 3

A SHORT HISTORY OF SALVATION ARMY BANDS AND THEIR MUSIC,
Part II: (1904–1939)

Ronald W. Holz

The purpose for which music is used in the Army necessarily determines its character and form. It must be such as to make a direct and immediate appeal to the minds and hearts of men. We make no endeavour to meet the tastes of the cultured few. Our appeal is to the masses.

Those few who have any acquaintance with our operations are fully aware how inappropriate would be music of a complicated nature in Army meetings. To reach the masses the music called for is that which goes direct to the souls of men, not such as demands a measure of culture and an intellectual process for its comprehension. The Army music is therefore popular in style, depending for its effect more upon melody than harmony, simplicity of style and structure characterise it, and it is thus universal in its scope and direct in its effect. Richard Slater, 'The Music of The Salvation Army', Musical Salvationist (XIII, 1898–1899), p131.

The period chosen for review in this chapter may be considered the most dynamic in the history of SA bands. By the beginning of World War II SA musical culture had experienced an explosion of both compositional and performing talent. The early march, selection, and meditation-style forms evolved in remarkable ways, joined by programmatic works, technical display pieces for soloists, variation forms and festival arrangements bordering on symphonic proportion, and a host of practical short pieces suitable for various worship settings or evangelical outreach. No longer did just the members of the IMED push forward Army band music. Aided by a series of composition contests designed to encourage and identify new talent, the department soon began to receive works from all over the world, including men like Leidzén, H. C. Goffin, Gullidge, Kirk, and Soderstrom. IMED would gain the services of Arthur Goldsmith, later in the era to be followed by George Marshall, Eric Ball, Albert Jakeway, Bramwell Coles, and Philip Catelinet.

World War I severely affected SA bands, particularly in Great Britain, but during this same time the SA was at work studying means to further boost the efforts of SA music, via the deliberations of the 1915–1916 Commission of Inquiry.

SA banding continued to be a way of life, the corps being the religious, cultural, and educational centre for thousands worldwide. Youth training programmes were given special attention, the modern era of SA musical education commencing with the success of the emerging summer music camp programme (See Chapter 9 USA). Adults leaders were not ignored, the era beginning with the institution of training courses and exams, supplemented by Bandsmen and Music Leaders' Councils and Congresses all across the globe, as territories world-wide established music departments and, in some cases, their own band publishing. Recordings and radio only enhanced and widened SA bands' mission and audience.

In the heart of the Depression the SA administration found itself the caretaker of a vibrant, sophisticated worldwide musical fellowship. Bands began to tour widely beyond their borders and the resulting impact was incalculable in terms of the rich growth of SA bands and their music.

Composition Contests

Starting in 1905 the SA ran a series of international band composition contests designed to encourage developing writers, as well as to alleviate the burden placed on members of the IMED to constantly produce music for the now bimonthly *Band Journals*. IMED chose the march as the form for the first series of contests, the march being the most needed in the minds of the department at that time.[1] The March, 1906 *Band Journal* (GS 505–509), entitled *Special Prize March Number*, held the four winners, two of whom were new to the journals – Gore and Young – and two who were well known figures in SA banding in the UK:[2]

> No.1 (GS 505) *The Melbourne March.* Staff Captain Gore, Melbourne, Australia
>
> No.2 (GS 506) *The Southall March.* BM E. H. Hill, Southall Corps, UK
>
> No.3 (GS 507) *The Christchurch March.* Bandsman J. Young, Christchurch, New Zealand
>
> No.4 (GS 508) *The Cadet March.* BM William Boyd, Paisley Corps, UK

George Bernard Shaw, who before his success as a playwright was a professional music critic, attended the December 7, 1905 festival at Clapton Congress Hall and then provided, at the request of the SA, a critical report of

Clapton Congress Hall Band, c.1906.

the event. His report was not made public until it appeared fifty-five years later in *The Musician* (UK), December 3, 1960.

His criticisms of the prize-winning marches not only discussed technical matters, they went to the heart of the problem faced by the editors at IMED—just what is Salvation Army music? He also addressed broad stylistic issues, suggesting in the process that the generally excellent Army bandmasters and good arrangers needed to attend concerts by the finest orchestras and military bands in order to continually improve their craft. The following excerpts go a long way in broadly evaluating a vast quantity of music published by the SA for its bands in the period 1900–1925:

> *...The Chalk Farm Band began by playing a march which was rowdy to the verge of profanity. Later on the Regent Hall Band played another which, though it had a quasi religious title, made me feel at once as if I were in the Hippodrome. It was followed by the announcement of the band March Competition Award; and I listened with much curiosity to the winning piece. It was a very creditable composition, neatly constructed and effectively scored, But it had absolutely no religious character. It was a military march pure and simple. Anyone hearing it at the Promenade concert, or on the pier at a fashionable seaside place, would never have suspected that it had any religious antecedents.*
>
> *Now the march which was judged second-best, though not so smart, had a trio in which there was an attempt at devotional feeling* [hymn setting]. *The award convinced me that the view of the judges was that the Army's secular music cannot be too secular.*
>
> *I suggest that this view is a mistaken one. If the only alternative to thoroughly secular music were the solemn, churchy, joyless so-called 'sacred' music, I should cordially agree that the whole success of the Army depends on its avoiding anything of the kind. I am also quite alive to the fact that the music must not be over the heads of the people.*

At the Festival I sat next a labourer who had probably worked half as long again that day as any man should work at heavy physical toil: at all events he was partly stupefied with mere fatigue. If the band had played very refined music for him...he would have been fast asleep in three minutes. And when the Chalk Farm Band played a piece of empty but exciting circus music for him in the most violently spirited way, he woke up and was pleased, as most of the audience were. But it woke him up at the cost of switching off the current of religious enthusiasm and switching on the current of circus excitement. It woke him up very much as a tablespoon of brandy would have woken him up. And with all the racket, which was powerfully reinforced by the low roof and the terrific clatter of the overtones set up by the instruments, it was not nearly as stirring as 'I'm climbing up the golden stairs to glory' [famous SA song by Emma and Frederick Booth-Tucker] *or 'When the roll is called up yonder'.*

Music can be impetuous, triumphant, joyful, enrapturing, and very pretty into the bargain without being rowdy or empty. I know the difficulty of keeping up the necessary supply of good marches, and the dangers of wearing out the best ones by too frequent repetition. But after making all allowances, I think it a pity that the SA, which has produced a distinctive type of religious service and religious life, should not also produced a distinctive type of marching music...

[Under Suggestions to Army arrangers of band music]... *They do not make half enough use of the individual character of the instruments and the way in which they can be made to relieve and contrast each other. I longed to hear a passage for the trombones alone contrasted with a passage for the euphoniums and tubas alone, or similar contrasts between the horns and saxhorns, the trumpets and cornets, etc. They were always mixed up in the same mass of harmony. And the scorers seem to have no idea of the effect of a unison passage for a mass of wind instruments breaking finally into harmony, or of a pedal point. They harmonise all the time in the same way, using all the instruments indiscriminately. In a word, they neglect variety, though variety is far more needed in brass band playing than in orchestral playing, where the use of strings and wood instruments, harps and kettledrums, etc., supplies variety and contrast almost automatically.*[3]

In 1906, the selection was added to the composition contest, and the May, 1907 issue of the *Band Journal* contained the three winning marches and three winning selections. [Illustration 9 contains the programme for the January 26, 1907 Bandmasters' Councils, which included the premiere of winners of the 1906 competition.]

In the process Arthur Goldsmith was introduced for the first time in print with a band work (First Prize Selection, *The Mercy Selection*, GS 534), as was Bramwell Coles (third place march, *Ambition*, GS 537). Most SA arrangers have made their first appearance in a SA *Band Journal*, at least until very recently, by way of a march. This was true for H. C. Goffin of New Zealand (father of Dean Goffin). Later to write one of the most popular of all marches, *The Red Shield*, Goffin made his debut with the release of his second prize winning march, *Plymouth*, in the March, 1908 *Band Journal* (containing winners of 1907 march and selection contest).[4]

William Broughton's (grandfather of the current composers Bruce and William Broughton) first march appeared in July 1909, but with the note *Revised by the Editor* [appearing several times on successive pieces by Broughton and others] added to show that he was in an apprenticeship of sorts with Slater. This was something Slater and Hawkes carried out with love and care for years, encouraging such writers as John Pattison, Harry Kirk, and George Marshall, whose first published marches appeared in 1909, 1911, and 1912 respectively.

Several other important 'firsts' via marches came as follows: 1915 Erik Leidzén and Harold Scotney; 1920 Albert Jakeway; 1921 Emil Soderstrom; 1922 Frederick J. Dockerill, Eric Ball, and Herbert Mountain.

While most contests rarely unearth masterpieces, the 1926 international band composition contest brought forth at least two works that have remained popular in the repertoire to this day, Erik Leidzén's first prize solo air varié, the Cornet Solo: *A Happy Day*, and Emil Soderstrom's march, *Fighting for the Lord*.

The categories were expanded to include not only the march and selection, but variation form (still labelled *air varié*), extended instrumental solo *air varié*, hymn meditation, and simple solo melody with band accompaniment. The winnings were spread internationally, with three Americans (K. M. Fristrup joining the above-named Scandinavian-Americans with his first place short euphonium solo, *Calvary's Stream*), and the Australian Harold Scotney (First Prize for Meditation—*Nearer to Thee*) taking a majority of the prizes.[5]

Great Britain could be proud of its new writers, as well, and by January, 1927, the home territory began an intermittent series of Composers' Festivals designed to both encourage and honour what was being achieved in its band music.

One of the most famous of these took place the following year, on February 15, 1928, in the presence of the Duke and Duchess of York. Bands featured included Cambridge Heath, Chalk Farm, Clapton Congress Hall, Penge, Regent Hall, and the ISB, who combined for several massed items. The 'old school' was represented by Goldsmith's selection, *The Cleansing Current,* (GS 742) and Hawkes', *The Call to War,* (GS 668). The new generation was given prominence:

> Eric Ball: *Adoration* (FS 26); *Hanover* (FS 42); Harry Kirk: *Songs of Happiness* (GS 953); George Marshall: *Army of the Brave* (FS 6); BM Vanderkam of Belgium: *My Fortress* (FS 7); Bramwell Coles: *Under Two Flags* (GS 876); *Sound Forth the Praises* (GS 957); *Man of Sorrows* (FS 13).

Vocal music was required on SA festivals, and the International Training Garrison Singers presented Charles Coller's 'Song for Full Chorus', *I am the Resurrection and the Life* (MS, Vol. XV) and a soon-beloved 'Salvation Song', *I Know a Fount,* by Oliver Cooke. Many of the composers conducted their own work, perhaps the most memorable aspect of that was George Marshall leading Regent Hall from his wheel chair. This kind of festival became the prototype for the many that have been held throughout the world, at the territorial, national, and international level. Recognising artistic achievement in the context of the Army's clear mission to reach the unsaved had come a long way from the days when composers—whether Army or classical—could not be identified on band scores, parts, or on public programmes.[6]

Training Leaders and Administering Bands

Bandmaster and Songster Leader Training Sessions commenced in 1905–1906, with 259 entries. In the period 1905–1913, for which Richard Slater kept figures, a total of 1486 participants took the examinations, with results showing that they did not suffer from grade inflation: 618 Firsts; 314 Seconds; 124 Thirds; 430 Failures [!]. Such courses were run intermittently over the next several decades until the establishment of the Bandmasters' Training Correspondence Course was developed, which could be monitored worldwide.[7]

An outline of the course of study, or Curriculum for the Bandmasters' Training Session of 1927 held July 15–July 24th has survived. The ten-day session met at the Men's Training Garrison, Mildmay Conference Hall, Newington Green, moving on Sunday, July 17th, to Clapton for the full Bandmasters' Councils led by General Bramwell Booth. The following weekend concluded with a Partnership Festival at Regent Hall on Saturday, the 23rd, and Field Corps visitation as arranged by the Bands Department for developing leaders.

Other visits during the course included a tour of the St. Albans instrument factory and printing facilities, SP&S at Judd Street, Men's Social Institutions, and a band practice at Chalk Farm. In addition to spiritual talks and devotions with such leaders as the British Commissioner and National Band Secretary Staff Captain Wilfred Kitching (later General), technical lectures were given by a wide range of successful leaders, teachers, and members of the SA musical staff. The ISB was on hand as the demonstration group for a number of the lectures.

Among the sessions held were the following: *The Reading of a Score* (Lt. Colonel Hawkes); *Practice-Room Methods* (Band-Inspector Saywell); *Interpretations* – with Illustrations by the Staff Band (Lt. Colonel Goldsmith); *The Art of Teaching* (Y.P. Sectional Davies of the London Polytechnic); *The Tuning of a Band* (Goldsmith); *Instrumentation* – with ISB (Goldsmith); *Dynamics* (Hawkes); *Controlling and Directing the Band and its Business* (Territorial Bandmaster Punchard); *An Hour on Band Training* – with the ISB (Staff Bandmaster Fuller).[8]

In 1907 the first Band Inspector for Great Britain was appointed, Edward H. Hill, bandmaster at Southhall Corps. Hill had lost his job in a brick works just as the Army was contemplating this new position. He was an ideal choice. The Band Inspector travelled a great deal, frequently touring for a month at a time because he was responsible for 19 Divisions. Brindley Boon observed to me that it was *quite an occasion when he arrived at the corps.* Hill inspected and placed a financial value on the instrument inventory in addition to evaluating the musical and spiritual health of the corps ensembles he visited. His spiritual impact was probably as great as his administrative assistance. He maintained this hectic pace for 18 years, until 1925.[9]

However, by early 1900 L. Halcrow was serving as Provincial Bandmaster in the Northern Province of the UK; Halcrow's home corps was South Shields. In one week he would normally visit six bands. A March, 1900, *Local Officer* (p308) feature on him reports that in one week he visited South Shields, Howden, Tyne Dock, Sunderland No.1, Blyth and Backworth. Another notable person to later fill a similar position in that same region was Bandmaster George Marshall.

In America, city or regional music directors were functioning by the late 1890s. The first truly professional divisional music director was evidently Erik Leidzén, who in the 1920s and early 1930s held several professional appointments, including the Scandinavian Department, New England Staff Band, National Capital Band of Washington, DC, and the New York Metropolitan Division.

Colonel Brindley Boon, noted SA music historian, composer and former National Secretary for bands in the UK.

The modern system of the Divisional Bandmaster in the United Kingdom was established by Brindley Boon in 1968 while he served as National Secretary for Bands. The old 'levy' system that had been in place gradually faded out and the new one being an honorary appointment, with the recipient usually acting as an encourager throughout the division, with the added perk of directing massed bands on certain occasions![10]

A major step in the support bands received was the establishment in 1921 of a Bands Department, a unit operating in tandem with, but separate from, the old music department, the IMED.

The first official National Secretary for Bands and Songster Brigades for Great Britain was Colonel Alfred Braine, who received his first musical training on cornet as a member of an Orphanage Band under the patronage of the great philanthropist, Dr. Barnardo. Converted at age 16 in the town of Battersea, he soon took over the small corps band there.

In 1882 he moved to London and began work as a junior clerk at IHQ. In addition to ISB duties he served as bandmaster of Hackney Band (Cambridge Heath), and Croydon Citadel, as well as the IHQ Trade Band.[11] While only in the position for a relatively short time, he established an administrative support system very much needed, one that just could not be fulfilled by members of the IMED, even though as far back as 1905 General Booth had tried to add that to Slater's duties.

Braine also wrote practical articles in the weekly SA music paper, *Bandsman and Songster* and in the monthly journal, *The Officer*. Several of his principal efforts were aimed at gaining clearer communication between corps officers and their local music leaders as well as wiser use of the fine musical forces corps officers had at their beck and call week after week.

Alfred Braine gave one commentary on these subjects in 1922. A second, related observation about these problems, is drawn from a book published in the 1930's by General Edward Higgins. Both give a summary look at issues facing bands and their officers in the post-Word War I era:

> **Braine:** *It is no uncommon criticism of Bands and Songster Brigades that they monopolise too much time on Sunday evenings, playing and singing pieces that are not only too long but unsuitable to the character of the Meeting, and the subject of the Corps Officers's or Leader's address, and that the 'atmosphere' has to be re-created after the Band or Songster 'performance'. There is an element of truth in this, but it arises mainly from a lack of system, or coordination... The Corps Officers should arrange with the Bandmaster or Songster Leader for the Song tunes, as well as the Band selection or Songster piece, in harmony with the Bible address. This can be easily done if they select their subject, and the songs to fit it, and give a memo to each before their practice night. If the Corps Officer could attend the practices and hear the tunes played and sung through once, it would add to the interest of the members, and the Officer would be sure of the musical side of the Meeting being satisfactory. The Bandmaster and Songster Leader should both be urged to keep the object of the Meeting before them and select what will best help to realise that object. It is not always the 'latest' or the best they can do that will meet*

the need. They therefore avoid 'National Pieces' and cut out all the 'performance', even to the extent of shortening Selections like 'Atonement' to less than five minutes, by omitting the last movement, or everything that is not a direct appeal to sinners. It will frequently be found that a simple appealing hymn tune will be more effective than any more elaborate selection...[12]

Higgins: *Our indoor Meetings in some places are becoming much less alive in their character than once was the case. I have been in some, and heard others, <u>in which the congregation has taken part only once in the whole service</u>, and that was the opening song! Such a procedure is ruinous in the long run, and is altogether contrary to <u>the method of the Army, which is to link up everybody to do as much as possible</u>. This system of having the whole Meeting by Bands and Songster Brigades will kill its life and spirit, strangle the activities of the ordinary Soldiers, and drive people away from sheer monotony and lack of interest instead of drawing them to us...<u>I would also insist upon having presented to me a list of selections which the band could play</u>, and would, in cooperation with the Bandmaster, select for each Meeting one which would bring some definite Salvation thought to bear upon the minds of the audience. I would refuse to have my Sunday night Meeting cut right in two by <u>a mere performance of music unconnected with any definite spiritual theme</u>.*[13]

These calculated exhortations came as a result of soul-searching on the part of Army leadership concerned with the loss of momentum in its overall work. The first great 'think-tank' in the history of Army music, the 1915–1916 Commission of Inquiry, began to bring together all the different webs and strands of the Army's music programme, allowing for concentrated study.

Commission of Inquiry

Perhaps the most significant and detailed deliberations ever held concerning Salvation Army music, its music forces, and their mission, took place during 1915–1916 at the request of General Bramwell Booth. Booth asked that a Commission of Inquiry [CI] be formed that consisted of ten upper-level staff officers (four commissioners, five colonels, and one major, the General's daughter).

This body interviewed members of the IMED, representative officers (six corps officers, four divisional commanders), local officers (seven corps bandmasters, four corps songster leaders), a divisional bandmaster, and a divisional songster leader. Their task was to study the development of SA music, both in terms of repertoire and musical practice, in light of the Army's mission of *salvation of the people, and the building up of a simple and zealous soldiery.*

The suitability of current publications for the ability level of SA groups and for its use in SA work was to be given thorough review. In addition, the degree to which *Orders & Regulations* were being observed, and the means by which these were maintained rounded out the agenda.[14]

Appendix 3 (see end of Chapter 2), shows the Summary of Report sent to the General on March 23, 1916, a two-page condensation of the 18-page report, itself a highly concentrated distillation of over 60 hours of interviews, all properly recorded in word-for-word transcriptions. This is followed by my annotation showing when formal action was taken on the issue listed. Some of the major achievements included the expansion of band music to include a consistent quantity of music for smaller bands, the *Second Series (Triumph Series)*, as well as more advanced music for the most proficient groups, the *Festival Series.*

Perhaps more significant was the Army's clarification of its mission, the three-fold primary functions of both SA instrumental and vocal music as highlighted in Chapter 1 of this book being embraced and firmly set as the guiding principles for all SA music activity.

The CI concluded that the recent developments in Army music had been of general advantage to the movement, especially in its ability to attract people to outdoor, and to a lesser extent (less provable) indoor services. Band use in congregational singing was given high marks, but the Commission strongly suggested the revision of both the *Song Book* and the *Tune Book*, both for content and, especially, for correction of the too-highly set keys chosen for many songs.

The main criticism was levelled at instrumental music: *It has undoubtedly cheered and inspired our own people and has often brought hope, comfort, and encouragement to sad hearts; but, while this is indisputable, the evidence indicates that the music has not fulfilled expectations in reaching the hearts of the unsaved to the extent hoped for and earnestly desired.*[15] The causes of this failure were identified as 1) an insufficient supply of suitable music, both in character and length, for Salvation services; and, 'much more serious' 2) *The leader of the Salvation Meeting, whether he be a Field of Staff Officer, does not seem to make any effort to link up with the Bandmaster or Songster Leader with a view to a suitable selection of music* [whether it be congregational songs or items by various musical sections].

This remarkable, honest document highlighted abuses where bands and songster brigades were not following *O&R* by playing or singing unauthorised (i.e. non-SA publications) in their festivals. When asked why outside pieces (solo and band) were being featured, BM Punchard

Wakefield (UK) Young People's Band, 1922.

of Chalk Farm responded that *it is because we have not got enough published to take the place of it* [especially solos, quartets, small group features]. He readily admitted he gave Festivals that had not been cleared with the corps officer or divisional commander, and clearly felt the entertainment factor to be essential.

The major crux of the situation had to do with the role of the corps band, which at this time was the heart of the corps, in some cases, the only vibrant expression of soldiery at the local level.

When Commissioner Carleton asked Divisional BM Brand whether the typical corps band in his region bore *a fair and reasonable share of the corps work?* Brand responded: *Saturday night Open Air and indoor Meeting; Sunday all day; and say one night per week, in addition to Practice night...fair? – I should say 'yes', Commissioner.* When studying the earlier periods of SA band history we should never forget the incredibly time consuming commitment that was required of SA band members. Bandmaster Brand's observations are not in the least bit exaggerated.

The CI concluded its report with a strong censure of officers who *do not appear to take sufficient personal interest in their Bands and Brigades*, while generally praising the quality of leadership found among its local music leaders and the dedication of its bandsmen and songsters.

Regaining a clear line of communication in the salvation war via a shared mission seemed obvious, but essential to the health and future of the Army, as its concluding paragraph put it:

> *The Commission feels strongly that if Bands and Songster Brigades are properly managed, Regulations wisely administered, and a reasonable amount of personal interest in them – individually and collectively – displayed by the Commanding Officer, there will not only be fewer breaches of Regulation, but it will be proved to a greater degree than ever before that, in Bands and Songster Brigades, the Army has a fighting force incomparable with that of any other Religious Organisation in the World.*[16]

The long-range implications of their findings and the subsequent actions taken in terms of administration of Army music groups and new publications that were soon launched defined the nature of Salvation Army music-making for the next 50 years. Just two years before the Commission had met, at the Fourth International Congress of 1914 (two years after the death of General William Booth in 1912), the SA could report it contained 1,674 bands and 26,000 bandsmen.

A Modern Publishing Firm

Richard Slater (1854–1939) retired from the IMED in 1913 after guiding Army music for 30 years. He continued to write music, articles, and serve as a consultant for the department. For a short time in the mid 1920s he returned to head the department *pro-tem* while Hawkes was on an extended sick leave (Slater was assisted by Bramwell Coles during that young officer's first stint with IMED).

In 1913, Slater's younger colleague, Frederick Hawkes, took over the editorship, with Arthur Goldsmith (who worked in the department 1908–1921) serving with him as joint editors-in-chief. The pace of the work was daunting. Goldsmith shared with the CI that he was required to produce one march and selection for each bimonthly issue of the *Band Journal* [GS] (Commission of Inquiry Goldsmith interview, p4). This was in addition to all other calls for vocal music, editing, proofreading, and encouraging young writers with whom the department corresponded. Refusing to work or compose at home, Goldsmith did all his work at the department. Hawkes, on the other hand, did all his creative work at home, demanding silence from his children, who, according to Brindley Boon, still whispered later in life.[17]

While the two men were a good team, they did have philosophical differences. Hawkes proposed to the CI a division and expansion of the *Band Journals* along lines that were eventually adopted (CI Hawkes interview, p17ff). While in support of more music for smaller bands, Goldsmith was adamantly opposed to an advanced series, maintaining a philosophy more in keeping with the old General's view on SA band music – keep it simple and make the message clear and plain. There is no direct evidence of ill will between the two, though no doubt tensions lessened when Goldsmith left the department in 1921

Besides the principal emphasis from the CI for launching new journals, another major effort was given to providing more solo and ensemble music, especially instrumental music. Until 1918, the *Musical Salvationist* used to carry a variety of small ensemble items for many different combinations of instruments, including strings, brass, keyboard, concertina, and even drum, fife, and bugle corps.

Starting in 1904 a series called *Bandsman's Companion* (Volumes No.1–9), commenced, in which was gathered both new and previously printed items of like nature into bound sets, like *Bandsman's Companion No.5* (Brass quartets and quintets, various combinations) or *No.9, Violin Solos, Duets, Etc.* These were followed by the long string of *Instrumental Solo Albums*, first begun in 1918–19 with *Instrumental Album No.1*, four quartets for two cornets, alto horn, and euphonium arranged by Hawkes, the combination being the most preferred among brass band chamber musicians.

In his Preface to *Instrumental Album No.1* Hawkes stated that the primary use of these arrangements would be in festivals of music. He acknowledged that there were many other uses for them, relating that many bands already had elite Quartet Parties that did special work on their own, and also enjoyed the pleasure, rare in those days, of simply making good music together. This series now numbers 34 volumes, although recently items from the older issues are available, if at all, only in single reprints.[18]

Other talent soon drawn to the department in this period showed prodigious ability. Henry Hall, later renowned as a popular band/orchestra leader, worked at IMED in the early years of World War I, until called into military service. Three of his marches for the SA have a clarity of melodic style that demand resurrection: *Holly March* (GS 787), *Nunhead March* (GS 751) and, above all, *The Sunshine March* (GS 810), which contained a tune soon to be famous all over the United Kingdom.

Eric Ball always considered his musical education having taken place, for the most part, under the guidance of

Hawkes and Slater with whom he interacted upon joining the department in the 1920.

Adjutant Albert Jakeway was assigned to the department in 1926, staying for 32 years and eventually assuming the editorship in 1952. Interestingly, Jakeway had spent part of his early career as an officer in Czechoslovakia, where he worked with the brass bands emerging there in SA work. Another young officer with fine compositional powers and skill as a pianist, Philip Catelinet, joined several years later. Bandmaster George Marshall was also enlisted to help with editorial duties at this time. What a pool of talent was present during this era!

The role of the editor-in-chief in shaping SA music publications can not be overestimated. He was the one who decided what band manuscripts are played by the ISB for the Music Board; he is the one who decided to assign members of his staff, or, which has been more likely, himself, to fill in the gaps when volunteer submissions failed to meet a need.

The precedent of editors and their staff providing the bulk of new music, especially pace-setting works, has created some curious problems in the history of SA band music. For years no one but a member of IMED could have a classical transcription published in Army journals, the rationale being that this decision helped stem the flow of unwanted manuscripts, but the unwritten implication being that they just preferred handling such music.

Erik Leidzén, one of the world's finest transcribers of brass and wind music, carried on an extensive correspondence in the 1950s with Albert Jakeway, as well as with the head of the International Music Board, but he never once succeeded in having any of the transcriptions he offered published.[19]

It must be said that Army bands have been well served for over a century by skilled and caring editors. The list shown below identifies the editors of IMED from its founding until the present, though the title of this department, or section, has changed several times in recent years.

Each man who led IMED faced a very demanding job, frequently with not nearly enough resources or staff to handle the job adequately according to 'outside' standards. Ray Steadman-Allen has told me, however, that he did not feel inadequately staffed during his tenure as editor and that the department in many ways maintained a very high standard in accuracy and quality. If there were problems, they lay more in the area of marketing and the occasional anti-music or anti-band posture from certain members of the upper administration.

Despite what some might call constraints, each editor has made an indelible and lasting contribution to Army music, both in their own creative work and in the musicians they encouraged and published. The balance between production from within the department and the voluntary submissions by gifted arrangers and composers actually acted as a strong benefit or catalyst in the first 90 years or so of SA band music (pre late-1980s).

In recent years, as the number of outstanding SA writers who make their living as professional composers/arrangers has increased, a new tension rather than balance has joined the equation, a tension that has led to a crisis in the evolution of SA music. This would include the kinds and quality of music being submitted for publication, and issues of copyright and performance rights. (See Chapter 4, *United Kingdom*, and Chapter 10 for further discussion).

In simpler days the Army naturally assumed ownership of all music sent in for publication. When a work was accepted for publication, the arranger was contacted with a simple release form, in which he or she relinquished all rights – royalties from sale of printed copies and performance rights/mechanical licenses – to the SA. Officer members of the IMED submitted a blanket cover letter each year for all their work, multiple examples of which, with identical wording, still exist. Here is one by Eric Ball, sent to then General Higgins, April 20, 1933, on SP&S letterhead (Music Ministries Unit files):

> *Dear General: In consideration of your printing or publishing any matter in respect of which I may be the author or have copyright or any other rights, I agree that all such rights shall belong to you, and I now assign them to you accordingly. Yours faithfully,*

Editors-in-Chief, The Salvation Army (1883

RICHARD SLATER

FREDERICK HAWKES

ARTHUR GOLDSMITH

ALBERT JAKEWAY

CHARLES SKINNER

RAY STEADMAN-ALLEN

ROBERT REDHEAD

TREVOR DAVIS

RICHARD PHILLIPS

Music Editorial Department, London -2000)

MUSIC MINISTRIES (2000 - 2006)
(See page 142)

BRAMWELL COLES

RAY BOWES

SLATER	1883-1913
HAWKES	1913-1936
GOLDSMITH	1913-1921
(Jointly with Hawkes)	
COLES	1936-1952
JAKEWAY	1952-1958
SKINNER	1958-1967
STEADMAN-ALLEN	1967-1980
BOWES	1980-1990
REDHEAD	1990-1992
DAVIS	1992-1994
PHILLIPS	1994-2000

Peter Ayling

Stephen Cobb

Andrew Blyth

An increase in the volume of SA music recorded commercially, played on radio, and eventually television, followed by the decision to sell SA music beyond the ranks have been bringing about a change in this complex area. It is no longer such a simple matter.

Below is a Chronological Listing of Editors-in-Chief of the SA Music Editorial 'Department' based in London; The label 'International Music Editorial Department' would apply to the period 1883–1992 (Richard Slater through to Robert Redhead), at which time the department became absorbed into the newly restructured United Kingdom Territory:

Chronological Listing of Editors-in-Chief, SA Music Editorial Department, London, UK

Name	Dates
Frederick Fry	1881–1883*
Richard Slater	1883–1913
Frederick Hawkes	1913–1936
Arthur Goldsmith	1913–1921 *(Jointly with Hawkes)*
Bramwell Coles	1936–1952
Albert Jakeway	1952–1958
Charles Skinner	1958–1967
Ray Steadman-Allen	1967–1980
Ray Bowes	1980–1990
Robert Redhead	1990–1992
Trevor Davis	1992–1994
Richard Phillips	1994–2000

In 2000 Peter Ayling headed up the newly formed Music Ministries Department. Recent practice (2001-2006) has seen Stephen Cobb appointed Territorial Music Director and Andrew Blyth as Assistant Territorial Music Director. Ray Steadman-Allen, Kenneth Downie and Peter Graham have acted in a part-time, consultancy capacity.

*Not technically an editor-in-chief, Fry worked as an editor under his supervisor, Herbert Booth

Musical Forms

New musical forms were gradually introduced into the *Festival* and *General Series* during the period 1904–1939 that would essentially, with very few additional exceptions, set the pattern for Army music for the rest of the century.

Programmatic music, variation forms, festival arrangements shaped in classical forms, solo features (both slow melody and technical), the suite, and more extensive transcriptions of classical works were the new areas of development. Older forms, of course, continued their carefully guided 'evolution'. The march would expand to include grander designs, such as the large festival march, as well as continued exploration of all sorts of variations on the quick march, processional march, and the march for general or 'ordinary' indoor or outdoor use.

Selections would gradually become more musically unified through consistent use of linking motives and intelligent tonal designs, and in the process become much more satisfying than the old potpourri selections. The most progressive work would be achieved in meditation forms, those that illustrate or 'meditate' upon a single given melody and associated text. Here the door would be opening for symphonic scale works, which, combined with related efforts in variation forms and programme music, brought Army music into the 'modern' era and established a literature admired as much for its musical excellence as for its spiritual usefulness.

Programme Works and Suite

The first programmatic work was Richard Slater's *Bible Picture: Stilling the Storm* (GS 601, January 1910), the first of four published, though Slater mentions in his unpublished *History* that he wrote a total of six. Intending to illustrate via a sectionalised musical narrative the biblical story told in Mark 4: 35–41, Slater provided descriptive notes in the full score, with additional song, poetic, or paraphrased biblical texts as appropriate: *The calm sea, The voyage, The sudden storm, Jesus asleep in the storm, The fury of the tempest, The terror of the disciples, The storm is stilled, Jesus is Omnipotent Lord.*

The stylistic effect strongly resembles music improvised for a silent film of the same era, though Salvationists would not have been encouraged to attend such worldly entertainment! The impact of this music must have been revolutionary. The placing of texts within full scores and even band parts was something that had been exploited for quite some time and was given further impetus by Commission of Inquiry requests that bands sing more in the midst of their playing. This type of descriptive piece called for a new kind of imagination on the part of the performers and congregation.[20]

Steadman-Allen has pointed out that Slater's series was not directly imitated by anyone until the tone poem was allowed in the 1930s. However, many of the selections and, especially meditations, of the 1920s attempt essentially the same thing (works by Vanderkam and Coles, particularly). In fact, in the sense that most Army music is intentionally referential – referring the congregation beyond the notes themselves or their purely expressive/musical power, to song texts, scripture portions, theological themes – all SA band music is programmatic. This is markedly the case in most selections and meditations of the period 1920–1935, in which the large majority of composers allowed their poetic imagination a great deal of freedom.

Musical coherence via motives derived from the tunes under development was emerging at this time in the hands of a few writers, most notably Marshall, Ball, and Leidzén. The compositional aesthetic of the day, however, stressed original introductions, episodes, and codas that were strikingly different from the straightforward tunes and songs that were a necessary part of the form. This is why so much of this music sounds to our ears as too violently contrasting, too emotionally 'over the top' in the 'original' portions, too common place, sentimental or hackneyed, in the settings of the previously written tunes.

The first use of the term *tone poem* came as the result of a vanity piece, General Evangeline Booth's Tone Poem: *Streams in the Desert* (FS 113, January 1937), arranged by then Adjutant Eric Ball. Ball had recommended the term to her. A complete choral version, for soloists, songsters, and organ, appeared later that year in Booth's revised edition (1937) of *Songs of the Evangel* (pp12–16).

It can be surmised that the text is certainly by Evangeline Booth, and possibly some of the melodies are also. Nearly all the other music (harmony, part-writing, scoring, etc.) is by Ball, even though the General would have exerted a great deal of interest in the band version. However, once achieved by the General (and the first composition in the band journals by a woman, as well!), the form was sanctioned, with Ball getting the first crack at it, *Exodus*, which came out in the very next issue of the *Festival Series* (FS 117).

Sonata process, which he and Catelinet had been exploring in several of their pieces while working at IMED, formed the basic framework, the loose three-part structure of the 'story' of the biblical Exodus aligned with exposition, development, and recapitulation (*In bondage, Night of the Passover, Deliverance*). Ball would return to this classic work when he wrote his masterpiece of contesting music, *Resurgam*, lifting out note-for-note some of his most dramatic music from the former tone poem (the death motive) and using it for the final transition, the shadow of the valley of death, of the latter.

SA writers embraced the tone poem more frequently following World War II, with Bramwell Coles' four movement (suite-like), *The Divine Pursuit* (FS 143, 1947), based on Francis Thompson's poem, *The Hound of Heaven*, ushering in the modern series of such works.

The first suite, however, appeared in the same issue as *Streams in the Desert*, Ball's, *Songs of the Morning* (FS 114). In this three movement work the first two movements are band arrangements of two choral pieces by Ball first released in the *Musical Salvationist*: Mvt 1 – Song of Welcome: 'Welcome Happy Morning', an Easter anthem based on a poem by Venantius Fortunatus, 'Hell today is vanquished, Heaven is won today'; Mvt 2 – Prayer: 'Begin the day with God', text by May Pike. Movement 3, 'Song of Faith', focuses on the expected final morning when 'Satan's Kingdom down shall fall at last' (*Hark, Hark, My Soul*, Frederick W. Faber's hymn as modified by the early SA pioneer George Scott Railton).

Resurrection morning, daily morning prayer, and the last morning in history become united not just in thought but by skilful musical means. The key of the first movement becomes the victoriously resolved key of the battle hymn heard in the finale. The beautifully reflective middle movement provides the listener the quiet repose from which such momentous dawns could be viewed.

Here was music that was technically challenging (the difficult cornet and euphonium *air varié* style *obligatti* have a certain period charm, as well), and superbly scored. This became a model that would be carefully followed in future decades.

Variation Forms

Variation forms, or *air varié*, took two paths, that of display pieces for soloists, and those for the entire band. The first published solo *air varié* was William Stevenson's cornet solo, *I Love Him Better Every Day* (FS 16, July, 1924). This opened the floodgate for the main type of festival solo published by the SA until works like Leidzén's, *Concertino for Band and Trombone* and Steadman-Allen's, *Ransomed Host* and *Eternal Quest* from the late 1940s–mid 1950s changed the nature of such pieces (See Volume II, Musical Study Part No.3).

Leidzén's, *A Happy Day* (FS 40, July 1927), winner of the 1926 solo *air varié* contest, evokes the great turn-of-the-century style pieces, with their 'Hungarian' sections in a minor key, but with a much more compact, economical

The Hallelujah Crusaders comprised of Officers and Sergeants from the International Training Garrison, London. They campaigned in the East of England during 1922.

approach to the form. *Ransomed*, George Marshall's famous euphonium solo which did not get printed in the *Festival Series* until after World War II (FS 152, January 1948), also exhibited a similar economy of means when it was released with piano accompaniment in *Instrumental Solo Album No.21*, 1938.

Here the old concert-waltz solo form is linked up with the bandstand-in-the-park *air varié*, the results being an enchanting blend, especially in the way the minor variation is linked to the stirring finale via a dramatic cadenza.

Leidzén had done the same thing in his challenging *Song of the Brother*, written first for cornet in 1916, and rescored for euphonium and band in the early 1930s (FS 136, July 1939). An interesting precedent was set for this work, in that, while there was an Army *contrafactum* in existence that had adapted the old song, *When You and I Were Young Maggie*, the score notes make no specific mention of it or its text other than to say *The theme is an old favourite which has been adopted to Army use*. In point of fact, Arch Wiggins had to come up with a new 'sanctified' text for the song so this piece could be more widely played![21]

The band *air varié* commenced with *While the Days are Passing By* (FS 31, July 1926), the form patterned on similar pieces released in the outside brass band press since the 1890s. As in the solo *air varié*, the tune itself is what gets developed, as in the manner Arban's *Carnival of Venice*. Technical display by individual players or sections, strong contrasts in instrumental colour, tempo, tonality, and metre are the order of the day. Some of the more popular from this period were those with a more humorous, or witty turn, like Coles' *Good Old Army* (FS 75), Herbert Mountain's *The Hardy Norseman* (FS 70), and Albert Jakeway's *Goodbye Pharoah* (TS 230), the latter from the *Second Series*. Jakeway's success points out the fact smaller bands were also provided with many of the new forms at this time.

The *air varié* that led SA composers gradually away from the old style was Eric Ball's *The Old Wells* (FS 58, January 1930). In his score notes, Ball pointed out the difference between his piece and previous variations in SA music: *A study...of the Score will show that as a simple air varié this piece is hardly true to the type, as it relies more upon thematic (as opposed to melodic) development than is usual, hence it approximates more nearly the form known as Symphonic Variations* [emphasis in the original]. This was, in one sense, also quintessential SA music, for the theme chosen was a grand old SA song, not some outside hymn or tune.

Ball begins with a lovely, straightforward arrangement of the original verse and chorus of the song. Five sharply contrasting variations on the chorus only follow, the last of which builds to a climactic point at which the chorus returns in triumph, rounding out the work in a very satisfying manner.

His colleague in the IMED, Philip Catelinet, followed him broadly in this trend, but with a programmatic twist, in another thoroughly Army-style piece, *A Sunbeam* (FS 115, January 1937), with the variations on *Jesus wants me for a Sunbeam* tracing the story. The score notes sequence reads *dawn; the clock strikes 7; playtime; school; release (the children make their way home with shouts of merriment).*

Classical Transcriptions

Classical transcriptions in this period followed the pattern set by Slater in the *Thoughts from the Masters* series, which reached a total of six by 1913. Gradually Slater moved away from merely using vocal models from the *Musical Salvationist* to direct transcription of short vocal or instrumental pieces, as well as excerpts from longer works.

Still, vocal models were preferred, for when Hawkes began his series of *Gems from the Masters*, most were drawn from oratorio, especially by Handel (*Messiah*), Haydn (*Creation*), and Mendelssohn (*Elijah* and *St. Paul*).

The range of composers and sources used by Slater, especially, clearly indicates a man well versed in operatic, chamber, and symphonic literature, a gift from his early days as an orchestral musician and amateur music scholar. Coles used the titles, *Moments from Tchaikovsky* (FS 90, January 1934), and, *Treasures from Tchaikovsky* (FS 174, January 1951) in his two most famous studies of his favourite composer, a writer whose style of symphonic sequencing he absorbed. Other Coles' transcriptions published after World War II included *Moments* with Spontini [spelled Sontini in FS 154], Mendelssohn, Schumann, Chopin, and Wagner.

In Coles' transcriptions Army band music was led toward more complete portions of symphonic or absolute music, though *Treasures* is fragmented, and does have one part-song, *Christ in His Garden*, which was loosely adapted for songsters from the Russian original. Movements from Symphonies 4–6 of Tchaikovsky make up the bulk of two these band 'chestnuts,' with some ballet and solo piano music thrown in for good measure.

The educational and fellowship aspects of Army banding come to the fore in this type of music. The commitment to providing more 'high-brow' material indicates a continued concern on the part of music departments and upper administration for the cultural/aesthetic knowledge/ experience of Salvationists. This naturally provided more challenging kinds of musical experiences, an aspect that only intensified after World War II.

The March

In band journals of this period, especially the *General* and *Triumph Series*, slightly more than 50% of the items were marches of one kind or another. Festival marches, not conceived for the parade, provided Army composers with ground to explore all kinds of modifications to the typical turn-of-the-century military march, especially in length, or in scale. For this, they would have models like Elgar's, *Pomp and Circumstance Marches*, or other symphonic models, like Hawkes' complete (a rarity in that day) transcription of Mendelssohn's, *War March of the Priests* (FS 8, July 1923).

Among the best in this genre were Coles', *Departed Heroes*, Eric Ball's, *The Torchbearers* and Leidzén's series, *Pressing Onward* and *Fling Wide the Gates*, the latter, based on an Evangeline Booth song, definitely of a grand, almost Wagnerian character. National pride played an element in these kinds of marches, an early example being J. Merritt's very demanding, *The Canadian* (FS 76, January 1932); there would be many parallel works.

The busy street marches of the 1904–1914 period continued to be written in large quantities. One of the most intriguing, Coles', *The Conflict* (GS 679, March 1913), would more likely be placed in the festival category in the next generation at least because of its stately flow, technical challenges, and larger form.

A certain elegant simplification took place towards the end of World War I, particularly through the example set by George Marshall in such march gems as, *'Neath the Flag* (GS 781, June 1917) and, *Stand to Arms!* (GS 799, March 1919). Economical in every regard – uncomplicated intros, music capable of being played by less than a full complement, and, especially, clarity of the accompaniments and counter-lines (usually only one) – these two marches provided melodies, and their settings, that immediately captured the general public's notice. They would be whistling them long after. (This is what John Philip Sousa had provided and what Kenneth Alford was offering at the same time as Marshall and Coles.)

Coles, Marshall, and Leidzén can be considered the finest of the Army march writers of the era, heirs to hard work by Slater and Hawkes. By the end of their careers they had seen 45, 42, and 27 marches, respectively, published in SA journals. A large number of good marches were written and march composers flourished from 1920 till the end of World War II.

Some of the more notable composers not already mentioned in this section on the march are listed below with one of their more famous, representative, but by no means only, quality march. The list also shows how international the pool of writers had become. Notice, also, the large number of marches named after corps, other SA organisations/programmes, or as with the first of its kind, Ball's *Star Lake*, music camps:[22]

United States: William Bearchell, *Brooklyn Citadel* (GS 1137, March 1939); William Broughton, Sr., *The Roll Call* (GS 1105, March 1936); Emil Soderstrom, *Army of God* (AFS No.1, 1930; revised GS 1776; April 1984).

Australia/New Zealand: Henry C. Goffin, *The Red Shield* (GS 986, Sept. 1928); Arthur Gullidge, *Army of*

Immanuel (GS 1057, March 1933); Harold Scotney, *Wellingtonian* (GS 934, June 1925).

Canada: Percy Merritt, *Dovercourt Citadel* (GS 1229, Dec, 1943); Norman Audoire, *Montreal Citadel* (GS 1084, Sept. 1934).

United Kingdom: Eric Ball, *Star Lake* (GS 1200, Dec.1941); Albert Jakeway, *Rosehill* (GS 1246, June 1946); Herbert Mountain, *Sheffield Citadel* (GS 1180, Sept. 1940).

The Selection

Below the march, the selection ranks as the next most numerous of forms in SA band music. A genre that unites two or more songs or hymns around a shared theme, the selection was the easiest to produce, yet the most difficult in which to succeed.

Getting beyond the stringing of tunes together with occasional cadential extensions, linking cadenzas, or even an extended introduction or episode proved even more difficult than in meditation-style works. Again, Marshall, Ball, and Leidzén led the way in providing more coherent works. These, along with Bramwell Coles, also worked at trimming the length of non-festival selections to within the requested time restraints, not always succeeding![23]

Two of George Marshall's best-known selections exhibit programmatic designs, a type of selection he and others enjoyed writing at this time. His highly dramatic *Visions* (FS 45, July 1928) is based on Matthew 7:14, and has subtitles in the score in a fashion very similar to Slater's, *Bible Pictures*: 1) 'The Narrow Way!' 2) 'Heaven!' 3) 'Temptation' 4) 'Doubt!' 5) 'Faith' 6) 'Conflict!' 7) 'Victory!'.

Three songs are heard in their entirety, including the opening song *Some Day* (MS Vol. 38, p98) from which Marshall seems to glean some of the motivic material for the 'original' episodes, though the process is not consistent. *Great and Glorious* (FS 93, July 1934), a sunnier work depicting Easter Morn, unites four of Marshall's vocal works in straightforward, and triumphant manner. The most intriguing part is the opening *Allegro con fiducia* which is built on the interval of a rising fourth and octave, the outline of which comes right out of the opening tune, *O Glorious Morn*.

Leidzén's *On the Way Home* (FS 106, Jan. 1936) is an even more obvious type of story-selection. This is brought into clear relief if you listen to his description of the travelling 'band of pilgrims' captured so well on his introduction to the work that appears on the *Erik Leidzén Memorial Album* produced by the USA East music department in 1963. *The Saviour's Name* (FS 98, Jan 1935) is of the more normal variety, five songs on the name of Jesus, the extended introduction to which is derived from the contours of several of the tunes to be sounded later. Like Marshall, Leidzén was looking for musical coherence in the midst of the highly emotional style of the period.

One of his earliest selections, *The Call*, did not see the light of day until 1952 (GS 1352), though he had entered it in the 1926 Competition. In this work Leidzén achieved a masterpiece of SA music wherein motivic, expressive, harmonic, and tonal components are united to make a musically satisfying whole. All the drama of the 'sermon in sound' is derived from the three tunes, underpinned by a tonal structure that juxtaposes a 'state of grace' or 'home' with a 'state of sin'. His slowly evolving ideas on text-motives were first tried out in this 'advanced music,', but he would not make full use of his experiment until much later, after returning to the Army after a long exile, 1936–1948.[24]

His close friend Eric Ball, who would musically evoke his own separation from the Army so beautifully in the selection, *Songs in Exile* (GS 1460, June 1958), also solved the problem of musical coherence within a selection, most notably in, *Constant Trust* (GS 1179, Sept. 1940). His score programme note reads:

> *Three well-known songs are the basis of this piece: Trust and Obey; The Cross is not greater than His Grace (Euphonium Solo); Trusting as the moments fly (Trombone Solo). The prevailing mood of the music is that of joyful confidence and hope, although the natural stress of life, bringing temptation to doubt, is illustrated before the music is brought to a restful conclusion.*

New England Staff Band (Erik Leidzén) on stage at Boston Palace Corps Hall, c. 1924.

He opens the work with what he calls his Trust motif, a quickly rising fanfare-figure that will show up in each of the episodes, as well as accompanying the tune presentations. This motif even makes a confident appearance in the second-to-last measure, the last statement of hope. To this Ball also adds material derived from the tunes themselves.

For instance, at Letter O, *poco agitato*, a fragment of, *Trusting as the Moments Fly*, sounds unsettled, insecure – the temptation to doubt – but new music did not have to be invented for this episode.[25] Therefore, Ball combines the old meditation-style 'original' music to the more classically styled technique of deriving unifying material from the tunes themselves, a happy compromise that many SA writers would follow.

In his festival selection, *King of Kings* (FS 67, Jan. 1931), Ball wrote a work bordering on a symphonic cantata, with very powerful original music that returns in various transformations throughout the work. Many of these selections work quite well when adapted for choir and band, which has been done often at the great Royal Albert Hall festivals.

Norman Bearcroft, who made many of these

arrangements, once shared with me that he felt one measure of success for many of these early SA selections was their adaptability to such situations, their power of telling a message further strengthened by the words being sung.

The Meditation and Hymn/Song Arrangement

The publication of Goldsmith's, *Rockingham* (GS 839, Sept. 1920) marked the official sanction of the new genre, meditation, or hymn tune meditation, the form that would be held up as the most difficult and most rewarding in which an Army composer could work.

Modelled on experimental works of the previous twenty years, the form offered an opportunity for musical development of both original material and previously composed tunes on a scale previously neither allowed nor explored in SA music. The illustration of the text associated with the hymn tune remained the underlying principle throughout the form's development.

However, the musical styles and techniques used in that illustration changed considerably over that 80-year history (1920–2000). Within the first twenty years (1920–1940), two principal changes were apparent; these centred around 1) the manner in which composers used original motives to unify their meditations and 2) the degree to which original motives were tune-derived.[26]

Very few meditations from this first period had a long performance life. The reason for that neglect lay in the highly subjective nature of the linking and episodic sections, the primary points in which the composer would provide, in the words of Steadman-Allen, *a written down form of contemplation.*

A typical meditation would consist of an extended introduction, verse 1, modulatory episode, verse 2, etc. (for as many verses as the arranger wished to portray), and then some kind of coda or codetta (See graph, Volume II, Musical Study, Part 2).

The pattern established by Goldsmith in *Rockingham* (and in previous works by Hawkes and Slater) is seen recurrently in future meditations:

1) Orchestrations/harmonisations of successive statements of the hymn-tune are sharply contrasted with each other.

2) Episodes and introductions are usually made up of asymmetrical phrase groupings, in contrast to the four-square structure of the hymn; 'traditional meditations' use fully original materials; 'classic' meditations derive them from melodic and rhythmic characteristics of the hymn tune.

3) The emotional climax in most meditations is found in the episode just prior to the final statement of the tune.

4) Tonal schemes are often centred in third-relation movement rather than motion by fifths.

The composers who fully embraced the 'traditional' meditation included William Broughton (7), Albert Jakeway (11), Eric Ball (12), and Bramwell Coles (7). Ball and Coles gradually moved towards the classic process, or at least a balance between the two, something achieved by the young Wilfred Heaton in, *Just As I Am*, discussed in Volume II, Musical Study, Part 2. [The number in parentheses cites the total number of published meditations, not just those of 'traditional' style.]

Way back near the turn of the century, however, Klaus Östby had composed a significant work, *Princethorpe*, in which there was a clearer relationship between the three unifying motives presented in the introduction and later episodes. These motives follow in a tenuous way either the general melodic contour or rhythmic structure of the tune.

Charles Skinner reported in his *An Appreciation of Lieut. Colonel Klaus Östby*, that, *Princethorpe* was composed during the summer 1907 (Steadman-Allen says 1904) but not published until 1923, in the first issue of the Festival Series (FS 2, Jan. 1923). Since that early date it had been played extensively by the ISB, in manuscript.

On the full score, in place of the usual Music Board 'approved' stamp, is the signature of the Chief of the Staff, Thomas Henry Howard, and in his handwriting the note *Passed for Staff Band – Defer publication till report.*

Ray Steadman-Allen reports it being played in the summer of 1904 by the ISB; see 'Evolution, Part 5'.]

The scale and complexity of the work must have caused the delay of publication until the *Festival Series* was launched, though it is not all that different than Goldsmith's, *Rockingham,* which evidently was considerably longer, as well, in its original form. What Östby had provided was a guiding light towards musical integrity in the form considered to be the pinnacle of SA compositional endeavour.

As in the selection, George Marshall (3 meditations) and Erik Leidzén (14 meditations) proved to be the progressive writers, with the former's, *Horbury,* being perhaps the finest and most representative meditation of the period (FS 62, July 1930).

Marshall derived two unifying motives directly from the hymn tune, yet in the climactic episode he also inserted truly original material. Also, when presenting the 14-measure hymn tune, he expanded the statement several times via the insertion of motivic material, almost in the style of a baroque chorale prelude, a form to which the hymn tune meditation is strongly related. Marshall's score note tells us that a verse-by-verse 'contemplation' of, *Nearer My God to Thee,* (the associated text) is not intended, setting up some interesting problems for future listening, especially when hymn tunes like *Horbury* can be tied to multiple texts:

> *Whilst no special endeavour to musically describe the verbal text of the song usually sung to this tune has been made, its theme has not been overlooked during the construction of this Meditation. Rather it has been employed as the guiding influence throughout, both as to point and substance.*

In Leidzén's, *Home Sweet Home* (FS 47, July 1926) there is a similar ambivalence, and it is also a work in which classic and traditional approaches are blended; it almost sounds like a tone poem:

> *The music of this Meditation is not intended to be verbally descriptive of the original words of the song,*

but endeavours to give expression to feelings about home viewed from various aspects. Introduction, built on thematic material from the tune. Home in its quiet, calm aspect; Home on the occasion of a farewell. The contrast to the outside world; Thoughts about home far away. Triumphant home-coming; the ending being suggestive of a calm deep peace (Score notes by Leidzén).

At the same time these larger, somewhat ponderous works were flourishing (either for festival or worship use), the music editorial department began exploring ways in which shorter versions of the meditation could flourish. They thereby provided more music for worship that lined up with the request by the Commission of Inquiry for many more works in a 3–4 minute length.

Several experimental short meditations appeared in the late 1920s, and in the 1930s four pieces that resembled the future song arrangement were released (beyond mere transcription of vocal items from *The Musical Salvationist*).

The regular production of the short hymn tune and song arrangement began with the release of Philip Catelinet's Song Arrangement, *Why Not Tonight?* (GS 1143, June 1938) and Hymn Tune Arrangement, *Weber* (GS 1239-No.2, June 1944). *Weber* consists of three successive harmonisations of the tune. The first presentation is scored note-for-note from the *Band Tune Book*. In the second statement the scoring changes every two bars within a generally thinner texture. The tune is sounded in the tenor range for the final statement, with the cornets playing a more florid counterpoint above. This economic approach would be used time and time again, sometimes within even fewer sections, in the coming decades.[27]

Honours, Abuses, Losses, and Gains

On May 8, 1910, the Regent Hall Band (BM Herbert Twitchin) was requested by Queen Alexandria to play in the courtyard of Buckingham Palace on the occasion of mourning the death of King Edward VII. Such an honour further symbolised the level of acceptance given the finest SA bands in the period under discussion.

A postcard commemorating Regent Hall Band (Herbert Twitchin, top left), in the grounds of Buckingham Palace, London.

By the end of this era Eric Ball would be leading the Salvationist Publishing & Supplies Band (a resurrected version of the old Trade Headquarters Band) in radio broadcasts from the BBC's Broadcast House. The same conductor and band would be asked by the leaders of the brass band contesting scene to read the manuscripts of the test pieces designed for the National Brass Band Championships [The ISB has, from time to time, also fulfilled this function]. Honours and recognition poured in. Bands toured wherever it was possible at the time to tour, the Chalk Farm Band perhaps being the most travelled of all SA bands at the time. Army bands seemed to be going, in the words of a famous song, 'from strength to strength'.[28]

However, this same period was marked by real difficulties: war, economic woes, tension between the SA and the 'outside' brass band scene, and internal strife due to the rigorous, and some times harshly applied, *O&R*. This would be the same period in which Army bands would be in the forefront of music's role in the electronic age, even if financial pressures kept them from fully exploiting these new media.

The story of British SA bands during World War I is

marked by great sacrifice and outstanding service to the Allied cause. SA bands were the first to help with morale by playing for regiments as they prepared to leave for the front and these same bands soon had a real ministry at the many military hospitals that soon had to be set up.

Large numbers of SA bandsmen enlisted, with entire bands, like Halifax and Long Eaton, joining *en masse*, finding themselves as military bands in Flanders within five weeks of leaving home. Of the approximately 25,000 brass bandsmen that enlisted during the war, a third, or about 8,000 were Salvationists.

Alf Hailstone has shared that in the first three months of 1917, 701 brass bandsmen were killed, 256 of whom were SA, including 7 on one day from the Keighley SA Corps Band. SA bands were admired for their work both on and off the battlefield. When rebuilding in difficult economic circumstances following the war, the SA would have an even greater support from the British public, and higher admiration from their comrades in the brass band scene.

The SP&S Band (Eric Ball) at BBC Broadcasting House, on February 4, 1939.

By 1926, the year of the General Strike, there were 1,050 SA bands in the British Isles alone! 'With a thousand bands' was not just a rhetorical blast.[29]

During 1909–1910 the *British Bandsman* brought up again the issue of Army music and the huge market that was denied men like John Henry Iles. The argument, though usually not supported by letters to the editor (many, of course, being by this time Salvationists), continued into the 1920s.

The editor continued to attack SA policy, but at the same time holding up once again the dedication and discipline of SA bands as a model for the brass bands in general. The SA had taken strong steps to curtail the involvement of SA bandsmen in contests, something that only heightened the tension between these two subcultures.

The brass press of the day frequently had short little reports that must have involved much personal anguish and bitterness, usually to do with a bandsman going from a contest band to an SA band, or *vice versa*. So, oddly enough, the discipline and tight autocratic control that had made SA bands respectable proved to be a problem by the late 1920s. Luring the best of SA bandsmen, 'sheep stealing', was not uncommon, and minor grievances could cause major splits. The *British Bandsman* mused on the strictness of SA banding, perhaps now too strict for modern life?...*so no wonder 11 of the 23 players of the Newton Abbot SA Band have left.*[30]

Part of the tension, in spite of the great strides in repertoire and in playing level, had to do with how SA leadership really viewed music's role. As SA bandmasters became better and better educated, as congregations became more and more sophisticated, officers did not always respond sensitively to their volunteer soldiers' needs. The problem existed from the very top to the very bottom of Army banding and would not be fully resolved for at least another generation. Added to this was the fact that many SA performers were taking their place in the ranks of the best orchestras and ensembles. This created divided loyalties that led to the loss of a significant portion of a whole generation of outstanding musicians.[31]

Bernard Adams, outstanding bandmaster of the ISB

1947–1975, wrote a revealing letter to Erik Leidzén (Jan, 31, 1955) that placed this kind of strife from the perspective of a gradually changing view of band music's role and the respect finally held for it by Army leaders:

Bandmaster Bernard Adams who led the International Staff Band from 1947 - 1975.

I am not the least surprised to learn of the way you feel about the right music being used in the right place and special attention being paid to its association with our particular form of worship...more and more musicians possessed of a sense of fitness as well as a certain amount of sensitivity are endeavouring to fit Army bands and their music into an ordered plan of useful functioning.

As recently as the days when Eric Ball was Staff Bandmaster [1942–1944] we would play during meetings conducted by the 'top' brass over here and the main function would be to fill time. I can even remember during the playing of a lovely hymn tune arrangement as the collection was being taken that the 'all highest' had Eric's coat pulled and he was told 'that's enough'.

When I took over the band [ISB] I asked General Orsborn whether at meetings conducted by him he wished the band to function in order to cover the sound of coins being dropped in the plate or whether he wished my choice of music to be a contribution to worship. He was most strong on the fact that he considered the contribution of the music an integral part of the design of his meetings. I am glad to say he allowed us to co-operate with him in this respect and did something for us and for Army Bands, hitherto almost unknown.

The contradiction between the Army's vigorous support of an unrivalled music publishing program and educational support network for its bands and songsters and its harsh treatment of both individuals and entire sections when the letter of law, or *O&R*, was not followed, is difficult to reconcile and fully explain.

The Army was proud of what it was achieving—musically, artistically—but it was also obsessed with maintaining its missional zeal and deeply concerned that its musicians no longer wished to 'blow salvation' into their congregations, but would rather bask in the warm glow of an audience's acclamation.

Reaching as many people as possible with the Gospel message via their music did continue to be the main goal for SA bands throughout the period 1904–1939. The Army and its bands were willing to try whatever would work, and so by the late 1890s they had dabbled in making recordings, the first evidently being made in 1896 on wax cylinder by the 1896 Trade Department Band. The New York Staff Band followed with some hymn tunes for the Graphophone Grand in the spring of 1899.

Other early efforts took place in 1902 (Herbert Twitchin, cornet, and Regent Hall Band), 1905 (ISB), c. 1911 (Stockholm Temple Band) and 1912 (Chalk Farm, on a French label), none of which, evidently survived.

Illustration 9: Bandmasters' Councils Festival, January 26, 1907

. . . PROGRAMME . . .

Opening Song ... ...

Tune—"Austria"

O THOU God of my salvation,
My Redeemer from all sin,
Moved by Thy divine compassion,
Who hast died my heart to win,
I will praise Thee;
Where shall I Thy praise begin?

Though unseen, I love the Saviour:
He hath brought salvation near;
Manifests His pardoning favour,
And within me doth appear:
Soul and body
Then His glorious image bear.

Angels now are hovering round us,
Unperceived amid the throng,
Wondering at the love that found us,
Glad to join our holy song:
Hallelujah!
Love and praise to Christ belong.

PRAYER

1. United Bands ... ... "God's Pardon." B.J. 496

2. Regent Hall Band. Selection—"Songs about Jesus." B.J. 518

Orchestra to sing verse

WHY should life a weary journey seem?
Jesus is my light and song.
Why should I my cross a burden deem?
Jesus is my light and song.

All the way is mark'd by love divine,
Round the path the rays of glory shine,
Christ, Himself, Companion is of mine.
Jesus is my light and song.

Congregation to sing the chorus

Jesus is my light and song.
I'll serve Him with my might,
Jesus is my light and song.

3. Congress Hall Band. March—"The Standard Be鄟rer," B.J. 517

4 The Staff Songsters ... Song—"The Soldier's Chorus"

5. Chalk Farm Band ... Selection—"Songs of Praise." B.J. 516

Our hearts are filled with praise because we are right with God! Are you?

6. Highgate Band ... March—"The Proclamation." B.J. 509

7. **Announcement of Band Selection Competition Award**

The Staff Band will play the Winning Piece

The Audience is requested to sing with us

Tune—"Falcon Street"

STAND up, and bless the Lord,
Ye people of His choice;
Stand up, and bless the Lord your God.
With heart, and soul, and voice.

Oh, for the living flame,
From His own altar brought,
To touch our lips, our minds inspire,
And wing to heaven our thought!

God is our Strength and Song,
And His salvation ours;
Then be His love in Christ proclaimed,
With all our ransomed powers.

Stand up, and bless the Lord,
The Lord your God adore;
Stand up, and bless His glorious name,
Henceforth for evermore.

8. United Bands ... ... March—"Southall." B.J. 506

9. Congress Hall Band. Selection—"Echoes of the Congress." (No. 2.) B.J. 503

10. Chalk Farm Band ... March—1. "Onward."
2. "Great Salvation." B.J. 519

The great Salvation of God is for you. Will you accept it, here and now?

11. Regent Hall Male Songsters. Song—"Our Army Bands"

12. **BIBLE READING** ... Commissioner James Hay

13. **Announcement of Band March Competition Award**

The Staff Band will play the Winning Piece

14 Highgate. Selection—"Songs of Heaven" (No. 1). B.J. 483

15. The Staff Songsters. Song—"I am the Resurrection and the Life" ... ... M.S., March, 1901

*Jesus said "I am the resurrection and the life;
He that believeth on Me, though he were dead, yet shall he live.
He that believeth on Me shall never die."*

16. Regent Hall Band ... March—"The Warrior." B.J. 521

17. United Bands. Hymn—"All hail the power of Jesus' Name"
(Tune—"Diadem")

. . BENEDICTION . .

--- NO ENCORES WILL BE PERMITTED ---

Recently, recordings of the 1914 Swedish Staff Band have been restored and featured in a CD that accompanies a book on Otto Lundahl (See Chapter 6). The first long-lasting 78rpm recordings were done by the New York Staff Band starting in the Autumn of 1922, for the Aeolian Company, Vocalion label.

This same band made the first radio broadcast by a SA band, in May 1922, when on a trip in Pittsburgh, PA. The band played regularly on local New York stations, some of which were picked up nationally, for years after that premiere. That band did not begin its famous nation-wide broadcasts until the mid-1930s. By that time many SA bands worldwide were being heard over the airwaves.

Meanwhile, the SA in Great Britain launched its first 'modern' 78s in 1927, with the Regal (later Regal Zonophone) label, the first disc containing two marches played by the ISB under George Fuller.

Deryck Turton has calculated that over the next 30 years 220 records containing 350 different pieces were recorded in 78rpm format on this label alone, with other territories around the world producing their own series, if not in quite the same volume. The long-lasting effect of these recordings on the Army's outreach and on the improvement in playing standards worldwide is by now considered commonplace. At the time, it was a revelation, as well as an embodiment of what had been achieved in the overall music programme of The Salvation Army.[32]

Notes

1. *The comparative amount of music played in this form of service* [marching] *performed by Salvation Army Bands, should be taken into consideration. On an average, there are three parades on the Sunday, and if three marches are played in each, this means that a total of nine marches are rendered during the day; whereas, as a rule, not more than about five selections are played in the same period. From the standpoint of quantity alone, this aspect is of real significance.* Frederick Hawkes. Chapter 17, 'The March', in *Studies in Time and Tempo* (London: SP&S, 1936), p103. Hawkes is referring to the days when most SA bands were on duty for three Open-Airs (with march to and from) and at least two indoor services per Sunday.

2. Boyd's 6/8 *Paisley March* appeared in May, 1905 (GS 484), and is one of the first military style marches for the SA; this is not surprising considering his military service and experience in the professional band world (*Local Officer*, May, 1905, p.380).

3. The entire report is a fascinating, entertaining, and humorous document by this great friend of the SA. See Shaw's *Music: The Complete Musical Criticism of Bernard Shaw*, Volume III, 1893–1950 (London: Bodley Head, 1981), 588–594. Blame for the cluttered part writing and scoring must lie with the examples provided by Slater and Hawkes. As late as the latter's *Studies in Time and Tempo* (see p27) he was holding up Slater's counterpoint and scoring as a model of clarity via an example from an old *Band Journal*, GS 313. In this march Slater had attempted a *tour de force* by combining seven different melodies at once, four of them in the same register, by horn, baritone, trombone, and euphonium. The result is a muddle, a curiosity of sorts.

4. Among the consistent winners through the last of the series were Coles and Twitchin. The names of composers first appeared on the pages of the score for the May, 1907 *Band Journal*, for prize issues only. In May, 1909, composers' names appeared for the first time within the score on a regular basis; then in March 1910, on the score cover as well. Goldsmith felt, as he expressed in his report to the 1916 Commission of Inquiry (see citation below) that such march contests were not helpful in truly identifying new talent and that only Bramwell Coles was the great discovery of that four-year effort. He is probably mistaken, but even so, what a discovery – the SA Sousa or march king, as he was so often called. That label embarrassed Coles greatly, just as it probably would Kenneth Alford, two great British march writers that achieved their work a generation after Sousa's best work. The impact of continental march styles and British Contest marches on SA march style and form also still needs to be given comprehensive study. Regarding these early march contests, Slater observed in his *History* (p75) that the best writers were found to be those already in the BJ. Some marches, because they were prize-winning, gained merit beyond their value.

5. Five awards went to the US, four to Great Britain, two to New Zealand, one each for Australia, Belgium, and Czechoslovakia. By far the largest number of entries was for the march – 48, and the selection – 21.

6. Printed festival programmes of this era had to list where the music was published, and if manuscript, that it was approved by a HQ. The February 15, 1928 programme is extant, in London Heritage Centre. Some other notable programmes from this era that survive, include the Bandmasters' Councils Festival, January 26, 1907 (See Illustration 9), and a similar one for January 18, 1913. Notice the declaration that no encores are allowed! A regional Bandsmen's Councils of 1926 was held at Belle Vue, Manchester, sight of the Open Brass Band Championships; the surviving programme lists the ISB, and corps bands from Barrow, Manchester, Burnley, Hanley, Chester, Rochdale, and Kensington.

7. Richard Slater, unpublished *History*, pp69–71.

8. Curriculum for the Bandmasters' Training Session, 1927. Outline program, two-page folio, London Heritage Centre. An Advanced level course was instituted several years later.

9. Author's interview with Brindley Boon, April, 1995. See Boon, *PMP*, Chapter 16, *Administration and Miscellany*, for an outlined history of the Bands Department and National Band Secretaries or Inspectors up through 1965. Those who followed Braine included Fred Adams (father of Staff BM Bernard Adams), Wilfred Kitching, Charles Durman, Edward Saywell,

Ernst Rance, Dean Goffin, and Brindley Boon, Leslie Condon, Norman Bearcroft, and Trevor Davis. Stephen Cobb fits into the new administrative paradigm.

10. See Ronald Holz, *Heralds of Victory*, Chapters 1–2, regarding men like Staff Bandmaster Straubel, who became a regional music director in the late 1890s; On Leidzén's early career in the SA, see *Erik Leidzén*, Chapter 2; Boon interview, April 1995.

11. Boon, unpublished ISB chapter, *Personality Parade*.

12. Alfred Braine, 'The Band and Songsters in Sunday Evening Meetings', *The Officer* (July, 1922), p58–59.

13. Edward Higgins, *Stewards of God* (London: SP&S, 1936), pp28–29. Underlined passages are italicised in the original. In the 1920s the weekly periodical *The Bandsman and Songster* ran a series entitled 'To Fit the Text' surveying bandmasters about what music they would choose for a Salvation Meeting given a particular scripture text. In one issue, February 13, 1926, to a text from Isaiah 59:1, 22 bandmasters of the Northern Division (UK) responded with 18 different choices. The only two works mentioned twice were *Songs of Exhortation* (GS 869) and *Mighty To Save* (GS 619). Two lengthy meditations were among the suggested repertoire: William Broughton's *At the Cross There's Room* (GS 877) and Frederick Hawkes' *Rousseau*. Such a wide variance emphasised not only the diversity of literature but also the need to more specifically educate bandmasters concerning the proper choice of music for worship. See 'To Fit the Text: No.4' *The Bandsman and Songster* (February 13, 1926), p63.

14. The complete report and a large quantity of the gathered testimony survives, one of the fortunate series of documents that survived the bombing of IHQ during World War II. This includes the testimony gathered during Sitting No.12, January 27, 1916, with 'Experts in Army Music': Goldsmith, Slater, and Hawkes. There were 8 pages of questions followed by 64 pages of testimony.

15. Report of the Commission of Inquiry, March 23, 1916, p4.

16. *Ibid*, p18.

17. Boon interview, April 1995. If the reader can find it, I highly recommend Arch Wiggins' book on Richard Slater, *Father of Salvation Army Music*, (London: SP&S, 1945).

18. See *Salvation Army Brass Band Music Table* in Volume II for complete listing of *Instrumental Albums* and *Bandsman's Companion*. SP&S maintains up-to-date lists of which albums or reprints can be purchased. The most recent instrumental solo album, *The Derick Kane Euphonium Album*, was released in the spring of 2005.

19. Copies of this correspondence in the author's possession. Leidzén was told once, for instance, that his transcription of Grieg's *Homage March* could not be printed due to copyright difficulties, only to see Charles Skinner's version show up a short time later! The bottom line was that only IMED members would be published, regardless of who sent them a transcription or how skilfully it was done. This policy was finally changed in the 1970s, with Ray Steadman-Allen the first to lift the floodgate. He has told me that most often it later became an issue of quality, not of origin, in the choice of what transcriptions were chosen to be published.

20. These *Bible Pictures* are unique in being almost entirely original, rarely quoting previously composed tunes. Slater's descriptive selection *The Valley of Death* (GS 591, 1909) pointed in a slightly different direction (more insistent use of tunes), one which he and Hawkes exploited fully. This sub-category probably reached a height of popularity in George Marshall's *Suffering* (GS 881, June 1922), later retitled *Olivet and Calvary* which Steadman-Allen transcribed for piano or organ as *Festival Feature No.5*, 1957. For more detail see Steadman Allen, 'Evolution, Part 10, Selection.' William Broughton's *Bible Picture: Paul and Silas* (GS 964) was transcribed for piano in the *Instrumental Solo Album No.13* in 1932.

21. The text became, in the hands of Arch Wiggins, *Oh! Live once again for the Lord, Brother*, published in the *MS* of 1936, 74–75. Leidzén's title was a type of pun, as he had written the work in honour of his own sister, Maggie, back in 1916. Eric Ball's famous trumpet solo *The Challenge* should be mentioned here, though it did not get published with band accompaniment until September, 1990, (FS 482).

22. A convenient way for studying some of the still popular early marches is found in *Instrumental Album No.13*, a piano solo and duet album containing mostly marches, including: original piano march by Slater, *March in C*; Hawkes' *Vesper Hymn March* (GS 451); Coles' *Under Two Flags* (GS 816) and *In the Firing Line* (GS 935) ; Marshall's *Our Army Brave and True* (GS 708); and H. C. Goffin's *The Red Shield* (GS 986). The arrangements were by two good pianists, Eric Ball and Philip Catelinet. Two transcriptions of early *air variés* (by O. E. Swanson and William Spencer) are also included.

23. That is not to diminish the achievements of Bramwell Coles in this genre, but it is my personal opinion his achievements here were not equal to these three.

24. For in-depth analysis of three Leidzén selections, see Holz, 'The Band Selections of Erik Leidzén', released as a series in the 1980 *Musician* (UK), as well as Chapter 12 of my book on Leidzén. The

selections studied include *The Call, The Children's Friend*, and *At the Master's Feet*. For coverage of Leidzén's break with the Army, see *Leidzén*, Chapter 2; on Ball's break with the Army, see Boon, *ISB*, pp145–149.

25. This passage bears resemblance to a passage in Elgar's *Dream of Gerontius*, 'Sanctus fortis, Sanctus Deus' – which is not surprising, as Elgar was his favourite composer. Ball once told me that in the brass band literature he learned a great deal from and admired the music and scoring of Henry Geehl, in addition to that which he gleaned from his superiors in IMED.

26. This entire section represents an extreme reduction of Chapter 3, 'The Meditation Initial Phase, 1920–1940' of my dissertation on the Meditation in SA band music.

27. *Ibid*, Chapter VII, 'Related Short Forms'.

28. See the *Chalk Farm Story*, Boon *ISB*, and Slater *History*, p92. See Chapter on Sweden for Torgny Hanson's account of British tours. In North America, the 'reciprocal' tours were becoming very popular, especially between Montreal Citadel Band and New York Staff Band, late 1930s.

29. See Hailstone, *British Bandsman Centenary Book*, (Egon) pp123–142 for story and data on SA bands in World War I.

30. *Ibid*, p83,102–103.

31. The most famous, and most representative 'split' occurred in the Coventry SA Band. By the mid-1930s it was a fine corps band led by the talented William Major, one of the first graduates of the SA's Advanced BM Training Course instituted in the late 1920s. Called 'the Army's Master Violinist', Major was also a composer, though his march *Three Spires* had been rejected by the Music Board. Major played it anyway, along with other 'forbidden' works like Robert McAnally's (Australian Salvationist) *Moments with the Masters*. The band's defiance went into the details of banding life – non-regulation band caps, instruments – something that could have kept them from being asked to record, despite being a very proficient ensemble. By April 2, 1939, Major had resigned, and four days later 29 bandsman had joined him. Ironically, the deputy bandmaster Greig, who rebuilt the band with the 20 or so that remained, would be asked to step down in 1951, shortly after the band's successful tour of Germany, for breaking regulations! He did so, but when not reinstated after an agreed-upon period, 20 members protested, resigned, and became the nucleus of a famous contesting band. And yet, by the 1980s the corps band was back up on top, touring all over the place. On Easter, 1994, BM Charles King, at the close of his successful tenure, was leading an efficient band of 31 members, 17 of whom had come in from the corps junior band. See Fred and

Ken Elliot, *The Band With A Name (A History of Coventry City SA Band, 1892–1993)*, p47ff.

32. For more information on early British recordings, see Deryck Turton CD booklet essay, 'The Heritage of SA Recordings', on *The Old Wells: Favourites for the 78rpm era, Volume One*, SP&S, 1997. Turton has extended the series now to four volumes (see Discography, Volume II). Also, see Brindley Boon's comments in a short article, 'Information wanted about old Army records', *The Musician* (Dec., 12. 1984), p786, as well as pp216–217, PMP. For information on early New York Staff Band recordings, and radio broadcasts, see *Heralds of Victory*, 17–18, 38–39. A vivid account of the use of Graphophone Grand recordings in New York City can be found in the *American War Cry*, April 22, 1899, p8, which included a recording of NYSB.

Chronology of Important Events in Salvation Army Brass Band Music and Publishing 1878-2004

1878   The Christian Mission renamed The Salvation Army. Fry family brass quartet becomes the model for the formation of SA brass bands.

1879   First corps bands begin to be formed and organised; bands use 'outside' publications and manuscript arrangements.

1880   William Booth encourages the widespread development of 'bands' (instrumentation not specified) in a General Order that appears in *The War Cry*.

1881   In February General Booth issues a second General Order concerning regulations and rules for 'brass bands'. Booth appoints Fred Fry to produce brass arrangements for Army bands.

1882   In July, Fred Fry releases the first SA brass music as a sixpenny card with seven tunes on it. Music publisher R. de Lacy of Brixton, London, publishes a band tune book of 42 tunes for *The Salvation Army*, with official SA sanction.

1883   *Salvation Army Music II* (Vocal/Piano) becomes the first music book containing original material by Salvationist authors and composers. In October, the first Music Department begins work. Richard Slater, Fred Fry, and Harry Hill form the first staff, under the general supervision of Herbert Booth.

1884   In August, the first *Band Journal (General Series)* begins monthly publication. GS 33, *Roused from my Slumber*, becomes the first classical transcription for SA band. In November, *Band Music for The Salvation Army* is published. This revised and expanded version of Fry's 1882 sixpenny cards contained 83 tunes, numbered consecutively and arranged for fourteen instrumental parts.

1885   In May a General Order in *The War Cry* states that *henceforth bands must use only music published by The Salvation Army*.

1886   In May *The Musical Salvationist* begins publication. It is the SA's regular vocal/choral publication subscription series. Originally this magazine included articles on vocal and band music, instrumental ensembles, solos, and choral music.

1895	BB Flat 'Monstre' Basses come into wider use in SA bands.
1896	The first music board, known as The International Headquarters Music Board, is formed to administer and control music publications and other aspects of musical activity. The Music Editorial Department (Richard Slater) prepares music for review, instrumental music played for the Board by the International Staff Band.
1898	Songster Brigades (Choirs) are finally recognised and formally allowed in SA worship and outreach.
1899	*Salvation Army Songs*, containing 870 songs and 216 choruses, is published. This *Song Book*, words only, becomes the first principal song book for congregational use that contained a significant proportion of songs written by Salvationists. The first Bandsmen's Councils are held on December 10th.
1900	*Band Music No. 1* is published. This brass companion to the 1899 song book, *Salvation Army Songs*, contains 303 tunes for the accompaniment of congregational singing. A Keyboard edition is also released.
1901	William Booth permits the use of band music for which no words had been composed or intended. The Music Board is thereby given further latitude, subject to conditions, for decisions regarding instrumentation, arrangement, and compositional style.
1902	The first 'Selection' for SA band, *Old Song Memories*, released in the January *General Series*. A prototype hymn meditation, *Jesus, Hope of Souls Repentant*, is released in February. The first SA March, *The Morning Hymn March*, released in April.
1903	Starting with the January *General Series*, scoring now resembles more closely that of most English brass band scores. Clarinets are dropped from scores. The first Bandmasters' Councils are held in January.
1904	The Third International Congress is held, June–July, in London. The Salvation Army is then established in 49 countries with 17,099 commissioned Senior (adult) Bandsmen. Flugelhorn added to *General Series* score.

1905	Original march competition held; Selection competition added in 1906; both continued for several years.
1910	GS 601, January, *Stilling the Storm* (Richard Slater), first published SA programmatic work, subtitled *Bible Picture No. I.*
1915–16	Commission of Inquiry meets to review all matters pertaining to SA music regulations. Leads to expansion of brass publications, including new band journals and instrumental soloist and chamber music albums.
1920	First 'official' Meditation published, *Rockingham* (Arthur Goldsmith), GS 839.
1921	*Second Series* or *Triumph Series Band Journal* begun, in support of smaller, less proficient bands.
1923	*Festival Series Band Journal* begun, designed for the most advanced music and sections.
1924	First instrumental solo in 'theme and variations' form published; *I love Him Better Every Day* (W. Stevenson).
1926	First band *Air Varié* (set of variations on a given tune) published; *While the Days Are Going By* (presumably by Frederick Hawkes). International Music Competition held; compositional forms requested are march, selection, meditation, and instrumental solo forms.
1928–30	Revision of *Band Tune Book* and congregational *Song Book* undertaken; *Tune Book* now has 542 melodies.
1936–37	First tone poems published; *Streams in the Desert* (Evangeline Booth/Eric Ball) FS 113 *Exodus* (Eric Ball), FS 117. First modern festival arrangement published; *A Glorious Hope* (Philip Catelinet), GS 1131. First suite for band published; *Songs of the Morning* (Eric Ball), FS 114.
1938	First true, short song arrangement; *Why Not Tonight?* (Philip Catelinet), GS 1143.
1944	First hymn tune arrangement, *Weber* (Philip Catelinet); GS 1239–2.
1948	*American Band Journal* (New York) launched via competition; designed for nine players; Erik Leidzén serves as editor.
1953	Revised *Song Book* published; *Band Tune Book*

Supplement published, with numbers 542–756. New York music department releases training journal for beginner bands: *First Marches and Selections.*

1955   First 'prelude' published; *Prelude on Three Welsh Hymn Tunes* (Ralph Vaughan Williams); FS 209. Regular short preludes not until 1970.

1957   *Unity Series* first published, designed for bands of four or more parts.

1970   First work for brass band and piano published [premiered 1965]: *Fantasia – Christ is the Answer* (Ray Steadman-Allen)

1976   *Song Book* and *Tune Book* supplement called *Keep Singing* released.

1978   Sixth International Congress held in London; 42,035 bandsmen; 60,407 songsters. Centennial Congress celebrates 100 years of SA banding.

1985   American Territorial Music Directors decide to coordinate music publication efforts nationwide in both vocal and instrumental music.

1986   *American Festival Series* begun, USA Central, edited by William Himes.

1987   *American Brass Ensemble Series* (USA, Southern, edited by James Curnow) is launched in new style; designed for four or more players; later renamed AIES. The series has as a feature the related *American Brass Soloist Series* (solo and piano accompaniment version). Band publishing carried out in Norway, Sweden, US East (New York), US Central (Chicago) as well as Great Britain.

1988   New *Song Book* and *Tune Book* produced; 871 tunes.

1991   The Salvation Army decides to allow the sale of all its music to bands outside the denomination; this policy managed at 'territorial discretion.'

1992   With the reorganisation of the British Territory, a truly International Music Council is established, which meets twice yearly to discuss matters related to SA music. It does not deal with specific publications, but recommends general policy worldwide. Changes in regulations allow more latitude for all SA band members, not just professionals, to participate in 'outside' performing groups. SA band music will gradually begin to be considered, and used, as test pieces at various levels in the UK and in North America.

1993	SP&S Ltd (London) and Egon Publishers Ltd jointly publish band arrangements for *New Christmas Praise*.
1996	The Salvation Army at work in 103 countries; 25,183 Senior band members; 11,763 YP band members (*1998 SA Yearbook*). Robert Redhead's *Isaiah 40* commissioned as the test for National Brass Band Championships, published by SP&S. First such piece by an active SA officer [Ray Steadman-Allen, in retirement, had already written several].
1997	International Catalogue of Salvation Army Music Publications first produced. By this time SP&S maintaining special manuscript and large-scale works brass series, via individual items rather than in sets of items.
2000	International Congress held in Atlanta GA; The International Music Council discontinued.
2001	International Music Forum holds its first sessions, July 2001. Canada and Bermuda Territory launches *Maple Leaf Brass* band series. USA East offering by this time two new brass band series, *Triumphonic Collection*, and *Philip Smith Signature Series*.
2002	The Salvation Army at work in 109 countries; 29,472 Senior band members; 13,957 YP band members (*2003 Yearbook*).
2003	Colonels Robert and Gweneth Redhead appointed by General John Larsson as the General's Representatives for the Development of Music and other Creative Arts for Evangelism and Worship.
2004	SP&S acquires the periodical *The British Bandsman*, and the brass band publishing firm R. Smith&Co. SP&S also operates World of Brass recording catalogue, including SP&S, Egon, and Doyen labels.

Chapter 4

UNITED KINGDOM TERRITORY: AN OUTSIDER'S VIEW

Ronald W. Holz

Generally speaking, our bands and songster brigades, once the 'spearhead of our attack', are now thought to be rather conservative, self-gratifying groups of musicians. There is some truth in this, and I would be the first to work hard, as I do, to engender an openness of mind to 'new things' among these with whom I am appointed to work. However, at the same time it is an irresponsible generality if applied to many who still do more 'outreach' (however inadequate) than most other Salvationists, certainly in the group setting, and who continually bless and inspire countless people in and out of the Army with their music. That is not even to mention the most important aspect of their music-making, which is an offering of self and gift to God himself. Lt. Colonel Trevor Davis, then Territorial Music Secretary, in his article 'Another World of Music', *The Officer* (December, 1995), p549.

The largest expression of SA banding is still to be found where it all began, in the United Kingdom. Chapters 2 and 3 of this book focused on the early history of SA bands and music, the main threads of that story having taken place within that same region. When organising and researching this study I realised that the huge subject of British SA bands called for its own book, or a whole series of books. Justice could not be given to the topic. What I felt could be done in this chapter was to focus on the immediate past, since the reorganisation of the British Territory.

I sought for patterns and trends in this important arena of SA music making, not to write a 'history' of the last dozen years or so! However, I have had support and cooperation from both 'official' and unofficial sources. I offer up an outsider's view, acknowledging that this can only be a small point of departure for continued discussion and assessment.

Some portions of this essay are speculative in nature, especially concerning music publishing efforts, aspects of which may have already been instituted or changed by the time this book goes to print. The bands I profiled at the conclusion of the chapter were purposefully not the better known, internationally famous groups. Rather, they were a representative sampler of various expressions of banding within the Territory, bands with whom I had had direct contact on several occasions.[1]

The last decade of the 20th century will be remembered by Salvationist musicians, particularly those in the United Kingdom, as a time of sweeping change and unsettling challenge. First, in late 1991 then Commissioner Bramwell Tillsley announced that as of March 1, 1992, SA band music would be available to the general public, though SA bands would still be restricted to their own journals.

Near that time, the British Territory was restructured as the United Kingdom Territory with the Republic of Ireland. The reorganisation included a significant change in the two principal music departments, Music Editorial, and Bands and Songster Brigades, whereby they came together as the Territorial Music Department, led by a Territorial Music Secretary, Robert Redhead.

Several years later, in 1998, in another refinement, the department became known as the Music Ministries Unit [MMU] and became part of the Evangelism Department. The title Territorial Music Secretary changed to that of Music Ministries Officer [MMO, Captain Peter Ayling]. In April 2001 Stephen Cobb was appointed leader of the MMU with the title Territorial Music Director, the first non-officer to do so in the history of music leadership in the UK. To top it all off, an amendment to *O&R* (Memo from Chief of the Staff, Commissioner Bramwell Tillsley, August 17, 1992) finally loosened the reins on Salvationist participation in non-SA music groups. *At territorial/command discretion, Salvationists may participate in non-Salvation Army music groups, provided that membership of such groups does not conflict with SA principles and service.* Army musicians in the UK faced major adjustments in their views towards their own music, music making in general, the manner in which their sections were supported, who could be a band member, and in the way bands functioned within SA worship and mission. Bands, and their personnel, would bear the brunt of criticism in the midst of change. They were easy targets.[2]

Stephen Cobb (who also serves as the conductor of the International Staff Band) heads the present Music Ministries Unit. He has instituted a departmental structure that is less hierarchic, much flatter in shape than previous practice. Within the new alignment he is stressing a multi-skilled and multi-task approach to the department's operation. He oversees general operations and administration and all

Territorial Music Schools have proved to be popular in the U.K. Bandmaster Stephen Cobb is seen leading a session.

sections of the department function under his leadership, including bands/songsters, special music events, and music editing/publishing.

The MMU staff in May 2004 was as follows [Note: Due to financial exigencies faced by the UK Territory, the MMU experienced staff reductions in the Autumn of 2004]. Andrew Blyth holds the position of Assistant Territorial Music Director, and oversees the day-to-day activities of the music editorial process.

The professional editorial staff who work from outside the department with Blyth include: 1) Dr. Peter Graham, Senior Editor (3 days/week); 2) Kenneth Downie, Creative Consultant with a mandate to write and/or arrange functional works for SA groups (3 days/week), as well as serve as Mentor to developing composers within the UK; 3) Lt. Colonel Ray Steadman-Allen, who in retirement continued to serve as a consultant and revered 'Senior Adviser.' Sub editors working in the London office with Andrew Blyth are Dean Jones, Nicholas Samuel, Simon Gash, and Paul Sharman.

All typesetting and origination is now done on computer, 'in house'; the two full time originators are Simon Birkett and Ira Thomas. Cobb has a music administration team made up of Kevin Ashman, Tristessa Aberg, and Bernice Cuthbert. Additionally, Derick Kane serves in a music education position, Training Specialist, a position described as somewhat along the lines of the old Territorial Bandmaster/Songster Leader, but with Kane available to all music sections. Retired bandmaster Don Jenkins, famous for his work with Bristol Easton Band, has worked two days a week as well, with some special attention given to archival materials.

The MMU is located at THQ, 101 Newington Causeway, just off the Elephant and Castle underground rail stop, The ISB band room has also been moved from IHQ to this location. Related to the MMU, but a separate entity, is Salvationist Publishing and Supplies, SP&S, Ltd. SP&S functions within the UK Trade Department, and is the publishing house of SA music within the United Kingdom.

Daily operations are currently managed and directed by Trevor Caffull (during the writing of the majority of this chapter Lt. Colonel Michael Williams held that position) with

Stephen Cobb designated as a Director of SP&S, Ltd. Thus there is clear communication between the MMU and SP&S. SP&S has recently relocated from Judd Street to a new location at 1 Tiverton Street, a building directly behind THQ.

A Territorial Music Council, chaired by the Chief Secretary on behalf of the Territorial Commander, meets regularly (usually monthly) to review matters of music policy, publications, and performance.

The membership consists of a representative corps bandmaster and songster leader, representative corps officer, the Territorial Music Director, Assistant Territorial Music Director, the Managing Director of SP&S, a representative of Publishing Department (not musical, but literary), and the Chief Secretary.

The International Staff Band and International Staff Songsters, while maintaining their title, belong to the UK Territory, not IHQ. These groups or ensembles formed from them are used for demonstration purposes at meetings of the Territorial Music Council [TMC].

The Band Programme and the Current State of Bands

(Interviews with BM Stephen Cobb, April 1995; May 1999; January 2003)

When he was Territorial Bandmaster Stephen Cobb worked three days a week relating to 510 senior bands within the UK Territory (Spring, 1999 figures). His appointment as staff bandmaster of the ISB is a volunteer assignment, separately administered, as is his local officer position, bandmaster of the famed Hendon Corps Band. To say that he was a busy musician is a gross understatement, as he also worked the remaining two days of the week as a school music teacher. Junior or youth bands did not come directly under his charge, nor did the summer Territorial Music School (both technically come under the Youth Department), though the MMU is connected to this youth work, as will be presently shown.

He would usually visit bands in the evening and on weekends, his main job being to reinforce and encourage all aspects of good banding, not being concerned with equipment and inventory issues (which are handled by various DHQs). He would bring new music, accessible music to each band, helping them understand how their support system, from the

TMC to the ISB, is there to help them. Not least, he tries to be of spiritual help, the most important part of his visits frequently being the devotional time he leads.

The greatest need within the territory seems to be for dedicated, trained local leaders in both vocal and brass areas. Stephen, as well as all members of the MMU, must emphasise the critical concerns of training new leaders and revitalising the 'veterans.' An Excellence Course modelled on the old Bandmasters Correspondence Course is underway, and an even more important programme to spotlight the best of SA young players is well underway, the Territorial Youth Band [TYB], the SA equivalent of the National Youth Brass Band of Great Britain. In this venture Cobb is catching the attention of the 'brightest and best'. He finds that bands are relevant to the younger generation and that kids want to blow brass instruments. The SA must not drag this interest into the dust, nor lose sight of the very best of what has been achieved in SA banding.

The TYB is currently meeting for one session or course every year for a week; the age range is 12–17. There is a strong SA component in addition to the rigorous musical study. The initial trial run at Boscombe, the concert for which drew over 500, featured such demanding literature as *Aspects of Praise* (Himes) and *Shine as the Light* (Graham). Beyond the course the band takes on special engagements and festivals. In the summer of 2002 the performance level of this group on Saturday, June 22, 2002 received high praise (*Brass Band World* report, July, 2002, p27).

The broad goals set for the Territorial Youth Band, as articulated by Cobb, are as follows:

1) Heighten the spiritual awareness of the young people in the course.

2) Begin to nurture and develop their leadership skills.

3) Provide a model group of its kind, to be the very best in musical and evangelical effectiveness.

By establishing such a high standard Cobb and his staff aim at not losing highly talented young people; they do not need to go elsewhere for musical excellence.

The number of bands currently within the UK is not overly encouraging. In 1983 there were 611 bands averaging 19

Cardiff Canton Band, Bandmaster Steve Martin, being conducted by Deputy BM Carl Saunders at Boscombe, Easter 2005.

members each in the UK; by 1999, 510 bands averaging 14 members per band. This latter figure is fortunately holding steady in 2004. The data points towards a possible stemming of the tide, the loss experienced during the 1980s and early 1990s. Cobb estimates that 66% of the 510 bands now are in the 14–20 member size. Above that, there are 50–60 band of 30 or more players and within that grouping about a half dozen truly superb bands, models of what an SA band should be in all aspects, especially in ministry and musicality.

While Cobb considers the ranking of bands a foolhardy endeavour he did supply, at my request, a representative list of 30 of the currently more 'successful' or 'notable' of the larger bands in the UK. The list, at early 2006, and in alphabetical order, also shows the bandmaster and, if available, the bandmaster's employment. Bandmaster Cobb could add another 30 bands to such a list:[3]

CORPS	*BANDMASTER* (and Employment, if provided)
Belfast Temple	Jack Birch
Bellshill	Ian Dickie (Payroll Manager)
Bexley Heath	Derick Kane (THQ Music Staff)
Birmingham Citadel	David Nicholson
Bristol Easton	Norman Cassells
Boscombe	Howard Evans (SA Netherlands)
Cardiff Canton	Steve Martin (Teacher)
Chalk Farm	Jonathan Evans (Accountant)
Chatham	Carl Woodman

Chelmsford	Simon Schulz (Medical doctor)
Coventry City	Hyw Ellis (Accountant)
Croydon	Paul Graham (Surveyor)
Derby Central	Alan Losh (Teacher)
Govan (Glasgow)	Brian Keachie (Music Teacher)
Edinburgh Gorgie	Keith Johnson (Engineer)
Enfield Citadel	Andrew Blyth (Music Ministries)
Hadleigh Temple	Ken Hillson
Hendon Citadel	Stephen Cobb (TMD)
Kettering Citadel	Richard Phillips (Musician)
Leicester Castle	Les Piper (Music teacher)
Maidenhead	Stuart Hall (Accountancy)
Norwich Citadel	Doug Beattie (Insurance)
Portsmouth	David Mallett (Teacher)
Reading Central	Paul Mortlock (Music Sales)
Risca	Ian Browning (Construction Building)
Peterborough	David Craik (Manager, computer company)
Regent Hall	Stephen Hanover (Representative, Electronic firm)
Sale (Manchester)	Ernie Young
Sheffield Citadel	Ian Wileman (Teacher)
Staines	Allan Martin
Sunderland Monkwearmouth	Nick Hall
Winton	Stan Randall
Worthing	Peter Downey (Corps Manager)

SA bands are supported and encouraged by upper administration. The five Territorial Commanders Cobb has worked for, Pender, Gowans, Hughes, Clifton and Matear, have all wanted bands to be effective and vibrant. No specific vision, however, comes from on high in these transitional days. Cobb does not expect it and does not think SA bands in the UK should look for it, but should grab the initiative. Given time, hard work, and continued/improved financial input, the band programme of the SA can be a growing part of the SA. After all, taken as a whole, the musical soldiers of the SA are still its most active contributors.

Channelling that dedicated service for optimum results is the main issue, one tied up to quality of music and texts, as well as musical styles chosen. He feels that, despite some polarisation in certain areas, most Salvationists are willing to work together, to be more discerning in the use of music for worship and evangelism, whether it is more traditional or 'contemporary' musical styles that are chosen.

To some, the main measures of success for a SA band involve what level of music they play, what recordings they've made, and where they travel, all models developed in the first 40 years of this century. UK corps bands have certainly achieved in these areas within the 1990s. While names like Enfield and Hendon come immediately to mind in all of these areas, other bands would include Norwich Citadel, Coventry City, Staines, Bristol Easton, and a host of others.

Recordings are a natural way for bands to extend their ministry and at the same time raise much needed funds. In 1994–1995 alone the Newsletter of the Territorial Music Department reported on the following overseas tours by UK corps bands: Boscombe (USA Florida); Romford (Holland); Reading Central (Korea/Hong Kong); Morriston (Holland); Birmingham Citadel (USA West). Tours, on the other hand, can create problems for bands, for they too frequently become vanity exercises, bands having to pick up the pieces following the big trip, because members were only in it for the short haul. This is nothing new for SA bands, but to the degree bands do not seek out local venues for ministry the temptation can become too great to rely on trips to build *esprit-de-corps* and as a means to enhance musical efficiency. This would hold true throughout the worldwide banding fellowship within the SA.

The International Staff Band is now the UK's premiere *territorial* band, yet still holds the responsibility to be the SA's premiere brass band. With only the finest expected of this

A Centenary photograph of Enfield Citadel Band in 1992 with Bandmaster James Williams

Actress June Whitfield CBE, filming for the BBC Golden-Globe-winning drama, 'The Last of the Blonde Bombshells', November 1999 .

group, it is satisfying to report that the current band is indeed among the very best in the entire history of the SA. Their duties have not changed, including these 3 vital tasks: 1) providing the highest standard in SA banding, both musically and spiritually via monthly visits to corps and in special territorial festivals and congresses; 2) recording and performing new music for the Territorial Music Council; 3) providing the finest models for the effective use of SA music in both worship and festival setting.

When you review the CD-Rom that accompanies their *Manuscripts* CD you find a focus on mission, calling, and witness, as much as on musical achievement. If we are perfectly honest, however, most people are interested in the ISB because they are or are not musically excellent. While not every past ISB was stellar, the days of Bernard Adams' leadership seem to hold a special warm spot with those with long enough memories. That is not to take anything away from the very impressive achievements by the succeeding bands under Ray Bowes and Robert Redhead (both bands were very musically sensitive ensembles). Many evaluations might line up with what Cyril Bradwell, Dean Goffin's biographer, shared with me concerning the ISB under Cobb that toured New Zealand in 1995:

> *In October we had a very brief visit from the International Staff Band, which greatly impressed under Stephen Cobb's leadership. I had always put Bernard*

Adams' 1967 band (with Roland Cobb and Terry Camsey
on top cornets) at the peak of my experience of SA bands,
but this 1995 ISB must now take precedence.

When I heard the ISB in Charleston, West Virginia, in April 1999, their programming, witness, and outstanding playing, especially in light of the fact that they had just arrived in the country, set the standard for all SA bands – they were true to their mission. My brother, Dr. Richard Holz, who travelled with them on their tour of the USA Southern Territory, observed that the band even got better. Most recently, I heard the band in Indianapolis during their Spring 2004 tour of North America, and I found the band performing at a very high standard indeed. Stephen Cobb and his colleagues honour the past, but they are not content to look backward; they would say that, with hard work and dedication, there is no reason why the best time for SA bands is not now.

The ISB continues to lead the way for a banding renaissance. Several times in the last few years they have been featured on the Gala Concert of the National Brass Band Championships, including the years 1997, 2001 and 2002. In addition, in 2002 SP&S released a double compact disc entitled *The Heaton Collection*, which was a joint effort by the ISB and Black Dyke Band, two of the finest bands in the world who have also shared the platform at three of those Gala Concerts. The discs contain nearly the entire output of Wilfred Heaton, from both SA and contesting band repertoire, a significant and symbolic venture. These bands joined once again, in Nottingham, October 2003, for a memorable festival in honour of the centenary of Eric Ball's birth.

Another model group that flourished during the 1990s was Egon Virtuosi Brass. The band was formed by John Street of Egon Publishers/Recordings in order to explore the heritage of SA music, to provide good recordings of material that people wanted to own and hear, and to provide a unique fellowship for outstanding corps band members from SA corps throughout the territory. Though certain key members of Egon Virtuosi were drawn from bands like Enfield, the large number came from a wide range of bands outside the London area. Under James Williams' baton (and Bram Gregson on one disc) the group released top-selling compacts discs of SA marches, concert music, devotional classics, and even profiled

Egon Virtuosi Brass (conductor James Williams) formed in 1993, essentially to record classic SA compositions. The band produced several CD recordings over a five year period.

several SA composers, Peter Graham and Kenneth Downie. Because it was perceived by many as a commercial venture, the group was on the receiving end of criticism, official or otherwise, from within the Army. Was it competition with the ISB, did its products cut down on SP&S sales? John Street, who subsequently entered into a cooperative venture with SP&S, was an entrepreneur with a vision for how to make SA band music interesting and accessible to a wider range of people. His success proved him correct, and he did no harm to the Army's mission, if anything enhancing it. He also was in the forefront of getting the SA and the brass band movement together, via Egon's sponsorship of a number of brass band Galas and Championships.

Another band that draws its membership from across the UK is the Household Troops Band directed by Major John Mott. Membership is drawn from a wide range of corps throughout the territory, and contains truly excellent players and soloists. Within the last decade or so this band, as formed for various seasons, has taken on the role of recapturing the old SA style of banding blended with contemporary techniques in both outdoor evangelism and in festival programming.

In the spring of 2002 the band successfully toured North America, retracing the pacesetting tour the original band undertook back in the late 19th century. A smaller group of 15 outstanding players, Festival Brass, has also formed on an intermittent basis. Their leader and principal cornet, Julian Bright, has effectively shown what a smaller ensemble can do, how flexible it can be in a wide variety of styles, from the most demanding *Festival Series* works to arrangements of contemporary Christian songs.

In June 2000 Festival Brass served as the representative SA band at the famous Great American Brass Band Festival in Danville, KY, during a year in which all the groups were from outside the USA. Their excellent programming and vibrant Christian witness in front of huge crowds proved again just how effective well-organised, musically proficient brass groups are.

Fellowship Bands have in recent years been one of the real areas of growth in SA banding both within the UK and in other territories. In these groups, retired or reservist band members, plus on occasion former soldiers or band members, join together for occasional rehearsals and concerts, many times using the income derived to support a variety of SA activities or local charities.

A marching display by The Household Troops Band, Bandmaster John Mott, at The Royal Albert Hall, London, 2005.

In the London area, former bandmaster of Hendon Band (and former ISB cornet soloist) Roland Cobb has taken up the baton again. He even convinced his brother, John Cobb (former ISB trombone soloist, professional musician, and arts administrator), to pick up his instrument and play in a SA-related band after a gap of many years. It may be that such groups can become the nucleus of a resurgence of interest in teaching young people, by a band member or retired member taking a personal interest in a handful of young players, providing them with a guiding hand. Such an idea of 'reproducing oneself' worked for years within SA bands and it is a self-sacrificing activity that can hopefully blossom alongside the almost hobby-like nature of fellowship bands.

The annual Bandmaster and Songster Leaders' Councils and Festival (usually held in late May or early June, and which no longer alternate) provide fellowship, instruction, model performances, and, hopefully, a general uplift to all who attend. These prestigious concerts and the instructional sessions connected with them have for years been top highlights of the calendar year in terms of the international music scene of the SA. The main festival event is now given the more inclusive title Gospel Arts Concert, and the Councils have been renamed the annual Music Leaders' Weekend.

In a recent issue of *The Salvationist* (UK) Brindley Boon recalled the tremendous impact this series of concerts, training sessions, and worship experiences have had not only on the UK Territory, but upon the entire music world of the SA.

In June 2003 the Gospel Arts Concert featured an international group, the New York Staff Band, who were completing a tour of the UK. With an emphasis on youth, over 500 young Salvationist musicians from various UK Territory's Divisional Youth Choruses made up a grand Festival Chorus. The Councils that followed met at the William Booth College, where technical seminars and joint worship were the activities again proving helpful in the nurture and health of corps music leaders.

In addition, the relatively new Adult Music School's structure seems to be right on track, as well, in this regard, as highlighted in John Stubbings' (Gloucester) report on the April 1994 course (TMD Newsletter, June 1994; this newsletter has now been changed to an e-mail version). The course ran April 4–8, attracted 47 delegates, and was led by Robert Redhead, Trevor Davis, Len Ballantine, and Stephen Cobb from the music department, and guest conductors Roland Cobb and Keith Prynn, an excellent staff indeed.

> *From 8:15 am each morning until 11 pm each evening, driven on by the gentle persuasion of Programme Coordinator [BM] Richard Carroll, they worked hard in band and mixed choir rehearsals, vocal technique classes, Bible forums based on a study of Colossians 3: 1–17 with particular emphasis on how this passage of Scripture relates to SA musicians, and nightly fellowship sessions. These took the form of lively discussions on various topics of current SA interest and here the varying backgrounds, experiences, and ages (spanning more than 50 years!) were especially relevant.*

In the spring of 2002 the Adult Music School was oversubscribed (nearly 70 delegates), always a good sign! The 10th annual session met April 21—25, 2003, and once again a full delegation attended. Another kind of fellowship that can only help are informal meetings of bandmasters, such as that organised by Jim Wright (Sheffield) in January, 1994, which also soon included deputy bandmasters. It would seem such individual initiative can only be a boost to the attempt at a comprehensive revitalisation of the SA's music programme in the UK

Summer music schools for young Salvationists (The UK prefers the term 'school' to music camp) still are held throughout the territory each summer. In 1994, for instance, 19 divisional or area schools were held, in addition to the Scottish National School of Music and the one that brings the 'brightest and best' together, the Territorial Music School. There is also now an Ireland School of Music. While Trevor Davis expressed concern in the Autumn 1994 department Newsletter that only 150 delegates were attracted to the top school (the facilities were capable of handling another 60 to 70 students), the achievement level was high indeed. There has been a recent surge in attendance at the Territorial Senior Music School (ages 16–29), the summer 2002 course being particularly successful. The long-range impact of these schools on the musical, social, and spiritual health of Army youth is incalculable.

One final factor when considering bands of the UK is the role their members have played in establishing or maintaining bands in other nations. You might think that such an issue remains a thing of the distant past. [See discussions of the impact of immigration on the growth of SA bands in Canada, Australia, USA, and New Zealand in subsequent chapters]. It is still a recurring event that some of the best and most talented move away.

In other words, it has been always going on, from the days when entire bands and their families were enticed over to America (see Chapter 9 USA) to form instant corps or staff bands to the more recent trend of hiring professional music staff. This might be considered a form of 'brain-drain,' but it has always been an aspect of Army music history. The motherland has indeed offered up many of her sons and daughters to the SA music scene in Australia, Canada, New Zealand, and the USA.

For example, starting in the mid-1970s America recruited a significant proportion of DMDs from the UK. Among the first were such talents as Ivor Bosanko, Pendel Division (who later became Territorial Music Director, USA West) and Terry Camsey, first as TMD in the West and then as DMD in Metropolitan New York. (Camsey returned to the West and became a commissioned officer.) Gordon Ward, from Hull, replaced Camsey as DMD in Metropolitan New York and became the soprano cornetist, and eventually principal cornet in the New York Staff Band. Richard Spicer went from Derby as DMD at Syracuse, and then on to Los Angelas.

More recently, James Anderson left Scotland to assume the DMD job in Dallas, later moved to Atlanta in the Territorial Music and Music Education department in Atlanta, replaced Ivor Bosanko as TMD for the USA West for a short time, and now assumes the DMD position in Washington, DC. The staff under Anderson when he worked in Dallas were almost entirely from outside the States: Philip and Stephen Burn (Bedlington), Anthony Thompson (Castleford), Nick Simmons-Smith (Chelmsford), and Eric Fyn (Windsor, Canada).[4]

Keith Wilkinson, a successful contesting band conductor who nonetheless kept his soldiership active in trying circumstances, was the DMD in Cleveland for a short time and until very recently directed the SA music programme for the greater Columbus, OH area. In addition, Ivor Bosanko was able to entice Christopher Mallett to Southern California as a DMD (The SA world mourned the untimely death of Bandmaster Mallett in the late Spring 2000). Ralph Pearce has held forth as a DMD in Phoenix, Arizona.[5]

In May 2005, Neil Smith, originally from Inverness, Scotland, assumed the position of Territorial Music Secretary for the USA West, after having served as DMD in the Sierra del mar (San Diego) Division. This is but a representative sample!

It has been my personal pleasure to work for the past ten years with a group of outstanding young musicians from the UK that were initially recruited by another expatriate. Christopher Priest, former ISB bass trombone and staff member at SP&S, has helped recruit staff for the summer conservatories in the USA South each year. These young adults then have the option of attending the two levels of the Advanced Leadership Seminar at South's TMI later that season. Most of the members of this class are upper-level university students majoring in music or recent music graduates, several quite talented, who are active in their corps and hoping to take on some kind of responsibility there, whether they be Americans or British.

I have been very impressed not only with the skill of the British students but with their spiritual focus, both of which portend well for the future of SA music in the UK. A handful of them have been employed in the States; most return home. Several have shared, however, that it can be difficult to break into a leadership position, even a minor one, in their local corps, a fact that must lead to frustration on occasion. Giving the young and talented a chance to lead will be a critical issue that local music leaders and corps officers must face.

Music Publishing and Music Sales

Interviews and Correspondence with Robert Redhead, Trevor Davis, Richard Phillips, Peter Ayling, Stephen Cobb and Michael Williams (July 1992; May 1999; December 2000; January 2003)

Stephen Cobb and Andrew Blyth recognise outright what has been until recently an unspoken principle of what was formerly the International Music Editorial Department – that publications are aimed primarily at sections within the UK, which represent approximate 70% of sales. Michael Williams confirmed this fact, with all three stressing that such an economic reality does not make them insensitive to overseas bands and choirs of the SA.

Cobb has overall responsibility for all musical decisions relating to publications, and he decides which items are presented to the Territorial Music Council. When he makes those decisions, in consultation with members of the MMU, he is primarily thinking of that British 70%. For band music, they seek material that is right for the medium and also music which primarily serves the SA's purpose, namely the communicating of the message of the Gospel. Communication, in a word, is the issue, regardless of style, though contemporary forms are certainly encouraged if they are tastefully handled.

Maintaining quality throughout all the band journals remains high on the MMU's list of goals. Arguably, there are not as many of the top SA writers these days as in previous generations who are sending in unsolicited pieces. However, as mentioned above, Peter Graham and Kenneth Downie, as part time professional staff, write quality but highly functional music for bands at all levels. This is possibly the first step toward embracing the commissioning of individual pieces, as is done in the USA South *American Instrumental Ensemble Series*. Whether they also embrace that same territory's method of releasing each piece separately is still a matter of speculation at the moment.

SP&S and the MMU will be facing copyright and performance rights issues more and more, which may lead to the consideration of establishing a contract system whereby each writer gets a percentage (standard 10%, for instance), or at least a manuscript preparation fee. While this seems to go against the spirit of SA tradition, it may be one way of keeping the quality of the content on a high level.

Also working in the MMU, in retirement, is that doyen of SA composers, Ray Steadman-Allen. One time head of the IMED, his skill and expertise (now in his 80s) are highly valuable to the MMU. In recent months Steadman-Allen had been serving not only as an editor - consultant but as a part of the music review panel.

Marketing SA music is a new phenomenon for SP&S. Prior to 1992 they had a closed market, SA bands having to buy what was produced, as they had no other choice. With declining sales in most journals due to the loss of bands within the UK, SP&S thought some of the loss might be taken up through outside sales. Williams has confided that *the only growth area subsequent to the general release of Army band music has been that of supplying photocopied out-of-print music.*[6] With marketing techniques in their infancy, SP&S admits that there are still many avenues to try for an increase in sales. Several obstacles still stand in the way:

> *There are a number of reasons why our normal journal music does not sell well to non-Army bands. One is that they do not like the policy of having to purchase four titles when perhaps they only want one. We would stand a much better chance of selling to a non-Army market if we published as separate titles... My guess is that it would still only be that composers whose names are known by the brass band movement in general whose music would be in demand. Think of the nightmare for the poor publisher in trying to determine print runs!! Another reason is that some of our titles are too 'religious' or 'meaningless' outside of Army circles.*[7]

More recently certain brass band sets and pieces published by SP&S have begun to sell in larger numbers to bands both within and outside the SA. For example, the bounded set *Favourite Marches and Hymn Settings* released in 2003-04, with accompanying CDs, which provide bands and bandmasters a model performance of sorts to follow for all the music, was originally intended to help market the band books in the initial launching of the set. The CDs are now in their third pressing and the booklets have sold very well, approximately 400 sets, sales coming from both within and without the SA.

New projects of similar bent are under development, including a new Christmas set, this time adaptable for from small *Unity Series* size bands [4 or more players] up to full ensemble [2006], something that should prove very useful world-wide.

Sales data for the period 1992–1997 support the picture of some decline in larger bands, but steady, even a slight increase, within smaller bands, especially those that use the *Unity Series*, a fact that supports Cobb's figures shown above. Printing runs for *Unity Series* were actually increased from February 1992 to October 1997, bearing mind that some journals will stay on the shelves for a while. In 1992, 600 sets of the *US* were published, all 600 have been sold; in October 1997, 809 sets of the *US* were published, 710 have already been sold. That trend continued up through 2002, with 655 sets published for October 2002, and 609 already sold as of April 2003.[8]

The picture for the other three series is not as favourable, bearing in mind that these sales also represent world-wide sales via the band subscription system. The number of sets printed is being scaled back in the larger journals as can be seen in this small, representative chart drawn from figures supplied by SP&S in April 2003:[9]

Festival Series

General Series

Triumph Series

Festival Series	Printed	Stock	Sales
March 1992	400	0	400
March 1995	405	55	350
Sept. 1997	410	58	352
Sept. 1999	350	64	286
Sept. 2001	350	65	285
Sept. 2002	319	70	249

General Series	Printed	Stock	Sales
April 1992	675	0	675
April 1995	665	103	562
December 1997	675	152	523
December 1999	562	107	468
December 2001	580	158	422
December 2002	462	139	323

Triumph Series	Printed	Stock	Sales
March 1992	925	84	841
March 1995	925	210	715
November 1997	930	248	682
November 1999	750	117	633

| November 2001 | 750 | 168 | 582 |
| November 2002 | 600 | 161 | 439 |

Even taking further shelf sales into account, this data is another indicator that smaller bands are the more numerous. It must be pointed out that the problem may be even greater, as some bands, who used to be 30+ in size, but now are really *Triumph Series* units, still order the *GS* and/or *FS* on the subscription plan.

The evidence strongly supports a move to release works for larger, more proficient bands, as single releases. When SP&S printed the test piece for the 1996 National Championships, Robert Redhead's *Isaiah 40*, the sales figures gave a more accurate picture of what to expect for the most demanding kind of literature: 38 sets sold for the Nationals, and approximately 600 scores.[10] Large test-pieces, of course, are probably not where the SA should be putting its energy! They have already recognised this by maintaining a list of large works individually available, as in the *Judd Street Collection*, items from which in very recent years have been selling in significant numbers.

SP&S projects a change in the *Festival Series* to single releases, Trevor Caffull explained that change as follows, this from a recent note to the author on June 1, 2005:

> *The switch from* Festival Series *to single set publication is effective from 2006, so we are in fact now in the last year* [2005] *of the* Festival Series. *In truth, this decision is partly practical and partly commercial. In practical terms we are trying to respond to the feedback we get from many SA Bandmasters that they only use 1/2 of the pieces from each* FS *publication, and are having to pay the complete set price meaning that they don't get good value. In commercial terms of course, having titles in single sets makes it easier to sell to non-SA bands. Titles that would have otherwise appeared in the* FS *will now appear in the* Judd Street Collection. *There is no plan to number these. Our intention is still to continue the same number of titles, approximately eight per year.*

As the SA in the UK has relaxed its restrictions on band participation in Sunday morning services [New *O&R* in the

UK, *Guidelines for Musicians*, released during the year 2000], there will be even greater demand for up-to-date music designed for worship and praise. The launching of the *TS*-scored *Scripture-Based Songs Series*, kept separate from the subscription system, and now into its seventh volume, has helped prove this, as has the recent *Magnify* contemporary band tune book. No figures are available concerning how many sets of the Central USA Territory's complementary effort, *Hallelujah Choruses*, have been purchased in the UK.

My personal thoughts favour a call for true international cooperation, rather than a mere broad understanding of each territory's efforts that thinly veils 'competition' in all areas of band publishing within the SA. The world is 'small enough' now to allow for intelligent sharing of the burden. Supply bands with the best music. The International Music Council discussed this matter, though the phrase 'territorial discretion' is not one that engenders full confidence. Recent conversations I have had with Trevor Caffull and several North American TMDs lead me to believe that things are turning in the right direction, with mutual support an underlying principle.

This cooperation is already evident in the most recent, world-wide band music subscription scheme administered by SP&S. Bands in the UK, and across the globe, can now not only subscribe to the UK journals, but they may also on the same form select several of the other consistently produced journals from the United States, including the USA East's *American Band Journal*, and the USA South's *American Instrumental Ensemble Series*. This demonstrates excellent cooperation and constitutes a major step forward in SA music publishing and marketing. I trust this will lead to a world-wide strategy in which all SA publishing firms not only work with one another in this manner, but also thoughtfully come to grips with the focus of their mission - what and for whom they publish and, especially, why they publish a particular piece or type of band music.

New Vistas and Interactions

During the 1990s the brass band movement and SA banding, always close but some times feuding cousins, have come together in a remarkable series of events that may become the means of a healing and long-term mutual support. With both areas still maintaining very high musical standards that are models for amateur music making, both subcultures are fighting losses of significant proportions. Yet it is now possible for a Salvationist to be involved in a contesting band, provided that person can balance their responsibilities, no easy task if he or she is aligned with some of the better, busier corps or contesting bands.

Conventional wisdom within the contesting brass band community always stressed how the Army was merely a source from which great players, writers, or conductors were gotten. No definitive study has been made that links the subtle interaction between these two. The issue is much more complex, however, than 'he was once a Sally, now plays with Black Dyke'.

The evidence confirming the SA origins of a large proportion of leaders in the brass band and professional musical world is overwhelming. Many absorbed the excellent discipline and training of SA bands, only to either face some crisis with SA regulations harshly applied, or simply did not embrace the call to Christian service, their musical careers making that

Bristol Easton Band with Bandmaster Nathan Jenkins.

decision for them. Howard Snell, whose father was a SA officer and talented brass musician, put it this way, emphasising the excellent musical experience and training he received at Paisley Corps (father was CO) under BM Bert McKay but how that was really all he took from the experience:

> *The Salvation Army is a unique institution – obviously a bit militaristic in terms of discipline. If you can work within it, I think it gives you some idea of organisation and discipline. It's a bit scrubbed, clean cut and polished Christianity, but it does actually rub off on people and they do behave in a more purposeful way...* [The period of training at Paisley] *gave me absolutely unrepeatable experience in terms of playing... There's nothing like it anywhere else that I know of. The standards were quite high too – if you didn't play well, you got told. That kind of background you can't find in any other sphere at all... When I went to the Academy in London, I started on the day I was seventeen. Within about six months I'd stopped and had no connection with The Salvation Army at all.*[11]

Yet there have been Maisie Wiggins Ringham (former principal trombone Hallé Orchestra) and Dudley Bright (current principal trombone with the LSO) who represent the other side of the issue, Salvationists who maintained their soldiership in the midst of the most demanding musical schedules and careers. Most churches lose young people when they go off to college or begin their careers. That the Army is as vibrant as it is, and still attracts top-notch people, the issue of losing talented people from the SA might be as much a matter of how they are treated, than one of personal theology or lack of sympathy with the Army's mission. [The usual estimate is that from 2% to 8% of the British public actually attend church on a regular basis.]

What it boils down to is how people have interacted, not whether they are anti-Army, or anti-Christianity. It has been a sociological issue, not a musical one, for the vast majority of former Salvationists have nothing but praise for their *musical* experiences.

Here is a representative short, alphabetical list (which could be duplicated many times over) of some famous brass musicians and conductors currently active within the UK who had initial musical training in the SA. *Brass players:* Dudley Bright, Mark Eager, Alwyn Green, Michael Hext, Nick Hudson, Don Lusher (now deceased), Don Morrison (now deceased), Maurice Murphy, Steven Mead, Harold Nash, Malcolm Smith, Denzil Stephens, Ashley Wall, Dennis Wick; *Composers / Conductors / Editors / Producers:* Geoffrey Brand, Ray Farr, Bram Gay, Peter Graham, Edward Gregson, Paul Hindmarsh, Elgar Howarth, Robert Simpson (now deceased), Howard Snell, Bramwell Tovey, Bram Wiggins.

The two main brass band periodicals in the UK have strong Army connections. *British Bandsman,* now owned by SP&S was previously owned by Trevor Austin, still an active Salvationist (High Wycombe). Until recently it was edited by Peter Wilson, while no longer a Sally (parents and grandparents were soldiers in Scotland), a person in sympathy with the denomination. Their allied music press, Rosehill Music, recently renamed Winwood Music, honoured in its name the old SA Rosehill Band of the SA.

The more recent monthly magazine, *Brass Band World,* has been run by three former members of the Stockport SA Band, or Junior Band, in the 1940s: Robert Mulholland, Junior (recently retired), Vernon Briggs and Alan Jenkins. Former Salvationist, Paul Hindmarsh, has recently been appointed editor. Brass band contests suffer in attendance when they choose a Sunday, because so many supporters come from the 'ranks.' Ray Bowes told me he tried to never miss the Nationals at the Royal Albert Hall, score in hand, when it met on a Saturday.

Harry Mortimer always stressed that *the one audience you can always count on would be the Salvation Army members* [both in the UK and overseas]. No wonder, therefore, there has been in recent years an explosion of cooperation between the SA and the brass band movement. The brass press encourages it. The ISB's role in the National Championships Gala Concerts, as noted above, is very significant.[12]

One of the first new-style cooperative ventures came in October, 1992, when Enfield Citadel (James Williams) and Black Dyke Band (James Watson) gave a joint concert at Regent Hall Corps. Since 1947 Enfield Citadel (then Tottenham) had taken advantage of the crowds of enthusiasts coming in London for the Championships to offer pre-Contest festivals. In 1995 they played one at the Royal College of Music, along with euphonium soloist Stephen Mead and his British Tuba Quartet.

By this time the SA aspect of the weekend was a major component of what has become a feast of brass music. [13] The Gala Concert of the British Open in 1996 brought together the SA-based Egon Virtuosi (James Williams), Black Dyke (James Watson), and guest soloists Philip Smith and Robert Childs. That same season, Robert Redhead, still an active officer, wrote the test piece for the Nationals, *Isaiah 40*. By 1997 the ISB was on the Gala Concert stage of the Nationals in the Royal Albert Hall, and in 1999, James Williams received the top brass band honorary award, the Iles Medal.[14]

The BBC Festival of Brass for 1994 included a programme of SA music by the Enfield Citadel Band. Two years later on the same programme, the Yorkshire Building Society Band (David King), a top-rated contest group, gave a programme of all-SA music: *Call of the Righteous* (Condon), *On Ratcliff Highway* (Steadman-Allen), *Just As I Am* (Heaton), *My Strength My Tower* (Goffin), and *The Kingdom Triumphant* (Ball). The repertoire became the basis of their award-winning *Essays For Brass, Volume One*, CD (Polyphonic, see

Norwich Citadel Band in concert with Trombone Virtuosi Don Lusher.

Discography), followed by *Essays For Brass, Volume Two* and *Volume Three*. King's achievement provided great 'shoptalk' in the SA and brass band community. Can 'outside' bands play such music with true understanding? Undoubtedly, as King's readings were judged to be among some of the most definitive for such classic pieces.[15] It is rarer nowadays to *not* find SA music of some kind recorded by top 'outside' brass bands and soloists.

Essays For Brass, Volume One, featuring Yorkshire Building Society Band (David King) on the Polyphonic label.

In another connected area, brass pedagogy, great SA players/soloists like Derick Kane and David Daws were being spotlighted in brass conferences and conservatory master classes.[16] If one stepped back from the entire scene and took an objective, non-biased look, the impression was that the two cultures were becoming interdependent and, if the new relationship was nurtured, mutually enhanced.

When you look at the back cover a recent issue of *Brass Band World* (see February 2003 for example) magazine you see another innovative effort by SP&S that is bringing the brass band world together: *The World of Brass*. In April 2002 SP&S became the proprietors of the entire Doyen Recordings catalogue, working in close cooperation with Nicholas Childs' corporation for a world wide distribution system. Adding the Egon merger several years prior to this, and *World of Brass* becomes one of, if not *the* most comprehensive sources for brass band recordings.

In the Autumn of 2004 Doyen/SP&S released the second volume in the History of Brass Bands Series, "The Salvation Army Connection," featuring Grimethorpe Band under Elgar Howarth, a program that profiled SA band music from the period 1900–1971. Additionally, in 2004 SP&S took over the management of *British Bandsman*, as well as the brass band catalogue of R. Smith & Co. These acquisitions have not been accepted without criticism from some quarters, as a review of Autumn 2004 issues of *Brass Band World* and *British Bandsman* will reveal.

If the SA music crowd lamented the metamorphosis of the weekly *Musician* (UK) into the *Salvationist* (UK) [March 1986], they could soon see their best and brightest profiled in the outside brass press. At least three UK SA bands have been given the 'centre-fold' treatment and well-written profiles by Alan Jenkins in *BBW*: 1) The ISB, in two issues on the occasion of their 100th anniversary (Nov. 1991, pp10–12; Dec. 1994–Jan. 1995, pp16–19); 2) Enfield Citadel, by Alan Jenkins (Dec 1993–Jan 1994, pp7–8); and 3) Hendon Band (Dec 1994–Jan. 1995, pp16–19); Household Troops Band (May 2002, p17). Interviews and articles on composers like Steadman-Allen (*BBW*, Dec 1993–Jan 1994, pp7–8) or Heaton (*BBW*, Dec 1994–Jan. 1995, pp6–9) addressed various aspects of these gifted men's contribution to brass band literature.[16] Here was writing and analysis not connected to any propaganda or jingoistic fervour, a tendency when the SA wrote about its own in the past.

Being under the glare of a public press only enhanced the prestige of the very best Salvationists and the best SA music. All this attention to things SA would naturally bring about even more interest in the riches of SA music, particularly solo music. Soloists like Steven Mead, Roger Webster, the Childs Brothers, Russell Gray, and Nick Hudson were pleased to include large amounts of SA solo repertoire on their CDs and in their programs, which continue to include appearances with SA bands.[17]

Brass Festivals entrepreneur Philip Biggs has recently launched a new brass quarterly magazine, *The Brass Herald*, which has featured in its first four volumes various personalities and selected bands within the SA tradition.

One other, lesser known development has been the establishment of the British Association of Christian Bands, begun 11 years ago by Trevor Austin and Barbara Butler following interest generated from a report in the *British Bandsman* about a similar group in Norway. While in Norway whole bands join their association, and they form an 'honours' band of the best players, in the UK the emphasis is on individual members. While still in its infancy, in light the availability of SA music to these musicians, it seems a logical place in which the SA could begin a reconnecting with other expressions of Christian banding that have existed in the UK for the past two centuries.

In America, church bands and orchestras are beginning to boom; perhaps that will happen in the UK. Trevor reported that in 2000 there were 5 districts, or chapters: Andover, Hants; Welwyn, Herts (covering Central London area); Faversham, Kent; Newcastle on Tyne; and Nottingham. In

Derby Central Band of The Salvation Army, Bandmaster Alan Losh, 2006.

three of the chapters (Welwyn, Newcastle, and Nottingham) the SA representation is only about 10%, but in the other two (Andover and Faversham) it ranges 30–40%.

My own experience with one chapter came in April, 1995, when Trevor asked me to do some guest conducting with a group of about 30 that had gathered for the Welwyn chapter, a minority of whom were Salvationists. It reminded me of a Divisional Bandsmen's Fellowship back in the States in a division with many small bands, except that these folks were from various denominations that used bands in their worship and evangelism.

Making music was only part of the activities, as other folk presented devotional thoughts or gave witness, and, of course, much talk and sharing of ideas. We found that everyone shared much in common, from practical concerns about music and music literature to issues of faith and commitment. Particularly remarkable is the fact that this British Association of Christian Bands holds a sacred service at Westminster Central Hall in London on the day after the National Brass Band Finals.[18]

Some Personal Experiences

When I toured England in May–June 1981 with the Cambridge (Massachusetts) Citadel Silver Band (Bandmaster

John Appleby), we experienced a wide range of UK corps and corps bands. It was encouraging to note those corps vibrantly alive in their musical ministry, not stuck in the past. It provided this young corps band with a needed lift in its own efforts back in the States.

The tour ended on a high note, with performances at the Songster Leaders' Councils Festival in the Royal Albert Hall, followed by an exhausting day at the Regent Hall Corps, a day that was normal for these stalwart folk. This involved three Open-Airs, two with marching, three indoor services and an afterglow service of praise.

It was at this Oxford Street corps that I was reassured that healthy corps might be more numerous than self-centred, irrelevant ones, though I did not think we could quite copy what this fine old corps kept going week-in and week-out. Bands still had a solid ministry both indoors and outdoors.

Love, caring, and open communication within a body of believers will boost everyone up in the ministry tasks assigned to each soldier. Cambridge returned to the USA not to become a Regent Hall – impossible! We returned to Massachusetts with a greater vision for what we were about, with new ideas about how to do it, with a certain satisfaction of having done well, but with a humble spirit and high admiration for the best of British music making and Salvationism.

In my last five visits to the UK territory (1992, 1995, 1999, 2000, 2003) I visited a range of corps, and their bands. Without engendering any sense that I was investigating them for my book, I frequently was visiting a friend in the area and went to the service or was invited to do a band practice, all very 'low key'. This is probably the best way to see things!

Only one of the corps I will briefly share about was on Stephen Cobb's list seen above, Chelmsford. My sample, therefore, is probably a good one, the bands ranging in size from 12 to 35, the music played ranging from *Festival Series* to the *Unity* and *AIES*. Two were what might be called village corps, three in mid-sized cities.

In May–June, 2000, the Lexington Brass Band, for which I serve as music director, toured England. SA corps bands hosted half our concert sites, several of which are profiled below. That visit was a wonderful confirmation of a new open cooperation between the SA and the outside musical world

[Host corps included Castleford, Chelmsford, Gloucester, and Portsmouth Citadel, plus Cambridge Corps, which lent us their hall for a rehearsal prior to the All England Masters].

In the Spring of 2003 I was only able to conduct Castleford Citadel Band and, a pleasant addition, the vibrant Yorkshire Divisional Youth Band, directed by the amiable BM Jim Wright, (now sadly deceased).

On the 50th anniversary of VE [celebrating World War II Victory in Europe] Day, May, 1995, the 12-strong **Harpenden Corps Band** served as the glue that tied together the community-wide celebration on the village green of this small town north of St. Albans in Hertfordshire.

As in many smaller towns the corps band is asked to play at civic services and united church events, the town considering it 'their band.' Led by ISB cornetist Nigel Hills, the band ranges from junior members just coming into the seniors to three highly skilled professional musicians. They can mostly tackle the SATB, or quartet series, with good success, but occasionally risk the *Triumph Series*.

Probably very typical of a large percentage of bands in the UK in size, skill, and function, they have a cheerful spirit, seem fully integrated into the congregation, and willingly offer up their sacrifice of praise to the best of their ability. I was struck by how the polished musicians blended in with the not so talented. On duty several services a Sunday, plus outreach in the form of an Open-Air or other visitation, the Harpenden Band seemed a happy, faithful, family-like group.

Stotfold Band play in front of the Mansion House, Dublin, prior to a Civic Reception, 1993.

Just to the northeast of Harpenden is **Stotfold**, where John Street, founder of Egon Publishers and a local politician, is the bandmaster. Numbering about 25 musicians, this band is likely to tackle some of the *General Series*, whether from the latest issues for a Sunday afternoon offertory, or a rousing march from one of old GS *Favourites* books on a Sunday night. 'Spirited' is how I would describe their playing, not unlike the personality of their director, who even encouraged his group to produce their first compact disc a few years back, though they would be the first to admit it wasn't one of the top sellers in John's catalogue.

Until recently this corps maintained three services on Sunday, but now the afternoon 'praise' meeting has been dropped in line with current practice. Here was another friendly band, people that seemed at ease with each other, the whole scene having a very traditional feel to it, but not in a stuffy, stodgy, or rigid way. The congregation was fair sized and a seemingly good mix of people in and out of uniform.

Gloucester Corps Band, where my friend and former CCSB cornetist John Stubbings is a band member, is directed by Bandmaster Cliff Matthews, who in 'real life' is Head of Music at a large high school in the area. When everyone is present there are 33 in the band, 15 of whom came into the band through the junior band, an impressive percentage in the early 21st century. The band can tackle *Festival Series* music with good effect and are keen to do so.

Gloucester Corps Band with Bandmaster Clifford Matthews.

Their Sunday service usually consisted of a prelude item, and the first hymn tune in the Sunday AM service. Then followed a 12-noon outreach activity (which could be a street

service, or nursing home/hospital visitation), and the 5:30 All Age Worship programme, during which they usually play a selection, accompany the singing, and offer a postlude. They give around eight festivals a year in local churches in order to foster inter-denominational relations, and take one weekend away from the corps, campaigning at another corps, per year.

The band is particularly active in offering charity concerts, organising approximately three a year on Sunday evenings after the worship service, for such groups as the Red Cross and Cancer Research, with many non-Army people attending. The band is also very active in civic and ecumenical events in the city including Palm Sunday processions, the annual Good Friday procession to Gloucester Cathedral, the St. George's Day parade and the Remembrance Sunday service at the War Memorial. A highlight of the band's season comes at Christmas, in the form of a high profile Christmas Concert in Gloucester Cathedral in aid of the Meningitis Trust, a major national charity. A media celebrity usually chairs the festival and the concert also features well-known instrumental and vocal soloists.

In the industrial north unemployment is extremely high, as much as 45% at times in the city of **Castleford**, where a SA band first formed in 1882. A corps as well known for its excellent songsters, as well as a famous junior band programme (Castleford is the home corps of former Staff Bandmaster and IMED Editor-in-Chief, Ray Bowes), Castleford was in transition between buildings. They were holding services and rehearsals at a variety of local churches supportive of the Army.

One night in May, 1999, I led their band practice. Sixteen members were present, some key players absent, but several other friends from nearby bands were helping them; when a full complement, they numbered 20 at that time, 14 of whom in whole or in part were trained in the corps YP Band. It is a small band for the music they tackle, but they host some excellent players. Among them were two young men I had known in the States, Anthony Thompson, a free lance professional trumpet player who had spent a short time in the States as an assistant DMD in Texas, and his brother Richard, who is now a Salvation Army officer.

The bandmaster at that time, Graham Woodhead had

chosen several festival-type pieces for me to conduct, as the band was not on duty that following Sunday and they were anxious to begin polishing some music for their upcoming weekend away down on the South West coast of England, at Paignton: *Pastoral Symphony* (Redhead) Mvts 1,2, and 4; the meditation *To Know Thee* (Himes), and Curnow's transcription of *Procession of the Nobles*.

After getting used to me, they settled into a solid, but congenial two-hour workout, the two 'rests' coming during a thoughtful devotional by the band sergeant and during the announcements towards the close of the rehearsal. (I was pleasantly surprised to see the corps officer present during much of the rehearsal.) After the rehearsal we drove by the site of the old hall, where the new one would soon rise. My friends indicated that the piles of the rubble at the edge of the property were to keep the gypsies out so they could not squat on the land before the building began!

In the spring of 2000 Castleford Band hosted Lexington Brass Band in a joint Festival of Music at the local civic centre, the new corps not quite completed. The grand evening ended with several excellent massed band items, including BM Woodhead directing *Procession of the Nobles*. It was an evening of triumph for both groups, and a credit to the work Graham had achieved with that corps band. BM Woodhead died suddenly in 2000 and is greatly missed.

The new corps building is now complete and the band continues to grow in size and have success in its local ministry. Brian Thompson succeeded Graham Woodhead for a while until his work took him elsewhere. Anthony Thompson, deputy bandmaster, took the band in the interim. When I visited the corps in March, 2003, Steve Roebuck, an area manager for a national Health Pharmacy, had become the commissioned bandmaster. Steve seeks to maintain a vital musical ministry with his very responsive band, moving forward in mission, while maintaining respect for the band's great tradition.

The night I arrived at **Chelmsford** in the spring of 1995 the band had just returned from a trip to the Continent where they had participated in VE Day activities. Everyone was buzzing about what had transpired, sharing photos, and especially looking forward to watching the 'highlights' video

Chelmsford Citadel Band marching through the local shopping centre, Easter 1999.

that someone had just finished editing, no doubt a video more for the band room than the sanctuary!

Here was a spirited group of about 35 members, ably led by Simon Schulz, a medical doctor by profession. The membership ranged through all age groups, another good sign. My visit was a last-minute affair but the bandmaster was very gracious in inviting me to take the band through some new music I had with me, as well as a particular request, Leidzén's *The Call*. Again, here was a hard-working band, a band that was quick to learn and work on getting things 'sorted out' quickly. They, too, were a pleasant, assured group, but not cocky or boastful, rightfully proud of their achievements, but able to place them in perspective. Here was another centre of Army banding that gave me cause for hope.

I returned to Chelmsford in May 2000, my Lexington Brass Band giving their premiere concert there, joined by Festival Brass, which shared the programme with us. Members of the band and the corps received us warmly, making the start of our tour, jet-lagged and all, a happy occasion.

There is excellent talent at this corps. One example is Nick Simmons-Smith, who had moved from Chelmsford to the USA for a number of years where he served as an assistant DMD in the Texas Division. Nick moved back home for a few years and has recently returned to Texas to work in various ministry opportunities in the Greater Dallas Command.

Top: Croydon Citadel Band, Bandmaster Paul Graham.

Centre: Hadleigh Temple Band on the march 1998.

Bottom: Sunderland Millfield Band play at 'Celebration' in York, 2003.

Closing Thoughts

Bands in the UK face the same challenges faced by SA bands around the world. Maintaining relevance in an increasingly affluent, 'pagan' society, where people merely yawn or vaguely tolerate a brass band as a Victorian anachronism, might be most difficult in the UK. My British friends tell me that SA brass bands in their street ministry are, at worst, regarded apathetically but at best, accepted with a great deal of warmth. Its rich heritage and traditions can tie up both SA administration and its laity just when flexibility within (even a multiplicity of) ministries, especially musical, are needed most.

SA bands will survive in the UK to the degree that new musical leaders are trained in a balanced way and to the degree that officers are similarly trained in leading worship and evangelism, so as to both preach the word effectively and use their troops wisely and compassionately.

Will the UK continue to produce lay leaders like a Herbert Twitchin, an Alexander Thain, a James Williams, a Michael Clack or officer musicians like Steadman-Allen, Condon, or Bearcroft?[19] I think they are there already, working in the trenches, so to speak.

A whole new group of talented composer, arrangers, and conductors are on the rise in the UK. Excellent programmes and support mechanisms are in place to nurture and develop leaders, develop fine players. Recent efforts of the MMU as profiled earlier give solid reasons for hope. (See Chapter 10 for further reflections on future projections.)

SA bands of the UK may be fewer in number, smaller in average size, but taken all together, it is a powerful force for the Gospel and for good. 510 senior bands are no small representative group of ambassadors for the Kingdom. The musical standard that these bands maintain is, in the majority of cases, high.

The finest UK SA bands are models of their kind. These bands and their members maintain an effective witness and strive for the highest musical standards sometimes in the face of indifference. I believe a vision for the future of SA bands is beginning to be articulated and shared amongst the general membership under the guidance of a dynamic music department, if not upper administration. This unique, dynamic chapter in the history of the Church and its music will not come to a close in the near future. I am optimistic that the SA bands of the UK Territory can be at the heart of a true revival within the SA. Brass bands, *per se*, are not the problem. They can and should be part of the solution.

Notes

1. I was not able to secure a British writer for this chapter, but not from a lack of trying! I am very grateful for the cooperation and direct input in the form of data and personal interviews of all members of the Territorial Music Department/Musical Ministries Unit. The successive leaders have been Robert Redhead, Trevor Davis, Peter Ayling and Stephen Cobb as well as Michael Williams, then managing director of SP&S, all of whom cooperated in specific aspects of this chapter. I have also had the opportunity to interview other leading musicians, both Salvationists and non-Salvationists, not all of whom could be fully represented in these few short pages. My own experiences within the territory began back in 1978, when I was a delegate to the International Congress. In addition to the 1981 tour of England with the SA Cambridge Citadel (Massachusetts) Band. My visits have included extended stays in 1992, 1995, 1999, 2000, and 2003 during which, in addition to research and teaching, I had the opportunity to visit a number of representative corps, both just as a visiting member of the congregation, a player, and as a guest conductor.

2. Commissioner John Larsson, 'The Territorial Commander's Column: Introducing the New Territorial Music Department', *The Musician* (UK) (April 14, 1992), p2. Way back in July, 1940, IHQ wrote to Bramwell Coles about the growing number of Salvationists that were becoming professional musicians, or who desired to be a part of other musical organisations. *We are inclined to the view that a distinction should be made between a Salvationist who earns his living as a professional musician, and a Bandsman who wishes to become a member of another Band or Orchestra in the town and who wishes to divide his time and loyalty between the two musical combinations...I shall be glad to hear from you at your earliest.* (Letter July, 31, 1940, signed Chief of the Staff for General Evangeline Booth) Coles' reply is not extant. The manner in which such restrictions were enforced caused untold bitterness and a loss of fine personnel.

3. Statistics shared by Trevor Davis, April 1995, and Stephen Cobb, May, 1999; reconfirmed by Stephen Cobb, January 2005.

4. The current staff in Texas has two Americans, Ben Howard and Jesse Fry, 2001 and 2002 graduates of Asbury College; the other two members came from the UK.

5. Keith Wilkinson's interesting story was profiled in the *Brass*

Band World shortly after his move to the US in 1996. A leading contest conductor, though his doctorate is in mathematics, he stuck it out as a soldier for years even though he was denied involvement or a leadership position until the change in *O&R*.

6. Letter from Michael Williams to the author, March 30, 1998, with confirmation on May 21, 1999, that this still holds true. However, income from mechanical licenses has been better. Williams shared that since 1992 the increase has been on average 3.5%

7. *Ibid.* Under Trevor Caffull's skillful leadership SP&S has very recently made great strides in its marketing strategies, which should have a significant impact on future efforts in music publishing.

8. Williams points out that there has been some marketing of this series to schools and churches, with some success, thus maybe influencing these figures.

9. In 1999 SP&S shared complete data for all issues of their four band series, 1992–1997. These figures would indicate, at least within the time frame 1992–1997, that total band numbers world wide had indeed dipped rather severely. More recent figures were not available at the time this book went to press.

10. Plus a few more sets when the piece was used in other contests, as at NABBA 1999.

11. *Labour and Love*, pp141–142. Colin Aspinall's experience is also told in this book. While he too tells of excellent musical training, he shares how he was barred from playing in the corps band one Sunday morning because he had played as a soloist with an 'outside' band at a garden party the night before at the request of his teacher. He felt some of the SA folk 'quite blinkered', and thus left. *Ibid*, pp142–144.

12. Harry Mortimer, *On Brass*, p98. Trevor Austin played in Rosehill Band, 1947–1951, and received then Bandmaster Albert Jakeway's 'blessing' for the use of 'Rosehill' for his companies, keeping alive the name of a great band. Robert Mulholland, Senior, was the bandmaster at Stockport in the 1930s and 1940s, one of the SA's finest bands at the time. He worked at Fairey Aviation during World War II. Along with thousands of others, he was made redundant at the end of war, but offered a chance at administration in the firm if he would play cornet in the famed championship band, Fairey Band, under Harry Mortimer. After accepting this offer of survival he was asked to leave the SA and for a while served as resident conductor of Fairey, 1951–1954, before emigrating to New Zealand. Robert Mulholland, Jr, shared a quote about the Fairey Band made by Harry Mortimer: *I'm thinking of issuing this band red jerseys, there are so many Army lads and so few who'll come for a drink with me after a concert!* Both Briggs and Jenkins have had very successful

careers as low brass performers and as music educators, with Briggs teaching at the Birmingham Conservatory and Jenkins serving as principal tuba of the London Symphony Orchestra. Letters to the author from Robert Mulholland, Jr. and Peter Wilson, July, 1999.

13. Review in *Brass Band World* (November, 1992), p23. Hints of what was coming might have been read from Ray Steadman-Allen's test piece, *Seascapes*, commissioned for the 1988 Nationals, though he was retired at the time. Steadman-Allen had been asked as early as 1974 to write a test piece but then Chief of the Staff Arnold Brown vetoed it with the comment: *It will happen one day, but not in my time*. Steadman-Allen has always regarded this SA contractual embargo on active SA officers publishing creative work as infringement of personal liberty, particularly as it was so severely applied to musicians, but not as harshly, if at all, to writers of books or poetry. He told me for some reason music was treated 'as a sacred cow'.

14. *Brass Band World* (November 1995).

15. *Essays For Brass, Volume 1* declared CD of the Year in 1995; *Essays For Brass, 3* was released in 2000.

16. Others written about in some detail in the pages of *BBW* in this same time frame have been composers Robert Redhead, Peter Graham, Kenneth Downie and performers like bandmasters James Williams and Stephen Cobb, and cornetist David Daws

17. See Discography; Philip Smith may have led the way with his *Escapade* CD recorded with the Rigid Containers Band back in 1991; His duo album with Dudley Bright, *Principals* (New York Staff Band), was another pace-setter in this regard.

18. Facts confirmed in a letter from Trevor Austin, July 2, 1999; A 'United Norwegian Christian Band' led by Roland Cobb produced a fine compact disc of mostly SA music a few years back.

19. Bandmaster Herbert Twitchin led Regent Hall Corps Band for 55 years. Alexander Thain, MBE, OF, a friend and correspondent of mine for a number of years, was a kind encourager. He received the Order of the Founder in March 1968, having led Edinburgh Gorgie corps band for 40 years. In his professional life he was the Entertainment Officer for the Edinburgh Corporation, including the famous International Festival of Music and Drama; in retirement he still served as assistant manager of the Edinburgh Military Tattoo (See Albert Kenyon, *In High Esteem*, p92–97). Michael Clack, MBE, has been, I believe, an unsung hero in SA music via his superb organ playing at great national events, but also until very recently as a faithful bandmaster at Chalk Farm, a modern day Punchard. In his professional life he served as a principal lecturer at the School of Music, Colchester Institute, a scholar and editor of early music.

Chapter 5

THE CANADA AND BERMUDA TERRITORY

W. L. (Wally) Court

Our music is an expression of service and commitment to God... If we ever lose the philosophy of the band we will lose something very fundamental to the Army... [I wish] there were more downtown street-corner bands reaching out to the unchurched... Robert Redhead, Territorial Music Secretary, *The Holy War of Sally Ann,* Robert Collins, Western Producer Prairie Books, Saskatoon, 1984, pp.179-181.

To fully appreciate the 125-year history of SA banding in Canada, the vast geographic stage on which the story has unfolded must be presented. Stretching 4,800 miles from the Atlantic Ocean to the Pacific Ocean, Canada has shared a 4,000-mile undefended border with the United States for almost 200 years. Since Canada achieved nation status in 1867, most of its population has lived in a 4,000-mile-long, 200-mile-wide, east-west corridor. Seven of Canada's 10 provinces border on the northern US. Its 20 major cities, including 9 provincial capitals, are located in this corridor.

Since 1896, except for five years in the late 1920s, Bermuda has been part of the Army's Canada and Bermuda Territory. And between 1898 and 1944, Army operations in several north-western US states and Alaska were also part of the territory. Further, while Newfoundland has been part of the Canadian Territory since 1886, it didn't join the Dominion of Canada until 1949. At 3.9 million square miles, the Canada and Bermuda Territory is the Army's largest administrative area. Today there are 366 corps and outposts in 13 divisions over half in Ontario and Newfoundland with about 25 in the country's larger cities served by full-complement brass bands. In a population of 31.6 million, there are 21,632 senior soldiers of whom 2,245 - one in ten - hold band commissions.[1]

Each of the present corps, as well as scores swallowed during a century of immigration, industry, residential expansion and changing demographics, has its own unique history of SA music-making. All the material presented here is worthy of amplification. It is hoped that space constraints limiting this account to an admittedly superficial overview will encourage others to explore their corps' evangelical and musical roots.

The first Salvationist to set foot on Canadian soil was British Commissioner George Scott Railton. His unplanned arrival occurred when the steamer returning him to England stopped in Halifax following his 1880 visit to New York to establish a beachhead in North America.[2] However, the Movement's evangelical zeal and spirited music arrived in Canada in the minds and baggage of immigrants from England, Ireland, Scotland and Wales. In fact, SA banding was not only introduced into Canada by British immigrants, but has been sustained throughout the century by successive waves of UK Salvationists.

As in England, banding in Canada was born in the streets where musicians—the appellation applied in its loosest form —improvised secular tunes on whatever instruments were available to attract outdoor crowds, produce recognisable melodies for singers to follow and provide cadence for marches to and from outdoor meetings.

One of the earliest references to a Canadian SA brass band came on October 26, 1882. A lady presented eight brass instruments to the fledgling Toronto corps with the expressed hope that the Army would *be able shortly to assume a more military appearance and parade the streets with greater prestige and prospects of success in recruiting than heretofore.*[3]

By January 1883, a band of three fifes, a snare drum, bass drum and concertina, had been formed in Hamilton; and a Kingston Band was reported as having played a concert to an audience of 800.[4] *But musical evenings notwithstanding, the most popular image of a Salvation Army Band...which came to symbolise the Army's special kind of evangelical outreach...was that of the Army band at the street corner with its familiar hymn-music reaching into the corners where no singing voice could.*[5]

In May 1884, two years after the first impromptu street meeting was held in London, Ontario, a city 1,600 miles inland, International Headquarters bestowed territorial status on Canada. Canadian Salvationists responded with the territory's first congress. This historic event included *the largest street parade to date*, as the 'Hamilton Band' and 'Toronto Band' led 2,000 Salvationists and their supporters to the corner of James and Albert streets in Toronto for the site dedication of their 'Great Central Temple' and headquarters building.[6]

The SA spread throughout Ontario like wildfire, with 62 corps operating by 1884, each with a loosely defined 'band'. A woodcut on the front page of the initial Canadian *War Cry* (November 1, 1884) depicted the St. Catharines, Ontario, band with four drums and a cornet. Brass and other bands were not the exclusive purview of the SA. Brass banding was a very popular and inexpensive pastime. As the *1934 SA Year Book* noted in the article *International Aspects of SA Music*, by Colonel Fred Hawkes: *Bands have done a great deal to make Army music popular, particularly with the working classes for to many, the brass band is the most popular of all musical organisations.*

Most towns had bands and a free concert was a sure-fire way of drawing a crowd, something Salvationist strategists were quick to embrace. No instrument was excluded, none discouraged. Various reports list fifes, drums, fiddles, concertinas, cornucopias, triangles, cymbals, ocarinas, autoharps, tin whistles, mouth organs, kazoos, even paper-covered combs – categorized by *The Toronto Globe* as *instruments of musical delight, or torture (according to taste).*[7] In 1889, Windsor, Ontario, citizens greeted 15-year-old Robert Keeler's newly-formed band with a fusillade of dead cats, rotten eggs, cayenne pepper, the appellation 'starvation army' – and jail.[8]

Saving souls was the Salvationists' prime objective, but if that soul was also a musician it was a bonus. Many of the Army's convert/musicians came from the ranks of town bands. In Moncton, New Brunswick, *to improve the drumming the SA converted one of the drummers of the Moncton Cornet Band and appointed him to preside over that department of their services.*[9] The drummer, W. G. Cook, subsequently *lost his grip on God* but while in Ontario *haunting the corners where the Hamilton Citadel Band held open-air meetings, he was encouraged to return to Moncton and was 'restored'.*[10]

If the convert wasn't musical he, or she, could be taught. Usually the person with the most music experience automatically became the bandmaster and it was his job to teach recruits on the instruments being acquired by enterprising officers. At Palmerston, Ontario, Ensign Dowell purchased 11 instruments and two drums for $65, though no one could play them. Two weeks later the band made its debut.[11] In nearby Chatham, Salvationists purchased an E Flat bass, baritone, tenor horn, E Flat cornet, two B Flat cornets and two drums from the Moraviantown Indian Band for $10.[12]

In Toronto, Professor George Wiggins, a Bachelor of Music, converted alcoholic and erstwhile accompanist for the Swedish Nightingale, Jenny Lind, became an Army officer. In 1884, he was appointed musical director for the SA in Canada.[13]

Canada-wide Expansion

From its explosive Ontario beginnings the Army and bands expanded eastward to Quebec in 1884, New Brunswick and Nova Scotia in 1885, and Prince Edward Island and Newfoundland in 1886. Moving westward with the flood of immigrants taking advantage of government offers of free, fertile land – 160 acres per homesteader – the Army arrived in Manitoba in 1886. Then it skipped 1,600 miles over the sparsely-populated Prairies and Rocky Mountains to open in British Columbia, then doubled back to invade Alberta in 1887, and Saskatchewan in 1892.

In 1886, an 18-member Headquarters Brass Ensemble was formed to accompany the Army's Founder, General William

Booth, on a tour of Ontario. Travelling with the General, the band formed up when the train stopped, played while he met local dignitaries, then led a procession to an auditorium for a public address.

The London Citadel Band, arguably Canada's most consistent and progressive Salvation Army corps band over 125 years, traces its roots to the Army's arrival in that city in 1882. Little more than a group of enthusiastic fifers and drummers, these pioneers soon found themselves under arrest. However, Booth's 1886 visit to the city provided the impetus to form an 18-piece band complete with drum major.[14]

Newfoundland didn't become Canada's 10th province until 1949, but the SA opened fire there in February 1886. A shipment of brass and reed instruments and a bass drum arrived in St. John's, the capital, the following month.[15]

On Canada's western shores, after Vancouver's original 1888 band *went to pieces largely because of laxity in the matter of regulations*, the band was reorganized by Samuel Redburn (Camberwell).[16] Across the Strait of Georgia on Vancouver Island, the Victoria Corps was benefiting from visits by British naval vessels and Salvationist servicemen to the Esquimalt Naval Base, and a brass band was formed there in 1890. Back on the mainland, a band was commenced in New Westminster in 1897.

Gaining a foothold in the predominantly French-speaking, Roman Catholic province of Quebec proved more difficult. Resistance peaked in Quebec City in 1887, when a parade of Salvationists, led by William Smith's 12-member 'Montreal Marvels' band, was attacked by a mob. When the dust had settled, 21 marchers had been seriously injured. Subsequent legal victories permitted Army street meetings and parades *as long as traffic was not compromised.*[17]

By 1890, 432 officers were holding outdoor and indoor meetings at 264 corps throughout the country and instrumental groups of one sort or another were operating in most.[18] In 1892, Fred Fry, who with his father, Charles William Fry, and two brothers, had pioneered Army banding in Salisbury, England, in 1878, was appointed to Canada as private secretary to the territorial commander, Commandant Herbert Booth.[19] Here, he met Canada's own pioneering family of Salvationist musicians—Major Richard Morris and sons

Harry, Frank and Arthur. Each night, father and sons participated in meetings at one of the 30 corps within travelling distance of downtown Toronto.[20] In 1885, *Satisfied that The Salvation Army could produce its own music, William Booth legislated that only music issued by headquarters was to be used by Army bands.*[21]

The British Invasion

The defining event that brought traditional SA brass banding to Canada was the 1888-89 visit of the 39-member Household Troops Band from London, England, led by Staff-Captain Harry Appleby. Full-time volunteers with only food and clothing guaranteed, they travelled steerage across the Atlantic and campaigned through the winter. The visit came at the invitation of Commissioner Thomas Coombs, head of the Army in Canada, who wanted to give his fledgling Army an effective evangelistic thrust and, coincidentally, raise needed operating funds.

The successful five-month tour through Quebec, Ontario and the eastern US, was all the more remarkable since William Booth had only commissioned the all-brass band the previous year. During the intervening months, the men had *learned to play, pray, and respond to discipline.*[22] They also embodied General Booth's *Regulations for Bandsmen*, issued in 1881, and only played music approved by the International Music Editorial Department.

These standards of excellence and effectiveness were not lost on their Canadian hosts. The uniformed, musically competent and evangelically motivated band so impressed Commissioner Coombs that after the band left Canada *The War Cry* announced the formation of a similar unit:

> *WANTED*
>
> *Salvationists who are good instrumentalists, to volunteer for service in a permanent brass band for the Household Troops. We are anxious to raise a good permanent brass band [similar to that led by Staff-Captain Appleby], to travel through the towns and villages of the Dominion, and for duty in special demonstrations. Also to conduct under an experienced staff-officer, weekly and fortnightly special campaigns, for the salvation of souls. No pay will*

be given. Any thoroughly converted bandsman who would like to devote himself altogether for the salvation of souls, should apply at once to the Commissioner. Let every applicant say what instrument he can play, and if he can provide a uniform or $12 to get one.[23]

A band was quickly assembled. Staff-Captain Robert McHardy was appointed its leader and Captain Christopher Leonard its bandmaster.[24] Three months later, the 20-member Canadian Household Troops Band sailed 23 miles across Lake Ontario to the town of Niagara-on-the-Lake and its first campaign.[25]

In 1889, *The War Cry* introduced a column devoted solely to the interests of bandsmen. With no false notions about the chief business of Salvationist musicians, the writer thanked God *for Bandsmen who are ready at any moment to put down*

Territorial Ensemble, Toronto (c.1895), including Robert Griffith, seated far-right, later bandmaster of New York Staff Band (1907 - 1912).

their instruments and pitch in at the Devil.[26] Immigration from the British Isles continued unabated through the 1890s. Corps and corps bands sprang up in many cities and towns across Canada. Toronto, with its size, predominantly British population and territorial significance, was especially favoured.

Photos of pioneering bands, member profiles and testimonies soon became regular *War Cry* fare. Among the more interesting examples: Winnipeg's Scandinavian Band, the white-uniformed Port Simpson, BC, Native Band[27] the New Glasgow, Nova Scotia, Band with *a black American on E Flat bass;*[28] and the St. John's, Newfoundland, Band with a dead seal recumbent in the foreground.[29]

In addition to corps bands, descriptively named divisional campaign bands were recruited from male and female officer and soldier ranks. The Maritime Musical Troupe and King's Own Band toured in Eastern Canada. The Red Knights of the Cross operated in Western Canada. Central Ontario District formed its Provincial Staff Band; Western Ontario, the Seraphatic Band and Marine Band. The Hallelujah Kooteney Brigade campaigned in British Columbia, and the Blizzard Band and The Harmonic Hurricanes, featuring two original marches, *Harmonic Hurricanes* and *Peck's Bad Boys*, conducted meetings in the north-west province.

British servicemen, members of the Army's Naval and Military League arriving at Bermuda's dockyards brought the Army and Army band music to that island in 1896.[30] In 1900, a United Bands Congress attracted 44 instrumentalists, and in 1903, a Bermuda band made a three-month tour of eastern Canada.[31] A third Canadian Staff Band led by Ensign Kenning was formed to accompany William Booth during his 1898 visit to Canada. By 1900, with 940 officers and cadets, 2,700 local officers and 436 corps and outposts, *The War Cry* reported an Army corps in every city and town with a population of 2,000, and weekly attendance in excess of 450,000.[32,33]

The late 19th-century flood of British immigrants became a 20th-century tidal wave, much of it the result of William Booth's Colonization Scheme. This massive social enterprise simultaneously dealt with the problem of poverty and unemployment in England and settling the vast tracts of uninhabited, arable land in Canada.[34] Between 1901 and

1914, over a million men, women and children emigrated from Europe, most from the British Isles, to work the land or find employment in Canada's expanding manufacturing base. Over 250,000, many Salvationists, were ferried to Canada on a fleet of 10 Army-chartered ships.[35]

During the century's first two decades, the country's population exploded from 5.4 million to 10.4 million.[36] This influx of instrumentalists and leaders was such that *hardly any large band in the Old Country can be found that has not one or more former members in the land of the Maple Leaf*, setting the stage for an even more rapid expansion of SA banding.[37] The Trans-Atlantic voyages were memorable. Daily open-deck meetings were held with scratch bands of Salvationist passengers playing brass instruments from the Army's manufacturing plant, established in 1889, being delivered to the Army bands springing up across Canada.[38]

With the new century came standardized uniforms with larger bands adopting military-style caps, high-collar and elaborately braided tunics, shoulder flashes and white-strap music pouches. In 1903, a Canadian ensemble attended the funeral of Consul Booth-Tucker in New York City.[39] In 1904, this group was expanded to form a 30-member Territorial Staff Band. Resplendent in distinctive scarlet tunics with white trim, maple leaf insignia and 'Mountie' hats, they represented Canada at the International Congress in London, England. A band from Bermuda also attended that Congress.[40]

One typical SA immigrant family, yet one to prove most untypical, was a 46-year-old shepherd, his wife and nine children. Originally Methodists, James and Annie Merritt joined the Army in 1881. James played cornet in the Petersfield, England, band for 26 years before bringing his family to Winnipeg in 1907.[41] James, and his five sons, James Jr., Ben, Henry, William and Percy, all bandmasters, made outstanding contributions to SA banding as instrumentalists and composers. James and Ben also became Salvation Army officers. James and Annie Merritt's legacy is now in its 13th decade and fifth generation of Salvationist musicians.

Flowing back to the 'Old Country' were glowing reports of the progress of these expatriates, reports that ran in the Army's international *Bandsman and Songster* publication. Its weekly *Across the Seas* column contains a wealth of

The talented Merritt brothers of Winnipeg; Left to right: James, William, Percy, Benjamin, Henry.

information on the progress of Salvation Army banding throughout the world in the early years of the 20th century. *Owing to the tide of emigration, a good many Corps in this country have had to part with valued Bandsmen, but, as we have already often had occasion to point out, what has been Britain's loss has proved to be Canada's gain*, wrote the editor in the October 31, 1908 issue.

Canadian bands from coast to coast received regular mention, among them Glace Bay, New Aberdeen, Montreal, Kingston, Belleville, Cobourg, Peterborough, Toronto, Hamilton, Brantford, Stratford, Wingham, Essex, Huntsville, Winnipeg, Brandon, Saskatoon, Calgary and Lethbridge. However, the literary output and zeal of the Vancouver correspondent was unmatched. *Our Band is in fine trim, and under the leadership of Bandmaster [Samuel] Redburn is making progress in every direction... Twenty-six Bandsmen from various parts of the world [Great Britain, Ireland, Australia, South Africa, United States and France] have arrived within the last few months, and the brotherly feeling that exists among us is good. The strength of the Band at the present is thirty-seven, so we can afford sometimes to split the Band in two.*[42] Bands throughout the territory were experiencing similar growth. *At the present time* [the territory] *has 60 bands some of which are very fine organizations containing 30-40 skilled musicians. During the past year numbers have increased by 160.*[43]

Bands large and small were also undertaking weekend campaigns in neighbouring cities and towns. In Peterborough, Ontario, where the band completed a 16-day tour of nearby centres, the bandmaster sought to upgrade his members' music skills by introducing a six-week study course and exam on music theory, with members expected to achieve a 60 per cent level. Less than a month later, the Peterborough correspondent wrote: *We are sorry to have to report that our Bandswomen have handed in their Commissions after years of faithful service, having taken up duty in other branches of Corps work.*[44]

One of the most enterprising and accomplished bands of the period was located in the country's geographical centre, the gateway to Canada's prairie 'bread-basket'. Begun in 1887 by W. Vinall (Bristol), the Winnipeg Citadel Band led by Bandmaster Charles Newman, completed a three-day campaign to Kenora, Ontario, in 1910, travelling the 450 miles by train.

Corps and bands proliferated in Canada's major cities, seven in Montreal, eight in Winnipeg, three in Hamilton and Edmonton, and two in several others. In Toronto, eight 35-member bands and several smaller units were functioning. A Territorial Young People's Brass Band of 27, led by Ensign Stitt, a Territorial Young People's Orchestra, directed by Captain Ernest Pugmire, and a Little Soldiers Fife and Drum Band were also operating.[45] Orchestras, with typical instrumentation, were also operating in many centres. With an eye to the future, larger bands began training young people's bands. Other junior bands operated in Corps Cadet Brigades and Scouting units. Indicative of growing administration, performer and public interest in banding, the October 29, 1910 *War Cry* carried a comprehensive, two-page explicit critique of a four-band Toronto festival.

Tragedy Strikes

In 1914, when Commissioner David Rees included a prayer *for the bereaved relatives of the* Titanic *sinking* during

SALVATION ARMY STAFF BAND WITH COMM. REES AND COL. MAIDMENT AS EMBARKED ON THE ILL-FATED S.S. EMPRESS OF IRELAND THOSE MARKED X WERE RESCUED

The 1914 Territorial (Canadian) Staff Band most of whom were drowned in the sinking of the Empress of Ireland.

Bandsmen's Councils, the future for banding appeared promising. However, the same ocean that had claimed the *Titanic* was not satisfied. The Territorial Band that represented Canada at the 1904 International Congress had proven so successful that plans were initiated to form a similar band for the 1914 World Congress in London, England:

> *BANDSMEN ATTENTION!*
> *Wanted! Bandsmen for the Territorial Staff Band. Must be first-class musicians and thoroughly recommended by Commanding Officer and Bandmaster. Those accepted must be in a position to accompany the Band when taking engagements outside the city. Applications stating instrument played, how long a Bandsmen, etc., to be sent to Colonel Kyle, Chief Secretary, James and Albert Sts., Toronto, marked 'Staff Band.'* [46]

These seemingly innocuous lines held dire consequences for the SA and SA banding in Canada. Subsequent issues of *The War Cry* listed the names of the band's 34 officers and lay musicians, and three last-minute substitute appointments.

The Staff Band's first contact with *The Empress of Ireland* was at Quebec City in 1906, when it played, *God Be With You*

Funeral cortege to Toronto's Mount Pleasant Cemetery.

Till We Meet Again as the Founder sailed from Canada concluding his final visit to the country. Its second contact had fatal consequences. The Territorial Staff Band and Peterborough Temple Band, a premier corps band, were chosen to represent Canada at the 1914 International Congress. The Staff Band, with a post-congress tour of

Memorial service for victims of the Empress of Ireland disaster.

Scotland planned, was scheduled to leave on May 28; the Peterborough Band on May 30. At the Staff Band's farewell in Toronto, Commissioner David Rees said he had already made three May crossings and had yet to have a decent voyage. Then, almost prophetically, he added *I learn that you love to be called 'the Commissioner's Band'. Why not come back to Canada branded 'God's Band?'* [47]

One of six ships carrying North American Salvationists to the congress, *The Empress of Ireland* left Quebec City shortly after 4:00 pm on May 28, with the Staff Band, 130 officer and lay Salvationists and 1,308 other passengers and crew on board. Ten hours later the outbound liner, having been rammed by a collier, was at the bottom of the ice-cold St. Lawrence River with the loss of 1,078 souls. Among the 145 Salvationists drowned were Commissioner and Mrs. Rees, Bandmaster and Mrs. Hanagan and 27 bandsmen. [48] Returning from the congress, the Peterborough Band saluted their departed comrades playing *Nearer My God to Thee* as their ship passed the disaster site. Later, 7,500 mourners

Servicemen's 'Khaki Band' that participated in the 1915 Congress.

Eastern Territorial Staff Band, 1915.

gathered in a Toronto arena where an assembly of comrade bandsmen from Toronto, Guelph, Oshawa, Hamilton and Chatham provided music for a massed funeral service.[49]

The Staff Band's untimely end and outbreak of World War I that same year, had a crippling effect on SA banding. Several hundred bandsmen, many recent emigrants, recrossed the Atlantic to defend their homeland. Indicative of the Army's musical contribution, the April 22, 1916, *War Cry* profiled 12 of over 20 Canadian Salvationists serving as battalion bandmasters with His Majesty's Forces.

Most eligible bandsmen volunteered for overseas service. Twenty two members of the Dovercourt Band enlisted with the Canadian Expeditionary Force. 31 of 38 Winnipeg Citadel bandsmen, and 20 members of the Riverdale Band volunteered for active service. In London, Ontario, senior members of the band formed the nucleus of the 142nd Battalion Reserve Band. In St. Thomas, Salvationists played in the 91st Battalion Band. Kingston bandsmen formed the core of the 59th Battalion Band. At Montreal Citadel, where 12 Americans who had enlisted in Canada were playing with corps bands, the band executive covenanted with *overseas members to hold the band together until their return*.[50,51] Japan was a World War I ally so when the Japanese battleship

Asama berthed at Esquimalt, the Victoria Band presented a fore-deck programme for the ship's 600 officers and crew.[52]

With the demise of the Staff Band and corps bands depleted, a servicemen's 'Khaki Band' provided the music at the 1915 Toronto Congress.[53] Such was the expansion of the SA into Western Canada that Western Territory Headquarters were established in Winnipeg that same year, a situation that lasted for 17 years. Also in 1915, an Eastern Territorial Staff Band comprised of *Empress* survivors and headquarters personnel was formed by Brigadier Fred Beer, a former bandmaster at England's Southend and Wood Green corps. However, either the desire or the need was not there, and the band ceased operating two years later. A headquarters orchestra led by Major Arnold also proved short-lived.

Banding's Golden Age

Salvationist bandsmen returned from the war with renewed appreciation for military tradition and regimental pride and found ample peacetime expression in the Salvation war. With enthusiastic administrative support, and spurred on by each other's exploits, they took SA banding in Canada to heights not experienced before or since. *The War Cry* launched the century's third decade and what is regarded as 'the Golden Age of SA banding in Canada,' with a photo-spread of 36 corps bandmasters. Their bands and others were making such an impact in Canadian music circles that *The Canadian Bandsman and Orchestra Journal* devoted its November 1920 issue to the exploits of post-war SA bands. The cover paid tribute to the ill-fated Canadian Staff Band: *The Toronto Headquarters Staff Band will long be remembered as one of the Dominion's leading musical organizations, not only by Salvationists but also by the general public.*

Bands featured, each with upwards of 40 members, were Montreal Citadel (William Goodier), Ottawa Citadel (James Harris), Riverdale (John Wood) and Dovercourt (Alfred Pearce) in Toronto, and Winnipeg Citadel (Henry Merritt). Excerpts provide critical insight into the quality of Salvation Army banding in Canada:

> ...*For the first 17 years of its existence* [the Riverdale Band] *remained a very small unit, practically making no*

improvement whatever, but in 1907 [they began] *to organize a band that would be a credit to a Corps the size of Riverdale...*

...Bandmaster James Harris [who conducted the Earlestown, Lancashire, Band between 1892-1906] *has conducted the Ottawa Band since 1906, and it is in better shape today than at anytime since its inception...*

...About nine years ago, the Dovercourt Band began the upgrade which finally lands them today in the place of being among the premier Salvation Army bands in Canada able to do justice to the Army's latest publications...

...[The Winnipeg Citadel Band] has attained a position second to none recognized by the highest authorities in its production of attractive melody, rich with impressive harmony, and possessing qualities of perfect balance in the intellectual as well as the emotional phases of the art... Every member of the band is possessed of characteristic chivalric instinct that has at all times distinguished the Salvation Army soldier. His ideality for service for Christ is supreme, and never is opportunity overlooked.

The journal also profiled Kneller Hall graduate Captain Robertson (Regent Hall), the newly-appointed divisional bandmaster in Toronto, and carried a photo of a 50-member Salvation Army Veterans' Band marching in the 1920 Canadian National Exhibition's Veterans' Parade. A SA band marched in successive Warriors' Day parades until the 1980s. In addition to the bands profiled in the journal, *The War Cry* reported substantial progress being made by Army bands in St. John's, Newfoundland, Charlottetown, Kingston, Peterborough, Toronto Temple, Earlscourt, West Toronto, Hamilton Citadel, Brantford, Guelph, Kitchener, London, Windsor and Vancouver. In 1926, *The War Cry* published a special issue devoted to 'The Bandmaster'.

In Cobourg, Ontario, Salvation Army band members holding an outdoor meeting were surprised when a visitor to the city who joined them in singing *Lead Kindly Light* and *Abide With Me* turned out to be the celebrated Italian tenor Enrico Caruso.[54]

Earlscourt Citadel Band led a parade of Veterans to open the Princes' Gate during 1927 Canadian National Exhibition's Warriors' Day observants.

Recognising the valuable contribution that bands were making to the Salvation war, and anxious to maximise this human resource, the administration provided its full support and encouragement. In 1922, Commissioner Charles Sowton suggested that 'Bandsmen's Day' should become an annual event. In 1927, Commissioner William Maxwell tirelessly chaired music festivals and conducted well-attended Bandsmen's Councils in Montreal, Toronto, London, Hamilton and Windsor on five consecutive weekends.[55] Lieut.-Commissioner Charles Rich, Maxwell's counterpart in

The Kingston, Ontario SA Band

western Canada, was equally active in encouraging musical excellence and spiritual integrity at regional Bandsmen's Councils.[56]

Canadian bands have always responded enthusiastically to invitations to undertake cross-border campaigns to US corps. Several US bands, mainly from border states, have also received warm Canadian welcomes. In 1923, while visiting Toronto, the Flint Citadel Band (William Broughton) joined several Toronto bands in a seven-hour marathon program at the city's central bandstand.[57]

Each week, the Canada East and Canada West *War Crys* carried pages of news and reports of special interest to *Our Musical Fraternity* in eastern Canada, and Of *Interest to Bandsmen and Songsters* in the west. Instructional articles by qualified writers on band training, technique, responsibilities of bandsmen, home practice, balance and blend, hints for young bandsmen, how to play the rests, and phrasing, were supported by photos of bands in the traditional front-centre-and-back-row configuration, and photos and biographies of bandmasters. Obviously operating without space constraints, the editors made sure that all bands, large and small, received fair treatment.

A 1923 Congress Festival in Toronto, featuring eight corps bands, further emphasized Canada's continuing dependence on overseas leaders – Arthur Delamont (Hertford), F. W. Robinson (Sheffield), Alfred Pearce (Newton Abbott), Arthur Higgins (Yeovil), Bill Walno (Stratford), Edward King

(Clydebank), Jack Robbins (Northhampton), and John Wood (Aberdeen).[58] In 1925, the Peterborough Band numbered immigrants from 13 British corps among its 43 members.[59] During the war and into the 1920s, Good Friday observances in Toronto were marked by mammoth parades. In these 'Easter Mobilizations', every city band and those from nearby centres would lead 2,000 uniformed Salvationists from the Parliament Buildings or University Armories to Massey Hall for a united meeting to contemplate Christ's crucifixion.

Things were equally progressive in western Canada, especially in the headquarters city of Winnipeg, where the Winnipeg Citadel Band (Henry Merritt) was becoming the century's most characteristically Canadian SA band. In 1924, the band undertook an extremely ambitious two-week, 3,600-mile tour visiting centres in the US Midwest and eastern Ontario.[60] In 1926, the band repeated its 1911, 3,200-mile campaign to Vancouver and Victoria.[61] Other bands receiving coverage in the Canada West *War Cry* included those of Edmonton, formed in 1907 by Bandmaster Horsman (Eastbourne), Drumheller, St. James, and The South Saskatchewan Divisional Officers' Band, and in Alaska, the Ketchikan Native Corps and Kake bands.[62]

World Depression and War

The 1930 Great Depression was also a depressing time for the Dovercourt Band when a disputed headquarters edict resulted in the resignation of the bandmaster and 29 bandsmen and much negative coverage in the Toronto press. The dissidents eventually moved to the Metropolitan United Church to form the Metropolitan Silver Band, currently in its 74th year of continuous operation.[63] Having been appointed to the editorial department in Canada earlier, Staff-Captain Bramwell Coles was assigned to lead the Dovercourt Band. Little needs to be said here about Coles' Salvationism, musical ability and life-long contributions to SA banding. Within a year, the Dovercourt Band had returned to the front ranks of Canadian SA bands.[64]

Great Britain's significant contribution to Canadian banding was not lost on Adjutant Eric Ball during a 1938 visit. *Most of the Canadian bands I heard are predominantly British in both personnel and ideals. This seemed especially so in*

Toronto where also is the influence of contesting bands... Make up your mind as to what you consider are the finest three corps bands in England; now think of Winnipeg as right in their company and there are three other Canadian bands following closely on their heels. Three soloists, bandsmen Ernest Parr, soprano, Ted Robbins, euphonium, and Ed O'Connor, E Flat bass, also received praise from Adjutant Ball.[65]

A precursor to the Reservist Bands that would emerge 45 years later, a 'Veterans' Band' comprised of bandsmen with over 30 years' service, was featured at the 1932 Toronto Congress.[66] In 1938, on the 20th anniversary of the end of World War I, a 45-member Salvationist Ex-Serviceman's Band was one of 40 bands participating in the Canadian Corps Reunion Parade reviewed by Prime Minister W. L. Mackenzie King.

In 1940, Brigadier Alfred Keith, territorial youth secretary and an *Empress* survivor, launched the territory's first summer music camp at Jacksons Point near Toronto. Today the Army provides practical instruction at some 14 divisional junior and senior music camps each summer. The camping season concludes with the performance-oriented Territorial School of Music and Gospel Arts at Jacksons Point. Since 1940, thousands of brass students have benefited from the opportunity to study under a pantheon of outstanding international and Canadian Salvationist composers and conductors supported by volunteer instructors. All are dedicated

Winnipeg Citadel Band, 1933.

to passing the skills, disciplines and responsibilities of SA banding along to the next generation.

World War II inflicted another heavy toll on the territory's bands. In addition to the men and women, many sons and daughters of World War I veterans, who enlisted for active service, several bands again joined reserve units *en masse*. Among them the Earlscourt (2nd Division Signals), Dovercourt (The Irish Regiment of Canada), Hamilton Temple (2/10 Dragoons), and London (142nd Battalion). Salvationists conducting military bands were fewer in number with Martin Boundy (RCAF Headquarters Band), Clifford Hunt (#6 Group RCAF Bomber Command Band), and William Habkirk (#2 Canadian Infantry Corps Band) taking their bands to England and the Continent. Wally Jeffries served as bandmaster on the Canadian Navy cruiser HMCS *Uganda*, and Harold Stuck led the Saskatoon #7 Air Force Band and Winnipeg #2 Air Command Band.

Salvationist War Hero

One name emerging from all Canadian Salvationist bandsmen serving in World War II is that of Brandon, Manitoba, Corps and Divisional Bandmaster Walter Dinsdale. The son of CSM George Dinsdale OF, an immigrant from Yorkshire, Walter earned the Distinguished Flying Cross for shooting down the first piggy-back flying bomb over England, and returned to serve as a federal parliamentarian and cabinet minister.

Following the war, the Army assisted in bringing another 10,000 immigrants to Canada under the government's Airborne Immigration Scheme and welcomed thousands more arriving at East Coast ports. However, this time most were displaced persons from Eastern Europe. Among Salvationists arriving from Great Britain were fewer bandsmen and only a few experienced bandmasters including Victor Kingston (Ilford), Bram Allington (Bournemouth), Aubrey Millward (Coventry), Ernie and Howard Livick (Penge and Cambridge), Roy Cornick (St. Helier, Channel Islands), William Gallagher (South Shields) and Kenneth Elloway (Weymouth).

At Earlscourt Citadel, Norman Audoire (Carlisle) led the band in the 1920s before becoming bandmaster at Montreal Citadel. After the war, four experienced English bandmasters – Wally Mason (Coventry), Derek Smith

(Clacton-on-Sea), later to lead the New York Staff Band, Brian Ring (Leeds), and Ron Clayson (Wood Green) took the Earlscourt Band to the vanguard of Canadian corps banding and tours of Great Britain (1965), Scandinavia (1981), and several major Canadian and US centres.

Many post-war bandmasters, all with contributions worthy of further research, carried familiar multi-generational Salvationist names. One such name was Delamont. L. S. Delamont (Hereford) emigrated to Moose Jaw, Saskatchewan, and formed a band in 1909. His four bandsman sons, Fred, Arthur, Herbert and Leonard subsequently led bands in Toronto, and New Westminster and Victoria B.C. Staff Bandsman Leonard died in the *Empress* tragedy.

Montreal Citadel Band (Norman Audoire) and Friday Evening at the Temple Chorus, Centennial Memorial Hall, New York, in late 1930's. Note the unusual seating formation and the chimes and timpani (despite no parts in published SA music of the time) plus usual battery including gong.

Banding: A Road to Officership

No more significant examples of banding's value in raising spiritual commitment to the higher level of officership exists than those of Generals Arnold Brown and Bramwell Tillsley, the Army's 11th and 14th international leaders.

In 1923, Arnold Brown's father, Charles, a British SA officer whose war wounds forced his resignation, immigrated to Belleville, Ontario, with his family. There, Arnold received his early music and band training from Bandmaster Jack Green (Maesteg, Wales) and entered training college in 1934. In 1978, General Brown admitted Bandmaster Green to The Order of the Founder.[67] Throughout his officership, especially in the years spent in Canada including those as territorial commander, Arnold Brown was banding's strongest administrative advocate, proponent and innovator. He was a cornet soloist, bandmaster at the Lisgar and North Toronto corps; helped launch the first Territorial Music Camp (1940), and participated in the territory's first Divisional Music Institute in Grand Falls, Newfoundland (1944), as well as the U.S. Central Territory's Music Institute. He initiated Toronto's popular post-war Spring Festivals. Several of his marches and selections have been published in the *Triumph Series* and *Canadian Brass Band Journal*.

In 1949, Major Brown conducted a 300-member composite band at a memorial service for 119 victims of a fire that destroyed the Great Lakes cruise ship *Noronic* while docked in Toronto. That same year, he produced the *This is My Story* series of Christian radio dramas that were broadcast over 67 Canadian and international stations. In 1957, he introduced *The Living Word* TV series. Music for both programs was provided by local, composite and visiting bands, with Colonel Bramwell Coles, having retired in Canada, serving as staff arranger, and Percy Merritt as music director.

General Bramwell Tillsley

Also with a strong banding background, Bramwell Tillsley, son of Kitchener, Ontario, Bandmaster Harold Tillsley (Kettering), spent his formative years as a cornet soloist in that corps' junior and senior bands.

As the Army matured and the first days of enthusiasm, and of people flocking to be saved, became a distant memory, corps became more inward looking and energy which had been expended on direct evangelism began to be spent on band and songster practices... In 1948, Commissioner Charles Baugh, Territorial Commander, confided to his executive officers his concern that the band and songsters were taking up too much time in Sunday meetings.[68] Despite such concerns, Commissioner Baugh championed the territory's first Spring

Festival of Music. Held off-season in a Toronto hockey arena, the inaugural event featured the Chicago Staff Band, and celebrated soloists and guest conductors in subsequent years. These popular territorial-sponsored festivals, since concluded, provided a welcome platform for Ontario corps bands and others from distances as far away as Bermuda, St. John's, Newfoundland, Halifax, Winnipeg, Vancouver, the US and overseas. Similar festivals have since been held in Hamilton and Vancouver.

Music Department Established

In 1948, the territory made the first tentative move to establishing a permanent music department by appointing Percy Merritt to the voluntary, part-time position of Territorial Band Inspector. In 1954, *The Canadian Brass Band Journal for Smaller Bands* was produced by the territorial youth department. A permanent music department was established in 1955, with Major Kenneth Rawlins as Secretary for Bands and Songster Brigades and, in 1959, Territorial Music Secretary. The mantle of successive appointments to this post fell on two UK officers, Major Norman Bearcroft (1969) and Major Robert Redhead (1977); and to two non-officer appointees, Leonard Ballantine, (1987), and Brian Burditt (1989). Captain Ballantine returned to head the renamed and refocused Music and Gospel Arts Department in 2002.

The department's initial projects included publishing volumes two and three of *The Canadian Brass Band Journal* and standardising national music camp curricula. In 2002, the department introduced a *Maple Leaf Brass* series featuring work by Canadian composers and arrangers. Production costs have been significantly reduced by storing scores and parts on disk and printing on request. Since 1982, the department has benefited from the estate of Canadian virtuoso pianist Glenn Gould. Among programs funded: a composition competition and travel subsidies for out-of-province National School of Music delegates.

Staff Band Revived

One of territorial commander Commissioner Clarence Wiseman's priorities in 1969 was reviving the Canadian Staff

In 1989 the Canadian Staff Band (Brian Burditt) joiined the Red Army Chorus, Orchestra and Dance Ensemble in Toronto's Massey Hall.

Band, and in Major Norman Bearcroft he found a willing and capable ally. A small headquarters ensemble led by Major Ernest Falle had operated in the late 1950s, but the concept of a territorial band had lain dormant since 1917. The waters were tested in 1967 at a Canada Centennial Year Massey Hall Festival, when a composite band led by Bandmaster Wilf Mountain (Sheffield) played Eric Ball's *Resurgam* and Goffin's *My Strength, My Tower*.[69] In 1969, under Major Bearcroft's determined leadership, the hand-picked founding ensemble, all members of established Toronto and area Army bands, became the focal point of the territory's music program. Commissioning the band under colours carried by *Empress* survivor Colonel Ernest Green, Commissioner Wiseman said it was being formed with the stated intention of providing a musical and spiritual role model for Salvation Army bands and bandsmen throughout the territory.[70]

The Canadian Staff Band has maintained quality musical standards under its founding conductor and successors, Major Robert Redhead (1977), Brian Burditt (1987), and Bermuda-born Kevin Hayward (2002). The band has travelled extensively in Canada and the US, and has taken its ministry of music to the UK and the Continent on several occasions, to Australia and New Zealand (1985), and Brazil (1997). In 1989, the band joined the Red Army Chorus, Orchestra and Dance Ensemble in a Toronto concert marking the Army's return to Russia. In 1994, the band celebrated its 25th anniversary with extravaganza afternoon and evening programmes featuring the Chicago, New York, International and Canadian Staff Bands.

Brian Burditt is another product of Canada's British Salvationist heritage. His grandfather, William Burditt, son of Army officers, came to Canada from Hereford in 1926 to lead the Hamilton III Band. His father, Bill, has led the Hamilton Citadel and Toronto Reservist Band, and Brian conducted the Hamilton Argyle Corps band before assuming leadership of the Canadian Staff Band and most recently, the Oshawa Corps Band.

New Horizons

The latter half of the 20th century brought a succession of technological breakthroughs that opened new avenues of Christian service for SA bands. Wax cylinders gave way to 78, 45 and 33 rpm records, cassette tape and CD recordings. Wind-up Gramophones were superseded by Victrolas and portable Walkman units. Light shows spawned moving pictures and, in the late 1930s, television. Public radio arrived in 1920. and several Canadian bands made early broadcasts. In 1930, broadcasting from an auto repair shop, the Brantford Citadel Band commenced a live, weekly half-hour radio broadcast that continued for over a half-century.[71] In 1934, the Montreal Citadel Band was heard nationally over the Canadian Broadcasting Corporation's network.

At mid-century, always anxious to hear and learn from their British counterparts, Ontario bandsmen eagerly lined up at Trade Headquarters to put down 75 cents for the latest Regal 78 rpm record. Bandsmen in other areas of the country had to wait for the mailman. Few Canadian SA bands made 78 rpm recordings, but one featuring Canadian Salvationist soloists was made by the RCAF Overseas Band in 1944. One side featured Ted Robbins playing Handel's *Harmonious Blacksmith*, the other, cornetists Cliff and Gib Williams and George Chapell playing Victor Herbert's *Three Solitaires*. In 1959, the major Canadian bands began producing 33 rpm records and, later, cassette tapes and CDs. By far the most prolific recording bands have been the Canadian Staff Band and London Citadel Band.

By 1967, with immigration from Britain in steep decline, the Dovercourt Band (William Habkirk) invited the UK Tottenham Citadel Band (James Williams) to visit Canada. Subsequently, 10 bandsmen and their families emigrated—among them, Bramwell Gregson who assumed leadership of the London Citadel Band, and virtuoso soloists Deryck Diffey (cornet), and Ivor Snell (euphonium). Several Ontario bands have since benefited from this mini-emigration. Under Bram Gregson's direction, the London Band, having already completed 85 years' service, reinforced its position as the century's pre-eminent corps band. In Owen Sound, Ontario, Bandmaster Harold Stuck, son of 1912 immigrant Bandmaster William Stuck (Woodford), launched his own immigration scheme personally arranging for some 40 British Salvationist bandsmen and their families to come to Canada for jobs in Owen Sound.

Maintaining its coverage of bands, band members and their contribution to their corps' evangelical programs, *The War Cry* devoted countless columns to band histories, personalities, photos and social items under such headings as *The Bandsmen's Column, Of Interest to Musicians, Band Chat, For*

The London Citadel Band during its tour of Britain in 1976.

Ted Marshall has achieved international acclaim for his expertise in sound recording.

Bandsmen and Songsters, The Bandsman and Songster Page, and *The Arts.*

In 1972, a new chapter of Salvation Army banding began when the Vancouver Reservist Band (Stan Collier) was formed. A Toronto Reservist Band (Victor Kingston) followed in 1987, both having received generous funding from government grants to senior citizen organizations. Both bands, and another since formed in London, Ontario, are among the most active in the country.

In 1978, the music department launched *Theme* magazine. Territorial Music Secretary Captain Robert Redhead described its purpose as *an attempt to help Salvationist musicians to feel that they are not alone, but part of this great territory, sharing one another's successes and failures, aspirations and disappointments, sensing that affinity with one another which is unique to Salvationist musicians throughout the world.*[72] Following a four-year hiatus, the magazine began a regular quarterly schedule in 1983. Articles are instructional and informative, but with few reports from the field and a press run of only 400, *Theme* has had difficulty achieving its founding purpose. Reflecting the renaming of the department, *Theme* is being refocused to include news and features on gospel arts.

Also in 1978, Captain Gwenyth Redhead's play, *The Bandmaster*, was performed at the International Congress in

London, England. Written to mark the centenary of SA banding, the play explored *the world of Salvation Army banding, the pressures, ambitions, temptations and the spiritual motivation of the men and women who 'play to the glory of God'.*[73] The play also underlined the bandmaster's role and responsibility as a contributing member of the corps' administration, representing a corps' most organised, uniformed, disciplined and dependable body of soldiers.

A review of Army banding in Canada would be incomplete without citing the contribution of Ted Marshall in making recorded SA music available to a vast domestic and international audience. The unseen, unheard artist behind many Canadian SA band recordings, as well as others from the US, Europe and Australia, Ted's recording expertise has earned international acclaim. As a Canadian Broadcasting Corporation technician, Ted, now retired and operating his own studio, engineered over 400 recording projects earning a score of prestigious awards including the CBC President's Award for outstanding achievement in sound recording.

Also deserving of special mention is the outstanding contribution of women band members, a role unfortunately defined in large measure, especially in the larger bands, by the lack or absence of available male musicians. In the formative days, women 'band lassies' served with their male counterparts in the ensembles, bands and orchestra combinations, often in equal numbers. Jubilee Project 45 of 50 announced by the territory in 1894 to celebrate the 50th anniversary of General Booth's public ministry, was the formation of a Lasses' Brass Band.[74] A Lasses Band was already operating in Victoria and another Lasses Brass Band was formed in London in 1896. While women have always been represented in the medium size and smaller bands, as bands grew larger more uniformed standards were introduced and demands on time increased, many women turned to other areas of service.

During World War I, women picked up the instruments left by bandsmen serving in the armed forces only to relinquish them to the returning men. The pattern was repeated during and following World War II. Today most bands, large and small, include capable women instrumentalists. Most tend to be younger and without family responsibilities. In 1989, the

Canadian Staff Band welcomed cornetist Melody Stepto, its first woman member. A few women, most notably Melinda Ryan (St. John's Citadel), now in the United States, also serve as bandmasters.

Contemporary Canadian-born virtuoso instrumentalists still living in Canada include Douglas Burden, Douglas Chaulk, Steven van Gulik and Robert Venables, each with symphony experience; as well as Robert Merritt, Captain Kevin Metcalf and Robert Miller. In 1998, Robert Venables was the featured cornet soloist on the Brighouse & Rastrick Band's CD *Exaltation.*

Isaiah 40, composed by Robert Redhead, was the chosen test piece for the 1996 National Brass Band Championships in London, England.

The list of published Canadian Salvationist composers is short, in some respects the result of the early demise of *The Canadian Brass Band Journal.* However, the advent of the photocopier, the *Maple Leaf Brass* series, and relaxation of regulations governing permissible music is providing opportunity for Canadian composers and arrangers. Those listed in the Chicago-produced *2004 Instrumental Music Index* – including those born elsewhere and now holding Canadian citizenship – number fewer than 20. Included are Eric Abbott, Norman Audoire, Arnold Brown, Morley Calvert, Ken Elloway, Bill Gordon, Paul Green, Wayne Knight, Henry, James and Percy Merritt, Kenneth Rawlins, and contemporaries Leonard Ballantine, David Chaulk, Douglas Court Jr., and Robert Redhead whose, *Isaiah 40,* was the test piece for the 1996 National Brass Band Championships in London, England.

The National Contesting Council presents the

BOOSEY & HAWKES

National Brass Band
CHAMPIONSHIPS
OF GREAT BRITAIN

PATRON – Her Majesty Queen Elizabeth II

TEST PIECE
"Isaiah 40" (Robert Redhead)

Championship Section Finals
SATURDAY 19TH OCTOBER 1996

The Royal Albert Hall
London

finals '96

Programme £2.50

EGON

Interestingly, apart from marches bearing the names of corps and music camps, only a few compositions have sought to capture the essence of the Canadian culture. These include James Merritt's festival march, *The Canadian* (FS 76), Bramwell Coles', *Maple Leaf* march (GF 1021), Percy Merritt's, *Golden West* march (GS 1117), Morley Calvert's, *Canadian Folk Song Suite* (FS 331), Norman Bearcroft's, *Songs of Newfoundland* (FS 504), and Robert Redhead's, *Deus Vobiscum* (God Be With You) tribute to the victims of the *Empress* disaster.

The roster of proficient native-born bandmasters is still comparatively short, the result of years of deferring to emigrating Salvationists with brass band experience and failing to develop potential Canadian leaders. Some notable

At the Bermuda Music Camp, students were given the opportunity to display their new skills to the Honourable John W. Swan, Premier of Burmuda, who took time from a busy schedule to visit the children at the camp.

exceptions over the past half-century include Morley Calvert, William Habkirk, Fred Merrett, Brian Burditt, Leonard Ballantine, David Moulton and Douglas Burden, and Bill

Bandmaster Stephen Bulla and Lieut-Colonel Norman Coles (son of composer Bramwell Coles) standing in front of photos of guest conductors at Metro-Toronto Division Music Camp.

Gordon and Ed Freeman, now living in the US. From the military establishment – Ted Robbins, who led the peacetime RCAF Air Transport Command Band; Herbert Jeffries, The Royal Canadian Princess Patricia's Light Infantry Band; Hugh McCullough, the Canadian Navy's Stadacona and Naden bands; and Ken Moore, who conducted the RCAF Air Transport Command Band and the Royal Canadian Mounted Police Band. Ken Moore's accomplishments and those of Martin Boundy, Cliff Hunt and Bram Gregson have earned them membership in the prestigious American Bandmasters' Association. Since relinquishing leadership of the London Citadel Band, Bram Gregson has formed his own Intrada Brass Band, with most of its members recruited from SA band ranks.

At present, most larger corps and a few smaller corps still actively support credible brass programmes. The London Citadel Band (John Lam) is the leading corps band. Other corps, all in major centres, enjoying quality banding include Halifax Citadel (Peter van der Horden), Halifax Fairview (Wayne Haggett) in Nova Scotia, Ottawa Woodroffe (Bill van Gulik) and Ottawa Citadel (Peter van Gulik), Hamilton Temple (Ron Heintzman), and some 10 corps in the Metro Toronto and surrounding area. In Newfoundland, St. John's Citadel (Melinda Ryan), St. John's Temple (David Rowsell) and Corner Brook Temple (Wayne Thompson) are the exceptions. Cariboo Hill Temple Band (David Michel), formerly Vancouver Temple, is the best in the west, with effective corps bands operating at Calgary Glenmore (Peter Yetman) and Edmonton Temple (Bruce Coley) corps in Alberta, and at Victoria Citadel (Trevor Lewis) in British Columbia. Sadly, several mid-century first-class bands, including the famous Montreal and Winnipeg Citadel bands, have disappeared or are shadows of their former selves. Several others continue to operate under their relocated corps names.

What of the Future?

To anticipate the future, evangelical optimism must be tempered with objective realism. Canada has changed and continues to change. Today, the Canadian SA operates in a multi-ethnic, multi-faith and increasingly secular society.

London Citadel Band in concert with Bandmaster John Lam.

Immigration from Britain has dried up. Since 1960, newcomers from Europe have declined from 69 to 19 per cent, and Asian immigrants have increased from 12 to 57 percent.[75] Toronto, the largest 'Italian' city outside Italy, is home to people from over 200 countries, and Vancouver has the second-largest Chinese population of any city outside China.

Operating in this milieu, the SA, its membership now almost entirely indigenous, is in an adaptive mode, especially in the larger centres. Few of these recent adaptations, especially the transition from 'evangelism' to 'worship', have served to support its banding heritage.

Since the outset, banding has been an integral part of the Army's evangelical, corps ministry. Statistically, this aspect of the territory's work has been in significant decline for several decades. Canada's population is nearing 32 million, but the Army has not shared in this growth. In the past 25 years, the number of active officers has declined by 10 per cent (1,274 to 1,050), with fewer than half in corps appointments. The number of corps and outposts has dropped (495 to 362). Since 1980, senior soldier rolls have seen marked declines (26,235 to

21,721), and adherents, a perennial numerical strength, have dropped from 65,329 to 54,645.[76]

As significant as the drop in senior ranks is, the loss of over 2,500 junior soldiers (7,563 to 4,663), the future Army, is even more disturbing. For those that remain, learning a brass instrument and joining the band is no longer the rite-of-passage for young Salvationists it once was. Not surprisingly, attendance at the territory's music camps is also in decline. Coincidental with the decrease in Corps junior bands, six divisional youth bands are now operating.

Unlike its US neighbour, Canada is not a military-minded country, a situation that causes some Salvationists to question the Army's image. The exodus of corps from city-centre to suburbia is redefining the Army's status from 'Movement' to 'sect'; its focus from 'evangelism' to 'worship'; its *raison d'etre* from 'mission' to 'community church'; its music more likely provided by so-called 'worship bands'. While competent and creative, such groups do not embody the music and deportment disciplines implicit in the banding experience, nor can they match a band's intergenerational continuity or provide a band's proven corps-building family component.

Numerical decline, refocused mission and relaxed regulations are impacting the leadership role. Unlike their predecessors who were schooled in and committed to the aggressive proselytising, disciplined British military and contesting band conditions, and the Army's high moral standards, today's leaders must operate in a less structured, less authoritative society, and in corps where officers serve as 'pastors' and whose programmes are directed more to indoor 'worship' than militant evangelism.

For over 100 years, SA band music has been inextricably linked to SA hymnody. Composers have been required to infuse their work with melodies and themes from The Salvation Army *Song Book*, melodies and themes to which congregations could relate on cognitive and emotional levels. As corps turn from the *Song Book* in favour of songs and choruses from TV and mainstream evangelical sources, this spiritually-sensitive, band-congregational bond is eroding.

Street meetings, the international cradle of Army banding, no longer play a significant role in corps or administrative evangelical strategy. Today's Salvationists seldom parade, so

General Arnold Brown

regimental street marches have given way to stage-friendly festival marches. Titles and themes that once encouraged Salvationists to spiritual warfare, are now more esoteric than exoteric.

Declining administrative regard for band members is reflected in the Army's relaxed, *Orders and Regulations for Bandsmen and Songster Brigades* are now *Orders and Regulations for Music Organizations.* Bandsmen and songsters are no longer regarded as 'local officers'; and provision for 'non-commissioned musicians' has been included.

Former General Arnold Brown lived in nine of the 12 decades reviewed. Commenting on the current state of banding before his death in 2002, he saw *more devotion to the spiritual aspect of banding than there was 30 to 40 years ago, but lesser acceptance of discipline, rather aiming at musical perfection.* The increasing complexity of the programme music being published by the Army and the relaxing of regulations would seem to underscore his observations. *Today's instrumentalists may be more spiritual and musically proficient than their predecessors* (he said) *but their numbers are fewer and the keenest and most experienced are finding outlets for their talents in other religious and secular groups.*

In Canada, Salvation Army Banding, once a tactical means to a righteous end, is well on the way to becoming the end itself. In some corps the signs are already there: *Your services are no longer required!*

In recent years there has been little evidence of administration concern about the decline in what Major Robert Redhead regarded as *something very fundamental to the Army*, in his 1984 quote that prefaced this chapter. The General's representative for the development of worship and evangelism through music and the other creative art internationally, Colonel Redhead, now retired, remains optimistic, in response to questions raised by the author:

> *We must remember that the Army's use of music is primarily a means to a glorious and very satisfying end. If that 'means' becomes the 'end', it can no longer serve its prime purpose. In the last 30 years, the SA has faced major challenge by a movement throughout Christendom which many have entitled the 'rediscovery of worship'...*

*therefore it is inevitable that brass banding has [also]
been challenged, and is now generally regarded as a
'niche' music form. In my view, the challenge
for SA bands is to accept this, and assess how they can
contribute in a valid manner to the newer forms of
worship and impact the world 'out there' by:*

*...Accepting modern trends in worship and working with
'worship teams' and other forms of music to facilitate
even more glorious worship of Almighty God;*
*...Using modern technology in communicating with the
general populace within and without the church;*
*...Developing an interest in the 'art-form' among the
young.*

*The worst thing SA banding can do is to entrench itself
and refuse to adapt. That will be the death knell and,
sadly, has already proven to be so in some situations.*

Can the Army, a 'niche' denomination if there ever was one,
afford to distance itself from its founding 'saved-to-save'
dogma as it searches for a new niche in contemporary
Canadian society? If there is to be a significant role for
bands – and songsters, for the two services are linked – to fulfil
in the 21st century Salvation Army, attention must be given
at every level to maximising the potential of these valuable
human resources. The responsibility for this lies as much,
perhaps even more, with the administration as it does with the
bands themselves.

Author Wally Court

About the Author

Wallace L. (Wally) Court, BA (Sociology), York University, Toronto, 1970.

A fourth-generation Salvationist, Wally was a junior and
senior bandsman in Brantford, Ontario, before moving to
Toronto where he played in the Dovercourt and Earlscourt
Citadel bands and, presently, in the Etobicoke Temple Band.
A music camp volunteer for 35 years, he also conducted the
Etobicoke Temple Youth Band on extended tours in all four US
territories between 1978 and 1986.

During a public relations career with Gulf Canada he received over 100 domestic and international awards for communication and publishing excellence. He is a Fellow of the International Association of Business Communicators, and a Life Member of the affiliated Canadian organisation. In retirement he worked for five years as assistant editor of the Canadian *War Cry*. He is currently writing a biography of Colonel Bramwell Coles.

He and his wife, Evangeline (Roberts), have three sons. Stephen, a SA officer, recently established The War College in Vancouver.

Notes

1. Canadian Territorial Headquarters, 2001 Statistics; SA International *Year Book*, 2002.
2. Arnold Brown, *What Hath God Wrought?*, Toronto, SA Printing and Publishing, Toronto, 1952, p3.
3. Maxwell Ryan, *The Canadian Campaign*, Toronto, Matthews, Ingham, and Lake, Inc., Toronto, 1982, p79.
4. *The British Whig*, September 3, 1883, as quoted in James Tackaberry's, *The King's Musicians*, unpublished, chapter 11, p3.
5. Gordon Moyles, *The Blood and Fire in Canada*, Peter Martin Associates, Toronto, 1997, p 43.
6. *What Hath God Wrought*, pp36, 37.
7. *The Toronto Globe* as quoted in *The King's Musicians*, Chapter 11, p4.
8. Donna J. Dunkley, *All Through The Years*, Preney Print & Litho Inc., 1986, p4.
9. *The King's Musicians*, Chapter 11, p7.
10. *The War Cry*, December 8, 1908.
11. *The War Cry*, March 28, 1886.
12. Chatham (Ontario) Corps history.
13. *The King's Musicians*, Chapter 11, p7.
14. *Ibid.*, Chapter 11, p7.
15. *The St. John's Evening Telegram*, March 15. 1887.
16. *The Bandsman and Songster* (UK), May 9, 1908.
17. *The Blood and Fire in Canada*, pp55-59; *The War Cry*, March 26, 1887.
18. *The Blood and Fire in Canada*, p11 and Appendix E.
19. Arch Wiggins, *Father of Salvation Army Music*, London: SP&S, 1945, p28.
20. *The Canadian Campaign*, p87.

21. *The War Cry*, May 27, 1885.
22. Brindley Boon, *Play the Music Play*, The Campfield Press, St. Albans, UK, 1966, pp24-26.
23. *Ibid.*, p54.
24. *The War Cry*, December 7, 1889.
25. *The Toronto World*, August 14, 1889, and *What Hath God Wrought?*, p83.
26. *What Hath God Wrought?*, p84.
27. *The War Cry*, March 3, 1906.
28. *Ibid.*, February 15, 1896.
29. *Ibid.*, February 19, 1896.
30. C. Palmer Curtis, *Bermuda Ablaze*, 1995, pp5-6.
31. *Ibid.*, p40.
32. THQ Statistics from the 1900 *Disposition of Forces*.
33. *The War Cry*, October 7, 1899.
34. *The War Cry*, December 2, 1903.
35. *The Canadian Campaign*, p121.
36. *The Blood and Fire in Canada*, p139.
37. *The Bandsman and Songster* (UK), September 5, 1908.
38. *The War Cry*, July 14, 1906.
39. *Ibid.*, October 18, 1947.
40. *Ibid.*, July 2, 1904, and Bermuda Ablaze, The Salvation Army, Bermuda, p41.
41. *The War Cry*, June 27, 1987.
42. *The Bandsman and Songster*, UK, March 21, 1908.
43. *Ibid.*, March 7, 1908.
44. *Ibid.*, July 11 and 20, 1908.
45. *The Toronto Star*, April 11, 1909, and *What Hath God Wrought?*, p77.
46. *The War Cry*, October 6, 1906.
47. *Ibid.*, June 6, 1914.
48. *The London Illustrated Times*, June 6, 1914.
49. *What Hath God Wrought?*, p124.
50. *The War Cry*, October 19, 1918.
51. *The Canadian Bandsman and Orchestra Journal*, 1920.
52. *The War Cry*, November 6, 1915.
53. *Ibid.*, October 30, 1915.
54. *The Holy War of Sally Ann*, p174.
55. *The War Cry*, April 2, 9, 16, and 23, 1927.
56. Canada West *War Cry*, March 30, 1927.
57. *The War Cry*, July 14, 1923.

58. *Ibid.*, October 27, 1923.

59. *Ibid.*, March 14, 1925.

60. *Ibid.*, September 20, 1924.

61. Canada West *War Cry*, June 19, 1926.

62. *Ibid.*, January 20, 1923.

63. *The War Cry*, August 20, 1988.

64. *Ibid.*, February 21, 1987.

65. *Ibid.*, July 23, 1938.

66. *Ibid.*, November 5, 1932.

67. *The SA Year Book 1979;* and *Fighting for His Glory*, p57.

68. *The War Cry*, June 19, 1948.

69. *Ibid.*, May 20, 1967.

70. Clarence Wiseman, *A Burning in My Bones*, McGraw-Hill Ryerson, Toronto, 1979, p175.

71. *Theme*, Volume III, Issue 2, The Canada and Bermuda Territory, 1984.

72. *Ibid.*, Volume I, Issue 1, 1978.

73. Gweneth Redhead, *The Bandmaster*, Triumph Press, Oakville, Ontario, 1969.

74. *The War Cry*, May 19, 1894.

75. *Time Magazine*, May 31, 1999.

76. SA Year Books, 1977 and 2003, and Canadian THQ 2001 Statistics.

Chapter 6

SWEDEN

Torgny Hanson

The soul in the music can be really manifested in playing a simple tune as in giving the most complicated piece. I want you to give your attention not only to playing the highly developed journals, but the same care, the same nicety of touch and style bestowed upon the most simple and commonplace words that the average man – such as I am – can understand. Make your music speak; make it say something to the crowd; play your very hearts into the people's hearts. Spoken by Bramwell Booth at the December 10, 1899, Bandsmen's Councils. 'Bandsmen's Councils', *The Local Officer,* January, 1900, pp224–228.

In 1920 the Chalk Farm Band from London visited Sweden for an extensive tour. This created the first major interest among Swedish Salvationists in the British-style brass band, even if the Chalk Farm Band during this time also featured saxophones, mellophones, and trumpets! This 'English style and sound' premiere was rather late in the history of SA brass in Scandinavia. Prior to this there had been bands made up of only brass instruments, but primarily as sextets that followed a continental-style set of instruments which were used by the Swedish military bands and in the national band movement. The sextets were then enlarged to form fuller ensembles by assigning several players to each part.

As corps opened around the country, bands were formed in several locations. The Salvation Army 'opened fire' in Sweden in 1882 and the first band was started as early as 1883, a sextet in Stockholm. The Army grew rapidly and consequently the number of bands increased. One notable early achievement was the formation in 1884 of a band of five women, commissioned at Gothenburgs 1st Corps!

These corps bands were normally not very large in number, many of them in the 5–6 range, but with a few as large as 18–20 bandsmen or women. The military bands, bands of the temperance movement, and national trade union movement became the models these early groups imitated. In terms of instruments used, you could find a clarinet or flute among the Swedish, German, or Bohemian brass instruments which featured rotary valves, but never a slide trombone and very seldom a euphonium. The slide trombone during this period was not even used in the Royal Opera Orchestra, other symphony orchestras, nor in the military bands in Stockholm. So, naturally, it was a sensational experience for Swedish Salvationists to hear and see the slide trombone section of the 1920 Chalk Farm Band.

In 1888 a Musical Department was formed at the SA National Headquarters in Stockholm. The first head of the department was a former military musician, Otto Lundahl, a newly commissioned Salvation Army officer who had been saved and become a Salvationist in 1886. His assignment was to develop the music department and train bandsmen for the newly established Swedish Staff Band. He was also charged with developing and publishing band music for the accompanying of congregational singing. The first editions consisted of single sheets with several tunes per sheet. The first *Swedish Band Tune Book* was printed in 1906, containing 420 tunes arranged for the typical Swedish brass sextet of E Flat Cornet, B Flat Cornet, E Flat Alto Horn, B Flat Tenor Horn, B Flat Valve Trombone, and F or E Flat Tuba.

The Swedish Staff Band, which had started in 1888, was such a sextet, plus one or two drummers. Later this ensemble was augmented to 12 players, yet even with a change to British-style instruments, never a slide-trombone! Under the name 'The Swedish Silver Band' the Swedish Staff Band had great success under Otto Lundahl during the 1890 and 1894

The first Swedish SA
Music Department,
1890s.
Otto Lundahl (right) with
Axel R. Assarsson and
Gustaf Hielm.

International Congresses held in London. At this time the band was a full-time activity. The members were not officers, but young lay Salvationists who were appointed to the band for specific periods of time. A profile of this 12-piece band appeared in Volume X of *The Musical Salvationist* (1895-96, p. 143-144): 2 E Flat Cornets, 1 B Flat Cornet, 2 E Flat Alto Horns, 1 B Flat Valve Trombone, 1 B Flat Tenor Horn, 1 B Flat Euphonium; 1 Circular F Bass, 1 E Flat Bombardon, Side Drum, and Bass Drum. Several former members of the band

The Swedish Territorial
Headquarters Band, 1899
(not Staff Band).

A Swedish-Canadian Corps ensemble in the Rotary-valve tradition. Winnipeg IV Corps (Canada), c.1905

had by this time become officers or cadets [officers-in-training] and were serving in the capacity of 'Band Teachers'.

Lundahl provided for Richard Slater's article lists of indispensable conditions for membership in this staff band and duties to be undertaken:

> *Indispensable Conditions: 1) They must be thoroughly saved and willing to give their lives to God without reserve; 2) Must have a taste for music, and be able to play a brass instrument; 3) Must possess a good singing voice; 4) Be willing to enter the Fight, remembering that no earthly advantages are offered or guaranteed, more than their necessary maintenance.*
>
> *Duties: 1) Be always and everywhere jealous of God's glory and the Army's honour; 2) To take part in the meeting – speaking and personal dealing; 3) Be careful of preserving the spirit and unity within the Band; 4) To take care of the instrument committed to them; 5) To sell* Stridsropet [War Cry] *while on journeyings.*

Such an appointment benefited both the individual and the Army. The bandsmen grew in their faith and salvationism as a result of their experiences. Several of them became bandmasters and band local officers, thus aiding the musical and spiritual development of the bands and the Army's ministry. This was an extremely important process in the growth of the band tradition in Sweden. The Swedish Staff Band ceased in 1923, though it was reformed for a short time during the 1930s.

In 1904, Otto Lundahl was succeeded as head of the music department by a Norwegian officer, Major Klaus Östby. Klaus Östby was a well-educated musician whose contribution for more than forty years to Salvation Army music in Scandinavia borders on the incalculable. His importance can not be exaggerated. In fact, Klaus Östby probably composed the first original brass band march for the SA. His *Kabelvåg March* is considered the very first full-scale march for the Army. Written in the mid-1890s to commemorate a rough sea voyage of the Norwegian Staff Band in icy, northern waters, it was published in the *Svensk Festmusik* band journal in versions for sextet (No. 6) and for larger ensemble (No. 187), but also for full brass band in the *General Series*, GS 1109 (June 1936). This highly imaginative programme music was years ahead of its time, a well-crafted work marked by much wit and humour.

Östby also composed four more substantial pieces scored for full brass band. These pieces were presumably composed between c.1908–1926. Two of them were published in the *Festival Series*, namely the meditation, *Princethorpe* (See Chapter 3) and festival march, *To the Land of Glory* (FS 12). The other two are in classical musical form – a *Passacaglia* dating from 1910 and an overture in the style of Mendelssohn's, *Harmoniemusik* called, *Feast in The Salvation Army*. These two compositions were surely thought as too intellectual or advanced for that time. Eric Ball once told me that he thought Östby was, in a way, fifty years ahead of his time as a SA composer.

In addition to arranging every tune in the 1906 *Swedish Band Tune Book*, he also started editing and publishing in the same year a Swedish band journal, *Svensk Festmusik*. This new journal not only contained further tunes for congregational singing but also 'band items' such as classical transcriptions, national gems, marches, and selections. The scoring at first was for the traditional brass sextet (Numbers 1–108) but as bands grew in size, the instrumentation expanded. Numbers 109–288 are scored for eight parts: B Flat Cornet 1&2; E Flat Alto Horn; Baritone/Trombone 1&2 [Tenorhorn]; Euphonium [Basun]; E Flat Bass or B Flat Bass;

[though early scores have Bass in F and E Flat], with optional E Flat Soprano and Percussion also available (See Illustrations 10 and 11). Full scores, which first appeared starting with Nos. 117–136, were, after a break, regularly produced for Nos. 201–288. Within *Svensk Festmusik* several marches by Klaus Östby and Erik Leidzén that first appeared here were later 'converted' to British-style scoring and were later released in the *General Series*. For example, Leidzén's *Livräddningsgardernas marsch*, published in the *Svensk Festmusik* in 1923, renamed *On to the War* when rescored as GS 939, Dec. 1925 (Illustration 11). Reversing the process, marches by George Marshall, Bramwell Coles, and others have been edited for *Svensk Festmusik* scoring and then published in Stockholm. Other important contributors to this journal have been Folke Andersson, David Berg, Gunnar Blomberg, Kristian Fristrup, Gustav Kjellgren, and Gustav Wallteng.

In 1963 a new journal replaced *Svensk Festmusik* and was called *Svenska Musikserien: Evangelisk musik för hornmusikkårer*. The score requires nine players and is identical to the *American Band Journal* ('Band Music for Evangelism') published by the USA East since 1948.[1] The numbering for this series commences with 301. Released irregularly, at present up to seven sets, music by composers

Illustration 10. Page 1 of Full Score to Svensk Festmusik No. 124; Marsch: Mot härlighetens land (Klaus Östby).

and arrangers such as Erik Silfverberg, Eric Ball, Rune Frödén, and Sture Petersson have been featured. Special editions of music for beginners' and youth bands have also been published, such as the four-part series entitled *Ungdomsmusikserien*, Volume 1 (1975).[2] In 2005 a new journal called *BrassScan* started, and plans are set for it to be published annually, each issue to contain four pieces. It's a common project between the Scandinavian territories with Erik Silfverberg as editor.

During the 1920s Swedish bands more frequently sought out British-made instruments, but still without changing completely to genuine brass-band instrumentation. Tenor slide-trombones and cornets with piston-valves were the first new instruments to appear. The last to come were the 'G' bass trombone and the 'monster' B Flat basses. Swedish bands saw an inevitable future in the British style. This must be considered as a remarkable step in Swedish band culture when you consider its very strong domestic tradition.

Swedish bands developed at a notably fast pace during the 1930s. This was surely because of the strong influences of visits by bands from England during the first half of that decade. Chalk Farm came a second time, 1930, and third time, 1934. Tottenham Citadel toured Sweden in 1933. In 1935 came the 'London Elite Band', a specially-formed ensemble of

Illustration 11: Page 1 of Full Score to Svensk Festmusik No. 133; Marsch: Livräddningsgardernas (Erik Leidzén) [On to the War].

London Elite Band (George Fuller) in the Stockholm Concert Hall. Notice G trombone with handle in use, far right.

very talented and experienced bandsmen under the leadership of Colonel George Fuller. The players were members of well-known corps bands as well as the International Staff Band. All these bands from England made a tremendous impression with their music making, but also with their organisation, discipline, and style of uniform. Further visits by bands from different parts of the SA world have, through the years, naturally meant a great deal for inspiration and broadening of vision among band members and bandmasters. Sweden has been visited by brass bands from Great Britain, the Netherlands, Germany, Switzerland, the USA, Canada, Australia, Korea and other Scandinavian countries. Add band personalities, such as composers, conductors, and soloists, and you find that such cross-fertilisation has been of great benefit in the growth of SA brass bands and musical performance standards in Sweden.

In a different but no less important light is the influence of recordings that were coming out from SP&S at Judd Street in London featuring the most famous of the English bands. Those groups were heard frequently via old-fashioned record players in the homes of Salvationist musicians, and thus new repertoire, opening a new world for banding in Sweden.

Thumb-nail Sketches of Representative Bands

The **Stockholm Temple Band** has through the years held a special place among SA bands in Sweden, because this band has fostered, and has had as members, most of the Swedish composers of SA band music. Names like David Berg, Gunnar

Blomberg, Erik Leidzén, Hans Nordin, and Sture Petersson are all well known as bandmasters or bandsmen of Stockholm Temple who composed or arranged good music for bands. During the bandmastership of Sture Petersson the Stockholm Temple Band toured England in 1966 and Germany, the Netherlands, Belgium, and France in 1973. Petersson also served as the territorial (national) music secretary 1983–1995.

At Stockholm 2nd Corps the young Erik Jehrin was appointed bandmaster in the late 1920s. He commenced a very purposeful and consistent work in developing the band after the English model. So, the **Stockholm 2 Band** became the very first genuine British-style brass band in Sweden. From 1935 to the beginning of the 1940s the bandmaster and the band had a very close relationship with Kristian M. Fristrup, then head of the SA music department in Stockholm. Many of Fristrup's manuscripts were played for the first time and tested by the Stockholm 2. This band toured in Finland in 1939 and in the Netherlands in 1950.

The **Vasa Band** is an inheritor of Stockholm 2 and Stockholm 5 corps bands, when these two corps were amalgamated in 1967 to form the Vasa Corps. Its first bandmaster was the then young Per Ohlsson, who in a short time created a young, very ambitious band, which as soon as 1970 was invited to tour England. The Vasa Band has also

Stockholm VII Band under BM Erland Beijer at 'Skansen', the annual Territorial Congress, 1976.

visited the Netherlands and Germany, as well as the United Kingdom for a second time.

Stockholm 7 Band is one of the best known corps bands of The Salvation Army, the reason being its several very successful tours of England, Europe, and North America. The first visit abroad was to Switzerland in 1948. The band is also renowned because of a consistently high musical standard that has been maintained for nearly 60 years. Bandmaster Karl Bengtsson, who led the band during its first decade of strong development, is an example of how former staff-bandsmen became important as local officers at the corps level. Bandmaster Erland Beijer, who conducted the band for 23 years, was in his younger days an outstanding soloist on the euphonium, one of the very first in a line of excellent soloists within the Stockholm 7 Band. Under Per Ohlsson, bandmaster 1976–1983, the band reached admirable heights in performance of the very finest SA repertoire. In 1999 the Stockholm 3 and 7 Corps were amalgamated into the **Stockholm South Citadel Corps**. Torgny Hanson directed the Stockholm 7–Stockholm South Citadel Band for nearly ten years, 1995-2004. During that time the band toured Great Britain twice as well as visited Norway and Latvia.

Södertälje Band was privileged during the 1920s and 1930s with weekly visits by Klaus Östby, who came regularly

Södertälje Corps Band (Torgny Hanson), 1985.

by train from Stockholm to instruct the band during band practices. This gave a sterling foundation for such a developing band. Under Torgny Hanson's 20-plus years of leadership, the band became an ensemble of international reputation. Tours have been made in many territories of Europe, as well as in Canada and the USA. Three visits to Great Britain have been undertaken. In 1993 the Södertälje Band was invited to take part and perform in the Royal Albert Hall, London, for the great festival of music held in connection with the annual Bandmasters' and Songster Leaders' Councils.

The **Örebro Band** is a band with strong traditions and is very much respected for its consistency in Salvationism and in musical standard. Bandmaster Folke Andersson, well-known composer, and his band local officers developed a solid band. Under Sven-Erik Karlssôn the band continued that effort and offered up fine contributions at congresses and festivals in Sweden. The Örebro Band has also been invited to tour in several SA territories, including Germany, Switzerland, the Netherlands, England, and Scotland.

When Colonel Albert Jakeway visited Sweden in 1951 he was very impressed by the little corps band of **Finspång**. Under Bandmaster Eugen Gustafsson, a musician with his roots in the old Swedish band tradition, the 10-piece Finspång Band became an ensemble with a very conscious musical style of high quality, especially in ensemble technique. The same can be said about the **Gothenburg 5 Band**. This quite small band performed in a very musically interesting way under the leadership of Bandmaster Sixten Forsell. This band is now a full-size brass band named **Hisingkåren Band**.

In the far north of Sweden a corps was opened at **Skelleftehamn** in 1940. Quite soon there was a beginners' bands for junior soldiers taught and led by Bandmaster Sven Johansson. The junior band became a corps band of very fine standard, which is still in evidence today. Very fine leadership has been the key to that success for a band that never benefits from players who transfer into the corps, but a band that must educate every new young band member from the very beginning.

The SA quickly thrived in parts of Sweden called the 'areas of revival' and particularly in the northern part of the

Huskvarna Corps Band with Bandmaster Henning Petersson, 1927.

Smaland landscape. This meant that soon several strong Army bands were functioning in the area. The corps bands in **Jönköping** and **Huskvarna** both had very special personalities as bandmasters during the period 1920–1955. At Jönköping Allan Petersson was bandmaster and in Huskvarna it was Henning Petersson. They were not related!

In Huskvarna the influence of Chalk Farm Band was evident, as the band for a period included saxophones and french horns. These two bands travelled extensively in Sweden and became models for Swedish bands to follow, not least because of their genuine and forthright wish to spread the Gospel and serve the aims of the SA. Huskvarna Band was the first SA band to visit Germany after World War II. The Jönköping Band visited Germany 1962, the Netherlands in 1965, Switzerland in 1979, Portugal in 1980, and twice in England, for the 1990 International Congress, and again in 1995.

No band has perhaps been so much marked by its bandmaster's style and character as the **Tranås Band** under Bandmaster Gunnar Borg, who was its leader for 41 years. This band has become famous in the brass band community through tours in Great Britain, Europe, and North America. Colonel Bramwell Coles was overwhelmed by its standard when he visited the band in 1946. He immediately invited Tranås Band to tour England at Easter, 1947. That tour was a great success musically and spiritually. English bandsmen and other listeners were very much inspired by the band's performances. Erik Leidzén became very attached to this band, which performed Leidzén's music with special understanding and sentiment. Bandmaster Borg created a style of musical phrasing and sound that is still alive in the band under Borg's successors, Torbjörn Cratz and Stig Uhner.

Educational Programs and Impact Beyond the SA

A very important reason for the comparatively high level of SA bands in Sweden in the recent past and even in the present, must be explained as the result of a purposeful programme of leadership training. This part of the territorial music department's activity commenced under Captain Rune Fröden, head of department 1957–1964, with support and cooperation of other professional Salvationist musicians like Sture Petersson. Other partners in this effort have been the territorial youth department and the Dalarö Folk High school, with its staff of music teachers.[3] The National Summer Music School has also played a vital part in this education and inspiration of young musicians. The senior staff at the Summer School give confidence-building assignments and tasks to developing young corps music leaders (or potential

The Tranås Corps Band in the Regent Hall, London, Easter 1947.
Colonel Bramwell Coles, Captain Charles Skinner, Bandmaster H. Twitchin and Bandmaster A. W. Punchard attended the event.

leaders) and this has created a desire for giving and an interest in musical and spiritual leadership at the corps level.

The British-style brass band movement is not large in Sweden. However, there are quite a number of brass bands in different churches and a few in schools at various levels. One can assert that the brass bands of The Salvation Army have been the inspiration and model for these brass bands. In many cases it has been Salvation Army musicians who directly or indirectly started these brass bands. For example, **Solna Brass** from Stockholm was started by Per Ohlsson and Rune Frödén. **Limhamns Brass Band** from Malmö was founded by the brothers Åke Hanson and Bertil Hansson, both SA bandmasters.

I also have ample reason to state that several professional musicians in the orchestral world, as well as in military bands and brass ensembles, received their first tuition and love of music in a Salvation Army brass band. Fortunately, several of these still continue to give service to the SA as either band members or musical leaders in the ranks of the SA. Here we can mention members of the Royal Opera Orchestra Stockholm, Gävle Symphony Orchestra, and Malmö Symphony Orchestra, as well as the Royal Navy Band, with its Salvationist music director, Andreas Hanson. The John Bauer Brass Quintet includes three musicians who are also very

Captain Rune Frödén conducts a combined band at the annual National Congress in Stockholm, 1957.

active as bandsmen in the Jönköping Corps Band. Additionally, Alexander Hanson is the current music director of The Swedish Air Force Band.

Important events in Swedish SA bands: a selective list

1882   The SA commences its work in Sweden.

1883   The first 'brass band' is formed, as a sextet in Stockholm.

1888   Music Department established at NHQ, Stockholm led by Otto Lundahl; Swedish Staff Band formed in same year.

1889   Swedish Staff Band at International Congress, London (First trip abroad for a Swedish SA band).

1904   Klaus Östby becomes head of Music Department.

1906   First *Swedish Band Tune Book* published (420 tunes) and the band journal *Svensk Festmusik* begins publication; both in sextet scoring.

1910s First 78 rpm recordings by a Swedish SA band, Stockholm Temple, released.

1920   Chalk Farm Band tours Sweden for first time.

1920s *Svensk Festmusik* expands to eight parts, with additional optional parts.

1934   Erik Leidzén returns to Sweden for a short time, and helps several bands focus on improving overall musical quality.

1935   Kristian Fristrup becomes head of Music Department.

1942   First Territorial Bandmasters' Councils held.

1943   First Territorial Music Camp for junior bandsmen is held.

1946   Bramwell Coles visits Sweden and finds surprisingly high standard of banding, which leads to tours in England for the Tranås Band, 1947, and Stockholm 7 Band, 1949.

1952   SA begins its own record label in Sweden, *Festival*.

1957   Rune Frödén becomes head of Music Department.

1963   The band journal *Svenska Musikserien* begins publication; scored for nine essential parts, similar to *American Band Journal*.

1974   The music branch at the Dalarö Folk High School is opened by Torgny Hanson and special programs for education of leaders and instructors of beginner and junior bands started.

1984   Sture Petersson becomes the first non-officer head of Music Department.

1996   Release by SA Music Department of first in series of historical books, with accompanying compact disc recording, on SA music in Sweden, *Klaus Östby: Skandinavisk Musikpionjär* (by Sven Nilsson).

1999   Second historical study, with compact disc, published, a study of Otto Lundahl: *Krigstrumpetens klara tonor: Otto Lundahl och Fräsningsarméns stabsmusikkår* (by Lars-Erik Lingström).

2005   Release of a new band journal, *ScanBrass*, by the joint territories of Denmark, Finland, Norway and Sweden.

About the Author

Torgny Hanson (b. 1945) is a third-generation bandmaster in the SA. Brought up in Malmö and educated at the State College of Music there, he became as a teenager the cornet soloist and deputy bandmaster in the Malmö 1 Band. After further studies in London (1971) he became national band instructor for the SA in Sweden starting in 1974. That same year he started the music branch at Dalarö Folk High School and became bandmaster for the Södertälje Band, a position he held for twenty-one years. He has been guest conductor at several SA summer music schools in Europe and North America, including Star Lake Musicamp in 1994. In 1995 he was appointed bandmaster for the Stockholm 7 Band, now named Stockholm South Citadel Band.

Torgny Hanson's professional career also includes positions as teacher and senior lecturer at the Royal College of Music in Stockholm. He is often asked for as a lecturer about brass and wind bands, their repertoire, and how to conduct and develop these ensembles. He has been conductor of The Swedish Army Band as well as the professional wind orchestras Stockholm Symphonic Winds and the Östgota Symphonic Winds. As Principal Music Director of the Swedish Armed Forces Music Centre, and now Inspector of Music he has held, since 1992, the highest positions for military music in Sweden. From time to time he travels as a professional conductor in countries like Finland, Norway, Netherlands, Great Britain and the USA, while also serving as a brass band adjudicator, including twice at the European Brass Band Championships.

Torgny Hanson

Notes

1. The similarity between the Swedish and Norwegian 9-part band journals and that of the USA East ABJ may be in no small part due to the influence of Erik Leidzén in his contribution as first editor of the New York journal and his strong links to his homeland and its brass culture. The first brass instrument he played as a young bandsman in Copenhagen was a rotary-valve E Flat Flugelhorn that would have played the top voice in the *Svensk Festmusik*-style sextets. See the early chapters of Ronald Holz, *Erik Leidzén: Band Arranger and Composer* for more details of his early training and experience in SA brass bands in Scandinavia.

2. A joint Scandinavian Y.P. Music Camp in 1973 provided the impetus for the *Norsk Musikk-Serie, Junior*, published by the SA in Oslo, Norway, starting in that same year. It is scored for 7 or more players: 2 cornets, 2 horns, trombone, euphonium, bass (E Flat or B Flat), percussion, and with full score. At least 8 issues, with 4 items each, were printed between 1973 and 1980. Norway also launched their own 9-part adult series, starting in 1968, *Norsk Musikk-Serie*. Like the *Svenska Musikserien*, it is released on an irregular basis.

3. A Folk High School is a post-secondary educational institution that shares some characteristics of an American two-year junior college and a technical training centre. At the SA's high schools in Sweden (Dalarö) and Norway (Moss) many Salvationists have both studied and served on the faculty. For example, in the past both Eiliv Herikstad (Moss) and Torgny Hanson, Per Ohlsson and Andreas Hanson (Dalarö) have served as teachers.

Sources and literature used for this essay

Anefelt, Paul V., *Sång och klingsande spel*. FA Press Förlag. Stockholm, 1963.

Kjäll, Thorsten, *De följde en fana*. FA Press Förlag. Stockholm, 1957.

Kjäll, Thorsten, *Korsets färger bära*. FA Press Förlag. Stockholm, 1972.

Private archive of collected material in the possession of the author.

Of additional interest

Band Life of Tranås, 1962 (Holz collection). A 20-page booklet, in English, produced by this band and sent to 'Composers of Salvation Army Music'. It is a detailed account of all music played by the band,

and every activity for the year. Includes a full listing of music performed, both by band journal and by composer, with a code showing when each piece was played.

Nilsson, Sven, *Klaus Östby: Scandinavian Musical Pioneer* [Text in Swedish, English abstract included] SA Music Department, Stockholm, 1996. Includes a CD with performances of Östby's vocal and band music, both in historic recordings and current readings.

Kjellgren, Gustav, *Sound Out the Proclamation: A Study of the History of Salvation Army Music in Sweden,* 1882–1982 (Text is in Swedish, 1-page English abstract included). Thesis written for completion of Degree of licentiate of philosophy in Swedish, Department of Musicology, University of Goteborg, 1992.

Lingstrom, Lars-Erik, *Krigstrumpetens klara toner: Otto Lundahl och Frälsningsarméns stabsmusikkår* ('The War Trumpet's Clear Sound: Otto Lundahl and The Salvation Army Swedish Staff Band', Text in Swedish only) SA Music Department. Stockholm, 1999. Includes a CD with various performances, including 1914 recording of Swedish Staff Band.

Chapter 7

AUSTRALIA

John Cleary

1880–1920 The Wide Brown Land

'Glory Tom' Sutherland was the first Salvation Army Officer to set foot in Australia, and he brought with him a pocket cornet. The instrument intrigued 10-year-old William Gore, son of the family with whom Tom and Adelaide Sutherland stayed for their first few days ashore.

A few months earlier Williams' father, John Gore, together with Edward Saunders, had conducted the first Salvation Army meeting on the continent of Australia, at Adelaide in the colony of South Australia. Following that meeting in September 1880, Gore and Saunders wrote to William Booth requesting officers. On February 17, 1881, Captains Thomas and Adelaide Sutherland stepped onto the colonial quayside with 'Glory Tom' resplendent in red tunic, navy-blue trousers, and a spiked white helmet with brass chain under the chin.

The Colony of South Australia was one of seven independent colonies making up what was termed Australasia: the five mainland colonies; the island of Tasmania; and the North and South Islands of New Zealand.

Brass bands were already integral to the emerging international Salvation Army culture. Sutherland quickly established a band at the first corps in the colony – Adelaide 1 – giving lessons to Will Gore amongst other aspiring instrumentalists. He then encouraged Fred Fry, a member of the Army's founding brass combination in England, to come and take responsibility for musical development at Australia's number one corps.[1] Sutherland established four Corps around the city of Adelaide, and in December 1882 received orders to open fire in Sydney 1,400 km (850 miles) to the northeast in the colony of New South Wales.

It was a blast from Sutherland's cornet at Sydney's Paddy's Market, on Saturday night, December 2, 1882 that heralded

Captain Thomas 'Glory Tom' Sutherland
First Officer appointed to Australia. Founded first band at Adelaide 1
(Adelaide Congress Hall)

the official beginnings of the Army in New South Wales. Supported by flag, tambourine and drum, four Salvationists: Captains Tom and Adelaide Sutherland, Lieutenant Alex Canty, and Sister Mary Ann Cox, played and sang the Army into town.

In one of the earliest editions of the Sydney *War Cry* a note appeared: *Will any friend who owns brass instruments and is willing to donate them to help God's work, send them to Captain Sutherland, 284 Castelray [sic] Street, as he wants to form a band at once.*

The band, when it appeared, consisted of five players with Sutherland on first cornet. *The War Cry* described how, as he led his band through the streets, the Captain marched backwards in the approved Christian Mission style. Some months later *The Salvation War* of 1883 reported of Sydney I, (Sydney Congress Hall): *An efficient brass band has been established under Brother Lewis as Bandmaster.*

The Army opened its work in Sydney three weeks before its official beginnings in Melbourne, but it was Melbourne, capital of the Colony of Victoria, that was to be the National Headquarters until 1921.

Though Sydney was Australia's foundation settlement, 'Marvellous Melbourne' as the city was called in the 1880s was riding high on the fruits of the great gold rush and the land boom that followed. Melbourne was also a natural first stop for the sleek clipper ships, coming up from the southwest and the gales of the Roaring Forties, that had sped them round the world. It had a vast natural harbour and flat agricultural hinterland. It was the base of the continent's fertile southeast triangle, which stretched 731 km (450 miles) to Adelaide in the west and, through Sydney, some 2000 km (1250 miles) north to Brisbane.

Tom Sutherland's order to move north had come from Major James Barker. In the wake of the Sutherland's success in South Australia, William Booth commissioned Barker to take command of *all the colonies of the Southern Seas.* His mandate included the six Australian colonies and New Zealand. His new bride Alice, who was later to leave her own mark on Salvation Army history, accompanied him.

James Barker arrived in Melbourne on September 21, 1882. He shortly proceeded to Adelaide for consultations with Sutherland and despatched him to open the work in New South Wales. Following Barker's return to Melbourne the No.1 Victorian corps, Hotham in North Melbourne, opened fire on Christmas Eve 1882. The meetings were distinguished by the ability of the officer Harry Edwards to deal with the push of roughs attempting to disrupt proceedings. He was immediately tagged 'Ironsides'.

In March 1883, Lieutenants Pollard and Wright, sailing from England by way of Melbourne, crossed the Tasman Sea to commence operations in Dunedin, New Zealand on April 1, 1883. Later they were joined by others including Harry 'Ironsides' Edwards, who started a band at Christchurch. In

November 1883, a party from Melbourne crossed Bass Strait to Tasmania, where operations commenced in the north coast city of Launceston and then moved on to the colony capital of Hobart. A party began work in the Queensland capital Brisbane in July 1885, and by early 1886 there were four thriving corps, Brisbane 1 & 2, Ipswich and Maryborough. Perth, the capital of Western Australia was 3512km (2200 miles) from Melbourne Headquarters, across a desert wilderness. It had to wait until December 1891, when William Booth, at the end of his Australasian tour, commissioned the first official party.

If distance and drought were the harsh characteristics of the Australian outback, affluence alongside squalor marked the character of its five capital cities perched around the coastal fringe of this driest of continents. Yet, Australia proved fertile soil for The Salvation Army.

Foundations

Founded as a convict colony in 1788, the Australian accent speaks of the origins of much of the colony's early population in the poor East End of London. The gold rush period of the 1860's brought new waves of immigrant 'diggers' who readily absorbed this Cockney working-class style. Australians were not overly religious and popular culture exhibited an explicit suspicion of institutional religion.

The culture was also somewhat chauvinist. Non Anglo-Celts were looked on with suspicion. Irish Catholics tended to be confined to the industrial ghettos. The Chinese who came with the gold rush were soon categorised as 'the Yellow Peril'. The native aboriginal population was treated with pity mixed with contempt for 'a dying breed'. This cultural chauvinism culminated at the turn of the century with the infamous Immigration Restriction Act or 'White Australia' policy. Agreement on this was one of the few things which united classes and interest groups in the debates leading up to the federation of the six Australian mainland colonies into the Commonwealth of Australia in January 1901. On leaving Australia at the end of his 1891 visit William Booth in frustration remarked, *As soon as a man lands on these shores he sticks up a placard and shouts, 'Australia for the Australians'.*[2]

The positive side of this culture was its aggressive egalitarianism, and sceptical attitude towards authority. These sentiments are clearly evident in the words of what became the unofficial national song, *Waltzing Matilda*, a song celebrating the defiant suicide of a 'swagman' (itinerant worker) in the face of rich landowners and police.

By the 1880s, reform was in the air. South Australia was pioneering political rights for women. In Queensland, rural workers were agitating to form a Labour Party. Workers in Victoria began the Eight Hours Movement for reform of working hours. In addition, the colonies were beginning to feel enough common identity to talk of eventually becoming one country.

William Booth, when writing, *In Darkest England and the Way Out* noted, *As Victoria is probably the most democratic of our colonies, and the one in which the working-class has supreme control, the extent to which it has by its government recognised the value of our operations is sufficient to indicate that we have nothing to fear from the opposition of democracy.*

The sentiments expressed by Booth against laissez-faire economics in *Darkest England* would have been welcomed in Victoria, the home of the economic protectionist parties.[3]

James Barker landed in a country ripe for invasion and his troops were ideally equipped. The Army offered a workingman's religion for a worker's country. They spoke the same language as the urban poor, and their colourful street parades matched the rising spirit of nationalism and confidence.

However, it was the practical compassion of the Salvationists that soon won over the sceptical locals. At the same time Salvationists were being arrested, charged and detained around the country, the Victorian Government voted James Barker an annual endowment to the funds of the SA.[4]

Persecution in some quarters was strong. Barker himself faced imprisonment more than once. From 1881 to 1907, more than a hundred Salvationists were fined or gaoled for holding street meetings or marches. There were at least two Salvationist deaths. But condemnation by local authorities, civil or religious, of the Army's irregular methods, simply served to further enhance its stature with the poor. A sentiment the *War Cry* of 1884 was very happy to exploit:

They say, 'That drum you must not beat,
That cornet must not blow;
Although we ring our lovely bells,
We're respectable you know.
The Army's only working men,
And therefore must not play;
It's an awful desecration
of the blessed Sabbath day.'

By June 1883, Barker was ready to open an Australasian headquarters at North Melbourne. A band was required, and for some weeks Staff Officer Jeremiah Eunson worked hard with a number of local soldiers centred on the Prahran corps.

Jeremiah Eunson
Full time Bandmaster

At the grand opening ceremony on June 12, all was ready to proceed when it was noticed that Eunson's band had disappeared. Their nerves had given way. They fled the field leaving only the disconsolate bandmaster. Hardly an auspicious beginning for the father of SA music in Australia.

For several months, Staff Officer Eunson had carried the official designation Bandmaster. As new corps opened, he moved around establishing bands and training players. His failure at the opening of Headquarters evidently proved salutary, for six months later he and his players were ready for another grand occasion.

On New Year's Day 1884, to celebrate one year of Salvation Army operations in Victoria, James Barker staged a rally, attended by over ten thousand people, in the Melbourne Exhibition Building, the largest auditorium in Australasia. It was a remarkable testament to Barker's methods, and a cause of some satisfaction for Eunson who presided over a band of more than forty players. Nerves were not evident.[5]

Jeremiah Eunson (1835-1919) had joined the SA in England. He was a contemporary of the Fry family, and played cornet in many of the Founder's early meetings. Now in his late forties Eunson found the headquarters appointment as a peripatetic band trainer more than fulfilling. The Army spread rapidly through the larger cities of Australia. One inner Melbourne suburb boasted three corps within its boundaries and most corps had musical aspirations.

The Australian Band Journal

In February 1885, only four years after the establishment of the first band at Adelaide 1, came the announcement of the first issue of the *Australian Band Journal* (AuBJ). Initially compiled and edited by Jeremiah Eunson, eight bound sets of the *AuBJ* would appear, under various editors, until replaced by the English Band Journal (*General Series*, GS) in 1913.

Two principal reasons were advanced for the publication of the *Australian Band Journal*. The first was simply a case of immediate need. Music ordered from England could take six months or more, depending on the vagaries of the shipping lines. More telling perhaps, was the complaint that English music was pitched 'outrageously high' for local congregations. They demanded a more suitable key. Eunson pitched his journal in a lower register than its English counterpart.[6]

Eunson wrote his original parts in green ink, suitable for reproduction on a primitive duplicator or 'Hectograph'. He worked in an upstairs room of an annexe next to the Melbourne Headquarters. It is said that as he wrote he hummed and at intervals he would *take up his cornet and play the arrangements, a few bars at a time. As he did so he tapped with his foot, beating time, much to the amusement of those working below.*[7]

The first issue of the *AuBJ* consisted of simple hymn tunes arranged for 10 instruments. The journal was issued monthly at one shilling per issue, or as time went on, in bound books at two shillings and sixpence each instrumental part. The first of these bound books contained numbers 1–48. Covered in black synthetic 'American leather', they quickly became known as 'The Black Books'. According to Colonel Percival Dale who first played from the books in 1912, *The most popular tune in these first sheets…was undoubtedly No. 9,* 'We'll Fight Till Jesus Comes', *which featured a second time repeat of the chorus as a bass solo, to which the cornet provided a vigorous trumpeting accompaniment.*[8] The music was simple and repetitive enough to be played by those still grappling with the complexities of brass, yet of sufficient colour to appeal. It worked well for both singing and marching.

The second bound set (49–96), introduced the words of choruses from number 78 onwards. A little later *Song Book* numbers were shown below the tune numbers. There was as yet no metrical classification, though appropriate tunes were designated, e.g. *Any L.M.* (any long metre). With the third and then the fourth set in 1890, technical standards began to improve. A calligrapher was employed. Eunson was editorially assisted by Bandmaster Hellings of Collingwood, and by a cadet from the Training Garrison, William Gore, the young man who had been so keen to learn the cornet from Tom Sutherland in 1881.[9]

On the Road - the Guards Band

1890 was an eventful year for SA music in Australia. There were now 255 corps and 419 outposts scattered around the rim of the continent. Some of these could be out of contact with headquarters for weeks at a time, and many of the soldiers knew little of the SA beyond their local district. In November 1889, the Training Garrison sent out their male cadets as two brass bands, campaigning for some weeks on foot through the Victorian countryside. Called 'The Royal Guards 1 & 2,' they tramped from town to town during the day, and found what accommodation they could at night. One member recalled marching out of a town at 10pm, camping in the fields at 1am, waking at 7am covered in frost, ready to march quietly into the next town, having covered some 23 miles. The campaigns were deemed an outstanding success.

On January 25th 1890, Commissioner Thomas Coombs announced the formation of a new travelling band, the 'Australian Guards Band'. Applicants were to be single young men who would be prepared to come *without receiving any salary (food and clothing, of course, being supplied).*[10] Recruits were encouraged from all colonies including New Zealand. By May 1890, the Australian Guards No.1 Band was marching the highways under Bandmaster Willie Norman. The Guards' uniform included waterproof cape-coats rolled military style to fit the straps provided on their haversacks. Their arms were free to carry their silver instruments and play as they marched.

At about the same time Australasian Headquarters began to rationalise the number of bands that had sprung up at the different colonial headquarters. Variously titled Staff and Headquarters bands, these existed for varying lengths of time in each colony. Eunson was commissioned to form an Australasian Headquarters Staff Band, later to become the Melbourne Staff Band. This small group of twelve had among its members Robert Sandall, future author of the first volumes of *The Official History of The Salvation Army*. Another who joined in those first few years was a future General, George L. Carpenter.

On June 7th 1890 the *War Cry* announced the formation of a second Australian Guards Band, under the control of Bandmaster Eunson, assisted by Lieutenant Will Gore. It took some time to gather enough recruits for this second Guards band and there may have been some rethinking of its structure. Almost a year after the first call a notice appeared in the *War Cry* calling for applicants for a Guards band who could ride, stating that *officers need not apply*. Lily Sampson in her book *Grassroots Army* records Commissioner Coombs speaking with Lieutenant John Sampson some months after the call for the No. 2 band appeared. Coombs asked Sampson to forgo his officer rank and salary, and travel with the band as long as it was needed. He told the Lieutenant that in

Jeremiah Eunson
The father of Salvation
Army Music in Australia

addition to its primary soul-winning purposes, the Army needed the band to raise money for property commitments at Headquarters and the Training Garrison.[11]

Whatever the difficulties, and minus the cavalry, the Australian Guards Band No. 2 was ready for action in August 1891. Jeremiah Eunson conducted the band for the first few weeks then handed it over to Will Gore. Both Australian Guards bands were on duty for the Founder's 1891 visit to Melbourne. From September to December Gore and the No. 2 Band accompanied the General around the country. Eunson returned to his responsibilities as Staff Bandmaster and head of the Music Department. Gore continued with the No. 2 Band, as both conductor and cornet soloist, for the next two and a half years, covering over 16,500 miles and registering some 1,400 converts. The No. 1 Band, travelling in different parts of the country, followed a similar pattern.[12]

William Gore

William H. Gore (1871–1927) was something of a prodigy. After his few lessons with 'Glory Tom' Sutherland in 1881, the 10-year-old became a member of the Adelaide 1 band. In 1883, he accompanied his newly commissioned officer parents as they opened corps across the South Australian bush. At Port

Pirie, aged 14, he established his first band, followed by another at Port Augusta. Back in Adelaide he helped start the band at Norwood. Gore now faced a challenge. It seems that until around 1886, it was possible for the 'unconverted' to be members of SA Bands in Australia. In Gore's words:

> *Up to this time I was unsaved, and a special order had been issued that prohibited playing by unsaved musicians in our bands, I was made the subject of some very earnest special prayer by the Officers at Headquarters. This was unknown for myself, but their effectual fervent prayers resulted in my conversion, and I was straight away put into harness at the South Australian Headquarters.*[13]

Upon his 'conversion', aged 16, Will Gore was asked to start a Staff Band at South Australian Colonial Headquarters. Among its members was William Peart, a future Chief Secretary to Evangeline Booth. During this period he was also bandmaster at Adelaide I. He developed a reputation as an instrumentalist and soloist. He was often called on to give 'one man concerts', and when conducting was known to pick up his cornet and play the solo part of any instrument that was missing. In 1888 he moved to Sydney where, like Eunson, he

William H. Gore (1871-1927)

William Gore, First manuscript tune book. Title page

William Gore Tune Book, First Cornet. Page One

took responsibility for teaching several suburban corps bands. In 1890 Will Gore was accepted into the Melbourne Training Garrison and into the Music Editorial Department under Jeremiah Eunson.

Will Gore's travels with the Australian Guards ended with the appointment of Captain Ebenezer 'Eb' Jackson from New Zealand in August 1893. Under Jackson's leadership the two Guards bands were merged. They continued to tour as a single unit of around twenty players for the next three years. Campaigning in the bush town of Wallaroo, Jackson was sentenced to 21 days for obstruction, but after only a few days the sentencing justice paid the fine himself. Jackson was released *very little the worse for wear save for a few blisters on his hands from unaccustomed toil.*[14]

In 1896 Eb Jackson succeeded Jeremiah Eunson as Staff Bandmaster and Head of the Music Department. The Australian Guards were retired. Will Gore married in 1895 and was transferred to the field. Jackson's leader in his new appointment was to be Commandant Herbert Booth, just arrived from Canada. Under Booth's dynamic leadership music became increasingly important. Spectacles were the order of the day. Fortunately Jackson had a reputation as an arranger for both vocal and brass.

The *AuBJ* continued to improve. Metal type had been introduced in 1893. Under Jackson between 1896 and 1903, twenty-seven issues (169–196) were published. A brief prepared for the Commandant listed the number of bandsmen in Australasia in 1896 as 2,049. Herbert Booth's arrival in Australia coincided with the fervent debates over Federation. Victoria was solidly in favour of colonial federation into one nation, but in some colonies sentiment against the idea ran high. No shrinking violet when it came to issues of great import, Herbert ensured the Army crest prominently displayed the motto *Advance Australasia*. And just in case the point needed reinforcement, he commissioned a new travelling band, 'The Federals'.

Adjutant George Cater (d.1928) was transferred from New Zealand to become Bandmaster. Commandant Herbert Booth commissioned the Federal Band and the Headquarters Cycle Brigade on Tuesday 2nd November 1897. The increasingly popular 'slouch' hat topped the Federals' blue serge and red trim uniforms. Cycling was still something of a risk in the ranks of the redeemed. Some feared the cyclists' wanderlust might promote other lusts. When the MSB cycled to one corps for a Sunday's meetings the congregation boycotted the Holiness meeting in protest.[15]

As the turn of the century approached and excitement for both the centenary and the coming Federation of the Australian colonies intensified 'The Federal Choralists', a mixed group of men and women, officers, cadets and bandsmen under Brigadier E. Holdaway, toured in several colonies. The role of both Federal units ended with the coming of the new nation.

On January 1st 1901 Herbert Booth took an honoured place in an open carriage, as part of the Grand Parade through the streets of Sydney to the ceremonies marking the Federation of Commonwealth of Australia. Seated beside him was the man who 20 years before had conducted the very first meeting in Adelaide, Will Gore's father, John. The Official Photographers commissioned by the Colony of New South Wales captured the events by means of the recently invented cinematograph. The cinematographers were all Salvationists, members of one of Herbert Booth's most remarkable travelling combinations – The Limelight Brigade or Biorama Company.

Bandsman Stanley Perry on tour in New Zealand (1907) with the Silver Biorama Band of the Limelight Department, led by his father Joseph Perry.
(Note the cap band, 'The Salvation Army' replaced by Biorama)

The Biorama Bands

The Limelight Department had its beginnings in 1891 when Captain Joseph Perry was commissioned to promote the visit of William Booth. Joe Perry had been converted as a result of Pollard's opening New Zealand campaign at Dunedin in 1883. He had built up some skill with the Magic Lantern and following the General's visit was kept in Melbourne to establish a lantern unit.

Herbert Booth's arrival in 1896 coincided with the invention of the 'cinematograph' or motion picture camera. Booth and Perry were soon cooperating on ever more adventurous displays. These developed into touring illustrated lectures with musical accompaniment. Limelight bands and orchestras doubled as the support crew for the film equipment. Applicants for these combinations needed skills as instrumentalists, vocalists, electricians, mechanics and 'bioscopists'.

In September 1900 at the Melbourne Town Hall the SA premiered *Soldiers of the Cross*, long considered one of the world's most important early film presentations. It lasted almost three hours and featured a choral and orchestral accompaniment. Four months later, limelighter, and future Army historian, Captain Robert Sandall was cranking the handle of the cinematograph that recorded the signing into birth of the Australian nation. For a further eight years Perry's Limelighters continued to enthral audiences in halls around the country.

Their 1907 tour of New Zealand featured the 'Silver Biorama' band of twenty-four multi-skilled musicians. Their cap bands replaced the words 'Salvation Army' with the word 'Biorama.'

In 1908 Biorama Bandmaster Captain Robert McAnally, was commissioned to write a score for a new film feature *Heroes of the Cross*. That score survives today in the National Library of Australia as one of the world's earliest original film scores.

In addition to film, the Limelight Department also possessed early recording equipment. During the years to 1899 the department is said to have made over two hundred and fifty phonograph recordings. The musical life of the Army owes another debt to the Limelighters. When Herbert Booth

resigned from the SA in 1902, in exchange for the rights to the film feature *Soldiers of the Cross*, he granted the Army copyright to all his songs and musical compositions, a legacy that continues to enrich the movement.

A New Nation

The effect of the early Army's comprehensive engagement with the life of the nation did not just show in the recognition of Herbert Booth at the Federation celebrations. In 1901 the first National Census recorded 0.82% of the population as Salvationist, a figure that has never been equalled.[16]

Following Federation and the departure of Herbert Booth in 1902 there was no slackening of pace. Commissioner Thomas McKie was as much the showman as his predecessor. To encourage and develop banding, a monthly newspaper *The Local Officer* began in 1902, followed in 1910 by *The Local Officer and Bandsman* [*LOB*], renamed *The Musician* in September 1947. In February 1903, the *War Cry* called for 50 bandsmen to form two brass bands to travel the Commonwealth and New Zealand. Applicants had to be prepared to be away for up to two years. A weekly allowance, with food and clothing would be provided. Former Federal Guards Bandmaster Adjutant George Cater would train both bands. They were to be called 'The Austral Guards'.

Later in the year Cater succeeded Eb Jackson as Head of the Music Department, with responsibility for the

TOP RIGHT:
The oldest known photograph of the 'headquarters brass band' (1896).
Notice: Back row 3rd from right Ensign Robert Sandall, later author of the Official History of The Salvation Army, 4th from right (with trombone) Ensign, later General George Carpenter; Front row far left Captain Eb. Jackson (bandmaster)

Headquarters Staff Band. The Staff Band through these years functioned very much as a support band for headquarters functions and some corps visits. Major occasions tended to feature one or more of the travelling combinations. Cater published numbers 197–210 of the *AuBJ*, and included some radical innovations. He began to publish material that was not Salvationist in origin, nor did it have any Salvation Army associations. He was apparently responding to the desire of

*Austral Guards Band
Robert McAnally,
Bandmaster*

more accomplished combinations for more challenging and complex music, which was beyond the capacity of the department to produce.

By August 1903, Cater was rehearsing the Austral Guards in Melbourne in preparation for their commissioning in Sydney at a Town Hall ceremony on August 31st. Their uniforms were the newly fashionable khaki with chocolate coloured trim.[17] The Austral Guards No.1 Band campaigned in Tasmania, South Australia, and Western Australia under the direction of Captain Robert H. McAnally (later of the Limelight Department). The Austral Guards No. 2 toured Queensland, New South Wales, parts of Victoria, and then proceeded on to New Zealand. The bandmaster for the mainland part of the tour was Harry Berryman, and in late 1904, Will Gore was transferred from his field appointment at Richmond 1, to lead the band during its six-month stay in New Zealand.

Upon his return, Gore was promoted to Major and appointed Head of the Music Department with responsibilities for the newly named National Staff Band, and the editorship of the *AuBJ*. It was to be his most creative period. That year his march *Victoria* won first prize in the International Composition Competition promoted by the Chief of the Staff. It appeared in the *AuBJ* under this title as number 215. In the English GS, it was published as *The Melbourne March*, GS 505 (See Chapter 3).

From 1905 to 1913 Will Gore published 134 numbers of the *AuBJ*. These were bound into three 'black book' sets, 217–256, 157–296 and 297–311. For part of this period Gore was assisted by Captain Robert McAnally who won First Prize in the International Competition of 1907 for a march published in the *GS* as *The Australasian*, GS 533.[18] Much of the music in these final eight years was written by Gore himself, bringing his personal output to more than 200 works.[19] With pieces such as *Hobson's Bay, Euphonia,* and *Sonorita,* Gore was credited with raising the level of harmonic complexity and introducing thematic development into his work. For special occasions such as the visit of the Great White Fleet of the U. S. Navy in 1908 Gore issued special arrangements of *Australian Melodies, American Melodies* and *New Zealand Melodies.*

During this final period of the *AuBJ* a number of young composers were published who would later take a major part in shaping the musical life of the Army. Most notable of these was bandsman Harold Scotney of New Zealand. His works include *Ruahine, Westeria,* and *Dannervirke.* The final issue of the *AuBJ* in 1913 featured an Australian Prize march, *Bendigo* by Adjutant Penberthy. What was lost by way of national music development with the closure of the *AuBJ* cannot be known. It is notable, however, that during this final period the *AuBJ* was producing international prize winning material from local talent.

Women's Bands

Whilst the practice of banding throughout the pioneering era was overwhelmingly male there were significant attempts to give effect to the Army's policy of full equality for women. As early as 1884 there is reference to an attempt to start a women's band in Launceston, Tasmania.

By 1889, New Zealand had had several women's bands in action. In 1888 there is again reference to a Lasses' band in Tasmania. By the early 1890s, women's bands were a regular part of corps life at North Fitzroy, North Melbourne and Brunswick in Victoria. In September 1895, these combined into a Melbourne Divisional Women's Band led by Brigadier Isaac Unsworth and conducted by the versatile Ensign Robert Sandall.

Captain Ruby Baker, Bandmistress of the Austral Lasses' Band.

In August 1895 Thomas Coombs called for applications for a Territorial Lasses' Band and the following month the *War Cry* reported that a number of applications had been received from New Zealand. The effort seems to have failed, as did another call issued by Herbert Booth in July 1897. It was not until August 1905 that Territorial ambitions were fulfilled when Thomas McKie commissioned the Austral Lasses' Band. The *War Cry* reported their uniform as: *neatly fitting speaker jackets, which hook face to face–military fashion–adorned with silver Ss, and four sets of two-yellow-braided fern leaves.* The fern was symbolic perhaps of the New Zealand women of 1889, or of the band's major destination. After touring five Australian states the 21 strong band moved on to New Zealand for some weeks. They travelled over 26,000km (16,000 miles) and played to crowds estimated at 60,000. The

conductor (bandmistress) was Captain Ruby Baker and her deputy Annie Oakes.

Annie Oakes was so keen to become a brass player she entered the Training Garrison in order to join the lasses' bands proposed for the mid-1890's. Perhaps her keenness counted when she was made deputy-bandmistress for the two-year existence of the Austral Lasses' band. At the disbanding of the Australs she returned home and within four weeks had charge of the Corps Band at Maryborough in Queensland. In 1910 a short article about 'Bandmistress Bainbridge' (*née* Oakes) the *LOB* remarked that for a woman to be *Bandmistress of such an important corps as Maryborough Queensland, is a position somewhat unique.*[20]

The Australs were the last of the travelling bands, but their influence and the spirit of their time was long remembered. Along with their evangelical and fund raising activities, they provided Salvationist musicians across the nation with something to aspire to. They overcame the isolation of the outback, and in doing so their playing, their dress and their commitment provided a role model for large and small groups across the continent. The demise of the travelling bands and the replacement of the *AuBJ* by the *General Series* in 1913 marked the end of the pioneering period of The Salvation Army in Australia. The death of William Booth in 1912 signalled the passing most clearly. In 1912 New Zealand became a separate Territory.

Consolidation

Just as the Australian people were growing away from the youthful self-confidence of the federation years and looking cautiously at events in Europe, so Salvationists in Australia became more conscious of their place in the international movement. Commissioner James Hay succeeded Thomas McKie in 1909. He was in his mid-forties and to that time the oldest commander appointed to Australasia. From young manhood he held tough administrative positions close to both William and Bramwell Booth. During his 12 years in Australia he would earn the title 'Bricks and Mortar' for his remarkable ability to build and consolidate.

The Thirtieth Anniversary celebrations held in 1911 featured a 'Bandsman's Week'. Four music festivals were held in Melbourne, and repeated again the following year. Corps bands were beginning to emerge from the shadow of the touring bands as strong combinations keen to tackle any musical challenge available. The Anniversary festivals even began to take on some of the characteristics of band contests. The structure and emphasis of these events leant more towards consolidation than to outreach. Full Programmes for each festival, held in different Town Halls around the city of Melbourne, were published in the *LOB*.[21] Each item that every band played was dissected: 400 words on the National Staff Band's playing of Gore's, *American Melodies* (AuBJ 270); 250 words on Hawthorn's performance of, *A Pleading Sinner* (GS 645). And so it went, column by column – Collingwood, Prahran, Williamstown, Footscray, Richmond – all got similar treatment. About this time *The Herald* newspaper of Melbourne said of the Staff Band that it had *attained a standard of musical excellence which compares favourably with the finest contesting combinations*.[22] Instrumentation had almost settled down. Whilst many bands carried clarinets and saxophones, the use of strings, from violins to guitars and even auto-harps, had largely ceased.

With longevity came some maturity. Adelaide 1, in 1911, became Adelaide Congress Hall, a well ordered combination of 26, under Bandmaster Jack Turner. Turner was converted as a boy of 12 at Semaphore. Handed a drum and given responsibility for music, he took his first cornet lessons from Captain Susie West. A few years later he helped form the band at Port Adelaide, and then moved on to Adelaide City. In 1902, Turner succeeded 'Teddy' Williams as bandmaster and by 1912, he had taken a band of 8 to 30. He considered the band's message in the meeting akin to the sermon. He went on to become Divisional Bandmaster and one of the most loved Salvationists of the era. Turner remained bandmaster for

Bandmaster Jack Turner, Adelaide I.

forty-three years. In 1945 he received the Order of the Founder (OF).

Operations in Perth had commenced 10 years later than Adelaide, but by 1913, there was a band of 30 at Perth City. The father of the band was Envoy Palmer who began his association with the corps in 1892. Palmer's son Bob was bandmaster for 12 years around the turn of the century, cementing an association between the band and the name Palmer that was to remain strong for over a hundred years. Perth City also boasted a boys' band of 21. The group included a very young future Commissioner, Hubert Scotney.

Prominent in accounts of this period from Brisbane, the most distant capital from Perth, is a description of the band which credits Band Instructor Baxter and Bandmaster Berghofer with *the present state of efficiency*, including new uniforms and instruments for the 20-strong combination.

The Sydney City Band was *in the front rank of Australasian bands*. With more than 30 members, it could boast soloists in every section. From the days when choice of uniform was left to personal preference, the band of 1912 was a sharp and disciplined combination under Bandmaster Sam Winley. He had been with the band for almost 25 years and bandmaster since 1904. Winley eventually became Divisional Bandmaster and retired in 1925 after 22 years leading the Sydney band.

Inner-urban corps were flourishing. Waterloo in Sydney had strong musical combinations right through the 1890's. One of the 20 young men in an 1899 photograph of the Waterloo band is the cornet player and future Guards bandmaster Robert McAnally. Petersham, growing rapidly in the suburbs could, by 1910 boast a band of 30 and a saxophone quartet. Regional centres were also thriving. In the growing industrial city of Newcastle, four women were prominent in the 1910 band of 20 players. Out on the edge of the desert, in far western New South Wales, the great mining town of Broken Hill boasted a band of 33 under Bandmaster Dixon. Their 1913 uniforms featured the latest *"new mens' summer hats,"* the military style 'slouch' hat.

World War I

The declaration of war in Europe had a profound effect on Australia. Hearts turned to 'the Mother country', and Imperial

*The Federal Guards Band
Note the 'slouch' hats.*

patriotism displaced Australian nationalism. Whilst Australia maintained a volunteer army, calls to king and country were strong, and following the great sacrifice made by the combined Australian and New Zealand forces in the Gallipoli campaign the call to arms affected almost every aspect of life. One old Royal Guards bandsman, William Mackenzie, became a national celebrity, as 'Fighting Mac', awarded the M.C. (Military Cross) for his frontline activities as a chaplain on the cliffs of Gallipoli and in France.

At Perth City, the boys of the 1913 Young People's Band moved into the chairs of senior bandsmen as over 20 of the members of the corps band of 1914 enrolled for military service. Throughout the war, corps musical activity remained strong, though Australian conditions did lead to the appearance of some unique individual characters. Among the most memorable was Adjutant Tom 'Mudgee' Robertson (188?–1927). Mudgee was a 'trophy of grace' and a musical freak. He possessed a range of five-and-a-half octaves encompassing six Cs. Mudgee claimed mastery from two octaves below middle C through three octaves above and was quite prepared to demonstrate it.

At an Adelaide Musical Festival, Mudgee delivered a slow melody to great effect:

The Adjutant played his solo in B flat, commencing on top F, and played through without a slip at this extreme ear-testing height. As he approached high F some folk seemed to be holding their breath as if to assist the soloist on the triplet run upwards, and all were astonished to hear him safely get the note and hold as a pause. This served only to increase the tension or suspense, for he proceeded to the A above that note, and finished at the B flat octave above.[23]

Just as memorable was his laconic bushman's approach to evangelism. Mudgee would trudge into town, play a 'Musical Blizzard' and then hold a meeting in the bar of the local pub. He confessed to one fall from grace. He took a dare to drink a cornet full of beer. *Done*, said Mudgee, and did it. He was suitably repentant. He never married and often, alone on the road, Mudgee would hitch a lift on a passing wagon and engage the driver in conversation about his cornet and the driver's soul.

The SA emerged from the war period a more disciplined and structured organisation. Standards were different. Many Salvationists served as musicians and some became military bandmasters. The world was a smaller place. Salvationists from West End in Brisbane had walked down the Strand and Piccadilly. They had seen the Army round the world, and they had experienced the military. Uniform wearing was a serious business. And so was war. Many halls in Australia still carry memorials to soldiers lost half a world away. One can sense something of the change in the photographs taken of bands through the late teens. Collars are fastened rather than undone; the rows are straighter and instruments better aligned. Something too of the old flamboyance began to go. Bandmasters that led from the front, playing as they marched, quietly slipped from the scene. Tightness and precision became the standard.

Salvationists were looking toward London. The more centralised structures fitted the temper of the times. The English *GS* and start of the *Triumph Series* in 1921 and *Festival Series* in 1923 suited the aspirations of developing bands; not only was the music more diverse and challenging, it was a tangible part of an international fellowship. However, it may be argued that in a way barely apprehended at the time, a profound shift was taking place in the Army's character, one reflected most clearly in its musical life. Army music, outward looking with roots firmly in popular culture, was becoming more self-confident, but also more self-contained and inward in character. Contact with the music of the streets faded, new idioms such as Jazz and the popular songs of 'Tin Pan Alley,' were considered worldly. A distinct genre of 'Army' music was emerging.

By the end of the war Corps in the major capital cities were growing quickly as manufacturing industries grew to meet growing population, and suburban centres spread. Dulwich Hill Citadel Band endured a number of ups and downs in the first part of the war, but by 1917, with the appointment of Harry Berry, a cornet soloist from Sydney Congress Hall (formerly Sydney City) as bandmaster, the band had grown from 12 to 40 players. It had traded its brass instruments for a 'Class A' silver-plated set, and the percussionists boasted Tympani. At Unley in South Australia, families such as Baldock and Camm were into their second generation of local leadership, encouraging a growing sense of tradition. In suburban Melbourne the old No. 2 Corps, Collingwood was bursting at the seams. It was for some years the largest corps in Australia. Many young bandsman trained under leaders like Bandmaster Charles Sharp, moved on to positions of musical leadership around the country.

1920 - 1960 Building the Temple

In 1919 Jubilee Congresses were held in Sydney and Adelaide, presided over by the Chief of the Staff, T. Henry Howard, who had succeeded James Barker as Territorial Commander in the 1880's. From Newtown in Sydney, to rural Inverell and coal mining towns like Lithgow, Army corps and their bands were flourishing. In that year the number of bandsmen in Australia was given as 1,075, though this cannot be accurately compared with the higher figure of the 1890s before the creation of a separate New Zealand Territory.

In 1919 also, Jeremiah Eunson, the father of Army music in Australia, was promoted to Glory from Brunswick, home to one of the bands he had established almost forty years before. The bandmaster then at Brunswick was a type that set the pattern for Army bandmasters in the years to come. Joe Rundle was the son of pioneer officer parents. One brother, William, was an Austral Guardsman then bandmaster at North Melbourne, Footscray and Moonee Ponds. His other brother Herb was a member of the Staff Band. Joe saw himself as responsible for more than music. He had taken on the band in 1913 and would eventually retire in 1946. Throughout those years he would stand aside and appoint as 'Conductor' anyone he considered more suited to the role than he. Men like George Dickens, Sid Rackham, and Arthur Gullidge developed their leadership abilities under his guidance.

Brigadier William Rook, bandmaster of the MSB for 15 years, was another in this mould. A Guards bandsman for six years, he became Staff bandmaster in 1914 after 16 years as deputy and retired in 1929. A competent arranger, though not eager to seek publication, his many arrangements for male voices can still be found in the possession of the Melbourne Staff Band. During his term he handed the conducting role to Robert McAnally, Herbert Dutton and George Dickens.

Herbert Dutton (d. 1966) first joined the Staff Band in 1913, and served 4½ years in a military band during World War I. He was cornet soloist for 16 years and conductor of the Staff Band for several periods during the 1920s. At one time Dutton and Joe Rundle cooperated on a novel venture. In January 1927, fifty prisoners at the Pentridge Gaol were sworn in as soldiers and the Pentridge Corps inaugurated. Dutton and Rundle took responsibility to train and conduct a singular SA band – The Pentridge Gaol Corps Band. After leaving the Staff Band Dutton moved to New Zealand where he became bandmaster at Wellington City and then at Petone.

Robert H. McAnally

It was under the baton of Robert McAnally that the MSB reached its post-war peak. McAnally was a product of Leichardt in inner Sydney. In the late 1890s, he was playing cornet at Waterloo. In 1903, he became an officer serving at various times with the Music department, the Guards, and Biorama bands. MacAnally is remembered as a somewhat flamboyant conductor who in the old style would put down his baton, pick up his cornet and play the cadenzas in his own compositions. William Rook gave McAnally control of the Staff

Band as deputy bandmaster in 1920. He was again in control in 1922 and 1923 as conductor. Already famed as an arranger from his days with the Guards and Limelighters, in 1920 McAnally revived the *Australian Band Journal* to distribute

Robert H. McAnally with the Austral Guards. Guards Bandmaster, Biorama Bandmaster, Staff Band Conductor, Composer.

three of his own compositions. They were published as numbers 312, *The Jubilee No. 1*, 313, *The Jubilee No. 2*, and 314, *Victory with Honour*. He wrote a series of 12 unpublished selections, six of these were arrangements of *Gems from the Great Masters*, which were at first only available to the Staff Band. These pieces anticipated the type of music soon to be available in the *Festival Series*. McAnally eventually resigned his officership and returned to Sydney where for many years he was engaged in the commercial music scene.

George Dickens (d. 1964) was the son of officer parents. He joined the Staff Band in 1918 after serving as conductor at Collingwood and at Brunswick. Dickens is best known to Army bandsmen for his marches, *Collingwood* (GS 918), *Beaumont* (GS 1001), *Herald of Praise* (GS 959), *Service Triumphant* (GS 1297), and *Shout for Victory* (GS 1530). He was appointed deputy conductor of the Staff Band in 1927, conductor in 1928, and bandmaster in December 1929 with the retirement of William Rook. In 1936, Dickens moved to Sydney where he was employed by a musical publishing firm. He then served as bandmaster at Rockdale for 19 years and was an active leader in the musical life of Australia's Eastern Territory. In retirement he had another number published in the British SA journals, the selection, *Joyful Pilgrimage* (GS 1468).

One of the final tasks of long serving Commissioner James Hay in 1921 was to divide the Eastern Territory from the Southern. The Staff Band journeyed up from Melbourne to combine in the celebrations with Sydney Congress Hall, Petersham and Dulwich Hill. Sydney Headquarters became responsible for Army activities in New South Wales, Queensland, and the soon to be created Australian Capital Territory. Eventually it was also to have responsibility for the developing territory of Papua New Guinea, which became a separate nation in 1975. The new Territorial Headquarters shared the same location as Sydney Congress Hall.

Orchestras

Through the teens and into the twenties as band instrumentation settled into a pure brass format, debates continued about the overwhelming dominance of Army musical life by this one form of musical expression. As early as July 1890 in the 'Official Gazette' section of the Australian *War Cry*, quoting *Orders and Regulations for Field Officers* (p233), an article appeared stating: *Every corps should steadily set itself to the formation of a string band... With very little trouble a band can be formed far more suitable for indoor meetings than the brass band.* The article goes on to point out that: *Brazen instrumentation is the most difficult to sing to, and in fact, seems to have a tendency to stop people singing. Everybody must have noticed this therefore the brass band should always be kept in subjection in indoor meetings.* It ends with an exhortation: *Each large corps should quickly raise a string band. Some have tried and failed. Never mind, try again.*[24]

On October 17th 1896, the *War Cry* welcomed the inauguration of Sydney's 'Musical Messengers' vocal and instrumental group saying *"The Messengers' strong point is its orchestra"* comprised of four violins, a cello, two cornets, a baritone, a guitar, and an organ. In April 1898 at the Inter-Colonial Congress Music Festival, attended by 9,000 people in the Melbourne Exhibition, Herbert Booth had an orchestra in pride of place with the Federal Guards and the Staff Band. The versatile Biorama bands not only had photographic, mechanical and electrical expertise, but many of their instrumentalists could switch from strings to brass as required. At their peak around 1907, they supported both a band and an orchestra.

In 1913, the *LOB* carried a report and photograph of an orchestra at the Newtown Corps in New South Wales. The report described how the orchestra was set up as a result of Envoy Watson being inspired by Commissioner Hay speaking on the topic at his welcome meeting in Sydney. [25] In January 1920, near the end of Hay's term, the *LOB* ran a half page 'Plea for the Orchestra' stating: *The Commissioner* [James Hay] *has expressed his strong opinion that orchestral music would greatly aid all our Corps, and that Corps Commanders should get to work and formulate small orchestral companies.* The article encouraged the idea of training 'double handed' musicians, and of running orchestras of up to twenty players. The article concluded by stating: *Some scores of our young women officers have recently taken up the violin, cannot they help the matter?* [26]

Throughout the twenties the *LOB* would occasionally feature an orchestra on its front page. Albury, Marrickville and Malvern had well supported combinations. By 1928, the Malvern orchestra had been in existence for 7 years. It had 21 members, and provided the music for all Sunday evening meetings except once a month when a change was made with the band. Bram Rose arranged most of the music played. At one time, the tenor saxophone player was future Staff Bandmaster Norman McLeod. Gradually the orchestras disappeared. But their legacy remained. Many years later a number of corps still encouraged their young musicians to take up the violin or another string instrument. Composer Major Howard Davies is one of those who in his youth often featured as a violinist. Neville Philpott was another. Max Percy who served as Bandmaster of both North Sydney and Sydney Congress Hall in the fifties and sixties was often featured as both a trombone and violin soloist.[27]

Through the twenties, Australian works do not appear in the British journals with the frequency one would have expected given the popularity of the old *AuBJ*. Whilst this certainly has something to do with different editorial standards, it may also be related to local inhibitions about stepping onto the wider international stage. Certainly from the unpublished works of Rook, McAnally and others held by the Melbourne Staff Band, material was still being written. One of those who did have material published in London was Envoy D. Garry (Paddy) Hollis. For nine years a member of the Staff Band, he served for a short period as bandmaster of Lismore in New South Wales, and later Box Hill in Victoria. His march *Hawthorn* was published in the GS (846) in 1920 and his *Redcliffe* march in 1929, GS 994. Many years later, in 1958, his *Brighton* (GS 1453) march was published. A fourth march, *Box Hill,* was approved for publication but not finally submitted.

Another who had a great influence on Army music throughout these years was Colonel Arthur S. Arnott, a composer of

Malvern Corps Orchestra (1930s)

scores of songs sung at the Annual Congress Young People's Demonstrations – unique programmes which he conducted for 39 years from 1902. He had a style which one observer termed *Rooseveltian*. Several of his original tunes from these events appeared in international journals over the years. Songs and choruses such as, *Christ for the Whole Wide Word; We're on the Homeward Trail; Some Glad Sweet Day; Jesus Thou Art Everything to Me*, enriched the work of many published arrangers.[28]

Immigrant Families

By the mid-1920s smaller suburban and country corps had begun to benefit from transfers from older more established corps. Later in the decade and on through the thirties and into the fifties, sponsored migration of British Salvationist families similarly benefited many corps. The family of future Staff Bandmaster Colin Woods, arrived together with the large Lucas family of five, and the Scarlet family, all from the North of England in 1927. It took the Rackham family a couple of tries before finally settling in Australia. The family of six first emigrated to Australia in 1912 from Lowestoft where they had been involved in the local corps since the earliest days. They served at Box Hill and South Melbourne before returning to England just before WW1. Back at Lowestoft 1 the father, William Rackham served as corps Treasurer, and son Sid as Bandmaster of a band of around 40 players.

The Rackhams eventually returned to Australia in 1923 and settled in Brunswick. Sid became conductor of the Brunswick band under Joe Rundle, and in 1927 also took responsibility for the Pentridge Prison Band. In 1930, the family moved to Hawthorn. Sid went on to become Bandmaster at Brighton through the Second World War. His younger brothers Lance and Victor became mainstays of the Hawthorn corps. In 1955, Lance was succeeded by Herbert Stevens as Bandmaster. His brother Vic became Songster Leader. In 1968, Lance became Divisional Bandmaster [DBM] at the same time Vic was serving as Divisional Songster Leader [DSL]. Officer families were sometimes quite large and as they moved from corps to corps (which was quite frequent) so the corps band went up and down. Two families in particular, Small and Knight each with several sons contributed considerably to the development of the band at Northcote in Melbourne. Norm Knight played solo cornet with the Staff Band and later moved to Petersham in Sydney where he served as bandmaster for thirteen years, establishing the band as one of the leading groups in the Territory. At Dulwich Hill in Sydney, Harry Berry Snr., and his son Harry, a fine trombone player, made a significant contribution. In 1927 Harold Boase transferred from Adelaide to become bandmaster. He was to have the band for 25 years retiring in 1951. He was also DBM of the Sydney West Divison.

The climax of the decade for bands was an extensive and remarkable – for the era – transcontinental tour by Perth Fortress in 1927 led by Bandmaster Joe Palmer. They crossed the Nullarbor Plain by train and journeyed up the east coast, a round trip of almost 10,000 km (6,200 miles).

The Stevens Brothers

Perhaps the best example of the style of Army banding which came to mark the inter-war 'golden age' of Army bands in Australia was the Hawthorn Band under the baton of the Stevens brothers. Arthur and Herbert Stevens led the band for more than 50 years through two World Wars and the Great Depression. Hawthorn was, by the 1920s, one of the leading Melbourne corps and a DHQ. Arthur Stevens had been bandmaster since 1902. He was first attracted to the Army in 1892 by the playing of the Australian Guards at the old No. 1 corps in North Melbourne. His parents soon followed the active 12-year-old into The Salvation Army. In 1897 the family moved to Hawthorn where Arthur became a bandsman, and in quick succession Band Secretary, Band Sergeant, Deputy Bandmaster and in 1902, Bandmaster. The band at that time consisted of eight players. By 1910 there were 22. Four of Arthur's five brothers were also in the band; Bob, Ernest, Jack, who was Deputy Bandmaster, and Herbert.[29]

Herbert Stevens (1897–1974) was a popular instrumentalist. He regularly featured as a vocalist and piano/accordion player, and was Hawthorn corps organist for many years. But it was as a cornet player that he became best known. As a contemporary stated, *His prowess on the cornet was well known and on two occasions his brilliant playing of* Maoriland *and* Memories *in the Melbourne Town Hall at*

Congress Festivals 'brought the house down'. In 1921 when Arthur Stevens was appointed DBM, he appointed Herb conductor until 1936 when he was commissioned Bandmaster. Under his leadership Hawthorn became one of the leading bands of Australia. They were the first SA band to play at the newly opened Federal Parliament in Canberra, and were among the first bands on the radio in November 1924 just two weeks after transmissions commenced.

From the twenties to the forties Hawthorn became the most travelled band in Australia visiting all states including Western Australia. They regularly featured in the pages of the *LOB* among the bands at Congress and Divisional Musical festivals, playing the most challenging music of the moment. During WW2, Herb Stevens and 18 of the bandsmen enlisted in the forces. Herb became bandmaster of the 39th Battalion Band composed mostly of Salvationists. He also conducted the 2/24th band. Arthur, as DBM, resumed the helm at Hawthorn. In 1948 Arthur led the band on a tour of New Zealand, the first Australian band to venture overseas since the Austral Guards almost 50 years before.

Later that year, upon his retirement Arthur Stevens was awarded the OF.[30] Herb resumed leadership of the band which he held until his own retirement in 1955. Herb then moved to Adelaide where he became Bandmaster of the Kensington and Norwood Citizens Band, leading them to the Australasian Championship. He was promoted to Glory in 1974.

Links between Salvationist, military, and citizens' banding were irregular but not unknown in Army circles throughout the inter-war period. Army bandsmen were becoming recognised as a distinct part of the subculture of 'Brass Banding'. The Hawthorn SA Band was, for many years, the recipient of an annual grant from the local council in recognition of its contribution to the life of the local community. The MSB had a long tradition of participation in civic occasions including the 1936 state memorial service to King George V.[31] They had performed on the second evening of radio transmissions in Australia, the first evening being a concert by Dame Nellie Melba.

By the 1930s, brass bands were an important part of local civic life in Australia. Each local town and municipality had its own band supported out of municipal funds. Some municipalities were quite generous, providing the bands with full facilities including rooms and instruments, others had to get by on grants and fundraising. Major public utilities such as Police, Fire Brigade, Ambulance, Tramways, and Railways also maintained their own contesting bands. Private industry, generally, was not involved.

Australia has never had a tradition, such as that of the great English 'Works' bands, of being fully financed by local companies. National contests were linked to major Eisteddfods such as those conducted annually at Ballarat in Victoria. Many a Salvationist bandsman followed the outcomes with as much attention as any in the secular scene. It was also the case that as the Army passed into its third generation, many who had grown up in the movement and left, had taken their love of banding with them. Often there were family connections between the Army and the contesting world. These informal linkages were strong. SA bands across Australia whether in major cities like Adelaide, Perth and Brisbane or regional towns like Newcastle and Launceston were recognised as among the leading bands of their communities.

The brass band was at the height of its effectiveness as an evangelical instrument. Outside pubs on Friday evenings around Australia, open-air meetings continued to attract crowds right through until the 1950s. This was particularly true in those states that enforced 6:00 p.m. closing of public houses. The Friday night rush at the pub was notorious for the number of drunkards pouring onto the streets.

Salvation Army bands of the 1920s were not averse to taking advantage of this particularly unfortunate aspect of mid-century culture. In what became known as 'Drunks Raids', bandsmen would descend on the hapless inebriates and 'encourage' them back to the hall for coffee and, if possible, conversion.

During the thirties Australian names began to appear more frequently in the English journals. Cecil Greig the Bandmaster of Norwood in South Australia had material published, as did Divisional Songster Leader Harry Harvey of Melbourne. In 1934 the New Zealand composer Harold Scotney (b.1889) transferred to Australia and was appointed Territorial Band Inspector for the Eastern Australia

Territory. Already well known to Australians for his publications in the old *AuBJ*, that same year he became bandmaster at Sydney Congress Hall, a post that he held for seven years.

In 1941 Scotney transferred to Petersham as Bandmaster for two years, and then returned to Congress Hall as Corps Secretary. He retired as Territorial Band Inspector in 1952. His compositions include 25 marches, 15 selections, four meditations, two solos, a duet, two quartets, and a quintet for trombones. In addition he produced several vocal works. Over a period of 40 years Harold Scotney had 43 works published in London, eight of them prize winners. He is perhaps best remembered among bandsmen for his marches, *Wellingtonian* (GS 934) and *The Quest* (GS 1016).

W. Arthur Gullidge

The early 1930s were significant years for another Australian Salvationist composer. In 1933 William Arthur Gullidge (1909–1942) won the Brass section of the Australian Broadcasting Commission's National Composition Awards with his composition, *Utopia*.

In 1935 he won the Military Band Section awards with *Spell of Venus*. Between these, in 1934, he won First Prize in two sections of The Salvation Army's International Competition, gaining the distinction of having his two winning compositions, the march, *Heaven-Bound Throng* (GS 1093) and the selection, *The Omnipotent God* (GS 1094) published together in *General Series*. He became Australia's most prolific composer of brass band music in the inter-war period. His marches particularly are instantly recognisable.

Gullidge developed a unique and still distinctive style of street march characterised by an aggressive introduction commonly featuring 'German sixths', a strong bass solo, and lilting counter-melodies in the trio and latter sections. The style has not been imitated, except once, as a tribute, by Ray Steadman-Allen, in his march, *Crown of Conquest* (GS 1401).

Brought up by his widowed officer mother, Gullidge spent his early years at Melbourne City Temple and then as a young man at Collingwood. Later, he and a group of bandsmen transferred from Collingwood to Brunswick. He served a printing apprenticeship at the SA Printing Works under the supervision of Bandmaster Arthur Stevens of Hawthorn. But the coming of the Great Depression did not spare the SA and, on completing his apprenticeship, Gullidge was out of work. He already had something of a reputation as an arranger and was offered part time professional conducting positions by several of the contesting bands around Melbourne. 'Massa' Johnson of the Fire Brigade Band and Harry Shugg of the

Bandmaster W. Arthur Gullidge Brunswick 1930s.

Tramways Band were both keen to use his material. The University Rifles Band offered him a retainer of fifty pounds a year as conductor.

Aware of this dilemma the Territorial Commander, Commissioner Maxwell, gave Gullidge two days' work a week at the Printing Works. It was here that Gullidge and fellow Brunswick bandsman Albert Redpath established *The Regal Brass Band Journal*. It was a journal designed for the secular brass band market and published periodically through the 1930s. All the compositions were by Gullidge, though some were published under his mother's maiden name, Greendale.

It was sold by subscription and delivered by mail or door to door by his wife Mavis. There is little doubt that headquarters gave tacit approval to Gullidge's publishing activities.[32] No complete set of the *Regal* journal exists but one of its numbers, *The Hussar* eventually found its way to London under the title, *Emblem of the Army* (GS 1572). It was 'sanctified' by Albert Redpath's judicious insertion of the chorus, *Lift up the Army Banner*.

Under Gullidge's leadership Brunswick made interstate tours to Adelaide in 1936, and Petersham in 1939. Among the works most talked about on the tour was Eric Ball's *Exodus*, which Gullidge had spoken movingly about before presenting it at the Melbourne Congress Music Festival.

At the outbreak of war in 1939, Gullidge signalled his intention to enlist. The former Tramways Bandmaster, now Major, Harry Shugg was responsible for military bands. He facilitated the enlistment of 22 Salvationists under Gullidge's leadership as the band of the 2/22nd Battalion. Gullidge was also commissioned by Shugg to arrange the Australian

Arthur Gullidge conducts 2/22 Battalion Band, Farewell concert, Brunswick Town Hall (16 November 1940).

(Note. Salvation Army flag with '2/22nd Battalion Band A.I.F.' inscription).

military journal of *Music for Ceremonial Occasions*. It remained in use until the 1970s.

In 1941 the Battalion, with Gullidge as Bandmaster, was posted to Rabaul on the island of New Britain, northeast of New Guinea. In the weeks following the Japanese invasion and capture of Rabaul in January 1942, Gullidge and all but one of the bandsmen of the 2/22nd Battalion Band were killed. Some died in the initial battle and some, in a later massacre, at the Tol Plantation. Most drowned when the ship *Montevideo Maru* on which they were being transported as prisoners-of-war was torpedoed by an allied submarine in July 1942. Family members did not become aware of the fate of the band until an announcement in Federal Parliament in late 1945. In 1956 the Military instituted the Gullidge Medal, awarded annually to the top musical apprentice in the Australian armed forces.

Arthur Gullidge was 33 when he died. In addition to his 27 published works in London, those in the *Regal* journal and the military publication *Music for Ceremonial Occasions*, there are two sets of unpublished selections of the *Gems from the Great Masters* variety (excerpts largely drawn from Offenbach's, *Orpheus in the Underworld*), and his ABC prize winning compositions *Utopia* and *Spell of Venus*. There is also an unpublished manuscript book of hymn tune arrangements, the most popular of which are, *Spirit of the Living God* and *Ivory Palaces*. The book also includes a number of original hymn tunes.

Aside from his marches, W. Arthur Gullidge is best remembered for the simple but evocative selection, *Divine Communion* (GS 1255; See discussion in Volume II, Musical Study Part 2).

In Western Australia a group of 12 bandsmen under Bandmaster H.E. (Bluey) Palmer of Perth Fortress also enlisted as a musical unit. As bandsmen in action they became battalion stretcher-bearers. Serving in Syria Bandmaster Palmer was shot and killed by a sniper's bullet whilst working alongside his brother Mick.

Post-War Continuity

The SA in Australia emerged from the war with its traditions enhanced and its military culture reinforced. The actions of

Red Shield officers working with the troops had become the stuff of popular legend. The familiar Red Shield bearing a kangaroo with the words 'Hop In' became part of the national iconography of war.

In local corps continuity remained strong. In November 1949 the *Musician* announced that Senior Major Harry Woodland had been commissioned as Bandmaster of West End Citadel Band. His father Envoy John Woodland had served there as Bandmaster, one brother Sid had been deputy Bandmaster, and his other brother, Senior Captain Woodland of the Melbourne Music Department, had also served as Bandmaster of West End.

Tom Roper took charge of Launceston Band in Tasmania in 1949, developing a strong combination that continued following his retirement in 1967.

At Unley in South Australia Bandmaster William Baldock led the band continuously for 50 years. Commissioned in 1909 at the age of 18, he retired in 1959, and was awarded the MBE in 1960. Norman McLeod succeeded George Dickens as Staff Bandmaster in 1936. He had come from Adelaide Congress Hall in 1917, moved to Hawthorn and thence to the Staff Band in 1917. He retired in 1963 after 46 years with the Staff Band. He was awarded the OF in 1955 and the MBE in 1966.

Bands were still the evangelical instrument of choice. Television had yet to arrive and traffic congestion in suburbia was unknown. Crowds still gathered for open-air meetings, and children followed the band down the street. In many places the band became the focus of local corps life. For a bandsman that life could be quite hectic.

A typical week might include: Sunday, five meetings (three indoor meetings and two outdoor 'open-air' meetings); a Saturday Night Programme; a week night rehearsal; and perhaps a Friday night open-air meeting. Divisional music festivals took the place of secular contests, and Saturday night programmes where one corps' musical sections – Band, Songsters, and Timbrels – would visit a neighbouring corps, became the staple of Army social life. For the better bands there was the opportunity for radio broadcasting through the Australian Broadcasting Commission's regular band programmes. Informally the local corps became identified with the quality of its Band. In many corps the Bandmaster

Bandmaster Harold Morgan. O.F., Sydney Congress Hall with Commissioner and Mrs Hubert Scotney.

assumed a status that only a courageous, or foolhardy, Corps Officer would challenge.

In 1947 the *War Cry* announced the establishment of Music Boards in the Southern and Eastern Territories. In 1949 a National Music Board was established to avoid the problem of appeals to London before works could pass between territories. Yet in the 50s and into the 60s few Australians were submitting work to London.

Following the lead of Harold Scotney, Bandmaster Harold Morgan of Sydney Congress Hall was one of the few. Born in England, Harold Morgan emigrated to Australia in 1924. He was for a short time Bandmaster of Lambton in New South Wales. In 1941 he succeeded Harold Scotney as bandmaster of Sydney Congress Hall, and took the band on their first overseas visit to New Zealand in 1952. A good speaker, reported as lucid and gripping, he was in frequent demand. He had works published in both *General* and *Triumph Series* and won several prizes in Army competitions. Harold Morgan was Eastern Territorial Bandmaster from 1956 to 1967 and received the OF in 1981.

Bandmaster Len Baxter, Brisbane City Temple.

Bandmaster Len Baxter of Brisbane City Temple was, like William Rook and Robert McAnally in an earlier generation, reluctant to submit his work for publication. He tended to keep his numerous compositions for his own band and for a select few others. Under his 44-year leadership from 1932 until

1977, Brisbane Temple Band maintained a reputation as one of the finest in Australia. The warmth and depth of its sound, particularly the tuba section, was renowned. During the war Len Baxter was for a time Bandmaster of the Armoured Division Band. His compositions include cornet and trombone solos written for John Allen and Ian Hankey, and several tuba solos for Colin Crawford. He is also known for his marches, particularly *Path of Duty*; and extended works including a *Great Masters* selection. In 1973 Len Baxter was awarded the MBE.

Bandmaster Frank Inglis of Melbourne who contributed several compositions to the international band scene.

Alan Pengilly of Maylands (later Morley) in Western Australia, was one composer who did maintain regular contact with the IMED; he kept a file of letters to prove it. He wrote for both bands and songsters. All his brass compositions but one were for *Triumph Series*. The first, *Westralia* (TS 556) appeared in 1956 and was followed by nine others. *Whosoever Heareth* appeared in *General Series* (GS 1621). Pengilly was Songster Leader at Perth Fortress from 1940 until 1959 when he transferred to Maylands. He died in 1983. Melbourne Salvationist Frank Inglis contributed several pieces to the international band scene including, *The Scene of Prayer* (GS 1303); *A Cavalcade of Choruses* (GS 1374); *The Singing Heart* (FS 207) and *Southern Skies* (TS 564).

During the fifties, constant improvement in international transport and communications at last enabled Australians to overcome what historian Geoffrey Blainey called, *The Tyranny of Distance*.[33] In 1952 Eric Ball made his first visit to Australia. The three great International Congresses of 1952, 1965 and 1978 saw the full flowering of a mature Army musical culture.

These International events acted as spurs to local performance. A stream of major works from composers such as Eric Ball and Dean Goffin, then Steadman-Allen and later Leslie Condon, continually lifted the horizons of Salvationist musicians. A plethora of music for big events encouraged local musicians to look to local celebrations, and set a 'Festival Series' stamp on the musical ambitions of a generation. Coronation Congress Festivals were held across the country in 1953, followed by Olympic Festivals in 1956. In 1959 Territorial Band Congresses celebrated eighty years of banding in Australia. These were of course in addition to regular Divisional festivals, Spring Festivals and State Congress gatherings.

In 1951 two notable bandmasters made their appearance, Max Percy at North Sydney and Len Collier at Dulwich Hill. Other bands to come on during the period were Geelong under Herbert Perriam, a recent migrant from the United Kingdom, and Earlwood in Sydney with Harold Jurd. Toowoomba in Queensland began to appear at Congress gatherings and Hobart in Tasmania was a band that began to be heard on broadcasts.

Suburban and country bands flourished largely oblivious to the social changes beginning around them. Pressed by waves of postwar migration from Italy, Greece and later Turkey, many of the old inner suburban corps declined. The original Victorian corps at North Melbourne, Collingwood, and Prahran eventually closed. They were replaced by growth in the suburbs at Box Hill, Camberwell, and Brighton and further out in new suburbs like Ringwood.

In New South Wales, declines at inner urban Newtown and Marrickville were matched by improving combinations at Rockdale, Paramatta, Campsie and Hurstville. Whilst the impact of migration in other states was less severe, new suburbs and new corps meant transfers out of some of the old.

These changes were less apparent in other states. In 1952 the Hobart Band from Tasmania visited Preston in Victoria, its first trip to the mainland. In South Australia, Adelaide Congress Hall, Unley, and Norwood were the bands appearing most often at major events. In Perth, the Fortress and Leederville bands remained the dominant combinations, though others such as Maylands were also heard on broadcasts. In Queensland, Brisbane City Temple, West End, Albion, Ipswich and Toowoomba were occasionally joined at major events by smaller combinations such as Cooperoo.

New Wave

In 1954 a new era of bandmaster, who led more by musical intelligence and excitement than enforced discipline, began with the appointment of Don McCoy as Bandmaster at Moreland. He succeeded James Maslin who had become bandmaster in 1926 at age 17. Maslin brought the band to a high standard particularly during the late 30s and 40s. Don

McCoy became DBM of the Melbourne Metropolitan Division; conducted the Southern Territory's 'Spotlight' Youth Band; and was the musical director for the Melbourne productions of Gowans-and-Larsson musicals. Don McCoy retired in 1981 after 27 years leadership at Moreland. He was promoted to Glory in 1982.

Through the mid-1950s and into the 60s, soloists became better known around Australia as interstate visits became more regular. In 1963 Leederville (later Floreat Park) in Western Australia, was to undertake a tour of the eastern states under Bandmaster Tom Russell with Murray Hicks as cornet soloist. Ern Harewood the Euphonium soloist at Unley in Adelaide, would eventually join the MSB. In Melbourne the leading soloists were Merve Preusker, trombone and John Butler, euphonium. Brisbane City Temple regularly featured Colin Crawford on tuba and the young John Allen on cornet. In Sydney, Allan Staines and Ian McComb were the featured trombone players along with Ron Bevan on euphonium and Edgar Smith on trumpet and cornet. Small but quality bands also appeared in several towns and suburbs, such as Chelsea under Keith Albiston and Morwell under Norman Hodgson.

In 1959 Ronald Smart, another of the new style bandmasters was appointed bandmaster at Campsie in the Sydney Central Division, holding the position for five years prior to moving to Los Angeles. In 1962, Irwin Palmer, continuing a great family tradition, became the Bandmaster of Perth Fortress and Keith McPherson took over at Box Hill. The following year Max Percy became the Bandmaster at Sydney Congress Hall, following 12 years at North Sydney. All four Bandmasters were to make significant contributions to banding in Australia.

Census figures indicated that by the early 1960s church attendance in Australia was higher than at any time since records began. Sunday schools were overflowing and Corps generally secure in their place within the local community. The *Musician* in 1960 advised that in Australia Southern Territory there were 5,500 senior and junior bandsmen.

1960–2003 Challenge and Response

The great social changes that marked the 60s and 70s had their beginnings in Australia in 1956, the year Australia first hosted the Olympic Games. The post-war affluence that enabled the Olympics to come to Melbourne coincided with the introduction of television, and all across the world young people were discovering rock 'n' roll. Within 10 years the world changed. The automobile was threatening the place of the band on the street; community organisations were feeling the impact of lifestyles where television provided diversion without effort; and youth culture was most clearly defined by one thing - music.

Youth Culture

The first Rhythm Festival in Australia did not take place until 1966 in Sydney. But the recognition of an emerging youth culture began a couple of years earlier when Southern TYS Brigadier Harry Goffin Jnr. set up the Territorial 'Spotlight' Youth Committee. The Melbourne 'Spotlight' annual festival and visits to Sydney, prompted a reciprocal response from the Eastern Territory. The Melbourne and Sydney Spotlight bands showcased inter-territorial talent and fostered many future musical leaders. Cornet soloist Brian Davies served a term as Melbourne Spotlight President and his brother Howard wrote one or two of his early contemporary vocal compositions for the Melbourne Spotlighters. Barrie Gott was active with the Sydney group, as were leaders like Vita Terracini, Bob Suey, and Max Percy. In the mid-60s Spotlight concerts with their array of young soloists and the best possible brass and vocal ensembles were the most anticipated of the year in both Sydney and Melbourne.

Young people's musical sections had a strong history in Australia. In the 1920s and 30s a number of Salvation Army Boy Scout troops featured brass bands, and several Corps had fife and drum bands. Joe Rundle of Brunswick was appointed Australia's first Divisional Young People's Band Leader in 1927. In 1961 the Brunswick YP Band under Alpha Yealland undertook an interstate visit to Adelaide. The average age of the band was 13 and included in their repertoire were Festival works such as Gullidge's, *British Melodies* No. 1 (FS 103).

Australia's first youth music camp took place in September 1948 at Mt. Evelyn, Victoria. However, it was Collaroy in the Eastern Territory that through the 1960s and 70s became Australia's equivalent of the Star Lake Musicamp. Both the senior and the junior music camp concerts, held at Sydney Congress Hall, were always booked weeks in advance. It was not until later, in the 1980s and early 90s that Melbourne's Territorial Music School at Whitley College, came to rival Collaroy. State and Divisional Music camps were also popular, and continued intermittently into the 1990s.

In 1970 and 1972 Preston Youth Group in Victoria, undertook two national tours. Both were by Motor Coach to enable visits to small centres along the way. The band leader Deputy Bandmaster Mervyn Collins, a former Air Force musician, commissioned several 'swing' style arrangements of well known hymns such as, *Crown Him with Many Crowns* and, more adventurously, selections from the rock musical,

John Wiseman, Cornet soloist, vocalist, pianist. Sydney Congress Hall, 1992

Jesus Christ Superstar. Wherever the band played, from small corps on the edge of the desert to key centres such as Brisbane Temple or Perth Fortress, musical taboos were broken.

In 1973 a group influenced by the sounds of commercial rock bands such as, *Blood Sweat and Tears,* and *Chicago,* was brought together by John Cleary and Ralph Hultgren. *Solid Rock* showcased the talents of largely untried young composers such as Brian Hogg, Ralph Hultgren, and Brenton Broadstock. For most of its eight-year life the band was led by Mervyn Collins and instrumentally anchored by jazz trombonist Michael Poore. Later in the decade Barrie Gott became involved, producing the album *Solid Rock*. It is perhaps the only Army group ever to make 'The (back) cover of the *Rolling Stone*'. The Australian edition of the rock industry bible highlighted the band's appearance at the 1975 Sunbury Pop Festival saying, *They're tight, the charts are good and all in all it's a terrific performance.*[34] Working the crowd as hard as he could while the band performed on stage, was the Territorial Commander, Commissioner Harry Warren. *Solid Rock* gave its final performance at the 1980 Australian Centenary Congress. A group with similar instrumentation but more middle of the road in its sound was *Blood & Fire* led by Barrie Gott in Sydney. Among the brass soloists were John Wiseman, trumpet, John Thompson and Ronald Prussing, trombone.

The surging popularity of youth culture and the 'Rhythm Group' era did not bring about a collapse in support or enthusiasm for the traditional brass band. Many of those experimenting with contemporary music were the best trained and most enthusiastic young musicians in the Army. They were equally enthusiastic in their commitment to traditional brass. Through the 60s and into the 70s brass bands, particularly those with a history as centres of excellence, set new standards.

The International Era

The 1965 Centenary Celebrations were the first International Congress gatherings that were accessible to more than a select few. International travel was within reach of many more Australians. And even for those brass enthusiasts who could not attend, the availability of quality Hi-Fidelity stereo recordings of Ray Steadman-Allen's, *The Holy War* and *Christ is the Answer*, brought sophisticated, mature, classic SA brass within the reach of everyone. The highlight of the period was undoubtedly the visit to Australia in 1967 of the ISB under Bernard Adams. The cornet playing of Roland Cobb; the tuba of Leslie Condon; and particularly the trombone playing of Ian Hankey and Malcolm Carter – both of whom later emigrated to Australia – had a great impact. The ISB visit also encouraged Australian bands to think of travelling beyond Australasia.

Box Hill had developed rapidly under Keith McPherson. McPherson also possessed exceptional organisational abilities. In 1970 Box Hill undertook the first world tour by an Australian Salvation Army band, visiting Canada, the USA, the United Kingdom, Switzerland and Germany. Two numbers especially written for the tour were, *Southern Cross* by Brian Bowen, and Leslie Condon's, *Song of the Eternal*.[35] Euphonium soloist Ken Melody and cornet soloist Robert Beasy were joined by Malcolm Carter and bass trombone player David Eldridge who transferred from Brisbane City and later joined the MSB.

Box Hill was followed, less than a year later, by Sydney Congress Hall under Max Percy, touring New Zealand the United States and Canada. Throughout these years both Box Hill and Sydney Congress Hall were supporting large 'No. 2' bands in addition to Young People's sections. A number of bands began to tour more extensively. Dulwich Hill went to

Brisbane City Temple Band, 1999.

New Zealand in 1970 featuring, *My Strength, My Tower*, and *Resurgam*. A guest of the Hobart Corps that year was a talented 16-year old cornetist from Perth Fortress, Margaret Fenn. Her solos included, *Tucker, Jubilate* and *Glory to His*

Major Howard Davies. Talented composer of both instrumental and vocal music.

Name. Strong country corps such as Wollongong appeared regularly at Congress music festivals, which remained popular. Bandsmen were keen to hear the latest from London such as, *A Song of Courage, The Joy Bringer, Themes from the Italian Symphony* and *Kaleidoscope*.

Principal cornet with the MSB during the mid-sixties was Brian Davies. He then spent some years in England as cornet soloist with the International Staff Band before returning to Australia to become bandmaster at Camberwell. His brother Howard, as a young officer, wrote two full musicals before his appointment to England with IMED and the ISB from 1972 to 1976. His skills as an arranger of both vocal and instrumental music demonstrate, like singer songwriter Joy Webb, an intuitive sense of the 'fitness' of words and music. Among the most popular of more than fifteen works in the GS, are, *Songs of Australia* (GS 1730) and *Wonder of His Grace* (GS 1653–2).

Creative Decades

The 1970s and 80s in Australia ushered in the most productive and creative period in Australian SA music history. Colin Woods became bandmaster of the MSB in 1969. Brian Davies was commissioned bandmaster at Camberwell the same year. In 1972 the internationally renowned cornet player Ken Smith succeeded Keith McPherson at Box Hill. In 1973 Barrie Gott became Bandmaster at Sydney Congress Hall, following Max Percy; and Ronald Prussing followed Barrie's father, W. Fred Gott, at Petersham.

Under Colin Woods the MSB developed a reputation throughout Australia as the standard setting unit, not only musically but as a force for encouragement and creativity. The band established its place internationally at the 1978 International Centenary Congress, with the premiere of Robert Redhead's, *Quintessence*, a work based on Australian melodies. Woods' skill as both trainer and conductor instilled both discipline and fire into performances which readily brought audiences to their feet. Woods encouraged Staff Bandsmen to become musical leaders in their own corps. He facilitated their involvement in innovative local music groups; and most significantly he fostered composers and arrangers such as Noel Jones, Brian Hogg, and Ian Jones.

The internationally renowned orchestral and brass composer Brenton Broadstock gained much of his early confidence working with the MSB. *St Aelred* was commissioned for the band's 1984 USA/Canada tour; *Come Ye Thankful* for the 1986 UK tour; *Rutherford* for the MSB centenary, and many more. Under Woods' leadership the MSB, through touring and recording was recognised as one of the world's leading brass bands, both inside and outside the movement. Colin Woods was awarded the Order of Australia Medal (OAM) in 1991.

The most prolific composer of the period was Noel Jones who served as Southern Territorial Music Director, a member of the MSB and Bandmaster at the rapidly growing outer suburban corps of Ringwood. Jones had his first number published in 1979. Since then over 30 compositions have appeared in Great Britain and 10 in American journals. Jones is not only prolific but popular. He specialises in music that is both playable and accessible. He writes for smaller bands, and he, perhaps sooner than others, caught the drift of what sort of music was really required at the local corps when 'the festival' was over. Of the Melbourne group of composers, it is Brian Hogg, Jones' successor as TMD, who is the most versatile; equally comfortable with traditional brass, big bands, or 'worship' bands.

Camberwell Corps was typical of a number of corps that went through extensive redevelopment in the 1970s and 80s. Corps such as Leederville in Perth became Floreat Park, North Sydney moved to Chatswood; and Hawthorn, one of the most historic of Victorian corps, moved to the suburbs and became Waverly Camberwell Band and under Brian Davies visited the UK, Germany, and the United States in 1982. In 1987 they went to the UK and Scandinavia. The band also produced a number of LPs and later CDs. Their featured soloists of the 1970s included Malcolm Linsell, cornet and Jeff McClaren, trombone. Later in the decade they were joined by cornet players Max Orchard and Ken Whittaker from Sydney

Both the MSB and Camberwell gained from the move of Whittaker and Orchard. David Harvey and later Ken

Preston Citadel Band, with Bandmaster Mervyn Collins, on tour in Taiwan.

Waterworth, both from Moreland, succeeded Ern Harewood and Colin Woods as the Staff Band euphonium soloists. Brisbane Temple's featured soloists were Deputy Bandmaster John Allen and former ISB member Ian Hankey. In 1977 Len Baxter retired as Bandmaster handing over to John Allen, who would be succeeded in 1986 by Malcolm Carter. John Allen transferred to Camberwell where he was later to serve a term as Bandmaster. Professionally trained Salvationist musicians also began to move into leading secular positions. Trombone players Ronald Prussing, Ken McClimont, Howard Parkinson and Graeme Liddel would at the same time be members of state Symphony Orchestras, three of them as Principal.

The 1980 Australian Centenary Congress festivals brought together the finest bands in the country and featured Enfield (UK) as the major visiting band. Adelaide Congress Hall Band under its long serving bandmaster Hartley Aberg welcomed visitors to the city where Thomas Sutherland had commenced the Adelaide I Band in 1880. Yet at the same time a cautionary note was sounded with the presentation of Gwenyth Redhead's play, *The Bandmaster*.

In 1981 Bandmaster Irwin Palmer of Perth established the 'Silver Threads' band. A quasi-Veterans' Band, it used the latitude of age to avoid regulation. From hospitals to social clubs, to elderly citizens groups, and straight concerts, the band mixed old time and contemporary music with SA and secular works, in a style that proved immensely popular. In 1987 more conventional Veterans Bands were established in Sydney under Fred Gott and Melbourne under former Staff Bandmaster Charles Scott.

Brass Encounters

Sydney Congress Hall under Barric Gott, began to chart a quite distinctive path, culminating in the 1982 premiere of 'Brass Encounters'. The catalyst was the visit of Hollywood Tabernacle band under Dr Ronald Smart in 1974. Hollywood's concert programme shifted the emphasis away from the performance of individual works and onto the impact of the whole concert. The music was chosen with a mind to its popular appeal, not just to an Army audience but to the wider public. Ronald Smart returned to Australia in 1975 to take up a post at the Sydney Conservatorium of Music, where he eventually became Director. Smart was awarded the Public Service Medal in 1990.

'Brass Encounters' took the Hollywood programme a step further. First conceived by Colin Calcott and Barrie Gott, the whole presentation was devised as a 'theatre piece' employing the full panoply of audio-visual special effects and whatever music, sacred or secular, was deemed appropriate to build to a

*Ronald Prussing
Bandmaster, Trombone
Soloist, Pianist.
Sydney Congress Hall
1992*

challenging climax. The format suited Barrie Gott's talents as both an arranger and conductor. Among his compositions for both the UK and the American journals, perhaps the most popular is, *Lightwalk* (FS 462). Colin Calcott later took the 'Encounters' idea to Wellington Citadel in New Zealand.

Following the appointment of Barrie Gott as Southern California DMD and Bandmaster of Pasadena Tabernacle in the United States, Ronald Prussing was commissioned bandmaster of Sydney Congress Hall in August 1983.

Prussing together with John Cleary developed 'Brass Encounters' for two international tours; to Canada and the USA in 1985; and the UK in 1991. Sydney Congress Hall had a particularly strong group of soloists during this period: Barry Garnon and Robert O'Brien on euphonium, Ronald Prussing on trombone, and John Wiseman on cornet.

Prussing maintained his demanding position as bandmaster at Sydney Congress Hall whilst continuing as Principal Trombone with the Sydney Symphony Orchestra. This was no easy task as Sydney Congress Hall followed one of the more rigorous schedules in the Army world, requiring the bandsmen to be in attendance all day on Sunday, eating both lunch and dinner at the hall, in addition to the normal week-night schedule of meetings and rehearsals.

Through the 1970s and 80s Hurstville Band in New South Wales helped change the meaning of 'the band trip'. Beginning in 1971 with a visit to Papua New Guinea, Hurstville began to focus on the developing world, visiting places where they could contribute as much in physical and material aid as they could in musical inspiration. They visited Fiji, Tonga and Suva in 1976; Indonesia and Singapore in 1979; Korea and the

Melbourne Staff Band Bandmaster Colin Woods Euphonium Soloist, Deputy BM, Ken Waterworth, USA ,1984.

Philippines in 1984 and Africa in 1995. Canberra South Band also visited the Philippines; Moreland and Perth Fortress bands visited Singapore; and Mervyn Collins led Preston on visits to Taiwan, Hong Kong, and Japan, featuring contemporary style concerts.

In its centenary year, 1990, the MSB travelled to Queensland, visiting relatively young corps like the Gold Coast and Carina and older centres such as Townsville. The featured soloists were Graeme Golding (trombone); John Collinson (cornet); and deputy Bandmaster Ken Waterworth (euphonium). The next year the band appointed its first woman member, Lieutenant Janette Shepherd. In Sydney, in 1990, the 400 musicians gathered for Musicians' Councils were treated to the sound of the 'Sydney Big Band' directed by Gavin Staines. At the Brisbane Congress, Carina band played Curnow's, *The Call to Arms* alongside the 'Brisbane Big Band' under Daryll O'Donoghue, while Brisbane City Temple, lead by Malcolm Carter since 1986, presented Ray Steadman-Allen's, *Daystar*.

In 1990 the SA in Australia had more than 200 brass bands involving almost 3,000 musicians. Throughout the early 1990s, traditional visits, band activities, and even tours continued much as before. Yet as the style of musical festivals showed, things were changing, rapidly.

In 1991 the MSB was again in Canada. In 1993, Dulwich Hill visited the Central and Southern Territories of the United States under the leadership of the talented arranger Graeme Press. In 1994 Camberwell visited Russia, the United States and Canada. Whilst maintaining a strong focus on classic brass band material the band developed a lighter more contemporary style. In 1992 The 'Crossroads Big Band', combined with the MSB for a joint festival. The Crossroads Band included a number of Staff Bandsmen and was led by Michael Harding, another young pianist and arranger who had been encouraged by Colin Woods

In 1994 Woods retired after 39 years with the MSB, 25 of those as bandmaster. At his farewell concert one of the final works Woods chose to conduct was Eric Ball's, *Resurgam*. His successor was his deputy Ken Waterworth. Waterworth was a skilled music teacher with a feel for contemporary music that would take the Staff Band in a new direction.

Resurgam

In July 1995, *The Musician* appeared for the last time. Though many of the old centres had faded or closed and many of the old bands such as Petersham and Thornbury and Subiaco were much diminished; new corps were opening in new developments across the major suburban areas all around the country. The question in the mid nineties was 'Do they want a band?' In some cases the answer was 'yes.' In other cases the answer was – 'maybe.'

Unlike the world engaging spirit of the 1890s, the mood at the turn of the millennium was unsettled and inward looking. The wider community shared a mood of uncertainty and suspicion of big institutions, including institutional religion.

The Australian National Church Life Survey[36] revealed that denominational allegiances were breaking down. Churchgoers showed a new willingness to shop around for a style of congregation that suited them. The Salvation Army was not immune. Salvationist distinctives had become 'brand variations' in an increasingly diverse 'Protestant Supermarket.' Unfortunately the Army 'brand' was becoming one suited to particular tastes only, a role which did not sit easily with the movement's oft declared purpose as a mission of mass appeal to the unconverted.

Other data from the survey demolished another commonly held view. Despite the military form of The Salvation Army and its widespread emphasis on the predominantly masculine activity of 'banding', the proportion of females to males in the Army – 63% to 37% – was almost precisely the same as in church congregations.

Commitment to the SA as an international movement, which had dominated much of the previous thirty years of centennial celebration, no longer seemed so important or relevant. What mattered in the first years of the new century was the local community, 'our' congregation and 'our' sense of meaning. Salvationists, just as other churchgoers, looked to their local communities to see what worked for those communities. At many corps the traditional pattern of Holiness and Salvation meetings were giving way to meetings held at different times and catering to different congregations. The use of general church praise and worship publications such as *Scripture in Song* helped simple guitar and keyboard combinations become the basic musical unit of many new and smaller corps. These 'worship bands' often proved more flexible and conducive to worship than a pure brass band or choir.

Where, in this changing environment was there a place for the great musical heritage of The Salvation Army? And, most importantly, what was its relevance?

In March 1993 Staff Bandmaster Colin Woods spoke out on the future of brass bands. In his characteristically direct fashion, Woods stated, *The demise of brass bands will spell the eventual demise of The Salvation Army.*[37] There is a sense in which he is right. Group music making is one of the most creative and cost-effective means of mobilising a significant body of people for a purpose that is both personally fulfilling and spiritually uplifting. Additionally, the brass band is one of the few group musical activities which is relatively simple to teach yet allows amateurs access to the best and most sophisticated music of the genre. For the past 125 years the brass band has enabled the SA to progress through those

Sydney Congress Hall Band.

strengths. But, the external culture has moved on, and to retain a relevant gospel Army music making must change. Bands have ceased to have the controlling influence they held for much of the last century. Corps require more flexible formats and differing musical combinations for worship. Perhaps the cautionary warnings of *The War Cry* of 1890 (see above) are now being heeded.

In October 2002 Box Hill Corps in Melbourne played host to its second annual week long Aggressive Christianity Conference. Nathan Rowe, the youthful Songster Leader and worship leader at Adelaide Congress Hall, conducted one of the electives. His series on music in worship included a session on renewing SA song. The highlight for many was the evening rally that brought together the corps band, songsters, and worship band in a powerful call to 'Send the Fire Today...'. In

The effervescent Barrie Gott, Bandmaster of Brisbane City Temple Band.

November 2002 Sydney Congress Hall held its 120th corps anniversary celebrations. The first appearance of the Sydney band led by 'Glory Tom' Sutherland was linked across the years, through multi-media technology, to a platform shared by the Sydney Congress Hall Band and the corps Big Band, *On Fire*. In April 2003, Gavin Staines led the *On Fire Salvation Army Big Band* on a five concert east coast tour featuring, as guest soloist, one of the world's greatest contemporary jazz musicians, James Morrison.

Music remains one of the most powerful tools in the evangelical armoury. Salvationist musicians must continue to confront the changes in musical culture going on around them. It is the necessary outworking of the sentiment the Founder shared with Martin Luther, *Why should the devil have all the good tunes?* And to the extent that the spirit of the movement is revealed in its art rather than its theology, the SA must continue to make its own music. Whether they are classic brass, local ensembles, worship bands, or big bands, the musicians of The Salvation Army must sing an alternative to the self-absorbed spiritual pap that passes for much Contemporary Christian Music. It is the clear message the founder sang: that salvation is for the whosoever; that the Gospel is as much about this world as it is about the next; and that without love of neighbour *I am nought but sounding brass.*

About the Author

John Cleary is a producer and broadcaster with The Australian Broadcasting Corporation. He is currently the presenter of the ABC's nationally broadcast Sunday Night Talk programme. In 1994 his history of The Salvation Army in Australia, *Salvo!* was awarded 'Christian Book of the Year'. John has been a member of The Salvation Army since being introduced to the Sunday School at Brunswick where he eventually became bandmaster. He has been a member of the Perth Fortress, Sydney Congress Hall, and Regent Hall (UK) Bands. He is the author of the entry on The Salvation Army in *The Oxford Companion to Australian Music.*

John Cleary

Notes

Citations from the periodicals *The War Cry, The Musician,* or *The Local Officer and Bandsman* are for the Australian version, unless otherwise noted. Band journal citations are given for Australian composers only; only titles are given for more current releases in the publications released in London.

1. Gore, W. *The War Cry*, SA Melbourne, Sept.14, 1907, p5.

2. Bolton, B. *Booth's Drum*, Hodder and Stoughton, 1980, p228.

3. Booth W., *In Darkest England and the Way Out.* Social Services Centenary Edition USA 1984, p286.

4. *Ibid*, p286.

5. Peeke, K. *Pressing Onward*, SA, Aust Sthn Territory 1990, p57.

6. *The Musician*, Oct 1960, p153.

7. *The Musician*, Aug 1957, p124.

8. *The Musician*, Aug 1957, p124.

9. *The Musician*, Aug, 1957, p124.

10. *The War Cry* (Australia) Jan 25, 1890, p4.

11. Lily Sampson, *Grassroots Army*, SA, Melbourne, 1980.

12. Dale, P. in *The Musician*, Jan 1947, p8.

13. Gore, W. *The War Cry*, Sept.14, 1907, p5.

14. Peeke, K. *Pressing Onward*, p59.

15. Peeke, K. *Pressing Onward*, p20.

16. Bolton, B. *Booth's Drum*, p36.

17. Dale, P. in *The Local Officer and Bandsman*, March 1947.

18. Peeke, K. *Pressing Onward,* p62.

19. Dale, P. *Salvation Chariot*, SA, Melbourne, 1952, p63.

20. *The Local Officer and Bandsman*, Nov, 1910.

21. *The Local Officer and Bandsman*, 1910.

22. Peeke, K. *Pressing Onward*, p106.

23. *The Local Officer and Bandsman*, July 1948, p175.

24. *The War Cry*, July 5th 1890.

25. *Local Officer and Bandsman*, May 1913, p10.

26. *Local Officer and Bandsman*, Jan 15, 1920, p3.

27. *The Musician*, July 1951, p99.

28. Dale, P. *Salvation Chariot*, p58.

29. *The Local Officer and Bandsman*, June 1910.

30. *The Musician*, July 1949, p9.

31. Peeke, K. *Pressing Onward*, p107.

32. Mavis Gullidge. Conversation with John Cleary. 15th May 1998.

33. Blainey, G. *The Tyranny of Distance*, MacMillan Australia, 2001.

34. Mac Crocker, 'Salvos and Skyhooks', *Rolling Stone* (Australia) No.181, Feb 27, 1975.

35. *The Musician*, 13th June 1970, p86.

36. Cleary, J. *Salvo! The Salvation Army in the 1990s*. Focus Books 1993.

37. *The Musician*, March 13, 1993, p8.

Chapter 8

NEW ZEALAND

Warren Baas

We are a permanent mission to the unsaved...and the primary purpose of our music should be to help bridge the gap between the saved Salvationist and the man in the street. I would like to hear more original songs with a real gospel appeal and intelligible to the average pagan – songs that can be used as a solo or by a songster brigade. They will need to be good enough to compete with the latest popular song and yet be of permanent value in our music repertoire. Men like Slater and Herbert Booth served their generation in this way... Our band music is technically excellent, but ours is the problem of making contact with the sinner through the playing of a band. Regardless of whether or not the style of composition is 'clear and plain' always the message must be 'clear and plain.'[1] Dean Goffin

New Zealand has ranked amongst the most enthusiastic and adaptable brass band nations in the world, not only in the SA but also in the whole brass band movement. This enthusiasm stemmed from the maintenance of a high standard of proficiency for a small nation isolated from traditional brass band countries and has been reflected by numerous successful tours and recordings bands have made.

This chapter sketches the formation of New Zealand society as a British colony and the SA's contribution to that process.

The roles which typical small bands play in SA ministry are outlined, and then bands which have international reputations: Christchurch City, Wellington South, Wellington City, Newton Citadel and Auckland Congress Hall, are discussed. Important personalities are mentioned in conjunction with the main band with which they are associated. The chapter concludes with a projection for New Zealand SA bands.

Early New Zealand History

Advertised as an 'antipodean Arcadia' New Zealand was settled by the British from 1840, inheriting many of the 'old country's traditions. When the first militia arrived to maintain British rule, they brought with them their sports, customs and military bands. At the height of the 1845–1846 and 1860–1870 New Zealand Land Wars between the Crown and indigenous Maori, there were nearly 10,000 British troops stationed in New Zealand with 11 of the 14 British Imperial Regiments having military bands. Civilian brass bands grew from garrison bands and brass band contests were first held during Easter 1880.[2]

The 1880s threw into relief the level of hardship experienced by settlers who toiled to produce wool, timber and gold. Social divisions based on wealth occurred. Christian faith and practice played a fundamental role in the shaping of colonial society, though early missions were focused towards the Maori rather than immigrants.

Charity may have been dispensed according to the degrading Victorian notions of the 'deserving' and 'non-deserving' poor, but it was the churches – not government social welfare – which helped the needy. Gradually church orphanages, 'refuges' for prostitutes, private and industrial schools for uncontrolled children grew up. Drunkenness, theft, assault and vagrancy were the principal causes of imprisonment but institutional reform could not attack the basic causes of crime, the most common of which was drink.[3]

By the 1880s nearly half of the 600,000 European population who had arrived since the 1840s were New Zealand-born and so grew up in a country without signs of an historical past. Many British immigrants were unable to regard the colony as home and so transmitted to their children and perpetuated a sentimentalised version of the British way of life.

The Arrival of The Salvation Army

The Salvation Army's 'invasion' of New Zealand was led by Lieutenants George Pollard (aged 20) and Edward (Ted) Wright (aged 19) during the height of the colony-wide recession. Working people, some of whom had religious backgrounds, were impressed by the forthrightness and zeal of the officers, and formed a ground-swell of support. However, many recruits were drunkards, criminals, prostitutes and unemployed people – victims of the recession who experienced real conversion. By targeting these people the Army helped fill a large socio-spiritual vacuum. Yet the Army was not without its critics.

The Reverend W. Morley, late President of the New Zealand Wesleyan Conference, received wide coverage of his lecture, 'The Salvation Army – its lessons and dangers'. He was critical of the 'questionable means used to attract notice when opening on a new battlefield', the 'want of reverence', and the 'autocratic control of General William Booth'.

SA music in New Zealand began with singing and Pollard playing his concertina. The first issue of the *War Cry*, reported that Captain 'Ironsides' Edwards was forming a brass band from among Christchurch converts; the second issue records that Dunedin was following suit. One of the objectives of forming bands was to imbue converts with a sense of urgency in committing their energies to prosecuting the salvation war. The success of these endeavours was shown in music playing an important role in the first congress meetings held in Dunedin at Christmas 1883.[4]

Participation in SA bands in New Zealand is not an exclusively male occupation, though it appears that except in rural areas where personnel was scarce, the sexes were divided into their own bands for some time. A 'Lasses Band' of eleven was created in 1888 in Christchurch under Captain Charles Robinson.

Herbert Booth remarked that he believed it was the first Lasses Band in the Army world. The Otahuhu Corps, in Auckland, formed its own Lasses Band of nine in 1889 under the direction of the Corps Officer, Captain Pallant. Early in

1892 volunteers were called for a Lasses Band to tour the country and attempt to raise funds for a new headquarters building in Christchurch. After three weeks training under George Jackson the twenty-four-piece band, led by Ensign Jim Wilson, toured for almost a year, achieving its financial objective, and gaining converts in its meetings.

George Jackson (b. 1866; d. 27 October 1893)

George Jackson was a gifted and versatile pioneer of the New Zealand SA. After his appointment as a SA officer in 1888 he served variously as *War Cry* editor, trade manager, financial secretary, and private secretary to Colonel Ruben Bailey, the

The versatile George Jackson, editor, composer and arranger, who died of tuberculosis in 1893, aged 27.

Colonial Commander. In 1893 Jackson was also involved with photography, in developing a zinc process for *War Cry* illustrations, and in producing slides for the early magic lantern programmes. Musically he trained the Lasses Band, was a contributor to the early issues of the *Musical Salvationist*, and was solely responsible for the early issues of the *New Zealand Band Journal* [*NZBJ*]. He is best remembered now for his song 'I want, dear Lord' (SB 426).

The remains of the pioneer *NZBJ* are fragmentary, only one second baritone part book in the Oamaru Corps band library is extant. This book reveals the first seven issues of the journal consisted of some 220 scored hymn tunes, though it is uncertain what the scoring of the band was. George Jackson was working on the eighth issue when he died of tuberculosis in 1893, aged 27.

George Jackson's younger brother, Ebbie, also became an officer, and shared with him the musical directorship of the ten-member Headquarters Staff Band which undertook several evangelical tours in 1891. Ebbie Jackson was transferred to Australia at the end of 1891, becoming famous as the conductor of the Australasian Guards Band which toured New Zealand and the Australian colonies in 1895, and as one of the early conductors of the Melbourne Staff Band [MSB].

Dunedin Fortress Band: the First Band

One of the early day Dunedin Salvationists, Robert Hughson, describes the development of the Dunedin Fortress Band from 1883 thus:

> *The first efforts were crude as there were many learners, but the enthusiasm was great. The first Bandmaster was Floyd, a New South Welshman. The first music was arranged by the bandsmen, one of whom, Mr. W. R. Don, was later to become a Doctor of Music. Other Bandmasters included: Herd, Harry Wilson and Tucker, under whom the band progressed in leaps and bounds. Sacred marches from the publishers Wright and Round were drawn upon for processional purposes.*
>
> *Captain Veitch was the officer who had to enforce the new SA policy of its bands only playing SA music. Although the edict was made in London in 1881 [sic] it was not until Ballington Booth visited New Zealand [in 1885] that it was enforced. Until that time the Fortress band played arrangements made by the competent musicians in the band. For Ballington Booth's visit the Dunedin bandsmen wore smart new tunics with loose*

Dunedin Fortress Band, 1929, with Bandmaster Arthur Millard seated 4th from the right, with euphonium. Deputy Bandmaster Howe, the solo euphonium, was absent when the picture was taken.

'frogs' and barrel buttons similar to that worn by General Booth... But Ballington Booth had no flattering praise for the band and rebuked them thus, 'When I came to Dunedin I did not expect to be met by a band in which all men were generals and playing the devil's music at that'... No marching tune was allowed that had what is known as an introduction, bass solo or trio. This seemed to some of the best musicians of the band as a travesty of music decorum and when leave was asked to play their own arrangements which had hitherto been acceptable, permission was flatly rejected. More in sorrow than in anger the doughty and in many cases talented bandsmen who had stood up to the contumely and scorn, the physical violence, the rotten eggs and flour bombs of the roughs, resigned from the Army and left it much smaller in number and poorer in musical ability. The band was composed of a residue to whom music as music held no great appeal, hence a less useful band was left in many ways.[5]

The instrumentation of SA bands in New Zealand took some decades to standardise. Early on, clarinets were used in the Dunedin Fortress Band so that music from the *Australian*

Band Journal (published between 1883 and 1913 in Melbourne; *AuBJ*) which included solo cornet parts with high B-flats could be performed. Other early bandmasters of the Fortress Band were Olly Judd, Albert Gould and Arthur Millard.

Arthur William Millard (b. Invercargill, 18 December 1888, d. Palmerston North, 26 December 1965)

The son of pioneer SA soldiers of Invercargill, Arthur Millard joined the Dunedin North Corps Band when he was about 15. Later he led the Dunedin Fortress Band for over twenty years. From the 1920s it broadcast over radio, playing his own compositions. Millard was a boot-repairer by trade and was largely self-taught as a composer, transcribing classical music for the family orchestra in which he played cello. The bulk of Millard's music remains unpublished, much of it written for special occasions such as incidental music to tableaux for band and songster trips. His first published piece, the Meditation, *Hursley* (FS 27), was the first SA composition to bear the rubric expressly forbidding bands from performing *Festival Series* music in other than music festivals. The composition itself is remarkable for its rich harmonic palette and use of unusually sharp brass band keys. Millard's published marches, *The Timaru March* (GS 1025) and *Palmerston North* (GS 1446) are typical of the genre written by New Zealand composers of the era, though Millard's hold more contrapuntal interest than do his contemporaries' marches.

Open-air meetings were a primary function of bands before broadcasting. They were not only occasions for putting the church onto the street in what Bramwell Booth described as 'peripatetic organs' but the effect of the marching band was something akin to a visible, audible and recognisable spiritual pied piper. Numerous early *War Cry* and newspaper accounts record the SA attracting large crowds due to people following the bands to the meeting hall. In order to have outdoor music it was necessary for early New Zealand bands to flout regulations issued from London restricting the type of music played. New Zealand is an isolated country, and music published in London was expensive and took time to arrive. Furthermore New Zealand bands were often smaller than their northern hemisphere counterparts. Evidence suggests that early bands used marches from secular Australian band journals like *Allens Brass Band Journal* (published by Allens, Melbourne), *The Inter-colonial Brass and Military Band Journal* (T. E. Bulch, Ballarat), and *Suttons Brass Band Journal* (Sutton Propriety, Melbourne) to supplement officially sanctioned SA music.

The 1905 competition run by the IMED in London saw, *The Christchurch Citadel March* (GS 507) by Bandmaster Arthur Young of the Christchurch Citadel win third prize. Yet it was decades before New Zealand composers became regular contributors to the Army's international journals. In the 1920s an attempt to encourage the composition and performance of New Zealand music was made with the publication from Territorial Headquarters of the *NZBJ* under the editorship of Henry Charles Goffin. The first volume contains 17 marches, four selections and one page of seven hymn tunes. No score was published and the instrumentation is the same as the 17 parts required for the *General Series* journal. The composers represented were Goffin, Harold Scotney, Arthur Scotney, Arthur Millard, Albert E. Greenfield, and Bandsman L. Francis.

The SA spread quickly through the island nation. Most new corps formed a band because they were an effective means by which people were attracted to the Army, and retained within its ranks as meaningful participatory members. Like all proselytising book religions, the missionary zeal associated with winning converts has the positive educational spin-off of creating a literate society. The SA went further, for many converts were also given a rudimentary musical as well as literary education. The structure of corps and brass bands also gave able members opportunities to exercise leadership qualities.

Small Bands

Most towns and localities in New Zealand have had a brass band of some description. Many corps bands in small cities and small suburban corps have had fewer than 20 regular players and would be best described as brass ensembles. The rural-urban drift has also been a feature of New Zealand sociological change since World War II. This has affected the size of rural corps and consequently the size of their bands. The effect has also been felt in suburban corps where soldiers have elected to commute to central city corps rather than soldier in the suburbs. Consequently many corps struggle to maintain bands of sufficient size to accompany songs in meetings. Even so, many corps have risen to such challenges and function with credit to their corps and local community. It is these bands which carry the bulk of SA music service in New Zealand.

Rural corps such as Stratford and Eltham in the Taranaki region rarely have had bands in excess of a dozen players. Country areas have always had difficulties retaining musicians because no sooner did players become proficient than they were enticed into non-SA music making or were attracted to larger population centres. Many bandmasters in small corps took on the responsibility of maintaining instrumental music as a personal challenge, serving their corps for many years like George Argyle of Ashburton for 45 years, and Philip Robertson who still serves Whangarei after more than 35 years. Bands in rural areas were not exempt from official censure either. In Stratford's early ministry, soldiers used to rotate in circles in open-air meetings so as to avoid prosecution for 'obstructing public ways'.[6]

From Whangarei in the north of the North Island to Invercargill in the south of the South Island small bands are involved in the routine of corps life. Small corps bands typically rehearse once a week for Sunday indoor meetings and may hold an open-air meeting. Open-airs are held when the public are about when shops open late or in residential areas. Many bands have succumbed to 'political correctness' by choosing to perform to rest homes and hospitals rather than conduct regular open-air evangelical meetings and risk causing 'offence' by proclaiming the gospel to secular audiences.

Street marching was on the wane in the 1970s and 1980s and is now practically unheard of except for Divisional or Territorial events. On Sundays most bands play in the morning holiness meeting and the evening salvation meeting, contributing an instrumental message in both. Bands' contributions may be an arrangement though often it will be the rendering of a tune from the *Tune Book*. In addition to their corps responsibilities bands are often called upon to perform civic duties such as accompanying hymn singing at

Anzac Day[7] services and community carol services at
Christmas. The Otahuhu Corps Band is one that has benefited
from its local council through the donation of money and
instruments so that it could act as the Municipal Band when
required.[8]

Perhaps the biggest undertaking for any SA band is the
annual Christmas caroling season. New Zealand is a southern
hemisphere country so Christmas falls in summer with long
daylight hours. Before private motorised transport was
widespread it was not uncommon in rural areas for one
caroling round to take from before dawn until after sunset on
a Saturday. Today bands' schedules are often as busy but the
commitment is spread throughout the week. This public
service is amongst the most popular, most visible and most
expected from the public that demands bands to perform at
many private and public Christmas functions.

The musical development and interest of bandsmen in
small bands has been encouraged by morale boosting yet
infrequent small bands festivals and tours. Feilding Corps
greatly appreciated the opportunities it had to have its band
perform at Congress meetings in 1914 and 1921 and its Drum
and Fife Band in 1916.[9] More recently city bands and visiting
overseas bands have visited smaller centres. Since 1988 the
National Youth Band has enabled talented young players the
opportunity of playing advanced music, creating an outlet for
musical expression without having to leave their home corps
because of mounting musical frustrations.

Serious efforts to produce music for the small bands in the
Territory were made in 1946 after a performance of Ray
Cresswell's, *The Victor's Day* scored for eight parts at the 1945
Band Councils. Local composers were invited by Senior-Major
Albert Chandler to submit pieces for the *New Zealand
Ensemble Journal* in a scoring that is now known as the *Unity
Series* distribution of parts. Further, Ray Cresswell also
appealed to IHQ for the establishment of a journal designed to
meet the needs of the Army's many small bands. His and
others entreaties were eventually answered in 1957 when the
first of the *Unity Series* journals appeared. The New Zealand
Territory's attempts to bring about its own ensemble journal
were finally abandoned after the change of appointment of
Albert Chandler in 1951.

Raymond Francis Cresswell (b. 30 May 1910, d. 1990)

Ray Cresswell, the son of SA officer parents, began playing in the St Alban's Corps Band from the age of nine, having been instructed by Bandmaster Joe Taylor of Christchurch City Corps. After taking an engineering apprenticeship, Cresswell transferred to Newton Corps where he undertook private

Ray Cresswell, composer of many prominent Army marches, and much more. Pictured here in his Motueka uniform.

music study with a retired music professor. His first pieces were written and rehearsed with the Petone Corps Band when he moved there as a fitter in the New Zealand Railway Workshops. *Maori Melodies* was his first success. Although it was not well received in London by the IMED, it was published in New Zealand without score in 1950 and found a ready audience when it was played and broadcast over the radio.

When Cresswell moved to Motueka (north of the South Island) upon seizing an opportunity to work the family farm, he doubled the size of the Corps band from one to two. He became bandmaster of a band that never exceeded twelve in number. Humbly conscious of his ability as a composer, Cresswell championed small ensembles and wrote vast quantities of music for them. He excelled in writing simple marches, selections and arrangements. His style was straightforward, unpretentious with SA melodies to the fore, and singable counter-melodies contained within a sound, if unadventurous, harmonic framework. His most frequently performed composition is the lilting 6/8 march, *Petone Citadel* (GS 1360) but his contribution to small bands extended into the far reaches of the Army world because he wrote them music which was performable.

Ray Cresswell was presented with a special Centennial Award in 1983 in recognition of his small band compositional efforts. In 1985 the Wellington Citadel Band performed a festival consisting entirely of his music as a gesture of thanks on his retirement.

Small bands and the types of activities that they participate in have carried the bulk of SA band service in New Zealand. The bands that are now examined are atypical of normal band service. They have often held a much higher public profile because of their depth of leadership, musicianship, Christian witness and overall exposure. In this regard these bands may be considered outstanding.

Ray Cresswell, the shepherd, in a 1962 photograph from the New Zealand War Cry.

Christchurch City Band

Since its beginnings in 1883 the Christchurch City Band has held open-airs in Cathedral Square, sometimes under difficult circumstances. In 1911 three summonses were issued for delivering an address and for praying aloud in the Square. Since the by-law preventing preaching was repealed, open-airs have been a regular feature of corps life, though rarely to the extent as this account from 1893:

> *Then on Sunday we beat the record for open-air meetings. One brother on Sunday said, 'Dear friends, this makes ten open-air meetings I have addressed this day'. And such was the case, for the Army held no fewer than fifteen open-air meetings during the day. While the Holiness meeting was in progress, there was a batch of old warriors scouring the district with the band, and holding*

meetings in places where the Army had not been for years.[10]

Joe Taylor probably had the greatest influence on the musical life of the Christchurch City Corps. From the time he was enrolled as a senior soldier in 1897 until he left the corps in 1928, he was at various times bandmaster, songster-leader and leader of the string band of over 20 instrumentalists, and at times all three. Each of these groups of musicians took part in services, with the strings playing regularly during prayer meetings.

Among the others who led the Christchurch City Band were: Brother Baker, Arthur Young (won third prize in the 1905 composition competition), Herb Walker, Les Sutton, Ern Smith, Norman Goffin (elder brother of Dean Goffin), Joe Hay, Alf Suter (who served the band for 45 years and was bandmaster on two occasions), Ken Bridge (later Chief Secretary of the New Zealand Territory), Edwin Danholt, Tom Brown, Ken Smeaton, Les France, Rex Arbuckle, Norman Gardner and Martin Robertson.

The Christchurch City Band raised funds for three new sets of instruments in 1937, 1949, and 1968. Further fundraising was also necessary as the band undertook trips within New

The Christchurch City Band.

Zealand from Auckland to Dunedin. In August 1974 Thomas Brown led the band on its tour to Australia. To help mark the 60th anniversary of the Singapore/Malaysia Command, the band toured the area in June 1995 under Norman Gardner. Other unique performance opportunities have been the 10th Commonwealth Games Interdenominational Church Service and the dedication of the Christchurch Town Hall Complex in 1974. More regularly the Christchurch City Band has performed at the now televised Christmas Eve Carol Service in Victoria Square. On a practical level, the bandsmen help staff the Civil Defence Emergency Caravan.

Wellington South Band[11]

The SA began its work in the Newtown district of Wellington on 28 January 1891 under Lieutenant Sam Renshaw and Captain Will Dawson. Initially Wellington City Corps assisted with music making but a small band was functioning by the turn of the century. Wellington at that time had a population of 49,000 and by April 1904 the corps had changed its name to 'Wellington South' to avoid confusion with Newton Corps in Auckland.

Commitment to musical presentation was also important for early Salvationists. In preparation for its first trip away to the 1907 Congress held in connection with the International Exhibition held at Hagley Park, Christchurch, the Wellington South Band rehearsed four times per week, two of the

Wellington South Band, 1946.

rehearsals being from 4.30–6.00 am. During the Great War the South Band managed a campaign to Levin during Easter 1918 despite many of the bandsmen having enlisted for military duty in Europe. After the War the South Band supported the Congress meetings in 1920 led by General Bramwell Booth, a function it has performed each time there has been a Congress in Wellington.

New Zealand's vulnerability to overseas agriculture prices and slumps in demand brought acute economic problems that became catastrophic after the New York stock market crash in 1929. During this period of social upheaval the band underwent numerous changes of leadership from the late 20s until the mid 30s. In May 1936 Captain Fred Searle invited 19 year-old Dean Goffin to transfer from the Wellington City Corps to become bandmaster at Wellington South. The *War Cry* suggested that the new Bandmaster's 'youth, musical capabilities and good Salvationism, should ensure rapid progress of the band'.

In 1937 Dean Goffin formed a corps orchestra which featured a number of the conductor's own arrangements in its repertoire. The South Band's presentation of Eric Ball's *Air Varié, Sound Out the Proclamation* in October 1937 provoked the *War Cry* reporter to write, *This band was knocking insistently at the door for recognition as a front ranker.* His comments were vindicated with the band's first radio broadcast on June 2, 1939.

The outbreak of war in Europe saw the progress of the band retarded because of the enlisting of many band personnel, including its bandmaster. Harrison Millard, son of Arthur Millard, strived to maintain musical standards but with the introduction of conscription for 18–46 year old men in 1940 his task was difficult. Dean Goffin resumed control of the Wellington South Band when he returned from overseas, but less than a year later he left to become a manager with the music firm Charles Begg and Co., Timaru, and Harrison Millard again took charge.

Dean Goffin travelled from Timaru to conduct his newly completed, *Thanksgiving for a Special Occasion* to mark the presentation of a new set of instruments to the Wellington South Band in 1949. This work was later revised and renamed, *Symphony of Thanksgiving* (FS 187) and used as a feature piece for the International Staff Band's 75th Anniversary celebrations. Dean Goffin, having completed SA Officer training, was appointed to Wellington South in 1953 and Harrison Millard was happy to give the baton to him. In September that year a 'Manuscript Festival' was held and the premiere performance of *Prelude and Fugue on 'Darwells'* (FS 230) was presented. Millard resumed control of the band upon the Goffins' farewell to London in 1956. Eric Rive in turn became bandmaster in 1957.

The Wellington South Band continued its demanding programme of corps witnessing, broadcasting, and Congress duties, and recorded its first long-playing record in 1963, *Inspired Brass,* under Rive's leadership. Wellington South Band made its first overseas tour to Australia in August 1971. Harrison Millard retired as Bandmaster in May 1972 after serving 22 years in the position.

David Howan continued the band's tradition of corps and territorial engagements, and recorded a long-playing record featuring Dean Goffin's music preceding the band's second Australian tour in August 1978. Domestic tours continued after the Centenary Congress (1983) and a third Australian tour (August 1987) marked the culmination of David Howan's bandmastership. Upon Bob Carrig's appointment as bandmaster David Howan became the first Divisional Music Director for the Wellington Division.

Bob Carrig was involved in the preparations for the busy Wellington South centenary celebration in 1991 including music festivals, one of which presented styles of Salvation Army music from its beginnings to the present. Stephen Stein became Bandmaster in 1991, having been principal cornetist in the Wellington Citadel Band. Stein continued the full and vibrant music programme of the Wellington South Band until his appointment as Bandmaster of the National Youth Band and Territorial Music Secretary in1998. The Wellington South Band has been served successively by Major Lindsay Chisholm, Ian Gainsford and Duncan Horton.

John Dean Goffin (b. Wellington, 9 July 1916, d. Auckland, 24 January 1984)

Dean Goffin's contribution to brass banding in New Zealand and Great Britain, where he served as National Bandmaster

Commissioner, Sir Dean Goffin.

(1956–1960) and National Secretary for Bands and Songster Brigades (1960–1966), has been immense. The third son of SA Officer parents Henry and Kate Goffin, Dean had a sound heritage of SA music. He was trained in the fundamentals of theory and composition by Cecil Fitzwater, Percy Tombs, the Napier cathedral organist, and his father. Although Dean Goffin confessed to being 'an indifferent performer on any instrument' he was offered the bandmastership of the Wellington South Corps because of his knowledge and leadership potential.

When Goffin enlisted for the First Echelon of the New Zealand Expeditionary Force his reputation as a band trainer went with him and he was promoted to sergeant and given the responsibility of forming and training the band of the 20th Infantry Battalion of the 4th Brigade. While serving in North Africa, Crete, Egypt and Italy Goffin not only conducted but also arranged and composed band music.

It was in Egypt 1942 that *Rhapsody in Brass* was completed. This original work, published in 1948, was chosen as the 'A-Grade' test piece at the British Open Brass Band

Championship (Belle Vue), Manchester in 1949. It was then that the SA realised that it had received a number of compositions from Goffin but had not published any of them. Consequent of Goffin's 'civilian' fame the SA began to publish his music: *Light of the World* (GS 1329) in 1950, a composition that still stands as the Army's quintessential meditation. *Symphony of Thanksgiving* and the Festival March, *Crusaders* (FS 173) followed shortly afterwards.

Dean and Marjorie Goffin entered the SA Officer training college in 1951. After initial pastoral corps appointments in New Zealand they were transferred to Great Britain where Dean became National Bandmaster, responsible for inspecting and rehearsing some 1,000 bands around the British Territory.

His schedule was hectic. As National Secretary for Bands and Songster Brigades he became responsible for organising musical events throughout Britain. Upon his transfer back to New Zealand in 1966 Dean Goffin was appointed to senior administrative positions which culminated in his appointment as Territorial Commander with the rank of Commissioner in 1980. In 1983 Dean Goffin was created a Knight Bachelor in the Queen's Birthday Honours List, the first New Zealand SA officer to accept the title, 'Sir'.

History will remember Dean Goffin for a handful of memorable compositions written in a relatively brief period at the height of his creative output before he entered full-time ministry.

Dean Goffin should be remembered first and foremost as a masterly band trainer and inspirational bandmaster. Preaching and pastoral care characterise the early years of his Salvation Army officership. His term in Britain was notable for its relentless travelling and rehearsal schedules. In his later career he was a capable administrator. His small corpus of compositions—that which the average band enthusiast remembers him by—were a fraction of his dedicated service to the SA. Dean Goffin was not a semi-professional composer. When the SA ordered his appointments it did not appoint a composer; it needed a bandmaster, and later it needed an organiser.

Dean Goffin's life was one of unceasing service as opposed to a life of enduring compositional productivity.

Wellington Citadel Band

The Wellington Citadel Band has been widely acclaimed as one of the foremost SA corps bands in the world, through its pioneering radio and television broadcasts, and recordings and international touring. Formed in 1887, it was under the direction of Herbert Tremain, who had moved south from Auckland in 1912, when Henry Charles Goffin arrived in 1913. Tremain, aware of Goffin's musical reputation, handed the band over. It was under both bandmasters, H.C. Goffin and Harold Scotney, that the Wellington Citadel Band built its reputation.

Harold Scotney moved to Wellington in 1916 and became Henry Goffin's deputy, playing soprano cornet and alto horn. Photographs of the era show 38 musicians in 1914 including two trumpets and mellophones. In 1918 the band had grown to 42 and additionally had two alto saxophones, a tenor and baritone saxophone. After Goffin's appointment to Foxton in 1919, Scotney introduced the band to live radio broadcasts in the 1920s. The two men exchanged command of the band upon Goffin's appointments in and out of Wellington. Scotney

Wellington Citadel Band, 1914, with Bandmaster Henry Charles Goffin. Note the two trumpets and mellophones.

regained the band in 1928 when Goffin was transferred to the new Auckland Congress Hall complex, but emigrated to Sydney in 1934 for health reasons. Goffin became the first Territorial Secretary for Bands, Special Efforts and Publicity in 1935. The quarter-century Goffin/Scotney era ended in 1938 with the appointment of Herbert Neeve as bandmaster.

Bert Neeve, a cornet player, demanded the highest standards of both spiritual and musical witness. World War II was the one major interruption of Neeve's thirty years of outstanding consistent leadership of the band. He led, by impeccable example, a group of dedicated men to new heights of Christian witness and Salvationist musicianship, being supported by band Secretary Selwyn Bridge, and soloists of renown such as Lester Harford, Gordon Hildreth and Ray Atherfold. Under Bert Neeve's leadership the Wellington Citadel Band became the first SA band to visit Australia in 1949 and 1964. The band's most ambitious and successful tour was the 1968 World Tour to the USA, Canada and Britain. Reviews of the tour speak of a band with immaculate tone control and precise musicianship.[12] The band's repertoire included a number of items by New Zealanders, including some written for the band including Thomas Rive's euphonium and band transcription of Mozart's *Fourth Horn Concerto* (K495) for Gordon Hildreth, Ray Cresswell's cornet duet, *Joyful Melody* for Lester Harford and Ray Atherfold, and Dean Goffin's, *Crusaders* which had been written for the 1949 Australian tour.

When television finally arrived in New Zealand in the early 1960s the Broadcasting Corporation wanted religious

By 1918 the Band had increased to forty two bandsmen and additionally had two Alto Saxophones and a Tenor and Baritone Saxophone.

Wellington Citadel Band. World Tour Photograph, 1968.

programmes made. Salvationists were prominent in creating programmes as opposed to treating television as an extension of a church pulpit. Eric Geddes featured the Wellington Citadel Band on air for the first time in 1963. He took full command of the band in the early 1970s, maintaining the band's high level of performance and undertaking two tours to Japan and the Far East in 1979 and 1985. He met Pope John Paul II after conducting the band at an open-air rally.

Bruce Hoare, the band's long-serving E-flat bass soloist, took charge of the band after the second visit to Japan. Although the band lost a number of experienced personnel through retirement and transfer around this time, it has continued its many engagements associated with corps and territorial activities but has not undertaken an overseas venture since Japan. In the early 1990s principal trombonist Ross McMillan became bandmaster. Among the innovative performance opportunities the band has undertaken in McMillan's tenure has been the Praise Proms, a New Zealand Christian adaptation of the famous BBC's Last Night of the Proms from the Royal Albert Hall.

Since then Eric Geddes has resumed control of the Wellington Citadel Band, taking it on a tour in 2002 of Canada and the United Kingdom with a professional dramatic and visual programme reflective of New Zealand and New Zealanders' acclaimed cinematic ability with motion pictures such as *The Piano* and *The Lord of the Rings* trilogy.

Harold Scotney (b. Treeton, Yorkshire 1888, d. Sydney, Australia 1973)

Harold Scotney immigrated with his parents to New Zealand in 1892. He became bandmaster of the Dannevirke corps band in 1904 at the age of sixteen. His first published pieces were the prize-winning marches, *Ruahine* (AuBJ 299) and *Dannevirke March* (AuBJ 308) appearing in the *AuBJ* in 1910. When Scotney emigrated to Sydney in 1934 he became bandmaster of the Sydney Congress Hall Band, and later Territorial Band Inspector, a position he held until his retirement. Dean Goffin described Harold Scotney as a 'thorough and conscientious workman' who did much to contribute to the 'golden age' of Salvation Army marches in the 1920s. Two fine published examples of these marches are dedicated to the Wellington Salvationists: *Wellington Citadel* (GS 887) and *The Wellingtonian* (GS 934). Both marches exhibit traits of Scotney's style: bold harmonic 32-measure introductions, strong bass solos, and occasional obbligato lines for soprano cornet – examples of Scotney writing for himself and illustrative of his belief in letting every part of the band make an important contribution.

Henry Charles Goffin (b. 8 March 1885, Plymouth, Devon, d. 3 March 1973)

Henry Goffin, a second generation Salvationist, was a bandsman at thirteen and appointed bandmaster of Plymouth Two, aged fifteen in 1900. He won second prize for the march *Plymouth* (GS 558) in the march section of the 1907 International Music Competition run by the IMED. This piece is remarkable because any direct religious reference by way of an identifiable melody is practically lost owing to the eclectic nature of the bass solo which comprised fragments of four tunes, including, *Grandfather's Clock*.

Goffin married Catherine Fergusson in 1909. In 1911 after the couple had been stationed in Glasgow as SA officers for some months and having witnessed severe social problems,

they retired from active service. The Goffins were nominated as immigrants by the Wellington Citadel Band and the family (sons Harry, born 1910, and Norman, 1911) sailed to New Zealand in 1913.

Goffin penned some of his most well-known compositions during the Great War: *The Red Shield* (GS 986), perhaps the classic SA march, was written for a deep regard for the Army's 'Red Shield' huts during the war, *The Salvation Army Patrol* (GS 1012) and *New Zealand Warriors* (GS 1041). The march, *Absent Comrades* (NZBJ 14) was written in memory of three Wellington Citadel bandsmen who died in the war. The popular cornet solo, *Maoriland* (GS 1114) was based on a tune from a Hawkes Bay Maori concert party heard at a festival in the Wellington Citadel.[13] It was written around 1921 for his second son, Norman, who was ten at that time.

At his various appointments around New Zealand Henry Goffin often took control of the corps band and encouraged boys to join junior bands or bugle bands. Much of the music he wrote remains unpublished or lost. His most celebrated conducting engagement was the rehearsal and performance of

Handel's *Messiah* at Congress, April 1949, in Wellington. This was the first time the SA in New Zealand had attempted to assemble a large chorus of 300 songsters for the performance of an oratorio. The event was a remarkable triumph and the feat has been repeated only once since, in Christchurch in 1974, when Dean Goffin was conductor. Henry Goffin was largely an independent character, a self-taught musician who expressed his independence by challenging authority as an officer and writing innovative music that tested established SA musical forms.

Herbert H. Neeve

Bert Neeve arrived in Wellington as bandmaster in 1938 from Newton Citadel. While engaged in military service he was decorated for gallantry in action against the Japanese. Resuming the baton after the war, he set about helping many of the band's former members settle back into civilian life. His musicianship, coupled with his disciplinarian methods, was self-evident from the quality of music presented by the band. His character earned him the unqualified respect and loyalty of his bandsmen and produced a consistently high standard of playing throughout the 40s, 50s, 60s and early 70s. Among the soloists of the era were Gordon 'Tubby' Hildreth, who became acclaimed through recordings of Leidzén's, *Song of the Brother* and Steadman-Allen's, *The Conqueror*, and Lester Harford, a cornet virtuoso renowned for his festival appearances, radio and television broadcasts, and recordings of Leidzén's, *Wondrous Day*, and *A Happy Day*, as well as Terry Camsey's, *Life Pageant*, which was written for Harford.

Newton Citadel Band

Within five months of opening in 1889 Lieutenant Whatford was leading Newton Citadel's first band of ten musicians. Bandmaster Bree, 'put in solid foundations and led his band faithfully in spiritual warfare' as the Corps' first commissioned bandmaster.[14] Notable bandmasters since the pioneering era include two former bandmasters of the Auckland Congress Hall Corps, Harry Deighton and Reginald Davies. Reg Davies particularly was a colourful character who commanded respect.

During his fifteen-year term as bandmaster the standard of playing rose enabling the band to broadcast over radio and record on vinyl. It was during this era that the two Auckland city corps bands of Newton and Congress Hall, based not more than three miles apart, became intense, though good-natured, rivals. Bandmasters who followed included Stan Neeve, Howard Parkinson, Ted Spice and Ron Sawyer.

Early in 1963 Newton Citadel Band came under the leadership of Frank Rawbone when he immigrated to New Zealand. Rawbone had succeeded the famous A. W. Punchard as bandmaster of the Chalk Farm Band in 1944. He had also conducted the Johannesburg City Corps Band in South Africa and the Clapham Congress Hall Band. Rawbone forged Newton Band into one of the finest ensembles in New Zealand, touring widely throughout the North Island and the east coast of Australia in 1968 with Doug Smith as cornet soloist. Periods of ill health led to Frank Rawbone relinquishing the control of the band to Neville Dew and James Denny.

In 1977 leadership passed to Dr Thomas Rive who had been a playing member for some three years. Tom Rive's term as bandmaster at Newton was cut tragically short by his sudden death in February 1978.

James Denny was appointed bandmaster in the second half of 1978 and under Denny's leadership the band undertook a number of short corps visits and made a number of recordings, including an LP of Christmas music.

Michael Craven was appointed bandmaster when James Denny retired in 1981. By recent standards Craven, in his early 20s, was a young leader. He came to the SA from a Brethren background and contest brass banding where he had toured with the National Band of New Zealand and had won the Amateur Cornet Championship of New Zealand in his teens. He had also studied at Auckland University with Tom Rive, majoring in composition, performance trumpet and conducting, gaining a Masters degree. Newton Citadel Band gained new impetus with its young conductor. His selection of new and adventurous scores extended bandsmen and left lasting impressions on audiences with the projection of the spiritual message.

The band toured Victoria and Tasmania during Easter 1983 with a band of 34 and a full repertoire of devotional and praise music including *Easter Glory, The Road to Emmaus, Psalm 100, The Holy War* and *Thy King Cometh.*

Following the Army's New Zealand centenary celebrations in 1983 the Army sought new paths to follow in order to remain relevant to an ever-changing society. The late 1980s in particular saw groups of officers and soldiers challenge Headquarters' position on a wide range of issues, not the least of which was the growing awareness of charismatic relevance. Challenges to organisational authority and the preparedness of people to act upon their convictions within the ranks of the SA was no more than a subplot of what was occurring at large on the stage of New Zealand society.

Since 1984 New Zealanders have elected a succession of free market-oriented governments. Many regulations that restricted the way people interacted have been abolished. Consequently people feel empowered to determine their own lives: they have choice. With respect to church practices individuals have become increasingly comfortable with changing congregations in a similar way they would change schools or jobs: brand loyalty is not an issue in the consumer society. Newton Citadel was one SA corps where large sections of the congregation chose to transfer to other corps or join other churches. As a result the size of the Newton Band fell dramatically. Maurice Robertson became bandmaster after Mike Craven accepted the responsibility of leading the Army's National Youth Band in 1988. While the roll of the Newton Corps remained sustainable, the distribution of ages skewed towards mature people.

Although the Newton Corps complex was situated in a sophisticated part of Auckland, the Army's brand of Christianity failed to attract any of the large numbers of *nouveau riches*, and gay and lesbian community who live there. On Anzac Day 1999 the Newton Corps closed. A band of a dozen played and a small Songster Brigade sang and the 70 soldiers of the corps were assisted with finding new spiritual homes.

Auckland Congress Hall

The main thrust of Auckland Congress Hall Band's ministry has been open-air services, playing at hospitals and institutions, the Sunday evening march through Queen Street, together with its musical contributions at the Auckland Congress Hall.[15] The first open-air meeting, held in

Auckland on April 13 1883 when 19-year-old Captain Ted Wright played his cornet, was witnessed by Herb Tremain (age 16), who was later to become bandmaster of the Auckland City Corps. The Auckland City Corps Band was formed shortly afterwards when two young local musicians were converted. Captain Wright was an able instrumentalist but within months Robert Little was appointed the first bandmaster. Regular playing took place after the opening of the Albert Street Barracks on Good Friday 1884.[16] Early in its history the Auckland City Corps met with resistance which often involved the band, as the following account by the son of an early officer shows,

> *One of the biggest battles took place when marching down one of the city streets with the band leading the march. All went well until the lower end of the street was reached, when round the corner came swinging a big muster of the 'skeleton army'. They were headed by their black flag on which was painted a large white skull and crossbones. There was a clash. The first thing to go was the Army flagpole, broken in half between the defenders and the offenders. The colour-sergeant and others fought bravely for the colours, but the opposing forces were too strong for them.*

Taken from a faded photocopy. Auckland Congress Hall Band, 1916.

A roll-and-tumble game followed… The big drummer was having the time of his life…beating the heads of some of these fellows 'double forte and quick time'… A number of the soldiers were badly knocked about by fists, kicks, and by coming into contact with pocket knives, while some faces were burning from the effects of wet lime that had been wrapped up in paper and thrown into the ranks. Quite a number of uniforms were torn in the scrimmage. This was one of the fiercest nights of opposition experienced since the formation of the corps.[17]

An early character of the period was 'Wingy' Hodgson. He earned his nickname because of the hook on one arm. This had been used in Hodgson's earlier Skeleton Army escapades to tear shirts off Salvationist's backs. After his conversion he used his musical talents for the Army by becoming bandmaster of Auckland Congress Hall and editor of the *NZBJ*. After the SA had become more accepted, the band was trained and fashioned by Herb Tremain who led the band for fifteen years. During this time the band travelled by boat to

Early New Zealand music leaders c.1921; Left to Right: Henry Goffin, Herbert Tremain and Harry Deighton.

the 1907 Christchurch Exhibition. Tremain's successor, Harry Deighton, conducted the band for sixteen years.

The Auckland City Corps moved from its original position in Albert Street to new premises known as the Congress Hall in Greys Avenue in 1928. Although a congress was never held on the site, the corps has since been known as Auckland Congress Hall. Architecturally the front façade of the new building resembled a Bavarian castle complete with ornamental parapets. The main auditorium had a high ceiling and a plastered dome above the platform increased the spacious feel and reverberation of the space. Henry Goffin took command of the band upon his appointment as Corps Officer. Many boys were introduced to brass banding through Goffin's boys' band, particularly during his first appointment to Auckland. Goffin also encouraged prison concerts with the bands.[18]

Following Goffin's appointment to Napier, Thomas Pace took charge. Pace had led bands at Newcastle-on-Tyne (England) and later Adelaide, Australia. Before transferring to Newton Citadel, Reginald Davies was bandmaster for a period in the early 1930s. By 1936 Territorial Commander Lieutenant-Commissioner Fred Adams, who wished to foster the growth of bands, led the band on a three-week tour of Wellington and the South Island with Pace as bandmaster. The period between the wars saw the Congress Hall Band on the streets of Auckland four times a week: Saturday night and three times on Sunday. The corps' three bands marched down Queen Street and open-air meetings were held en-route by the Junior Band, the Auxiliary Band, and the Senior Band marched the furthermost.

Thomas Rive was appointed the youngest bandmaster of Auckland Congress Hall when at 18 he took control of the band on the first of four occasions: 1939–43, 1952–56, 1959–65, and 1967–71. J. H. Wilson was also a bandmaster during World War II, and after the war, Alan Pike, who had played in Dean Goffin's Wellington South Band before hostilities, took charge. Rive's interest in sacred vocal music saw him in good stead to become songster leader in 1945 until he resumed leadership of the band. While Tom Rive was studying for his doctorate the bandmastership fell to Ken Mahaffie (1957-59) who stamped his own mark on the band by leading it on its first overseas tour, to Australia for three weeks in 1958.

Doug Smith, a cornet soloist with the Wellington Citadel Band, became bandmaster in February 1972. The following year the SA began its work in Fiji as a missionary effort. Congress Hall Band toured Fiji via a weekend in Sydney in 1974, and again in 1977 and 1980. It was under Smith's baton that women were first admitted into the band in the early 1980s. The period also saw the band undertake a modernisation of concert performance. Key to its upbeat presentations were a series of festivals designed with Colin Calcott, known as *Close Encounters of a Brass Kind*. These programs and their successors, *Sight and Sound,* were designed to be non-threatening introductions to the gospel message in a contemporary musical setting. The band's most recent album, *Victorious*, was recorded in 1983 and is a more traditional expression of celebration to mark the corps' centenary.

Allan Keay, a former songster leader of Hamilton City Corps and a leader at the first Salvation Army music schools, followed Doug Smith as bandmaster when the latter emigrated to Sydney. Keay held the post for five years before John Townend oversaw the band and its move in 1989 from Greys Avenue to its new complex in Queen Street. During the Keay-Townend period the Congress Hall Band ceased its regular marches through Queen Street and stopped wearing its distinctive red high-neck tunics as standard uniform.

A brass ensemble called *Celestial Brass* was created around this time from members of the corps band and other invited Salvationist musicians. Its function was to support Songster Brigade *Sight and Sound* presentations with top quality brass music. Celestial Brass performed its own contemporary repertoire and had Colin Calcott, Eric Geddes and David Chaulk, formerly of the Canadian Staff Band, as conductors at various times. Although not intended to compete with the corps band, *Celestial Brass*'s insistence on musical excellence excluded a number of less proficient bandsmen and created divisions between the groups.

A number of temporary conductors followed Townend as Bandmaster, including Ken Mahaffie and James Denny, until James Downey was appointed in 1993. Jim Downey served as a trumpeter with the Royal New Zealand Navy Band and had played with the Congress Hall Band for over a decade before his appointment. During the mid 1990s the role of the band in corps worship shrank considerably as it vied for the accompaniment of congregational singing with the corps' Contemporary Music Team (CMT). After a change of corps officer, Downey was encouraged to train the band for successful tours of Fiji and Tonga in 1996, and Chile in 1998. Following Jim Downey was the percussionist of the RNZN band, Brent Hayward, who occasionally led the group from the drum kit. Congress Hall Band is currently conducted by Mark Christiansen.

Thomas Rive (b. Waimate, South Canterbury 2 December 1920, d. Auckland 10 February 1978)

Thomas Rive, born of Salvationist parents, became a bandsman in 1931 and was appointed Waimate Corps

Thomas Rive in uniform of International Staff Band, 1958.

Bandmaster in 1936, aged fifteen. For a brief period in 1938 Rive was Dean Goffin's deputy at Wellington South, and the two musicians spent much time together exploring their skills as composers. Rive moved to Auckland to study music at the university and he joined the Auckland Congress Hall corps in 1938 where he became bandmaster. Between his terms as bandmaster Rive held the posts of deputy bandmaster and corps sergeant major respectively. Under Thomas Rive's leadership the band broadcast regularly over regional and national radio as well as maintaining a full witness in Auckland city. In 1968 he led the band on a successful tour of the central North Island.

Upon graduating Bachelor of Music in 1943, Thomas Rive married Audrey Skellon. Rive fulfilled his National Service obligations during the years 1941-1944 by serving with the New Zealand Home Forces. Following the War Rive worked as a lecturer in Harmony, Counterpoint, Fugue, Composition, Music History, Analysis, Instrumentation and Musical Form at the University of Auckland. In 1949 he undertook post-graduate study in composition at Oxford University and the resulting *Theme and Variations for Orchestra* was published by UNESCO in 1951. In 1958, having registered for a doctoral degree the previous year, Thomas Rive was in London researching his thesis. He was a guest member of the International Staff Band and he conducted his set of variations, *I Know a Fount* (FS 238) on several occasions. Rive graduated Doctor of Philosophy in 1963, the first Ph.D. graduate from Auckland University in Musicology. He was made Associate Professor in 1966, and in 1974 he was appointed to a personal professorial chair.

Thomas Rive was a renowned authority on the vocal music of the Spanish renaissance composer, Thomas Luis de Victoria. Elements of renaissance music pervade Rive's music: the easy flowing polyphonic lines in *Colne* (GS GS 1733 2), *A Pilgrim Song* (FS 309), and *I Know a Fount* are recognisable examples. [See Volume II, Musical Study, for further discussion] Following his retirement as bandmaster of Auckland Congress Hall, Thomas Rive maintained active Salvation Army service as a bandsman at Newton Citadel. On 1st January 1978 he was commissioned bandmaster of Newton Band but was Promoted to Glory just six weeks later.

Thomas Rive's contribution to The Salvation Army has been immense not just from his scholarly-crafted scores but also through his courageous Christian witness in the face of academic scorn. As a university teacher Rive was a target of ridicule from those who rejected faith. Despite the protests Thomas Rive regularly led the Congress Hall Band marches in Auckland's city centre as a witness to his faith. While at the University Thomas Rive was a sensitive counsellor to young Christians, particularly Salvationists and music students, sympathising with their concerns and offering sound encouragement.

Youth Bands

When Dean Goffin returned to New Zealand from Britain and was appointed Territorial Music Secretary he had the idea of forming a Territorial Youth Band following the annual May National Music School. This idea became reality in 1979 when Winston Hoare was selected to lead the band in the 1980 Congress in New Zealand and Australian Centenary Congress in Adelaide. The Youth Band performed with credit and impressed members of the Enfield Citadel Band who were on tour at the time, with its performance of Edward Gregson's, *Laudate Dominum*.

The resurgence of music education programmes in the early 1980s owes much to the charisma and intelligence of Territorial Music Secretary Trevor Davis. The annual Music School was enlarged to included girls' singing in 1981 under Margaret Kendall and many divisional junior music camps were also held. Davis was ably assisted by corps bandmasters Philip Robertson, Harry Ide, Graham Jameson, Mark Stone and Michael Craven. During the mid-1980s the annual Music School became so popular that it divided into two separate schools: Brass and Vocal in May, Contemporary Music and Drama in August. While this decision was taken to alleviate pressures on the Army's facilities at Camp Akatarawa, it also contributed to dividing young people between traditional and contemporary forms of SA music expression.

In 1982 Graeme Smith, formerly of the Wellington Citadel Band, formed a youth band in Auckland for the Northern Division's annual Youth Councils. The band performed a number of non-SA pieces at its evening concert that failed to impress Commissioner Dean Goffin who was the speaker that weekend. Nevertheless the formation of this band showed that there was considerable interest amongst young people to become involved. Divisional Youth Secretary William Millar asked Graham York, who had played with Palmerston North's *Swinging Brass*, to form legitimately a Divisional Youth Band in 1984. This band played at youth councils and undertook a trip to Rotorua before dispersing.

Winston Hoare was asked to form a youth band for the Youth Congress *Epoch* held at Palmerston North in 1987. The ensemble played well and was well received but while members were keen for the band's continuance, Headquarters was insistent that the band was a one-off phenomenon. This failed to prevent the band reforming unofficially for the Easter meetings at Auckland Congress Hall later that year under the title, *Band on the Run*. Following this event the group was formally disbanded.

Youthful determination prevailed and in November 1988 an official National Youth Band [NYB] was formed in response to the persistent enthusiasm shown by young people in spontaneously forming their own bands. It comprised auditioned musicians between the ages of 16 and 30 and was conducted by Michael Craven. The NYB's purpose is to allow young musicians the opportunity to extend themselves musically and develop spiritually through extensive rehearsal, Bible study and evangelistic outreach within the structures of the Army. Members remain active participants in their corps bands and pay their own way to up to six engagements throughout New Zealand each year. Much of the remarkable success of the band, which includes it being the first New Zealand band to record a compact disc, *Come Alive in Christ*, is due to the inspirational leadership of Michael Craven who led the band until 1995.

The NYB plays a wide variety of music including lively classical transcriptions, standard SA festival and devotional scores, and contemporary arrangements. The band featured Robert Redhead's, *A Pastoral Symphony* at the Wellington Congress in 1991 and was also invited to General Eva Burrow's Congress in Auckland the following year. Unfortunately, performing at the Christchurch Youth Congress, *Dunamis Down Under,* in 1993 revealed a distinctive gap between where the teenage audience was at and what the band was delivering. Since 1995 Eric Geddes and

Stephen Stein have both been appointed to conduct the NYB, Stein leading it on a tour of North America in Easter 2002.

Music Schools ceased in 1994 but were replaced by rehearsal weekends for the National Youth Band. In 1997 Territorial Youth Secretary David Noakes instituted the National Development Band with Stewart Stanbridge, a well-respected wind band trainer, conducting. The aim of the Development Band is to encourage 14–25-year-old musicians in Christian values and banding without the time and financial commitment of the NYB. In 2003 the NYB has 36 members, and the National Development Band 40.

Since 1990 the Dean Goffin Conducting Award has been presented in conjunction with the National Music School. The award, presented by Mrs. Commissioner Marjorie Goffin, was created for the encouragement of young conductors after recognising a dearth of young conducting talent. As a result of this award a number of bandmasters have arisen including Stephen Stein and Ross McMillan. The Award is now contested for at NYB rehearsal weekends.

Special Bands

Infrequently bands have been formed to cater for special occasions. Among these events has been the band to accompany Richard Philip's tour in 1994. This band was coached by Eric Geddes and its repertoire included a number of 'stand alone' pieces but also a selection of accompaniments for piano solo, notably the last movement of Rachmaninoff's *Second Piano Concerto* (op.18).

In the mid-1980s Mark Stone was appointed Territorial Contemporary Music Director. He had achieved success with a contemporary music ensemble known as *God's Army Band*, and was responsible for encouraging brass bands to tackle swing-style compositions. He also coordinated the publication of a useful brass tutor, *Blow Your Heart Out for Jesus* which was innovative in the New Zealand territory for its publication with an accompaniment cassette.

Jazz music, and swing in particular, has gained appeal throughout New Zealand as a performance idiom. Palmerston North's *Swinging Brass* caused a sensation at the Centenary Congress in 1983, particularly with improvisation. With the relaxation of the regulation not permitting Salvationist bandsmen to perform in non-SA bands a number of proficient young musicians have joined other groups. *The Brassed Off Big Band* is an example where Salvationist musicians, especially cornetists and trombonists, participate in an 'outside' Christian band led by Stephen Hornblow, who is of Methodist background.

During the 1990s a Divisional Band was formed in Auckland and conducted by James Denny with the aim to provide an outlet for able mature corps musicians in the same way the National Youth Band created an opportunity for geographically spread young musicians to perform. In 1999 a 'Golden Oldies' band fulfils this role.

Future Prospects

Perhaps the most insightful comment ever made about brass banding in New Zealand was when Thomas Rive ventured to say that he believed the significance of the brass band was sociological rather than musical. He believed that its position lay somewhere between sports clubs, service clubs and musical societies, and that a band could not afford to play the music it wanted until it had the backing of the municipality or corporate sponsorship which was only achieved after the band was seen and appreciated by the community. He added that although the popularity of brass banding seemed to be waning, he thought that the musical resources of the brass band had not been fully exploited.[19]

One plan of early Salvationists was to get converts immediately involved in the salvation war. Acknowledging that not all recruits were adept at preaching or able to leave their full time occupations, the formation of bands was a useful and meaningful way of occupying large amounts of human resources in a form of evangelism. The SA has been successful in evangelisation by being socially relevant: bands attracted crowds who could then be told about the gospel.

Having attracted an audience the role of the band changes, as expressed by Dean Goffin in the quote that heads this chapter. Regardless of whether, as in Goffin's phrase, the message – style of composition is 'clear and plain' – there exists the increasing issue of a disinterested secular New Zealand society which can hardly associate more than a few lines to a handful of popular hymns such as, *How Great Thou Art* and

Amazing Grace. The SA has long used the music of its bands as a metaphor for the gospel message. This necessitates that the messenger and audiences share some common ground so that communication occurs. This does not mean that New Zealand is not a spiritually minded country. Census surveys note that while many New Zealanders profess a faith, church attendance figures have been declining since the 1960s in liberally and theologically complex churches but are increasing in many fundamental faiths.

An inevitable question arises: 'Do brass bands get the message across?' Brass bands, especially proficient ones, can effect positive responses from audiences. The ISB toured New Zealand in 1995 and was very well received. Yet many corps bands struggle to achieve this. In New Zealand brass bands, SA or otherwise, no longer attract large concert audiences, particularly in cities. In 1980 when the National Band of New Zealand toured North America the farewell concert in the Auckland Town Hall was full. In 1995 the National Band embarked on another tour of North America and it failed to fill a school auditorium despite wide publicity. This concert was held shortly before the ISB performed and many wanted to make the comparison between the two bands, but the ISB played to a capacity audience.

However, there are times when SA bands attract audiences and get the message across. As Christmas recurs annually the New Zealand public seem to expect the SA to be on the street playing carols. To many this is Christmas. Santa Claus is a perennial figure that has existed for about as long as the SA but he is not perceived to be negatively traditional nor an anachronism. Both icons are eagerly awaited and appreciated during Advent. However, SA bands do not hibernate during Lent and Trinity. Perhaps they could, but for musicians it is unrealistic to exist seasonally. Bands are a sociological means by which members are held together.

Simply being together does not justify the existence of any band either. Societies use shared goals to give themselves a sense of progression and achievement. For musicians this means performance: parades, festivals, broadcasts, recordings and tours. And just creating performance opportunities is not enough either; they must be perceived to be successful. Cyril Bradwell writes about criteria used to determine the success of an overseas tour. His observations can be applied to any performance activity.

> *The criteria for success of an overseas tour by a Salvation Army band are not easy to define succinctly. The successful attainment of high musical standards, the warmth of fellowship with Salvationist comrades, the help and encouragement given to smaller corps outside the main centres, the impact on non-Salvationists and non-Christians, the fostering of the band's unity and spiritual dedication, the humble recognition that the band's musical offering is acceptable to God for the encouragement of his people and the furtherance of the gospel—all these elements and many others, must come into any assessment.*[20]

Corps are becoming increasingly aware that banding and especially touring, demands and consumes enormous resources. In recent years stewardship of scarce resources has been given much consideration. Recent tours overseas by New Zealand bands have contributed much more to the societies they visit than a bracket of festival selections and a street march.

Hamilton City Band's trip to Tonga in 1995 included a working party of tradesmen who helped repair buildings; the band also left the island nation brass instruments. Auckland Congress Hall Band's tours to Fiji and Tonga, and Chile also rendered practical assistance in a similar way. However motivating touring incentives may be, practical assistance is a recent initiative and has occurred in a period when brass banding as a whole in New Zealand has been declining.

Despite its long heritage the New Zealand Brass Band Association has recognised since the mid-sixties that all was not well and that there has been a steady decline in the numbers of active participants. The reasons for this are many. Since the 1960s two features which have had a remarkable effect on the lives of New Zealanders are the increased affordability of amusements and the increase in self-determination. Since the 1950s the greater availability of cars has made commuting more accessible. People now have greater freedom of choice of where to go to work and leisure.

New Zealand city churches have members who drive past smaller churches to attend services where they feel comfortable. Visual media enable people to be entertained within their own homes.

Brass banding now competes headlong with other equally meritorious pursuits. Even in music, banding has come against many alternatives. Since the 1960s there has been an explosion of music styles. In efforts to recruit young musicians brass bands now compete with rock bands, rhythm and blues, big bands, rap, and heavy metal bands.

The challenges faced by brass bands in New Zealand are also faced by the SA. Statistically the state of SA banding in New Zealand over the decade 1984–94 is one of decline. Since 1984 when there were some 59 bands in the Territory, with 1,077 members, there were in 1994 50 bands with 629 members – a decrease of nearly 42% of players in ten years. The statistics for young people's bands are worse. 1984 saw 33 bands with 271 members. By 1994 the number of bands had fallen to 20 with only 140 members, a decrease of 48% of players. The decline in the number of players has also affected the difficulty of new music that bands are purchasing. In 1984 there were nine New Zealand subscribers to the *Festival Series*, ten years on there are only five.[21]

In determining to keep their Christian faith relevant, musicians – particularly those in the youth programmes – choose musical styles in which to express themselves. There are also other attractions besides music groups that compete for the participation of a limited pool of performers, for example dance and drama groups. Many who get involved in more than one activity can become too thinly spread, and for some participation only increases when big events such as a tour or major performance loom.

The time demanded by any activity to pull off near-professional quality performances has also increased. As a result of exposure to top quality acts, especially through the media, many performers and some audiences are becoming less tolerant of second and third-rate performances. Once band broadcasts were live but now they are recorded and edited. An inevitable consequence of rejecting 'Anything for Jesus' and pursuing 'nothing but the best for the Lord' has seen quality musicians seek out ensembles of the highest standing so that they avoid time commitments to activities which could see them compromise or monotonise their artistic calling.

In this respect SA bands may have become victims of their own success. The SA is a part of the process of general improvement of education standards amongst those who have come into contact with proselytising book religions. Its band programme has improved musical literacy amongst those who have been through its ranks. There now exist Salvationist musicians who seek careers as professional musicians including the armed services, popular bands, orchestras, composers and teachers. Where professional musicians elect to remain in SA bands invariably the standard of performance rises. Some SA bandsmen have chosen to take advantage of the relaxed regulation prohibiting dual membership of a SA and 'outside' bands. Since the 1995 National Brass Band Championships in Rotorua there would have been a sufficient spread of Salvationist instrumentalists to form creditable A-grade contesting bands each year.

The issues that face New Zealand's SA brass bands are the same that have always faced it. Namely they must seek:

- to be useful and meaningful to the organisation, helping define its identity;
- to be useful and meaningful to the public, aiding ministry;
- to be useful and meaningful to the musicians, developing and enhancing self-worth and ownership

Regrettably the expectations of each of the three groups, the SA, the public and the musicians, are currently in conflict with each other. Where the organisation and the public want the bands on the street at Christmas some bandsmen find little merit in being a jukebox playing a handful of well-loved carols. Where the bandsmen wish to impart their skill in the presentation of a festival score the public may be overwhelmed with the length, complexity and abstract message of a technically difficult work. Further, the audience may not expect, appreciate or want anything more from a band other than simple hymn settings.

The SA wishes to remain a relevant evangelical force. Yet it must also deal with its past before it can tackle the future. If in wanting to become *more* relevant, the music and style of worship of the SA employs changes, to the exclusion of what it has developed as its heritage, the organisation risks losing a significant part of its identity and consequently alienating many who have devoted their lives to the Army's historically militant form of Christian expression.

SA bands no longer have the magnetic attraction on the New Zealand public they once had. Militarism, outside of peace keeping, in a legislatively nuclear weapons-free country is almost anathema. New Zealand society is such that individuals have been given more freedom and responsibility to choose how they wish to determine their own lives. There is no drama associated with rejecting any form of evangelism: social, political or religious. It is almost ironic that the freedom the bandsmen of the early Dunedin Fortress Corps Band did not have by way of dress and music is now possessed by today's bands and now there is little leadership to help guide this choice.

It is a sad indictment on the recent leadership of the territory when Territorial Commanders comment that they do know not how they will be received at some corps because there is no longer a single SA cultural thread running through the command.

If they are to survive, Salvation Army bands will need to adapt and take advantage of the opportunities and challenges presented them. In this respect current Territorial Music Secretary Stephen Stein is positive about banding, particularly in small corps like Linwood and Oamaru, but more especially the two national youth ensembles. Recognising that band members often have talents on more than one instrument and live lives outside of SA banding, Stein sees the roles of bands as Thomas Rive saw them: as sociological rather just musical groups. Stein's down to earth leadership focuses on music personnel as whole people who pursue a variety of interests rather than just musical, and his appreciation of this earns him respect.

> *If The Salvation Army finds it can use music to evangelise, it will do so. If it finds it is getting in the way it will drop it.*
>
> Thomas Norman Rive [22]

Stephen Stein conducting the NZ National Youth Band during a shopping mall outreach performance.

About the Author

Warren Baas was born and raised in Auckland, New Zealand, where his interest in SA brass banding was developed as a cornetist in the Otahuhu and Auckland Congress Hall corps bands, and the National Youth Band. He studied at the University of Auckland, gaining degrees in Commerce and Music where his post-graduate musicological studies resulted in a project on New Zealand SA composers and a thesis on Gustav Mahler. He currently teaches Economics at King's College, Auckland, where he has directed the band programme and the orchestra and arranged music. Included among his non-professional interests are hiking in New Zealand's national parks, travelling, and umpiring club cricket during summer.

Warren Baas

Notes

Band journal citations are given for New Zealand composers only; only titles are given for more current releases in the publications released in London.

1. Dean Goffin recorded in an interview with Leslie Fossey that was published in *The Musician* 8 February 1958, and is quoted in Cyril Bradwell, *Symphony of Thanksgiving*, p253.

2. The first contest saw only military bands competing. In 1891 the United Brass (and Military) Band Association of New Zealand was formed to organise national contests, but it was superseded by the civilian-oriented North Island Brass Band Association in

1900 and South Island Brass Band Association in 1909. The New Zealand band movement as a whole received an injection of enthusiasm during the visit of John Philip Sousa and his band in 1911 as part of the Sousa band's round-the-world tour but it was not until 1931 that a single national brass band association was formed. Summarised from Stanley Peter Newcombe's *Challenging Brass: 100 years of Brass Band Contests in New Zealand* 1880–1980 (New Zealand Brass Band's Association Inc., Powerbrass Music Co. Ltd, Takapuna, New Zealand. 1980).

3. Information on the pioneer history of New Zealand in this outline is drawn from: Jeanie Graham, 'Settler Society' in *The Oxford History of New Zealand* edited by W. H. Oliver with B. R. Williams (Auckland: Oxford University Press: 1987), pp112–13.

4. For a finely researched and detailed history of The Salvation Army's first 100 years in New Zealand see Cyril Bradwell's *Fight the Good Fight.*

5. Robert Hughson, *'Unofficial History' of The Salvation Army – Dunedin City Corps 1883–1936,* p19.

6. Allison Robinson, *The Salvation Army in Stratford and Eltham, 1893–1993.*

7. April 25th marks the anniversary day when soldiers of the Australia New Zealand Army Corps (ANZAC) began their amphibious assault on Gallipoli on the Dardenelles Peninsula, Turkey, in 1915 in the Allies' unsuccessful attempt to remove that country from the Great War. The day is a public holiday in both Australia and New Zealand. Armistice Day, November 11th, is not commemorated by a holiday.

8. Mina Carberry, *Otahuhu Corps Centenary 1887–1987,* p9.

9. *Feilding Salvation Army Centenary, April 26-29, 1985* p9.

10. H Bramwell Cook, *Christchurch City Corps 111th Anniversary, 28-29 May 1994.*

11. Wellington South Band has been fortunate to have in its ranks an historian in the person of retired Corps Sergeant Major Cyril Bradwell QSO, OF. Cyril Bradwell currently leads The Salvation Army's Territorial Archive in Wellington and is the author of the centenary history of The Salvation Army in New Zealand, *Fight the Good Fight,* as well as many other publications including *Make Music for Thy Lord,* a history of the Wellington South Band – the fullest historical account of any Salvation Army band in New Zealand, and a publication from which this summary is largely drawn.

12. John Bate, compiler, *Memoirs of the Wellington Citadel Band 1968 World Tour.*

13. While the melody may have been a repertoire item of a Maori

concert party, it is western in influence and construction, and in no way reflects the idiom of traditional Maori music, much of which is unaccompanied and chant-like.

14. Quoted in *Praise Him!* Newton Citadel Band brochure to accompany its Australian tour in 1983.

15. Auckland Congress Hall, *Centennial Celebrations 1st–4th April 1983.*

16. The Salvation Army Congress Hall: *A Review of the first 85 years.* Herb Tremain is the grandfather of Dr. Ronald Tremain, one of New Zealand's foremost modern composers. As a Salvationist Ronald Tremain never took charge of a SA band but did have a number of vocal compositions published by the Army. The band arrangements of his songs were not authorised by him as composers' rights are released on submitting music to IMED. He retired as Professor of Music from Brock University, Ontario, 1989.

17. Victor Brame quoted in Cyril Bradwell, *Fight the Good Fight*, p3.

18. *Auckland Congress Hall Band Souvenir Programme Wellington and South Island Tour 1936.*

19. Geoff Chapple, 'Bright, Primary Sounds and Colours' in *The New Zealand Listener, 5 July 1975*, p18.

20. Cyril Bradwell, *Symphony of Thanksgiving*, p183.

21. Statistics obtained from the Territorial Music Secretary, Songster Leader Eva Key, 7 September 1995.

22. Quoted in Stanley Peter Newcombe, *The Music of the People: The Story of the Band Movement in New Zealand 1845–1963* (Christchurch, New Zealand: G. R. Mowat, 1963), p95.

Chapter 9

UNITED STATES OF AMERICA

Ronald W. Holz

We have gotten to depend upon ourselves and our machinery so much that we are in danger of forgetting that there is a God. Nothing brings us closer to God than beautiful music. If you want to know one of the very good reasons why the world needs bands just ask one of The Salvation Army warriors, who for years has marched carrying the cross through the back alleys of life. Let him tell of the armies of men that have been turned toward a better life by first hearing the sounds of a Salvation Army band. The next time you hear a Salvation Army band, no matter how humble, take off your hat. John Philip Sousa, 'Why the World Needs Bands', *Etude Magazine,* September 1930, p. 48.

The first SA band to sound forth in the United States was actually Canadian, the Kingston (Ontario) Silver Band that supported a 'Monster Salvation Demonstration' in Syracuse, NY, November 11–12, 1883.[1] Early American pioneers were adept at throwing together 'pick-up' bands of a wide assortment of instruments, like the band made up of *drums, cornet, concertina, and tambourines* that played in Newark, NJ, in late summer of 1884.[2] General Booth's initial 1880 'General Order for Bands' first appeared in the July 17, 1884 *American War Cry* (AWC) but evidently brass bands may have got underway even before this date. The first commissioned corps bands in the USA were East Liverpool, Ohio and Grand Rapids, Michigan. East Liverpool can be documented as playing at a Steubenville, OH, SA rally in December of 1884. Grand Rapids' start is not as clearly defined, but they claim 1884, as well, for their premiere.[3] The Chronology shown below in this chapter lists representative numbers of corps and regional bands flourishing within the States within the first few decades of SA work in America.

Instruments began to be sold from the SA Trade Department in New York by late 1885, and a complete set of brass instruments could be purchased for $130 by early January 1886. SA band music was not advertised until the Fall of 1888, with the first tune book, *Salvation Army Band Music*, and *Band Journals* (GS) #1–50, on sale by the winter of 1889. The New York Staff Band, however, did have SA band music by no later than the fall of 1887.[4]

When the SA in Boston held its seventh anniversary rally in April, 1887, the Fall River Corps Brass and Drum Band showed up wearing old US Army uniforms, while the new

Grand Rapids (MI) Corps Band, the first commissioned band in the USA, c.1884. Bandmaster David Hay is in the front row, far left. Drum Major is Case de Blond, first convert for the Salvation Army in the town.

Boston #1 Brass Band made its premiere then by playing a total of three tunes. The Lawrence Corps Band and perhaps a group from the New York #1 Corps Band rounded out the musical feast that was available.[5] It was obvious to Commander Ballington Booth that models were needed, and these soon came in the form of the National (New York) Staff Band formed in June 1887 and by the tour of the Household Troops Band of the UK in 1888–1889 (See Chapter 2).

Travelling musical specials, like the small Ohio Divisional Band (soon to become the OH and KY Divisional Band, or O&K Band), also helped spread brass band fever, especially when there were talented musicians in the group. In this ensemble alone there were three musical pioneers who are representative of the origins of many early SA bandsmen. Their leader was William Halpin, a British officer out of Birkenhead 2, *a converted musician*, who was transferred from Fakenham, England to New York in December 1885. He soon formed the band at New York #1 Corps. Walter Duncan, who was playing a *large circular bass* with the East Liverpool Corps Band in the mid-1880s, evidently had noticeable leadership skills. He was soon made bandmaster of the Volunteer Brigade Band, then the National Guards Band, and eventually the Northwestern Divisional Band of Chicago, IL.

A musical star of the pioneering group was 'Trumpeter' Edward Trumble, a professional cornet player out of Elyria, OH, who became a kind of national bandmaster for a number of years, as well as director of the National Staff Band.[6] The combination of Salvationist immigrants/officer transfers and converted American town or professional bandsmen would hold true for several decades as the balanced source of both musical leaders and the finest players.

Band tours were established for both evangelical and financial reasons. The Grand Rapids Corps Band undertook the first American corps band tour in 1888–1889. Their trip, under the leadership of Bandmaster David Hay, stretched for 6 weeks, covered 1,000 miles, during which they held 136 meetings. This group had not had the encouragement of the Household Troops Band, so their initiative is all the more remarkable.[7] Such rigour would be duplicated, and then surpassed by the Volunteer Brigade Band, formed in May 1889, touring extensively by the fall of that year.

Renamed the National Guards Band in the summer of 1891, this group would visit 11 states in 1891–1892, raising thousands of dollars towards the new national headquarters building, while at the same time helping local corps raise their own money. In the process, by following the excellent example set by Appleby's Household Troops Band, they planted the seed for bands wherever they travelled. An interim tour report from the April 2, 1892 *AWC* cited the band having travelled 3,840 miles since September, 1891, 90 cities visited, 96 conversions recorded. In one location alone (Jermyn, PA) they raised $500 for the NHQ and $355 for the local corps, substantial amounts in those days.[8]

The published picture of the Grand Rapids Corps Band, *War Cry*, June 7, 1887, shows a band of 17 players, including several women (at least four) and two members of colour, African-Americans. The band was not only mixed in terms of race and gender, but also in age, including a very young snare drummer.

From what can been seen clearly, the band consisted of one clarinet, five cornets, two altos, a valve trombone, two euphonium-size bass horns, bass drum, snare drum, cymbals, all led by a drum major.

One of the earliest photos of the South Manchester, CT, Corps Band (established 1888) shows a band of 15, including a piccolo, clarinet, five cornets, two valve trombones, two baritone-euphoniums, an E Flat bombardon, bass drum, snare drum, and cymbals. (See chapter, *Instrumentation and Scoring*, Volume II for a chronological overview of the instrumentation of the New York Staff Band of this period.) This instrumentation would be typical of many American town bands of the era.

The Ishpeming Corps (MI) Brass Band featured on the cover of the *War Cry* of October 10, 1891, was praised for playing well and because it *uses nothing but Salvation Army music, playing the Brass Band Journal up to No. 90*. The cover was intended to be a sales plea, for it continued: *It is a spiritual band. The uniform is of the regulation pattern, and may be taken as a fair sample of that supplied by Headquarters to our bandsmen.*

This 18-piece band (including 2 flag-bearers and possibly the corps officer) used two circular helicon basses, two clarinets, and, somewhat rare in American SA bands of the 1890s, a slide trombone.

The New England Provincial HQ Band by 1905 more closely followed British models. Commander Evangeline Booth hailed them in the pages of the *War Cry* for playing only SA music. This band consisted of eight cornets (including possibly a Soprano Cornet), one flugelhorn, four altos, four baritones, three trombones (including bass in G), two euphoniums, two E Flat bass, one B Flat bass, and two drummers.[9]

As America had a thriving brass band scene in the 19th century, there was no lack of music for SA bands available from outside publishers. In addition to official SA journals, American SA bands sought out music published by such firms as Carl Fischer in the USA and Wright & Round and Boosey in Great Britain. Music from all three firms has been located in early band books and band programmes of the National

'South' Manchester (CT) Citadel Band, c.1890.

Staff Band [NYSB]. That American SA bands were making an impact on the wider American cultural scene, as well as attracting the interest of publishers, can be seen in Theodore Moses Tobani's band composition, *Salvation Army Patrol*, published by Carl Fischer in New York 1892.

A similar work appeared that same year, printed by Joseph Flanner of Milwaukee, Charles J. Orth's, *The Advance and Retreat of the Salvation Army* (later also published by Fischer in a revised band arrangement by Ellis Brooks). Orth's piece contained as the central theme a parody of the song and associated tune, *Oh, you must be a lover of the Lord*. He changed it to 'Oh, you must be with us by and by, Oh you must be with us when you die'. The work was so popular that Orth received a medal from Gilmore's Band recognising this fact. The description of this 'patrol' placed by Orth at the top of his *marche characteristique* score evokes a bygone era of the early SA and its bands:[10]

> *This composition is descriptive of a Salvation Army parade. Commencing with the drums in the distance, the army is heard gradually coming nearer. Passing by they make a short halt, singing one of their war songs, led by trumpets, amidst shouting and whistling of the street Arabs; after which they march on again, and gradually disappear.*

Staff Bandmaster Charles Straubel attempted a short-lived publishing effort in the spring of 1898, though the newly reorganised music department did not last long, and none of the early music sheets have survived.

In the midst of economic depression and internal strife, SA bands, however, did not fade away, but continued to grow after Commander Booth-Tucker regained the confidence of American soldiers following the defection of his brother-in-law, Ballington Booth, in the winter of 1896. Band festivals, beginning with those by the New York #1 Band and, especially, the National Staff Band under Charles Anderson, provided even more interest in SA music. Such efforts were duplicated across the nation.

The first Local Officers' and Bandsmen's Councils were called by Colonel Richard Holz in Cleveland, March 1904, with

THE BOSTON STAFF BAND

The Boston Staff Band c.1919.

his area bandmaster, another musical pioneer, William Bridgen, leading the effort.[11] In 1907 a second staff band, that in Chicago, got started under the highly efficient team of Major John T. Flynn, Bandmaster and Captain William Broughton, Director. While only starting with nine players, by 1914 the group was joining more established groups like the National Staff Band and Worcester #1 Band at the International Congress in London.

Another young band that travelled to that congress was the Flint, Michigan, Band, a corps band remade almost overnight through the efforts of Bandmaster Bearcraft, who also happened to be a manager of the Buick Motor Corporation and thereby able to employ large numbers of Salvationists.

This kind of recruitment was not uncommon, one of the more famous ones being that undertaken by the New England Provincial command, especially under William McIntyre, whereby bands in the Boston area got a real shot in the arm in the first three decades of the century. The corps of Iklestone, Derbyshire, for example, lost a fair number of families, several of whom would become important in the history of the SA in the USA: Needham, Walters, Wheatley, and Stevenson.[12]

While some SA bandsmen enlisted in the US Army during World War I, SA bands in the US were not greatly affected by the war. Shortly after the war, however, a decision was reached that American SA bands would all embrace standard

New York Staff Band, January 1899, Bandmaster Charles Anderson (second row, fourth from right).
Notice pocket cornet front left.

Chicago Staff Band, April 3, 1928. Bandmaster William Broughton, front, 5th from left.

concert pitch, A=440 (see *Instrumentation and Scoring*, Volume II), influenced in part by the US military and most American instrument firms making that same decision.

During the war SA bands gave wholeheartedly of their services in patriotic fundraisers and parades. These, combined with the enormous impact of the SA work on the battlefront in France, brought the SA a much wider public image. During the 1920s SA bands reached new peaks in numbers, types of bands, musical proficiency, and in new types of ministry. Bands were on radio and recording 78 rpm records by 1922. There would be a staff band in every one of the four territories after 1927. A modern system of music education and administration was gradually forming, with the establishment of the first music camp in 1920 and then with wide spread divisional and territorial music councils and congresses designed to both edify and encourage.

Composers featured at the 1930 National Congress.
From left to right;
Front row: K. M. Fristrup, William Broughton;
Back row: Emil Soderstrom, Bramwell Coles, Erik Leidzén.

On top of all that, the first more lasting band publications began in 1928 by the Eastern Territory under its newly appointed Territorial Secretary for Band and Songsters, Edgar Arkett, french horn soloist of the New York Staff Band. In this programme Arkett had the help and cooperation of three leading musicians, William Broughton of the Chicago

A typical US Corps Band in the 1920s. Note that the majority of players are women.

Staff Band, Erik Leidzén, DMD in Metropolitan New York, and Trade Secretary Sam Hodges, a man unsung in SA history for his contribution to the development of its music.[13]

This era reached a climactic moment in New York City on May 17–18, 1930, during the 50th anniversary National Congress, May 16–22. On the 17th John Philip Sousa led over 700 band members in his new, *The Salvation Army March,* inside the 71st Regiment Armoury at 34th and Park Ave.

On the following day, 15 bands performed in the Metropolitan Opera House, during which the Chicago Staff Band premiered the prize-winning marches and selections, including, *Army of God* (Emil Soderstrom), from among the 104 entries in the Golden Jubilee Music Competition. The judges were William Broughton, Bramwell Coles, Erik Leidzén, and another distinguished leader among secular American bands, Edwin Franko Goldman, director of the famed Goldman Band. The Festival of Music and Song on the 17th deserves examination because the bands, their leaders, and the music played provide a wonderful composite portrait of what had been achieved in 50 years. Here were some of the best items from the latest journals, as well as the influence of the American band scene via virtuoso solos from the outside repertoire:[14]

Right: Los Angeles Citadel Band, BM Edwin Taylor, with noted scientist Albert Einstein, at the Tournament of Roses Parade, 1932.

Band Programme Items, in Concert Order, May 17, 1930 Festival

March: *Mighty to Save* (Marshall)	Massed Bands (E. Leidzén)
Selection: *Visions* (Marshall)	Detroit Citadel Band (R. Herival)
Meditation: *Harlan* (Kitching)	Southern Staff Band (A. Baldwin)
Cornet Solo: *Air Varié* (Clarke)	Stanley Shephard, soloist, with New York Staff Band (G. Darby)
Songs of the Evangel (Booth/Broughton)	Chicago Staff Band (W. Broughton)
March: *The Salvation Army* (Sousa)	Massed Bands (J.P. Sousa)
Selection: *Adoration* (Ball)	New York Staff Band (G. Darby)
Meditation: *A Soul's Awakening* (Ball)	Flint Citadel Band (B. Smith)
Meditation: *When I Survey* (Coles)	Cambridge Citadel Band (G. Foster)
Xylophone Solo: *Russian Fantasia* (Levy)	Richard von Calio, soloist, with Southern Staff Band (A. Baldwin)
Selection: *Army of the Brave* (Marshall)	Chicago Staff Band (W. Broughton)
March: *American Commander* (Turkington)	South Manchester Band (D. Addy)

Other bands that participated in the massed bands that evening, and also in solo spots throughout the Congress included: New York #1 (G. Granger), New York #4 (G. Charleson), Brooklyn #1 (W. Bearchell), Brooklyn #2 (E.

Baxendale), Training College Men's Band (W. Maltby), Training College Women's Band (O. Warth), Newark #1 (W. Devoto), Newark #2 (Slaymaker), Passaic, NJ (R. Stillwell), Worcester (H. Brewer), Schenectady Men's Band (J. Ryans), Schenectady Women's Band (Jardine), Troy, NY (W. Streader), Buffalo (G. Smith), Carbondale, PA, Scout Band (McNally), Yonkers, NY (W. Wrieden), Pittsburgh Y.P. Band (no leader listed), Louisville, KY, Band (no leader listed). Additional bands were listed who had sent representatives. Many of these were bands from out west not able to attend due to cost of travelling such large distances.

Most American SA bands within the 1920–1940 era embraced a general pattern of activities. It was a dynamic period of growth for SA music throughout the country. By World War II most territories and a good percentage of their bands had experienced, sponsored, and/or participated in band exchange trips, regional, national, and international tours; nationwide radio broadcasts; summer music camps; music councils and congresses; band recordings; festivals—large and small.

Not all of these were pursued in detail nor were all fully developed or exploited. However, they were excelling in open-

Detroit Citadel Band, 1927.

airs and parades! Edward McKinley has noted that in 1926 alone the American SA hold over 200,000 open-airs. Most of these were manned by the Army's primary fighting force, the brass band. In 1941, *Newsweek* magazine could report that there were approximately 1,000 corps bands in the USA, the majority in the range of 8–14 members.[15]

The leadership and membership base had come from a balance of both talented immigrants and native-born citizens. The main centres of band activity were still in industrial cities of the East and Midwest, and California, especially in metropolitan New York, Chicago, Boston, Philadelphia, Detroit, Pittsburgh, San Francisco, and Los Angeles. The following chronology lists only representative events in the period 1880–1941. It is not intended to be comprehensive, but hopefully provides the skeleton on which an historical perspective of this formative period can be built:

Chronology of Representative Events in SA Music in the United States, 1880–1941

1880   The Salvation Army official established in the USA.

1883   First SA band to function in USA, Kingston, Ontario, Silver Band in Syracuse, NY, November 11–12; small pick-up bands of varied instrumentation abound.

1884   First Corps bands in East Liverpool, OH, and Grand Rapids, MI.

1885   Some instruments for sale from Trade Department; New corps bands in Oakland, CA; Fall River, MA; Danbury, CT; and Alliance, OH; A 'Divisional Cornet Band' formed for anniversary of Boston #1 Corps.

1886   Corps bands established at New York #1; Augusta, ME; Other 'Divisional' bands functioning in several areas of the country.

1887   National Staff Band [New York Staff Band–NYSB] formed; first appearance June 18, in Brooklyn. More bands functioning by then, including: Chicago #1; Barton, MD; Des Moines, IA; Lawrence, MA; Minneapolis–St. Paul, MN; New Brunswick, NJ.

1888   SA band music generally available in USA; Full sets of brass band instruments available from Trade Dept.; Seattle #1, South Manchester, CT, bands formed.

1889   Visit of Household Troops Band to USA; Volunteer

Brigade Band formed at NHQ, then soon renamed the National Guards Band [NGB]; Steubenville, OH, Girls' Brass Band functioning; Worcester #1 MA formed; First corps band tour taken by Grand Rapids Band.

1890   Music department established at NHQ, vocal music only (May Agnew, editor); other bands established at Ishpeming, MI; Chelsea, Boston #1 and #2, MA.

1891   Tours by Northwest Divisional Band (Illinois Divisional Band–Chicago), New York Staff Band, and National Guards Band; Georgia #1 (Atlanta Temple) Band commissioned.

1892   Continental Congress, Nov. 21–23; Massed band of 150; Solo bands include Ansonia CT; South Manchester; Worcester #1, MA; Bayonne, NJ; Swedish Band (Brooklyn), as well as NYSB, NGB, and a Field Officers Band. New bands at Butte, MT; Hyde Park, MA. Salvation Army Cavalry Band (later called the Charioteers) begins tours out West.

1893   Staff Captain 'Trumpeter' Trumble takes on tasks of organising bands and various major functions in a type of early bands department.

1894   New bands in Lowell, MA; Minneapolis #4; New England Jubilee Band forms for tour; William Booth tours USA, 1894–95.

1895   NHQ moves from 111 Read Street to 120 W. 14th Street; first record of a band festival, NYSB at Harlem Corps, July 24th.

1896   Ballington Booth resigns in January; replaced by Booth-Tucker in April; Divisional bands include OH and KY Div. Band; Quaker City Brass Band (PA); Pacific Coast and Golden State Brass Band (CA).

1897   First corps band festival, New York #1 Band (BM A. J. Pike); *War Cry* asks for 1,000 more bandsmen for 1897, bands not flourishing as a result of Ballington split. William Bridgen working as a type of regional music director, in Cleveland, leading the *largest band in the nation*– 40-member Cleveland Amalgamated SA Band.

1898   Music department reestablished at NHQ, under Ensign Straubel; first band publications released in April–short-term effort. Rudiments of musical notation added to curriculum at Officers Training school. First recording of NYSB done on Graphophone Grand machine; Staff Bandmaster Charles Anderson initiates 'modern' series band festival programmes.

1903   NYSB and Canadian "Staff Band" together in NYC for funeral of Consul Emma Booth-Tucker.

1904   First Local Officers and Bandsmen's Councils held in Cleveland, OH; NYSB travels to 1904 International Congress (June–July).

1905   New England Provincial HQ (Staff) Band hailed by Commander Eva Booth for playing only SA music; 'New' 1899–1900 *Tune Book* finally on sale in US.

1907   Chicago Staff Band (CSB) formed.

1908   Flint, MI band reorganised via Bandmaster Bearcraft, a manager at Buick Motor Co.

1913   New York-area Women's Brass Band flourishes, one of several throughout USA.

1914   June–July, London, International Congress: Flint, MI, Band, Worcester #1 Band, Chicago Staff Band [CSB], New York (National) Staff Band participate.

1915   First extensive Bandsmen's Councils held in NYC, for Central Province (24 bands); Papers presented by George Darby, John Allan, and others.

1919   *Local Officers' Counselor* magazine begins publication; until 1931; this is a valuable source of educational articles, and features on bands and their leaders.

1920   'Low' pitch A4=440, adopted as standard in USA; Territories reorganised into Central, East, West; First music camp held at Long Branch, NJ; SA band first plays in Tournament of Roses Parade, Pasadena, CA.

1922   NYSB and CSB first play on radio; NYSB makes first 78 rpm record on Vocalion label; Western Staff Band formed, lasts until 1932.

1923   Erik Leidzén serving as New England provincial music director in Boston and leading NE Provincial Staff Band.

1920s Large divisional music and band congresses being held throughout the United States, but particularly in New York, Boston, and Chicago area.

1926   Several Americans placed as winners in International Band Composition Contest, including Erik Leidzén, Kristian Fristrup, and Emil Soderstrom.

1927   Southern Territory formed, as is the Southern Territorial Staff Band.

1928   Edgar Arkett named Secretary for Bandsmen and Songsters in Eastern Territory; begins to publish *National Band Journal* ('American Brass Band Journal') and *American Festival Series*.

1930   May 16–22 Congress held in New York City; approximately 700 bandsmen attend and led by John Philip Sousa in his new *Salvation Army March*; Solo bands included staff bands from Atlanta, Chicago, New York; corps bands from Flint, MI, Cambridge, MA, Manchester, CT.

1934   First Central Music Institute held June 21–July 5.

1935   First Star Lake Musicamp August 28–Sept. 2.

1936   Central Territory prints first tune book for small bands.

1937   *The Musician* (US) begins publication.

1941   *Newsweek* magazine article estimates there are 1,000 SA bands in the USA, most ranging 8–14 players.

Post-World War II Renaissance

SA banding would reach a high water mark in the two decades following World War II. Corps bands began to flourish again, with particularly strong and proficient expressions in and around greater metropolitan Boston, Chicago, Detroit, Los Angeles, New York (as well as upstate New York), Philadelphia, Pittsburgh, and San Francisco. All four territories had established, or reestablished music departments designed to support regained momentum in the SA's evangelistic campaigns, fuelled again, primarily, by its musical forces. There were four essential aspects to this planned renaissance, some territories able to handle all four, some less so:

1) Large music congresses where corps groups could play for and learn from one another, as well as listen to some of the finest SA musicians, either as soloists or as guest bands. Supplemented by music leaders' councils in the form of continuing education programs for established leaders and for the

Erik Leidzén conducting massed bands at Star Lake.

encouragement and identification of new leaders.
2) Bandmaster training courses.
3) Emphasis on the summer music camp at the divisional level, and upgrading the standard at territorial camps wherein young leaders could be identified.
4) Music publishing as necessary for bands within the territory.

Harry Otway in the Central led the way with huge three-day congresses that involved as many as 20 corps bands and 20 songster brigades. Richard Holz in the East developed an alternating series of biennial music congresses and music leaders' councils that lasted for 17 years. Tours by overseas sections were calculated to boost morale and spur the locals forward via these excellent examples. Several notable ones include Tranås Band, Sweden (1954), ISB (1957, 1962), Netherlands National Band (1959), Tottenham Citadel, UK

New York Staff Band c.1948 with Bandmaster Brigadier W. E. Bearchell. Richard Holz (later Commissioner) playing flugel.

(1964), Govan Citadel, Scotland (1966). Exchanges between American territories also took place, Chicago and New York Staff Band exchanges at respective music congresses in the 1950s being notable.

Problems of distance kept the West and South from doing quite as much in this regard, except at the yearly congresses connected with the commissioning of cadets. However, within these territories divisional events were encouraged on an intermittent basis.[16]

Most bandmasters learned their trade by growing up in a SA band and eventually taking on responsibility as the opportunity presented itself. These conductors rarely had any formal training or guidance in their position except the occasional congress clinic or a helpful article in an SA periodical. The SA certainly was conscientious in providing educational materials and in providing meticulous score notes with rehearsal suggestions in its band journals. What was needed was practical, hands-on training in conducting/band training and a deeper understanding of what it meant to be a Salvationist music leader.[17]

The most impressive endeavour in this area was launched by Richard Holz and Erik Leidzén, the Bandmasters' Training Course, which held its first graduation in the spring of 1949. Over a 13-year period (1949–1962) Erik Leidzén saw over 800 soldiers and officers graduate from the 12-week course sequence that met within the East in centres like Boston, Cleveland, Dayton, Hartford, New York, Philadelphia, Pittsburgh, and in the South at Washington, D.C.

Not every participant became a commissioned corps leader, but a large proportion did take up a leadership role at the corps level. Equally important, a whole generation of young officers who took the course became much more attuned to how SA music could be effective in their ministry, whether they were eventually to lead a group or not.[18]

When this course was stopped in the mid-1960s no comparable programme replaced it, though the revised Correspondence Course from England, especially with new input from Dean Goffin, Charles Skinner, Ray Steadman-Allen, and others did help somewhat. I ran a more extensive leadership course for three years in the Massachusetts Division, 1978–1981, that had an impact within that division.

Other DMDs have tried similar patterns of one kind or

New York Staff Band Male Chorus, Chorus Leader Thomas Mack, at the USA National Congress, Kansas City, 1980.

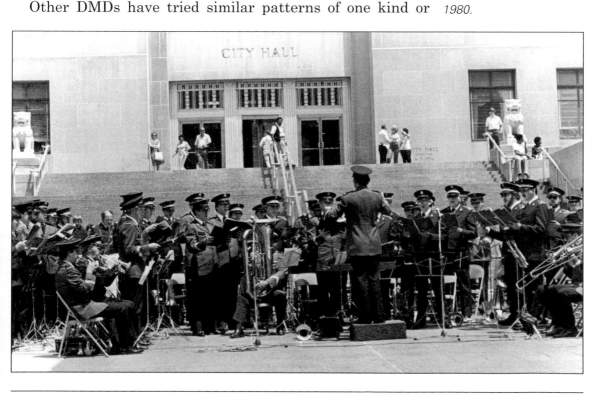

another. However, a consistent approach to leadership training, one of the greatest needs within the USA, is only now emerging via special emphasis given at the territorial music camps or institutes. For example, within the South a two-year intensive course is offered at the Territorial Music Institute in both instrumental and choral leadership. The courses are much more strenuous than what was ever attempted in the old Leidzén classes. Parallel efforts are being run at Star Lake, WMI, and CMI. Divisional music directors can target potential adult leaders knowing that there are special programmes to which they can be sent that will be of substance.

The Southern Territory Music Department has begun a pilot programme for courses during the regular year in cooperation with the Divisional Music Directors. Some of the DMDs have already begun their programmes, especially in connection with their own summer conservatories.[19]

The music camp programme of the SA was started by John Allan at Long Branch, New Jersey in the summer of 1920, soon moving to Star Lake Camp in Butler, NJ for the next few years, but at this time still a regional camp for junior band members.[20] Music camps soon spread across the nation.

By 1934 Central Music Institute, the first of the famous territorial music camps, opened its doors and Star Lake Musicamp was underway the following year. By the late 1930s nearly every division in the US was attempting a summer music camp of some kind. Territorial camps, or institutes in the West (WMI) and South (TMI) followed after World War II.

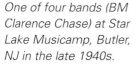

One of four bands (BM Clarence Chase) at Star Lake Musicamp, Butler, NJ in the late 1940s.

The music or band camp phenomenon is one of the American SA's greatest contributions to worldwide SA music. Other territories might call them Schools of Music, the age range might be slightly different, but the essentials were the same. Music camps were designed to give beginners the very best start on a brass instrument and allow intermediate players to broaden their musical horizons and improve their technique. The territorial level camps challenged the most 'advanced' players to much higher achievement and encouraged them to take up the responsibility of being guiding lights in SA musical ministry.

Eric Ball with Leslie Condon and Divisional Bandmaster Alfred Swenarton of the Northern New Jersey Division at Camp Tecumseh, 1963.

Among the first new wave of DMDs were Kenneth Strehle in Philadelphia and Alfred Swenarton in New Jersey. Strehle began his position as early as 1943, dividing some of his time with duties in correctional services. Swenarton moved from the East's territorial music department to Newark, NJ, as DMD, in the early 1960s, with some added responsibilities in public relations and fund-raising. Both men were dedicated corps bandmasters (Philadelphia Citadel and Asbury Park,

NJ, respectively) who also established excellent divisional youth bands that were soon copied across the world.[21]

Significant losses in the number of SA musicians during the late 1960s and early 1970s led SA leadership to soon begin hiring full-time DMDs on a wide scale. Ronald Waiksnoris was hired as Boston's Divisional Music 'Consultant' in 1974; Philadelphia (Ivor Bosanko, 1975) and Pittsburgh (Ronald Holz, 1975) followed shortly after. With some consistent successes and with some lamentable setbacks, primarily for financial reasons, the DMD position was firmly established in all four territories by the late 1980s. McKinley reported that in 1992, 27 of 38 DHQs had full-time DMDs (Central, 6 out of 10; East 8 of 11; South 8 of 9; West 5 of 8).[22]

Another advance in the SA music training programme came in 1986 with the establishment of the summer music conservatory, first launched in the Georgia Division under the patronage of Colonel Jack T. Waters. Usually an addition to the normal 8–10 day divisional music camp, the music conservatory gathers a smaller, hand picked group of young musicians in the general age range of 10–15, numbering anywhere from 30 to 70 students.

The course is held over as short a time as 3 weeks to as long as 6 weeks. While festival performances play a positive role in the conservatory, the main emphasis is on skill development, musical knowledge, and personal Christian growth, essentially a highly concentrated music camp without the great pressure to put on festivals to show how much has been crammed in within a few short days. The learning pace is stretched out, students are nurtured on a more personal level.

With support from the territory every division in the South now maintains a music conservatory and several divisions schedule 3–4 week Senior Conservatories [ages 12–18] and one-week Junior Conservatories [ages 9–12]. Conservatories have been started in all three of the other USA territories.[23]

If there had been a precipitous loss in the number of bands and bandsmen within the period 1960–1980 (at least 35% loss), recent figures seem to indicate that in the 1980s this broad trend was at least stalemated. The number of senior musicians from 1980 to 1990 had essentially remained the same (3,983–3,964). However, over that same period junior members increased by 30%.

*James Curnow
rehearsing the SASF
Brass Band at the 1980
USA National Congress.*

While no doubt more detailed analysis is required, more along the line of Thomas Mack's study of music in the Eastern Territory, it is now apparent that the combined efforts of a nationwide network of DMDs, supported by the four territorial departments, are keeping SA music alive. Without such attention it would surely have faded away to the most marginal of programmes.[24] What has been particularly important in the last two decades of the 20th century and into the 21st has been long-term, consistent leadership from territorial music departments: Central – William Himes (1977– –); South – Dr. Richard Holz (1979– –); West – Ivor Bosanko (1979–2001); James Anderson (2001–2004), and East – Ronald Waiksnoris (1984– –).

A more detailed review of the leaders cited in the lists that follow might show the reader that in long periods of stable leadership, like that from 1946–1962 under Richard Holz (Eastern Territory), the music programme within a territory made its greatest gains. With this professional expertise has come nationwide, even continental cooperation. The Territorial Music Secretaries (Four USA and, Canada-

Bermuda) now meet every year discuss Army music policy and programme, and to coordinate any number of programmes.

An early success in this cooperative venture came in the 1980 National Congress in Kansas City, which included not only sharing the various musical assignments in many different venues, but also in running a nationwide musical composition contest.[25] At one of the largest festivals of the congress each territory put forward a representative band, with even NHQ having its band present.

Derek Smith leading the New York Staff Band, c.1980.

The bands by territory or command were: Central–Chicago Staff Band (William Himes); East–New York Staff Band (Derek Smith); South–National Capital Band (Campbell Robinson); West–Santa Ana Corps Band (Ed Freeman); NHQ–SASF Brass Band of Asbury College (James Curnow). The last-named band contained band members from all four

SASF Brass Band of Asbury College (Ronald Holz) playing in a shopping mall near Cincinnati.

US territories as well as from Canada, and in a way, was a truly national group. The NYSB demonstrated one of the pioneering uses of video with live band music at the National Congress via Stephen Bulla's, *Suite of Overtures*. Bulla had written one short overture for each of the four territories in which regional songs and cultural references blended with the unifying *idée fixe*, the hymn tune, *The Eden Above*.

Five years later, at the International Youth Congress (Macomb, IL) the four territories coordinated a massive, 3-hour music marathon on July 21, 1985 called, *Music from Around the World*. Four simultaneous concert series featured bands, choral music, contemporary gospel music, and soloists/ensembles. The brass bands that participated ran the gamut from existing corps and divisional youth bands to groups formed especially for the Congress:

> Ontario South Divisional Youth Band (Roger Davies).
> Pendel [Eastern Pennsylvania and Delaware Division]
>   Brass (Harold Burgmayer).

Royal Oak, MI, Corps Youth Band (Ed Rowland).
Southern Territorial Youth Band (Richard Holz).
SASF Brass Band of Asbury College and Theological
    Seminary (Ronald Holz).
Western Territorial Youth Band (Ivor Bosanko).

The music programme in the United States has recently, in many respects, taken a major role in SA music throughout the world. With proper communication and sharing of tasks, the present situation could bring about a second renaissance, like that experienced in the 1950s, within the brass bands of the SA of America.[26]

Chronological Listing of Territorial Music Secretaries/Directors or Music Department Leaders in the Four American Territories of The Salvation Army (Data provided by each territory)

Central Territory: Leadership of Music Department
(latest rank while in position given)

1940–1947	Lt. Colonel Harry Otway
1948–1954	Captain Bernard Smith
1954–1958	Major Victor Danielson
1958–1963	Brigadier Cyril Everitt
1963–1970	Major Ernest A. Miller
1970–1972	Brigadier Hubert Rawlin
1972–1977	Brigadier Ronald Rowland
1977–	Bandmaster William Himes

Eastern Territory: Leadership of Music Department
(latest rank while in position given)

1890–	May Agnew
1893–1896	Staff Captain Edward Trumble
1898–1899	Bandmaster Charles Straubel
1928–1933	Ensign Edgar Arkett
1933–1935	Major William Broughton
1946–1963	Brigadier Richard E. Holz
1963–1972	Major Vernon Post
1972–1975	Major William Simons
1975–1981	Major Thomas Mack

| 1981–1983 | Bandmaster Charles Baker |
| 1984– | Bandmaster Ronald Waiksnoris |

Southern Territory: Leadership of Music Department
(latest rank while in position given)

1948–1961	Lt. Colonel Frank Longino
1961–1967	Brigadier Leslie Hall
1967–1968	Lt. Colonel Harry Ward
1968–1970	Captain Harold Anderson
1970–1972	Major Raymond Cooper
1972–1979	Brigadier Hubert Rawlin
1979–	Bandmaster Dr. Richard E. Holz

Western Territory: Leadership of Music Department
(latest rank while in position given)

1943–1949	Brigadier William Broughton
1955–	Lt. Col. Charles Dodd
1956–	Lt. Col. Frank Wilmer
1957–	Colonel Edgar Arkett
1959–1961	Brigadier Harold Barry
1967–	Bandmaster Harry Hartjes
1974–1976	Bandmaster Terry Camsey
1977–1979	Lt. Colonel Ruby Adams
1979–2001	Bandmaster Ivor Bosanko
2001–2004	Bandmaster James Anderson
2005	Bandmaster Neil Smith

Composers and Publishing

Taken as a group, Salvationist arrangers and composers in America in the period 1970–2005 must surely be considered as a highly significant part of SA music's development. Composers of international acclaim in the professional world have included one of the world's finest wind band writers, James Curnow, one of Hollywood's most successful film composers, Bruce Broughton, and the United States Marine Band's chief arranger, Stephen Bulla. William Himes, who puts most of his creative efforts into SA rather than 'outside' compositions, must also be included in that elite grouping. But that by no means finishes the list. Consider the following other names, who have enriched SA repertoire, some of whom are highly skilled professionals, others talented amateurs: William Broughton, Harold Burgmayer, Jim Cheyne, Paul Curnow, Stanley Ditmer, Karen Krinjak, Thomas Mack, Lloyd Scott, or Robert Schramm.

Then there are the writers who have moved to the States to pursue work, most of them within the SA: from Canada – Douglas Court, William Gordon; from the UK – James Anderson, Ivor Bosanko, Terry Camsey, Dorothy Gates and Ralph Pearce. The list could go on! The SA in America has tried to encourage its writers, having held composition competitions in 1930, 1947, 1965, and 1980. Territorial music camps offer excellent opportunities for developing writers to enhance their theoretical knowledge and to study their arranging craft in an ideal laboratory situation.[27]

In January 2002 the four USA territories and the Canada– Bermuda territory cosponsored a North American Composers' Forum, a three-day intensive seminar held on the campus of Asbury College in Wilmore, KY. Twenty-seven delegates worked with a faculty made up of William Himes, James Curnow, James Anderson, and Drs. Ronald and Beatrice Holz.

Delegates and Faculty at the North American Composers' Forum, SASF Student Center, Asbury College, January 2006.

Various sessions on arranging, scoring, song writing, and the philosophy/theology of SA music were complemented by one-on-one tutorials that each delegate could pursue with a member of the faculty. The delegates particularly appreciated these intimate work sessions.

On the final evening the SASF Band and Vocal Ensemble, as well as several ensembles from the college music department, presented a recital-demonstration of works sent in prior to the Forum by various delegates. The Forum was repeated in 2003, with Len Ballantine, TMD for Canada and Bermuda joining the faculty. Ballantine led the meaningful worship service on Sunday morning wherein delegates and faculty focused on the renewing and dedicating of their creative gifts.

As the staff person who received delegate manuscripts for performance consideration, I was somewhat surprised to find the large majority of submissions in both years were for brass band and brass ensemble. Once again in 2004 another excellent group of emerging composers gathered at Asbury College, and Lt. Colonel Norman Bearcroft and Stephen Bulla joined the faculty for the first time. The Forum met again in January 2006, with Dorothy Gates, Aaron Vanderweele, and Phil Laeger added to the faculty. The curriculum expanded to include more attention to contemporary styles and song writing, as well as discussion of the needs of each publication series.

Prior to the 1980s SA band music publishing in the States was sporadic, the only consistent programme being New York's *American Band Journal* and its related brass ensemble and occasional youth band journals. Financial resources had been slim and pressure from SP&S (and IHQ) to block the sales of American products outside the originating territory added to the difficulty of maintaining any reasonable market.

Most of the publishing went in spurts, starting with William Broughton's Western band journals or graded booklets released in the late 1940s. The Central Territory followed up with several 'easy' band books (the Kelly series of *Easy Marches* and *Easy Selections*), as well as one ensemble series volume edited by Soderstrom in 1962.

Music publishing currently takes place in all four territories. Only the Western Territory is not involved in

A nine-piece Metropolitan (New York) Ensemble in 1932, without instruments, model for the American Band Journal *(begun 1948). Erik Leidzén, director (third left) with Divisional Commander, Alexander Ebbs (fourth from left), founders of the Friday Evening at the Temple series.*

printing brass music, deciding instead to concentrate on vocal series. The East has as its main band publication the *American Band Journal*, the 9-piece series started by Richard Holz and Erik Leidzén in 1948. In addition, they release intermittently the *New York Brass Sextet Journal*, the *Triumphonic Collection* (individual concert works scored for festival series size bands) and most recently, *The Philip Smith Signature Series*, cornet and trumpet solos with brass band accompaniment.

The South specialises in its four-part, *American Instrumental Ensemble Series* and the parallel, *American Instrumental Solo Series*, while the Central handles the *American Festival Series*. You could claim that there is a certain division of labour here, in terms of the size of bands targeted. The East and Central have also published several complementary brass tutorial methods and beginner band music. The East maintains a now wide ranging solo brass series, *American Soloist Albums*, as can be seen in the SA Brass Band Music Table in Volume II.

It is very possible that with the success of American band publications these music departments are poised to take on more responsibility toward the worldwide Army band market. The stature of current editors of American band music speaks highly for the level of work expected and being achieved: Atlanta – James Curnow; Chicago – William Himes; New York – Kevin Norbury, until 2001, after 2001 Dorothy Gates. The acknowledgement by the MMU in London that they are just as much a territorial unit as are the four American departments and, in recent years, the frequent interaction between all these departments and SP&S has led to a more balanced international cooperation and the mutual sharing of methods and formats in a wide range of band publications (See Chapter 1).

Four Representative Bands

Choosing just four corps bands, one from each territory, in order to offer up a representative sample, was a difficult task, a necessary if frustrating one! How do you ignore, for instance, the bands of Eastern Michigan (Flint, Dearborn Heights, Port Huron, Royal Oak), New Jersey (Montclair, Asbury Park), the other fine California bands, or the emerging corps bands of the new South?

You have to leave someone out, some band that perhaps better deserves the profile. Yet the four bands selected tell a story of consistency, innovation, and dedication to the Army mission that can stand for other solid programmes around the nation.

I present these bands in chronological order of their founding. Two originated in the 1880s; one in the 1970s; and one has had a remarkable pilgrimage not unlike many corps bands around the world, corps that have had to change their location in the face of suburban flight and ongoing social change. Each band deserves a full chapter, but I hope these encapsulations give the essence of each band's spirit and contribution to Kingdom-building through music.

Manchester Citadel: Bandmaster Michael Orfitelli

The Manchester (Connecticut) Citadel Band is one of oldest, continuously active corps bands in the United States. Formed in June, 1888, two years after the founding of the corps, the band has the visit of the Fall River (Massachusetts) Corps Band to thank for lighting the spark of Army banding in this former mill town just to the east of Hartford. The first set of instruments was purchased from Cheney Mills, a local textile firm that employed Salvationists, but which by the mid-1880s no longer supported a band at the mill.

The small nucleus of the first SA band was trained by a local musician, Jimmie Hall, who was paid up to $1.50/week for his teaching, depending on what was in the band treasury. Playing indoors by late summer, the band first ventured outside on Christmas, 1888.

The 'South" Manchester Band, as it was known for many years, played an important role in regional and territorial events in the first 50 years of the SA in America, culminating in their performance at the 1930 National Congress. BM David Addy proudly led them in a march by their own Harold Turkington, who found out that night he was among the winners of the composition contest. It is interesting to note that Turkington was later to serve as the elected mayor of the town of Manchester!

In that same year (1930) the band began its series of park concerts directly across the street from the hall. They also renewed their active prison ministry, especially their long-standing visitations at the state correctional institution in Somers. The band is a recognised part of the community and has played for various civic, school, and religious observances throughout the 20th century.

Frequently considered a self-sufficient corps, Manchester has maintained a solid soldiery for over 115 years from which a highly dedicated group of local officers has been found, including those who led the band and the junior band. For this has been a corps that always trained its own, usually giving away to the rest of the Army world some of its finest players rather than gaining them.[28]

Among its bandmasters have been such unsung heroes as George McCormack, Hamilton Metcalf, Fred Clough, Harold Turkington (on two separate occasions), David Addy, Robert Lyons, William Hanna, C. Peter Carlson, Robert Richardson, Jr., and Robert Jackson. The current bandmaster, Michael Orfitelli, has held this position longer than any other leader of the band, 34 years. A product of the corps junior and senior band programme, Orfitelli has, until recently made his living as a specialist in the telecommunications industry, though he has taught music in public schools and holds a Master of Music Education degree from the Northern Illinois University. He now holds the position Territorial Disaster Training Coordinator for the USA East (Emergency Disaster Services).

The songster leader of corps and flugelhornist of the band, Karen Krinjak, also came up through the ranks at Manchester. She is a noted piano soloist and arranger/composer. Both were featured soloists with the proficient Southern New England Youth Band that flourished in the period 1964–1979, a group in which many Manchester young people played. The long-term commitment of these two leaders is particularly noteworthy, as the current health of the corps music groups is the result of hard work after a difficult time in the late 1960s when the corps was rocked by a major controversy within the band. Both Karen and Michael were young band members at the time.[29]

The Manchester Band was exclusively male until the late 1940s, except during both World Wars, when women were allowed to fill in for the men in the armed services. The band in the 1998–99 season was made up of 20 men and 11 women. Slightly more than half the members of the band had grown up in the corps. Members of the band held a wide variety of jobs, including work in teaching, law, engineering, social work, insurance, finance. This band has always had not only a solid musical reputation, but equally important, Manchester has endeavoured to be a spiritually focused band.

In the very first year of the band, after a visit by Samuel Logan Brengle, membership in the band was restricted to

Manchester Citadel Band, Connecticut.

those who professed the *blessing of sanctification*. While such litmus tests would not be applied now, the band is as serious about praying together and discipling one another as it is about playing great music. The current band maintains a solid standard, being perhaps the finest corps band in New England at the present moment. They get featured in territorial events, they take their weekends away, they put on their festivals of music, but above all the Manchester Citadel Band goes about its business in a generally unheralded way, without fanfare, and other band razzle-dazzle.

Generation after generation of band members and leaders has been faithful to their calling. The town of Manchester, CT and the SA have been the better for that consistency.

Atlanta Temple: Bandmaster Robert Snelson

Atlanta Temple Corps moved to a new, impressive building next to Territorial Headquarters in 1996 following 40 years at the historic Seminole Avenue location, adjacent to Georgia DHQ [Formerly THQ, 1955–1976]. A typical headquarters

Atlanta Temple Band (Bandmaster Doctor Richard Holz) in front of the old Seminole Avenue corps hall, 1990, on the occassion of the 100th anniversary of the corps.

corps, with many soldiers and officers employed in some aspect of SA work either within the city, division, or territory, Atlanta Temple at one time or another seems to have attracted some of the finest leaders and players from across the South. Among these have been such guiding lights of Southern music as Lt. Colonel Albert Baldwin, first Southern Staff Bandmaster, and territorial music secretaries Lt. Colonel Frank Longino (who served as corps bandmaster several different times), Brigadier Leslie Hall, and Brigadier Hubert Rawlin. George Pyke, Sr., Major Stanley Jaynes, Captain William Powell, and the late Commissioner Richard Holz also held the baton for short tenures. The earliest bandmaster was cornetist Clinton Collins, who founded the band in 1891, when it was called the Georgia #1 Corps Band. The earliest extant photo of the band from approximately this date displays an all-male band of 12 players made up of two cornets, five saxhorns, one E flat bombardon, and three percussion (bass drum, snare drum, and cymbals)

The establishment of a THQ in Atlanta in 1927 gave a boost to the band when the Atlanta Temple Corps occupied the first floor of the new THQ building at 54 Ellis Street in downtown Atlanta. Ever since then, however, it has been subject to a high turnover rate in both players and conductors, at least until recent years. The band has never lacked players, and at some times in its history has nearly exceeded 50 members, after which, according to the old O&R, the band would have had to seek permission to maintain such a size or divide into several different ensembles! It was, in many respects, the showcase band of the South, except on special weekends when the Territorial Band would be formed, and then with quite a few Temple band members holding down principal chairs.

The most notable achievements of this band have come under the baton of Dr. Richard Holz, 1979–1993, a time during which the band became a paragon for the reviving music programme within the South and a band that could be ranked among the finest in the country. In addition to its weekly corps duties, divisional and territorial functions, ATB during this time can point to several notable, historic engagements:

1980 Concert at the American School Band Directors Association Convention (subsequent recording by *Crest Records*)

1981 Concert at the National Convention of the Hymn Society of America
1986 Trip to Santiago, Chile; first SA band to visit South America; South America West Territorial Congress
1988 Second recording, *The Guardian of Our Way*
1989 Guest band at the Eastern Territory's Commissioning, in New York City
1991 First SA band to play at the Great American Brass Band Festival, Danville, KY; return visit in 1993

During this same period the band also visited Chicago, IL, Dallas, TX, and Tampa, FL, as well as taking other regional trips in the South.

A significant aspect of the Atlanta Temple Band's ministry during the past 20 years has been its active role in the religious and cultural life of the South's hub city. Monthly concerts and participation in services at many Atlanta churches gave the Atlanta Temple Band a prominent visibility in the community. The band has been a regular guest at nationally-known churches, including Peachtree Presbyterian Church (Dr. Frank Harrington) and Wieuca Road Baptist Church (Dr. Bill Self).

Richard Holz's former colleague in the music department, Christopher Priest [First Songster Leader of the USA Southern Territorial Songsters] carried on within this tradition from 1993 until the Fall of 1998. At that time Dr. Holz took a leave of absence from his responsibilities as corps sergeant major to direct the band for a one-year interim period due in part to Priest's official work in preparation for hosting the 2000 International Congress.

Bandmaster James Anderson, out of Edinburgh Gorgie Corps, Scotland, and DMD in Texas for seven years, succeeded to the podium in the Fall of 1999. The spring 1999 Roster of the band included seven parents sharing band fellowship with their children. The list included William Broughton/David Broughton; Ron Livingston/Jennifer Livingston; Major Steve Hedgren/Matt Hedgren; Jerry Sjogren/Greg Sjorgren; Bert Gotrich/Lars Gotrich; James Anderson/Timothy Anderson; and one three-generation family, Brigadier Louise Pertain/ Mary Pertain Miller/ Hillary Miller.

The instrumentation of this 37-member band included 12

cornets, six alto horns, six euphonium/baritones, five trombones, five tubas, and three percussionists.[30] When James Anderson moved to Los Angeles in 2001 the baton was taken up by John Zanders, who had served a number of years as the DMD for the Georgia division. Robert Snelson, currently Territorial Music Education Secretary in Atlanta, became bandmaster of the now 36-member Atlanta Temple Band in August 2004.

Pasadena Tabernacle: Bandmaster Bill Flinn

Band names can be confusing. The name 'Pasadena Tabernacle' signifies not only a city and an old SA title for a type of corps, but the fact that this corps, and its famous Tab Band, are the result of the 1983 merger of the Pasadena Corps and the Hollywood Tabernacle Corps. Hollywood Tabernacle had moved out of downtown Los Angeles, the Los Angeles Tabernacle Corps, which began humbly under the title Los Angeles #2, its band under BM Joe Norton in 1909. Moving to Fourth and Main in the 1920s, the band became the Los Angeles Citadel Band and was led by such stalwarts as Captain 'Dutch' Higgins.

Pasadena Tabernacle Band with Bandmaster Bill Gordon.

In the late 1940s, the Citadel became a Harbor Light corps; this necessitated another move, and another title: Los Angeles Tabernacle! In 1964, and at the end of Ray Ogg's term as bandmaster, the corps moved to Hollywood, the band soon being led by a young Australian, Ronald Smart. Harry Sparks tells a lively account of the whole matter in his charming book, *With a Thousand Bands: 50 Plus Years in a SA Band*. For him, it brings his band pilgrimage full circle because he grew up and trained in the Pasadena Corps Band and was involved in the last move of the Tab Band from near Hollywood and Vine to his 'home' corps. His father had been converted in an Army Open-Air service in Pasadena, 1915, back when the 'band' consisted of a cornet, a drum, and several tambourines (Pasadena Corps was founded in 1888).

Tab Band has been in the forefront of SA music making since the days it was asked to play in the Tournament of Roses Parade in 1920 when Harold Gooding was bandmaster. It was a pioneer in radio and television ministry and can even claim to be the first band to fly as a group to an engagement, in 1946, on an old freight vehicle. *The instruments were stacked in the centre aisle while bandmembers sat on jump seats which were previously used by paratroopers* (American *WC* May 1983). One of the most widely travelled bands of all time, their record is indeed an impressive one:

1959 San Francisco World's Fair; Canadian and USA East Tour
1963 Billy Graham Crusade, Los Angeles Coliseum
1964 United Kingdom and European Tour
1967 Expo 67, Montreal, Canada
1972 Australia–New Zealand Tour
1978 Third International Tuba–Euphonium Symposium (T.U.B.A.)
1986 Eastern United States Tour
1995 Canadian Maritimes–Ontario Tour
1999 Chile, South America, Tour

Their leadership roll through the years reads as a 'who's who' in SA music out West, as well as for folks that have moved to these sunny climes: Ray Ogg, Ronald Smart, Wilf Mountain, Ivor Bosanko, Barrie Gott, William Gordon, Lambert

Bittinger, James Anderson, and Bill Flinn. Interim leaders included William Broughton, Sr., and Bernard Verkaaik, former leader of the Netherlands National Band. Dr. Ronald Smart and William Gordon are the names most linked to the adventurous spirit of this band, particularly when it came to contemporary music styles. Smart did not hesitate to experiment with jazz-style orchestrations back in the late 1960s-early 1970s, while Bill Gordon brought the band into the modern rock era, with his effective treatment of many 'Praise and Worship' tunes, arrangements which are now standard issue for most SA bands. This aggressive, progressive approach can be traced through the more than 15 recordings the band has made, including the *Crowns* CD, made for their 1995 Canadian Tour. The CD was also used as an effective piece of outreach ministry within the band's normal sphere of influence.

Until very recently the band was led by Lambert Bittinger, formerly the band's solo cornetist. He has had a musical career representative of many West Coast Salvationists. Trained in the Eastern Territory, where he received his bachelor's degree in music education from Montclair State College, Bittinger developed an outstanding corps band in Kearny, NJ.

For a number of years he was a member of the East's territorial music department and cornet soloist with the New York Staff Band. He moved to the West Coast in the late 1970s, playing in Tab Band for several years before moving to Atlanta, GA, serving as principal cornet in the Atlanta Temple Band with his college friend, Richard Holz, and eventually moving back to Los Angeles. His colleague at Pasadena, Bill Flinn, is also a product of the East Coast, but out of the Pendel or Philadelphia scene, having moved to LA in 1976. Bill did an outstanding job leading the songsters until 2000, and then led the corps Youth Band 2000-2004. The songsters under Flinn blazed their own trail of glory via innovative worship and concert formats, so much so that the two sections represent one of the most dynamic centres of Army music anywhere on the globe.

In March 2002 James Anderson, at that time TMD for the Western Territory, assumed the bandmaster position at Tab, with Bittinger continuing as a very active deputy bandmaster. Bill Flinn took over the band in June 2004, somehow finding time to lead this outstanding ensemble while maintaining his professional position as Chief Operating Officer for the Tournament of Roses Association, an organisation he has served for 24 years. Bittinger's band in 1999 consisted of 43 members, six of whom participated along with him in the Hollywood Tabernacle Band. The numbers in 2005 are just slightly larger. The band is committed to growing home grown talent.

The Youth Band has a wide programme of musical training organised in a series of groups of varying experience. On alternate Sunday afternoons there is now an impressive array of music and gospel arts programmes for the large youth population in the corps. The Band's recent commitment to implementing their Vision Statement included extensive community involvement. This was actualised during their recent trip to Chile where the band and timbrel brigade painted the exterior of a three-storey, children's home. Dr. Robert Doctor, a significant leader in the history of corps himself, in a document sent to me in 1999 succinctly concluded his overview of the band is this manner:

> *The band currently enjoys several father-son/daughter combinations, a few husband-wife participants, four SA officers, several teachers, three university professors, some financial consultants, a computer administrator, and a number of students. The average age of the band is young as it seeks to build a commitment in following generations for the rich tradition handed them by those who have gone before.*
>
> *Over the years, through geographic change, international and local adversities, this band has been and is a cohesive force for Christ, ministering in music with a contemporary message designed to attract and hold listeners.*[31]

Norridge Citadel: Bandmaster Peggy Thomas

When the 40-piece Norridge Citadel Band toured Great Britain March 24–April 4, 1999, they took with them their innovative ideas about SA worship, marked especially by their presentation of Robert and Gweneth Redhead's 'worship experience', *Revelation Hope*. This suburban corps in the northwest Chicago area has been home to experiments in new worship techniques and evangelism via the medium of the brass band. The primary force behind this effort is their dynamic and talented bandmaster, Peggy Thomas, assistant territorial music secretary for the Central Territory and principal cornet of the Chicago Staff Band. She and her Norridge colleagues launched, *Hallelujah Choruses*, the contemporary chorus/song accompaniment series that has allowed SA bands to serve not only in their traditional role, but also as a 'praise and worship' band. They also have produced compact discs like, *The Beatles Theology?*, not so much as a typical fund raiser, but as something to be given out in the neighbourhood as an enticement, an attraction, to worship services at the corps. Their *Spring* and *Summer Song Festivals* are directly designed to attract people in their area.

This is not a band-driven corps by any means. It is a corps led by a talented, committed group of local officers chosen for their spiritual gifts, men and women who have proven that SA corps can grow significantly in a worship environment that balances both traditional and contemporary musical styles.

BM Thomas has led Norridge since 1983. Her most recent predecessors included Art Shoults, Edward Lowcock, and John Jones, for this is a relatively new corps, historically speaking. Shoults was an excellent euphonium soloist with the Chicago Staff Band, and Ed Lowcock was a great developer of SA bands throughout America, including stints on the podium of Brooklyn Citadel, Patterson, NJ, and Inglewood (now

Norridge Citadel Band, Chicago (Bandmaster Peggy Thomas).

Torrence), CA. John Jones took over the band upon the sudden death of Lowcock in 1978. He carried on the young but fine tradition established by Shoults and Lowcock, taking them to the 1978 International Congress, where they premiered Curnow's *Psalm 100: A Psalm of Praise*, a work commissioned by Lowcock for the tour.

Always a youthful band of mostly homegrown Centralites, with quite a few serving in the Chicago Staff from time to time, over a third of the spring, 1999 band were students, seven high school – seven college. Ten adult members work in some professional capacity for the SA in the greater Chicago area. Other jobs represented in the membership would be engineers, marketing manager, housewife, computer programmer, nurse, social worker, salesman, and an anaesthetist.

In her thought-provoking article *Worship Evangelism* Thomas tells of the pilgrimage that led this band to explore new ways of worshipping and reaching out in their neighbourhood. Essentially, they have found that they needed to 'repackage' the Sunday AM service, making it more dynamic, making it more like the old SA Salvation meeting in its liveliness and excitement, but with a true vertical orientation – praise to God, not just about God. When the SASF Band visited Norridge several years ago, the worship committee (a marvellous innovation) had no problem at all with that fact that the band wanted to play Ball's, *Kingdom Triumphant* in the 'Holiness' Meeting. This fitted in with exactly where our leader, Major Juanita Russell, was aiming the service, and who had requested that stirring music.

Peggy had already learned that sometimes playing a rock-style hymn arrangement as the last prelude item, followed by a balance of contemporary choruses and traditional hymns, would keep the audience fully involved, all generations. Music would have great power if the choices, whatever the type, style, length, were selected as part of whole experience designed to enable change, the essence of worship.

The repertoire chosen by Thomas for the UK tour models this balance as well. Two CDs were recorded for the trip. One, entitled, *Church Windows* after Bill Gordon's adaptation of Respighi's tone poem of the same name, was organised around the theme of windows – windows of love, promise, heaven...witness. The central band piece of *Revelation Hope*, Redhead's, *Omega*, a work that uses contemporary songs by Twila Paris and Graham Kendrick, was included, though the entire worship experience had its own separate CD. Traditional band music, from classical transcriptions to hymn tune arrangements, blended with rock and jazz style pieces to form a programme that would reach many.

On top of all that, when performed publicly, *Revelation Hope* contained visual components, from timbrel drills to multi-media projections coordinated with some of the music. The only thing missing, if you purchased both CDs, was the brief message given by the accompanying officer, a direct challenge and appeal that followed the second half of the festival, *Revelation Hope*. One UK officer wrote to the *Salvationist* after hearing the band's 'festival':

> *I must write in praise of the Norridge Citadel Band...I attended a packed house at Staines Corps and can honestly say I have never been so impressed by the content and presentation of a band programme... What a delight to sense Christ taking centre stage and an Army festival using music to attract our attention toward him* (Captain Stephen Poxon, April 24, 1999 *Salvationist* (UK) p10).

Norridge Citadel seems to have found a way to maintain their primary mission while still offering up interesting, and demanding music literature played at a high level of technical achievement. They do this not only on tour, but week in–week out, at home. Mission and music work together, with the music, the band, being the 'handmaiden of the Lord,' so to speak, allowing true worship to take place, lives changed, redirected, and a congregation on fire in their Christian walk. They have sought Biblical principles in their methods, and this has proved a revelation of hope, indeed.[32]

Reaching Out to Share the Wealth

This brief study of SA bands in the USA should not conclude without mention of the continuing support US territories, divisions, and individual corps give to the growing SA in countries less blessed with financial resources. Some of these efforts have already been mentioned above. One can think way

John Allan, founder of the SA's music camp program, noted cornet soloist and later SA Chief-of-the-Staff, wearing the US Army Chaplain's uniform during World War I.

Hollywood Tabernacle Band (Bandmaster Ronald Smart), June 1964 on their tour of England.

back to the establishment of the Erik Leidzén Memorial Scholarship in the USA East (mid-1960s) that has brought outstanding young camper musicians from a host of countries to Star Lake Musicamp. This started a trend that has continued to this day in all four regions. In the early 1990s Star Lake also instituted the Richard E. Holz Scholarship that brings from Territories outside North America outstanding junior faculty members (rather than campers) with great leadership potential.

Sometimes in these cultural exchanges musicians are brought to the states, sometimes teams from the US travel abroad. For example, the Central Territory is just completing a five-year partnership with Caribbean Territory, a partnership combining the longstanding music leadership and expertise of the Midwest with the talent and mission of the Army's vast work in the Caribbean islands. In this partnership the Central Territorial Music and Gospel Arts Department provided the faculty for Caribbean Music Institute (CariMI), a nine-day training session held in Kingston, Jamaica on the campus the Army's School for the Blind. In addition, the Central has provided instruments, music for CariMI and two travel/tuition scholarships for the top students to Central Music Institute.

Recent efforts in the Western Territory have included the following. In 2001 Envoy Nigel Cross led a group from the

Chicago Staff Band with Staff Bandmaster William Himes, November 2005, at the Annual Thanksgiving Festival of Music.

Northwest Division to a children's home in Mexico City and did everything from maintenance work on computers and basketball courts to services at a children's home, concerts at corps, open-airs and street concerts to holding a music school. The American band and chorus members became the music school staff. They taught vocal, timbrels, recorders and whatever brass instruments the people had.

Ivor and Janette Bosanko became seasoned travellers to South America East. They went every year from 1995 to 1998. In 1995 they also went to the music camp in South America West. Each year they would select a student, at the conclusion of the camp, for a scholarship to the Western Music Institute. In 1996 they led the music camp in the Hong Kong and Taiwan Command. In winter 2003 James Anderson travelled to Santiago, Chile, to serve in a similar capacity.

In the Southern Territory the Texas Division has long standing ties with the Latin America North Territory. Florida and Carolina divisional music programmes work closely with Argentina, and most recently the Territorial Music Department travelled to Brazil to help staff and run the first divisional music camp for Brazil. Like other territories, the USA South financially supports delegations to its TMI from various countries in Latin and Central America, and the Caribbean.

These are representative examples of substantial contributions in personnel, musical expertise, and financial resources that the USA gives for the betterment of SA music throughout the developing world.[33]

Notes

1. See cover of *American War Cry* [*AWC*], November 8, 1883, p1, and subsequent coverage. I am grateful to Fred Creighton and Major Jim Tackaberry for confirming the fact that the Kingston Band was functioning by this date, and had had contact with Thomas Moore, American Commander, who would have enlisted their support for Syracuse.

2. *AWC*, September 11, 1884, p1. Another 'Military Band' procession took place in Pittsburgh (July 1st).

3. East Liverpool's claim may be more solid. See *AWC*, Dec. 27, 1884, p.6; The yearbook *The Salvation War* (London: SA, 1885), p61, reports that East Liverpool had 250 soldiers after only 13 weeks of campaigning. The Grand Rapids claim is supported by a notation appended to a photo of the band now housed in the Central Territory archives. That photo appeared in print in the *AWC* of June 11, 1887. Grand Rapids corps history claims 1884 for the 'commissioning' of both the band and the bandmaster.

4. Both Holz, *Heralds of Victory*, Chapter 1, and McKinley, *Marching to Glory*, p52–55, provide more detail on the early days of bands in the USA. One remarkable event in this period was the founding of the Danbury, CT, Corps Band, which received its first lessons from the local town bandmaster, George Ives, a famous Civil War musician and the father of noted composer Charles Ives.

5. *AWC*, May 7, 1887, contains full report.

6. Career sheets on Trumble, Duncan, and Halpin, USE Archives. New York #1 and Halpin – see *AWC*, Feb. 20, 1886, p1 as well as March 27, and April 24. Duncan listed his nationality as Scottish, though he was converted in America; report on circular bass appears in *AWC* Feb. 23, 1889, p8. See *Heralds of Victory* for more details on each individual.

7. Reports on the Grand Rapids Corps Band tour appear during the winter months of 1889, *AWC*. See *WCC*, December 10, 1933, for article on 50th anniversary of Grand Rapids Corps.

8. *Heralds of Victory*, pp5–9.

9. Article by Evangeline Booth, *AWC*, January 28, 1905, p3; A picture of this band appeared in *AWC* April 15, 1905, p4. This band started as the New England Life Guards, in imitation of British models, was renamed the New England Jubilee Band, and eventually the New England Provincial Staff Band, reaching its peak under Erik Leidzén, 1923–26.

10. For an overview of 19th-century American bands, see Margaret and Robert Hazen, *The Music Men*, in which it is estimated there were as many as 10,000 brass bands in the USA in the late 19th century. For the music of these bands, see Raoul Camus' volume

on 19th-century American brass band music. Tobani, a leading band arranger of the day, published his patrol piece under the pseudonym Andrew Herman. See articles on Orth, Tobani, and Brooks in *The Heritage Encyclopedia of Band Music* (Rehrig, edited Bierley).

11. *AWC*, March 19, 1904, p10; and Bridgen with Cleveland Citadel Silver Band of 27 members, *AWC*, Nov. 5, 1904, p4, with Bridgen giving testimonials for Trade Department goods. Bridgen, by all accounts very talented, had quite a chequered career, ending up by following Holz to Philadelphia in 1909 and leading the Atlantic Coast Province Band there. He was, in many ways, an early Divisional Music Director. In addition to other bands, he formed the famed Patterson, NY, Corps Band; see *AWC*, February 8, 1890, p11.

12. Chicago Staff Band 75th anniversary programme, November 27, 1982. Having two leaders like this was very common at this time. Broughton conducted the band on four different occasions – 1907–1909, 1913–1916, 1927–1932, 1943, while Flynn was the great stabilising presence in the band's early years, 1907–1924. On the Flint band see *Local Officers' Counselor* (Volume 8, No. 2), Nov, 1926, pp16–17. *The Local Officers' Counselor* provides a rich source for articles on American SA bands and their leaders.

13. For one band's contribution to the war effort, see *Heralds of Victory*, pp34–35. Hodges was not only a talented brass player, but a gifted organist who prepared various songbook collections released by Commander Eva Booth in the USA. He probably assisted her with her first songs, like *Fling Wide the Gates*, while Leidzén completed the work on the first edition of *Songs of Evangel*. Broughton became her pawn in a power struggle over the Friday Evening at the Temple Series, in remarkable series of events that led to Leidzén's departure from SA music for 15 years. See *Erik Leidzén*, pp26–32.

14. The programme also included congregational songs, scripture reading, items by a large Festival Chorus led by Arkett and Darby, a Scandinavian Chorus and Orchestra led by Sam Toft, two songs by The Hawaiian Singers, and an address by Commander Eva Booth. Sandwiched into this was a demonstration of a new quartet-based hymn tune series for bands that Erik Leidzén was developing for small bands.

15. *Marching to Glory*, pp182–186; *Newsweek*, December 15, 1941, p69.

16. In particular, see *Heralds of Victory*, pp78–79; I also recommend as an overview of this whole period, Commissioner Richard E. Holz, 'The Development of SA Music in America', *War Cry* (March 13 20, 1982), pp4–6.

17. McKinley reported that in this time period there was only one American graduate of the British BM Correspondence Course, BM Sam Collins of San Francisco Citadel; *Marching to Glory*, p217.

18. Both *Heralds of Victory* and *Erik Leidzén* books contain information on this course, which stressed leadership skills/organisation, basic music theory, and introductory conducting. Graduations frequently took place at congresses, where graduates conducted a Bandmasters Band. The course continued after Leidzén's death, first taught by Richard Holz, and then, into the mid-1960s, Vernon Post.

19. The USA South's TMI Advanced Leadership Seminar meets for 5½ hours a day, alternating between a conducting lab, lecture, discussion, and analysis. Each student is video taped extensively, both within the lab session and in front of TMI ensembles. Goals and objectives of the class: 1) Conducting skills refined and improved (including physical technique, score reading/preparation, and rehearsal techniques); 2) Practical knowledge of SA band repertoire (Scoring/instrumentation, suitability, etc.); 3) Broad study of SA music in historical and theological context, especially in terms of worship and evangelism; 4) Study of two SA band works, in cooperation with the guest conductor, who holds a master class.

20. Commissioner John Allan is one of the musical giants of SA music. At a very young age he was playing in corps bands where his officer parents were stationed, and soon was soloing on cornet with professional bands like the American Band of Providence (originally under Reeves). He not only organised the first music camps in America, but was instrumental in the founding of Star Lake Musicamp. His fine playing, which he considered recorded after his prime, can be heard on the 1922–23 Vocalion records of the NYSB, on which he plays his own composition, *Memories*, a

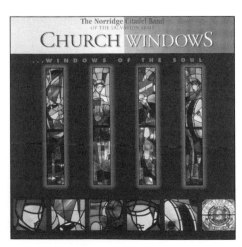

Two enterprising CDs from Norridge Citadel Band.

piece later published in the *Festival Series*. During World War I Allan served on the staff of General Pershing, American Expeditionary Forces; he eventually became the Chief-of-the-Staff for the SA.

21. The impact of these two men is difficult to overestimate. So many leading musicians in the Army played under them as teenagers in the Pendel or Northern New Jersey Youth Band, or witnessed their dedicated service as corps bandmasters. Each territory has these kinds of people – Max Wood in the Central, Frank Longino in the South, Harry Stillwell in the West, who are but a sample.

22. *Marching to Glory*, pp334–34.

23. I have the annual reports from DMDs in the South for several years (1994–1999) prepared for the annual meeting of DMDs in Atlanta; within these are comprehensive profiles of their conservatories, their students, curriculums, in addition to complete reports of their yearly activities.

24. Figures from *Marching to Glory*, 268, 282. Thomas Mack, *The Future of the Brass Band Ministry in the SA Eastern Territory*, USA. B.S. Thesis, Nyack College, 1998.

25. I was privileged to serve as a judge for the contest (Along with Ivor Bosanko, Max Wood, Richard Holz, Vernon Post, and James Curnow). Among the winners were William Himes, choral, and Stephen Bulla, band.

26. So many things must get left behind in such a short review, like the Army's forward-looking involvement in early TV. The NYSB alone played every year from 1952–1961 on shows like the Today Show, Gary Moore Show, I've Got a Secret and others. The Living Word TV Series (See Chapter on Canada) developed by the SA in the mid 1950s–mid 1960s, which featured many instrumental groups, songsters, and vocal soloists, was another example of more direct televangelism. One of my earliest band memories is playing on an early TV show with the Arlington-Kearny, NJ, Y.P. Band, in the late 1950s.

27. The minute you make such lists, others suggest themselves, like the entire generation preceding this one, including men like Bernard Ditmer (brother of Stanley), and a host of others, some of whom may have only had a few pieces printed, but the experience was enriching and of great benefit to their careers as SA music leaders: Harold Gustafson, Lloyd Reslow, and Harold Zealley from the 1947 contest, for example.

28. The band's prison ministry is among the first by any SA band in the States, the first visit recorded in the Fall of 1895, when National BM Edward Trumble accompanied them to the Wethersfield State Prison: *AWC*, November 30, 1895, p7. Among the materials shared with me by the band, via BM Orfitelli and Major Richard Munn (CO at the time) was the interesting corps

history completed in 1947, and subsequent documents at later anniversaries.

29. The so-called Richardson split came as a result of insensitive application of the bandmaster's (Robert Richardson) 'evaluation' of individual band members just as the band had reached a new peak of musical efficiency. Charge and counter-charge in this battle of prides nearly shattered the corps. I was a young 'ringer' with this band throughout this terrible event (my father was DC at the time), and the memory of what happened has always been a caution to me in my musical ministry, as I know it has for BM Orfitelli.

30. Data provided from the Southern Territorial Music Department.

31. Data provided by William Gordon, Lambert Bittinger, Robert Doctor, Ivor Bosanko, James Anderson, and Francis Dingman, the latter on the staff of the USW Archives. Dr. Robert Doctor, long-standing leader in the corps, provided me with a lovely short history of the band which I wish there had been room to include in its entirety. Bittinger works in Institutional Advancement at the University of Southern California. James Anderson has recently moved from Los Angeles to Washington, DC, where he has assumed the DMD position in the National Capital and Virginia Division and where he directs the National Capital Band. In May 2005 Neil Smith, a Scottish Salvationist out of Inverness, Scotland and former member of The Band of the Scots Guards, assumed the position of Territorial Music Secretary for the USA West after serving several years as DMD in the Sierra del Mar (San Diego area) division.

32. Data provided by Peggy Thomas. The band also provides free CD Christmas cards (*Let Heaven and Nature Sing*) and free Christian music, hymn settings or various style, *Thinking of You*. The corps even sends these and other CD products out to other corps so they too can use them in their outreach. The Norridge Citadel is one of the finest examples of recent church growth principles and Evangelism Explosion ideas working successfully in a SA setting.

33. I am grateful for reports provided in February 2003 from territorial and divisional music departments from which I made this very small summary. It is gratifying to see the intensity of support given in this area. I have personally been able to train a group of talented musicians from such nations as Brazil, Argentina, Panama, and Jamaica at the USA South's Advanced Instrumental Leadership Course at their annual TMI. My experience is but representative of what also goes on at Star Lake, CMI, and WMI.

Chapter 10

FUNCTION, MISSION, AND MUSIC IN THE FUTURE OF SA BANDS

Ronald W. Holz

...I have always regarded music as all belonging to God. Perhaps some of you have heard me say in public that there will not be a note of music in hell, it will be all in heaven, and God ought to have it all there, and God ought to have it all here... The church has strangely lost sight of the value of music as a religious agency. I think God has used the Army to resuscitate and awaken [it]*...and while the bandsmen of The Salvation Army realise it to be as much their service to blow an instrument as it is to sing or pray...and while they do it in the same spirit, I am persuaded it will become an ever-increasing power amongst us. But the moment you, or any other bandsman, begin to glory in the excellence of the music alone, apart from the spiritual results, you will begin at that moment to lose your power... You see, when you separate the divine from the human, it ceases to have any power over souls. Don't forget that.* Words by Catherine Booth, the Army Mother, as preserved by Commissioner Catherine Booth, on the occasion of the visit of the Household Troops Band to her at Clacton-on-Sea, June 1890, shortly before her death.[1]

Brass bands are but one part of the SA's vast work, though a highly visible and audible one! Yet, as has been observed several times in this book, they do not exist in isolation. Bands, therefore, have always been easy targets for critics, internal or external, who love pointing out what is wrong with the SA or its music. Yet the SA band sub-culture, for all its perceived weaknesses or faults, has also been one of the crowning achievements of the denomination. What has been achieved for good, or what has gone astray, has taken place within the greater programme of the SA, which itself has sometimes been led with vision, and sometimes lost its way. The scope of this study does not allow a more comprehensive examination of that relationship, but when top ecclesiastical leadership has projected an all-inclusive vision and concrete plans for carrying it out, SA music forces have been among the most aggressive, adaptable, and consistent partners in that noble task. This chapter must focus primarily on SA bands. However, if bands face a tentative future, it is because the SA, as a militant denomination made up of committed laymen and clergy, also faces that same future with similar, and perhaps even greater, concern.

By reflecting on the observations and opinions shared in Chapters 4–9 of this book the reader can easily reach the conclusion that SA bands and their culture face a crisis at the start of the new millennium, perhaps the greatest challenge they have ever faced. Using international statistics listed in SA *Yearbooks* as a guide to assessing the current state of SA band culture, the overall trend seen in band membership does not lead to giddy optimism, figures that are supported by previous reports already cited in this book's chapters on representative territories and regions. The *Yearbook* report date is listed first, then the year for which the statistic was drawn:

Yearbook	*Actual Year*	*Senior Band Members*	*Y.P. Band Members*
1980	1978	41,333	26,967
1985	1984	44,244	28,350
1990	1988	41,998	31,681
1995	1993	39,838	11,020
1998	1997	25,183	11,763
2000	1999	24,837	9,780
2001	2000	24,057	9,422

2002	2001	26,479	11,618
2003	2002	29,472	13,957
2004	2003	24,753	14,740
2005	2004	26,642	13,400

These statistics show generally that in the last twenty years of the 20th Century the numbers of band members, both senior and junior, declined significantly. Then, within the past few years modest gains are evident in both categories. However, a cautionary note must be inserted here. The rather precipitous losses in youth band members, for example, between 1990 and 1995 may or may not be related to a new statistical listing, other Senior or Y.P. musical groups (excepting songsters brigades and singing companies). What has been reported as a 'band member' may have fluctuated widely between territories. The losses over this period in those areas of the SA world that were traditionally strong in bands is the great concern, one matched by parallel losses in adult soldiership within the same period - something again reflected upon within this book by each of our authors. We do not yet have complete enough data, however, to make a full and accurate assessment along the lines of Thomas Mack's report referenced in Chapter 9 (USA).

We cannot dismiss these numbers. SA bands are losing ground, alternative means of music-making and arts ministry are on the increase, and the SA is growing significantly not in territories with great band traditions, but in so-called 'Third World' areas, some of which embrace traditional brass bands. This final chapter will contain a broad investigation of the various issues facing SA bands in terms of membership, mission via function in worship and evangelism, and the music they could be playing. My colleagues and I have all pointed out the losses, while at the same time reflecting on the many incredibly vibrant programmes within the countries profiled. I can confidently list, in broadly drawn terms, the following seven optimistic observations:

1) SA brass bands are the best they have ever been – at least technically and musically.
2) The best SA players rank among the finest brass musicians in the world, and the finest SA conductors are highly respected.

3) The pool of talented arrangers and composers will remain strong, and even improve over the next generation, representing an even wider range of nationalities, cultures, and backgrounds.

4) SA publication and music education efforts have never been stronger, more widespread, nor more diverse.

5) The SA music programme is backed up by the finest administrative support system the SA has ever had, and one that finally is being monitored on an international scale.

6) Youth music programmes are generally again on the rise, as are music leadership training programmes in some territories, the two key areas that will lead to a renaissance in SA bands.

7) In many 'non-traditional' territories and regions of the SA world where significant growth is apparent, Salvationists there embrace brass bands and traditional SA music to the degree finances allow them, in addition to developing their own cultural resources.

Yet many in the Army entertain the nagging thought that the whole SA band scene could be, in the words of then General Frederick Coutts, when reflecting on the SA in its 1965 centenary year: *Has it any future? Is it not a Victorian anachronism which is inevitably on its way out?* (From sermon delivered in St. John the Divine Cathedral, New York City, October 24, 1965).

These sweeping generalisations must, of course, be put in some kind of context. That is what is attempted in this chapter, perhaps not definitively, but with enough integrity to set the stage for further study and dialogue – for who can claim to have all the answers? Speaking globally about SA bands is, of course, very difficult, but certain broad issues can be faced and discussed, indeed, already have been raised on a consistent basis in Chapters 4–9. These range from the changing nature of Salvationist worship and bands' role within that change to the difficulty of reaching audiences outside the corps hall with the Gospel message. Thomas Rive's observation, shared in Warren Baas' New Zealand chapter, that brass bands must be looked at as a sociological phenomenon first, rather than a musical or even spiritual one, may be the wise starting point. This will be followed by three areas of inquiry and reflection: 1) The future mission/function of SA bands; 2) The music that will assist that mission; 3) A concluding summary that points toward a regained vision for SA brass bands.

Before that discussion begins in earnest, I want to emphasise the fact that SA band activity is primarily run by willing volunteers, who may or may not be backed up by regional, administrative professionals. Any assessment of what has been achieved or what might be achieved in the future must be done with the understanding of the great personal dedication and sacrifice that goes into being a SA band member or bandmaster. We cannot forget the human dimension in our sweeping generalisations. Most of what has been wrought in SA music has been done through high moral, spiritual and altruistic motives. No matter how off centre some individual leaders or bands might have strayed, this great strength makes me believe that bands can face with hope what is sure to be a tough future. In the 20th century SA brass bands survived two world wars, epics it was predicted they would not survive; bands have survived radio, television, urban renewal-demographic shifts, the self-centred consumer society, and the emergence of worldwide web technology.

Most people like issues to be plainly drawn, black and white. It is not that simple. Many people might belong to SA bands for reasons that have, on the surface, little to do with music, aesthetics, or Christian vocation and ministry. This would include, but not be limited to, fellowship, belonging to something 'meaningful', the benefits of a disciplining activity, a vague sense of calling to help others, keeping family together and many others, including the idea that music is generally 'good' for the individual. In the theological tradition within which the SA grew, the Wesleys encouraged musical participation, whether secular or sacred, by believers, for precisely these kinds of benefits. Amateur music making within the UK had this moral underpinning, something that transferred easily into SA bands on a global scale. The best of music and musical participation, as understood in the great liberal Western tradition, could and should ennoble, enrich the soul.

Army band experience provides a great training ground for the developing musician. Many families have sought out the SA band scene for their children not for any moral or spiritual purpose, but merely because of the high musical standards demanded therein. How many times have SA readers heard an older young person testify to how only the music of the SA kept them involved in the church, until such time as they had what they considered their first true spiritual experience? How many profiles of the world's leading brass band personalities, for example, include an off-hand compliment to the unparalleled practical musical training they received before 'leaving the work'? For many, the quality of the music and the music making are what kept them 'in the ranks', if but for a while.

It is easy to point out that in the history of SA corps life, music groups became the steady pillars around which corps thrived, within which families flourished, from whence the best local leaders and then officer recruits were found. Bands and choirs are intergenerational, and their music, at its best, appeals to the widest range of people both within the corps and outside the corps. There may have been abuses due to incompetent, arrogant, unregenerate leadership, badly chosen or out-of-balance functions, poorly set priorities, but the model, the paradigm was solid for many years. Then put the truly spiritual aspect into it, the desire to serve Christ, to spread the Gospel, to help others grow spiritually and for the band member to likewise grow deeper in faith and spiritual development. What a positive model the ideal corps brass band experience was for Christian service and personal spiritual nurture. A SA band is much more than a social club or an amateur musical society – or at least it should be!

I vividly recall during my first years as a young bandmaster – the 1960s – the many prophets of doom who predicted the immediate demise of the brass band in SA worship and practice, soon to be replaced by ubiquitous rock bands. Their predictions were premature. In fact, in my own experience, my friends and I who became involved in Christian rock bands (these observations are echoed in John Cleary's Australia chapter), whether supported or not by SA administration at the time, also kept fully involved in SA bands. Most of us had or would take on band and other music leadership responsibilities. Taking one group in the USA East alone as a sample—a 'rock' band led by Charles Baker (currently bandmaster of the excellent Montclair, NJ, Citadel Band) in the period c.1971–1975—there were six future bandmasters and other leading SA musicians, among them Charles Baker, Stephen Bulla, Len Ballantine, Jude Gotrich, Michael Orfitelli, Philip Smith and Ronald Holz.[2] We enjoyed contemporary rock styles, tried to be effective evangelists in an 'alternative' world, but we did not abandon our past, either. We were at home in both worlds.

Was the issue sociological, musical, or theological? Perhaps a combination of all three, for our lives had been strongly touched through SA band music and experience. It was within our SA musical activity that our spiritual lives had the opportunity to be transformed; SA music was the channel through which we were drawn to Christ. There was depth, as well as integrity to this part of the Christian walk, and our transformation and commitment has compelled us to share that experience.

Plus, our rock bands involved but a small, elite group, where the dangers of egotism, selfishness, small group or individual domination of worship are even more highly magnified compared to that in larger, all-inclusive groups like a choir or instrumental ensemble. How could anyone think that smaller praise or rock bands would be less susceptible to typical problems of church music, behaviours that William Booth lamented about before he even started the SA (See again Chapter 2)!

Several years ago Phil Wall, a leading 'radical' Salvationist from the UK, visited with me while he was at Asbury College to speak in a chapel service.[3] A product of the SA band 'subculture' (he would modestly describe himself as someone who once upon a time was a reasonable euphonium player), Phil has been one of the leaders of a movement in the UK Territory that has organised 'alternative' gatherings of Salvationists called *Roots*. *Roots* has been a force for renewal in several territories, and is now recognised on an official level, as indicated by *Roots* in the USA South and Canada in recent years. As we talked about the future of the SA and its bands, Wall pointed out that so much of the future of the SA is in the hands of its musical leaders, because they are some of the

Belfast Temple Band playing at the Scottish Congress in Glasgow.

brightest and best soldiers, and therefore hold the greatest responsibility. He later put it in an email message to me as follows: *Their's is such a key responsibility before God as they have oversight over the most able of our personnel. Their capacity to lead well in a time of massive change and to lead us into renewal will no doubt be decisive in our future.*

Connecting in a relevant manner in the increasingly multi-cultural nature of the SA and, more importantly, the world around them, is the other obvious concern. 'Getting rid' of brass bands, however, would be, as Bill Himes puts it later in this chapter, *throwing the baby out with the bath water.* In fact, in a gesture to be more inclusive, a *Roots* gathering of 3,200 Salvationists, in May 1999, included a small-size brass band called Roots Brass, led by Matthew Wells (Hendon Corps). This group demonstrated the flexible nature of a brass band for less 'traditional' SA worship, perhaps bridging the gap of relevance, and showing the way towards reconciliation in an arena that is becoming, unfortunately, more and more polarised in certain parts of the Army world.

During our conversation Wall suggested that the main issue facing SA bands was, globally speaking, a missiological problem that the brass band sub-culture must face with sociological sensitivity and spiritual insight.

The debate is not about the intrinsic merits of brass versus electronics versus 'ethnic' instruments. It is about what will best communicate the character and message of Jesus Christ in a given social and cultural setting. Within that debate, Wall suggests bands and especially, their leaders, must consider four broad issues or trends that will effect this effort, trends seen globally not just within the SA but throughout the Christian world.

The first is the danger of maintaining or reverting to a kind of tribalism in which bands recognise only the narrow boundaries of their self-built microcosm. From there they can refuse to adapt within a constantly changing society, becoming locked in time, playing music history.

The second and third concerns Wall pointed out were the shifts from formal worship to informal as well as from structured to spontaneous worship. These two trends also threaten bands, because their sophisticated repertoire, their accomplishments, are seen in the best light within an ordered worship experience, or at least within a more formal setting. That borders on the ironic when viewed in the light of entire history of SA bands and their music. Finally, the military model of the SA has long since lost its appeal, yet a brass band can been seen (and heard) as an icon of 'militarism'.[4]

If bands feel threatened and undervalued, they could very easily 'circle-the-wagons' and reinforce the image of a narrow cultural enclave. On the other hand, should brass bands be imposed in all cultures where the SA works, or should that be up to the local population to decide what expressions are best suited to them?

The final three trends can be understood best by reflecting on the great success of the Pentecostal movement worldwide and the gradual decline in 'main-line' denominations. The SA has not escaped this, except to note that the early Army was informal and spontaneous, but that back in the late 19th century military models were favoured, now they are not. Bands and their increasingly sophisticated repertoire soon outgrew the very conditions that made them attractive in the first place. They and their corps became 'tribalistic', they favoured structure over improvisation, they preferred 'liturgy' to 'free and easy'. Military-like discipline and uniforms were of great benefit – friends indeed of the brass band.

A new openness is needed in Army worship and evangelism so that cultural baggage can be removed to allow true ministry to take place. Wall's general trends summary could prove helpful as more reflections are taken concerning the mission of SA bands and the music and musical styles chosen for those tasks.

The SA faces many other grave concerns besides the state of their banding programme. The SA probably needs its brass bands and band members in many of its territories, but in recent years the focus, the priorities have been placed on spiritual, educational, and theological renewal first. If anything, the success of the SA music programme, in whatever dimension it is examined, is one of the great achievements of the SA and one of its great gifts to Christendom. It is not surprising that bands, or traditional SA music in general, are not at the top of the list of priorities to be addressed in reviving and expanding the Army.

The recent report of the International Spiritual Life Commission dwells on major theological and worship issues without earmarking any specific programmes. Guidelines and strategies cannot be drawn that suit all countries, territories, and cultures.

One of the Army's greatest strengths is its diversity of culture, methods, and resources.[5] Recent efforts like the International Education Symposium, the International Spiritual Life Commission, and the 1994 USA National Forum rightfully focused more on the essentials of Christian faith and practice, to which the means to develop and implement these will follow once priorities are set. The report of the International Education Symposium includes a list of *Faith Education Strategies for the New Millennium.* Not surprisingly, neither music, nor specific SA music programmes are addressed directly, but under the heading 'Context' there is a turn towards a more open, inclusive view of the arts in SA mission, something that could make the 'tribalistic' band supporter all the more concerned. Such folk might see the category 'creative arts' as implying 'all other arts but the traditional band and songsters'–activities that will compete with and drain away resources from the 'real' SA. That, of course, would be a very narrow-minded reading of the intent of the report:

The Creative Arts in Faith Education: *We propose that the Army actively promote the use of the creative arts as a powerful tool in spiritual formation and discipling.*

Action Steps:
a. Develop in each territory a system for creating, resourcing and sharing creative arts materials and ideas both within the territory and internationally.
b. Use the [World Wide] Web for the profile and dissemination of materials and ideas concerning the use of arts in faith education.
c. Broaden divisional music camps, where conducted, to include other creative arts (for example – drama, dance, story, music, visual arts), and invite the participation of people on the periphery.
d. Encourage the appointment of local lay leadership specifically for these kinds of ministries.

As another example of what could cause concern among the traditionalists, only one of 25 recommendations from the USA Territories 1994 National Forum (June 4, 1999 report) directly mentioned music, no types or styles of music discussed. Recommendation 2, concerned *Quality Worship*, identifying that as a 'key to growth'. Two of the 'innovative' ideas listed dealt with music:

a) That each division establish and mobilise a divisional worship resource team which should include officers, soldiers, and music directors who will provide support and training while sharing resources in every way possible to all corps in the division.
b) That territorial music camps and institutes incorporate classes and/or tracks in their curriculum which focus on planning, leading, and supporting worship.[6]

Recommendation 22, addressed the issue of whether to hold Sunday evening meetings – *Survival, termination, or slow death* – and requested *Flexibility* at the local level in determining what is best in the mission of each corps.[7]

To these I can add again the continuing concern over whether uniform should be worn by just officers, by soldiers, by just soldier musicians, or perhaps only worn on special occasions. Do we drive people way with our unusual appearance or is the uniform an attractive element as well as a 'witness', or, even symbolically sacramental? Does the uniform identify us, its loss meaning the loss of a clear identifying role in the greater Church? Music groups like uniforms for the simple reasons of visual 'uniformity' and as an attractive aid in performance. In past eras the uniform was seen as a social leveller of sorts, everyone, at least soldiers, on an equal footing, gaining the wearer a sense of belonging and, in some cases, their first good piece of clothing! SA bands, I believe, whatever else is decided, will most likely be choosing some kind of 'uniform'!

In addition, should local officers serve shorter terms of office, rather than the old 'for life' pattern? While some corps benefited greatly through long-standing leaders, in others it has been 'deadly' when the wrong person maintains 'power' over a long period of time. Several American corps already set term limits for their locals, both to avoid such problems, but also to avoid 'burnout' on the part of their talented soldiers. One problem with setting limits in length of musical leadership, of course, is that long periods of time are needed to establish programmes, especially youth programmes, or the support network that feeds senior ensembles. It would seem only corps with great depth of soldiery could set up such a plan. Rotation plans might assist in the process.

What else is of concern that starts as a sociological problem and becomes a musical and theological one? 1) the issue of the quality or lack thereof in much P&W texts and music while experiencing loss in the use of theologically sound song and hymn repertoire; 2) the widening gap and possible lack of cooperation between Gospel Arts sections, a category under which all groups are now being grouped (See below for further discussion).

On a positive note, within another social front Army bands are interacting with the 'outside' music community in ways they have never done in the past. The old regulations restricting individual participation in other musical organisations have been lifted or modified; SA bands join with all kinds of other organisations for joint concerts. As a result, SA brass bands and their members have wider influence. This can be musical and, if you allow, at least 'moral,' if not directly or overtly spiritual in such contexts. Remember the ISB's recent performances at the National Brass Band Championship Gala Concerts! Another arena that has borne much fruit has been the cooperation between the SA and the North American Brass Band Association. NABBA has relied on the resources, guidance, wisdom, expertise, and leadership skills of key Salvationists. For example, many have served as adjudicators at NABBA contests, guest clinicians for developing bands, and even as officers on their Board of Directors. NABBA has featured the finest SA bands as models of their kind in the majority of its Gala Concerts that close each year's contest.[8] This is also happening in a slightly different way in Great Britain. Brass band pundits can no longer say that the influence of SA bands on brass band culture is simply that of who was wooed or driven away from the SA into the other fold!

I am convinced that such 'outside' involvement is a powerful way for the SA musician to be "in the world, but not of it". We are not an isolated movement anymore. How often have SA publications profiled the 'star' SA soldier musician without reflecting that this kind of influence can and does go on throughout the world through the agency of thousands of SA musicians.

The Future of Bands and their Mission

What will be the roles SA brass bands will or should play in the 21st century, bearing in mind the 'supreme aim' of all SA music-making to proclaim the gospel message? Are they not the same broad roles articulated in Chapter 1 of this book that can be condensed into worship, outreach evangelism, and, to a lesser extent, supporting other SA endeavours as well as cultural and civic duties that do not compromise the SA beliefs and mission? Should not SA band musical practice be 'salvation worked out in sound'?

Typical SA band shop talk is usually aimed at the pieces the band is playing (particularly festival music), perhaps an up-and-coming recording session, or, especially, what tours are on tap for the future. For many, these are the functions that greatly define their band, and banding practice. You might think they would talk about whether anyone was 'reached' during a recent meeting, anyone 'saved', anyone 'recommitted'? Perhaps it is human nature to dwell on the perks of banding, of belonging to something musically significant. Spiritual issues are personal, and make some uncomfortable. I know of what I speak, for I have fallen into that same rut. All bandmasters, from leaders of staff bands to corps bands, know that they need incentives of a less lofty kind to keep interest at a high level. Week-to-week duty is hard, and maintaining enthusiasm in midst of daily pressures a daunting task. Music festivals, congresses, exchange trips, and tours have been proven to be of long-term benefit for several generations in Army music history and mission. The question must be asked as to the relative balance struck in band activity, the emphasis given to these special, enhancing or enriching programs.

This is a major issue. Do tours, recordings, and festivals drive many bands' agendas? If we are truly honest, we must state that they can and frequently do. In this respect, the SA's great musical and administrative successes may have become spiritual millstones around our necks, and the words of the Army mother at the head of this chapter haunt us.[9] The human element is ever in the forefront. Musicians are not without strong egos and personalities, whether individual or corporate, and these seem to need lots of reinforcement.

As the shop talk continues you might hear band members lamenting the growing Praise and Worship 'problem', the loss of limelight in services as drama, mime and other ministries start sharing the stage, or the simply 'terrible' reliance by other sections and soloists on 'canned' backgrounds and accompaniments. Much of the latter are no longer SA at all, but drawn from the Contemporary Christian Music [CCM] world. It is true that many of the new creative arts rely on non-SA sources, unlike the timbrel brigade, which has gone so hand in hand with band ministry. That is to be expected in fledgling activities, many of them led by first generation Salvationists looking for meaningful avenues of service and ministry according to their perceived gifts. Until seasoned music leaders seek out leaders of a mime or dance troupe, for example, and suggest cooperative efforts (supplying them with

recommended recordings to which they can develop 'routines'), these groups will take the 'path of least resistance'. They would not know any other way of operating. Putting together a mime presentation with a band or songster selection is hard work! Some territorial music and gospel arts departments are already giving guidance in this area, but much more is needed. The models have been developed. I will never forget the impact of a mime-dance troupe from the UK performing to Leslie Condon's *The Present Age* during the Holiness Meeting at the International Youth Congress, the summer of 1985. That's 20 years ago!

Let's summarise some of the major concerns and issues bands face in relationship to their mission and their traditional functions. We need to do that from the perspective of the corps band, the heart of SA banding, rather than from the viewpoint of occasional groups (divisional, regional, territorial or staff bands). The corps band is on duty each week for whatever is deemed best by their corps officer, corps

Members of the Japan Staff Band taking part in an outdoor community concert.

council, and their commissioned leader for missional activity at the corps level. The three primary functions of an SA band, which have remained unchanged for a very long time, are used as the focus points:

1) Attracting people to 'meetings' where the Gospel can be shared

The open-air and a parade back to the hall are frequently not options, are all but non-existent for many bands, and for a wide number of reasons. What alternatives exist? Most alternatives would not create an immediate attraction to a worship service, or traditional Salvation Meeting, but can have an impact, nonetheless, whether or not folks are drawn back to the hall or a gospel message has been proclaimed. Mall programmes, park concerts, radio and TV broadcasts, visitation at prisons – hospitals – nursing homes, civic events at which an SA presence projects the Gospel at least in image. Design festivals with careful regard for the message to be proclaimed in attractive, easy to grasp presentations that include more than just the band playing a series of pieces. Work with other sections like songsters, drama, mime, timbrels, youth sections, guest groups, soloists and personalities to investigate multi-media possibilities. Publicise what is to be done. Make it attractive and exciting to be at an Army event, meeting or concert once again!

2) Accompanying the congregational singing

Still a major role, but the nature of SA 'hymnody' is changing, and some congregations want more Praise and Worship-style singing. What alternatives exist? Bands can share the stage with Praise bands (alternating and or combining with them), or they can embrace the many fine accompaniments available so that the band is both the traditional hymn and song accompaniment, and also becomes the P&W group. Done well, this is a function the brass band can do better than most alternatives, including the Praise Band.[10]

3) In meetings, speak Salvation messages to the hearts of the hearers

With the finest instrumental repertoire of its kind available, the issues here are knowing the background of the given audience or congregation, using the band wisely (why and when), and choosing appropriate music. Our repertoire is so rich, deep, and stylistically diverse! SA leaders must give local groups more flexibility in deciding where best to use their musical gifts and exercise their musical ministry.

Flexibility seems to be an attribute bands and their leaders must possess, something that has been demonstrated by several pace-setting corps bands throughout the world (Several profiled within the pages of this book). Models are certainly available and constantly being offered in a wide variety of venues.

Take, for instance, the inclusive nature of the USA Central Territory's Festival of Gospel Arts (first of its' kind), June 1999. Headlined groups included the decidedly non-traditional ensembles from urban Chicago, like Walt Whitman and the Soul Children of Chicago or the Midwest Pans of Thunder. To these were added the more traditionally-oriented massed youth chorus and youth brass band, the Chicago Staff Band, and Norridge Citadel Band, the latter demonstrating their new *Revelation Hope* worship experience (See Chapter on USA for discussion).

A *War Cry* report, in discussing three concurrent afternoon festivals, performers, stated: *The concerts displayed a wide spectrum of worshipful expression from traditional bands and songster brigades to interpretive movement, a timbrel and flag corps, and a steel drum band* (AWC, July 10, 1999, p.15).

A similar event planned for the spring of 2003 took advantage of the excellence of Dr. Harold and Priscilla Burgmayer, headliner clinicians. These two Salvationists have had notable success in implementing and articulating a well-balanced gospel-arts program in the Pendel Division, from sacred dance to traditional brass and choral ensembles.

When the Old Orchard Beach (Maine) Camp Meetings were planned for August 1999, the organisers advertised a balanced list of their own headliners. These included the New York Staff Band plus God With Us by Ron Moen, Stephen Bulla and Bill Broughton's "Spirituals to the Bone", and Ron Kenoly in Concert - *a celebrated figure in praise and worship music* (Advertisement, Eastern Territory's *Good News* June 15, 1999). Something for everyone and the entertainment factor right up front - not exactly a new part of SA strategy.

That strategy can lead to bad tactics, however, and distort the whole point of a band's function and purpose. When sharing his concerns about SA bands and their music, Len Ballantine speculated that in some SA circles the primary spiritual focus, driven by an innocent altruism, had perhaps been lost. He had noticed that in the UK the days of the SA revolving around bands were definitely gone, that Army musicians need to exercise much more flexibility and careful, critical thinking in their approach to musical ministry. A return to communicating a text, a message, was essential, and he definitely did not buy into the need for more large-scale works for bands, at least in the quantity with which they had been produced in the past. For decades bands had embraced entertainment and aesthetic pleasure as *acceptable* motivators for what they did. He concluded with a story about attending a late 1990s SA musical programme, 'A Night at the Proms with the SA', in which the name of Jesus was never mentioned. How could this display of show tunes honour God? Why bother to be an Army band anymore? He was not talking about in-house, fellowship gatherings, but rather events aimed at the general public.[11]

So many issues, so many concerns—it seems an overwhelming and unending task to take it all in! Can this be put in a clearer, simpler perspective? A fine summary dealing with the relevance of the brass band was written by Bandmaster William Himes of the Chicago Staff Band. Himes' observations help us make the shift from the functions brass bands fulfil within the SA to the music that will be written for and chosen by them for those tasks. Himes emphasises the flexible, versatile, and practical nature of the brass band. Behind his argument, of course, is the understanding that if the leadership and members of this 'flexible, versatile, and practical' tool of the Gospel do not have these same characteristics, it is all for naught.

THE BRASS BAND: DYNAMO OR DINOSAUR?
William Himes (Reprinted with the author's permission)

With each historic milestone of our Movement, such as the International Centenary of 1965, we have spent a time of introspection and self-scrutiny. During these times, we can be tempted to jump to simplistic solutions which usually climax with the proverbial tossing out of the baby with its bath water. I would offer as exhibit 'A': the present state of brass bands in the USA.

With growing frequency I have sensed attitudes which could be summarised as follows:

1: The brass band is an outdated idiom to which we cling tenaciously, solely out of a feeling of tradition.

2: Brass banding is old-fashioned and out of touch with contemporary Christian music.

3: Brass instruments are extremely expensive and not cost-effective given the limitations of most corps finances.

4: If we must have an instrumental programme, why should it be brass and percussion only? Why not use strings and woodwinds, after all, these conform better with school programmes.

Answering these opinions in a positive context, let's identify the merits of that dinosaur, the brass band.

In the first place, a brass band is flexible. Whether in parade or festival, prison or cathedral, outside or indoors, the brass band can function more efficiently and effectively than any other instrumental combination. Having taught high school band, I know that weather can render woodwinds ineffective or inoperative, but brass instruments can function in wide temperature extremes that leave their woodwind and string cousins in the dust (or snow)!

A brass band is versatile. Those who think its music is out of touch with contemporary Christian music have not been paying attention to the style and sound of our brass publications in the last few years. [We are] leading the way in the production of quality brass music, often effectively playable with as few as four, which swings, rocks, and sets toes (and hopefully hearts) a-tapping with gospel tunes known in and out of our Movement.

Have you ever heard a symphony orchestra play a march? It sounds pretty lame, doesn't it? Have you heard a jazz band play a hymn tune? It just doesn't make it! Have you heard a concert band try to swing or rock? Not convincingly, I bet.

Bandmaster William Himes conducts the Chicago Staff Band at the International Millennial Congress, 2000.

Yet, from *Star Lake* to *Treasures from Tchaikovsky,* to *Deep Harmony*, a brass band can play in all of these idioms and do so convincingly! In fact, it has taken me forty years to reach the conclusion that no other musical combination can match its adaptability and versatility.

A brass band is acoustical. In this age of electronic music, with its synthesisers, drum machines, sequencers, recorded tape tracks and mega-watt amplifiers, it is refreshing to hear music produced by a group of committed Christian musicians that is pure, natural and unamplified!

My final point is at least as important as all the others combined: a band is practical. The wonder of the brass band is that it is, technically speaking, a model of simplicity. From cornet to tuba, only one set of fingering and a working knowledge of treble clef is required. With this minimum working knowledge, participants can play, teach and conduct brass ensembles with surprising proficiency. No one who conducts a concert band or orchestra can make that claim.

With its versatility, flexibility and practicality, it would be a tragedy to abandon our brass bands at this point. Let's not succumb to the 'bath water syndrome'. Given the fact that the largest churches in our community are developing instrumental programmes at an unprecedented rate, it would be an unfortunate irony to lose one of our greatest assets. [William Himes, OF, Territorial Music Secretary, Central Territory, USA]

The Future of the Music for Bands

The kind of music written and published for SA brass bands in the 21st century will naturally be shaped by the activities or functions bands undertake. Artistic/aesthetic issues are secondary; how SA music 'evolves' is directly tied into mission. Certainly supply and demand issues enter into the picture, especially as Army music is now available to all. How does the SA market this material to reach as many as possible? If the SA is a global Army, is it reaching all Salvationist band members and giving them the right tools, the right music? How easily can they access it – is it as easy as surfing on the World Wide Web? Yet the sociological frame of reference is always present – what about multi-cultural issues? What about a 'dumbing-down' of our high quality music? What about copyright and performing rights issues for our arrangers and composers? Can we keep the 'best of the best' still writing for us?

In the midst of this confusion, pause and consider what now is available for SA bands worldwide. Pick up a copy of the latest International Catalogue of Salvation Army Music Publications - an embarrassment of riches, when you think of it! SA bands have never been better off, and have never been better served by their publishers. Some might argue that quality fluctuates in the journals. That has indeed always been the case, the remarkable thing being what a high standard has been maintained. Compared to many outside brass publishers, SA brass band music has been generally of a higher standard of craftmanship, as has the editing and proof-reading undertaken.

The post-1921 'compositional-goals-to-be-admired' pointed to large-scale, 'big-piece efforts' being produced for major Congresses or tours. Regular 'Ordinary' fare was churned out on a consistent, if not always inspired level. This is changing. Editors must now manage their journals more carefully, several commissioning specific types of arrangements, therefore managing the repertoire in a more meaningful way. The need to produce large-scale festival works is less a priority, as the handful of bands that can play them can access them through collections like the SP&S, *Concert Works Manuscript Series* or *Judd Street Collection.*

However, both SP&S and the USA East have been led into temptation via the release of test pieces that would be of little practical value to the vast majority of SA bands, *Isaiah 40* (Redhead), *Odyssey* (Norbury) and *St.Magnus* (Downie), being three recent, respective efforts. If they are not printing large inventories, and able to print on a 'by-request' basis, it may be a helpful, worthy endeavour.

In further defence of these decisions, one can make the argument that it demonstrates the SA's willingness to interact with the larger brass band community and to offer music that at least gets the players thinking about the spiritual, something akin to the SA mission.

Of course, most of Philip Wilby's test pieces have that slant as well, but one does not think of this Christian gentleman, who frequently signs his scores *Laus deo* (Praise be to God), as an overt evangelist![12] In fact, as certain SA territories lift their restrictions, there is much in the contest repertoire, both past and present, that could be of use within the context of SA goals. There are many other pieces in the brass band repertoire besides *Resurgam* that can speak to the human soul.

While I was preparing this book and chapter, I asked Peter Graham to reflect on his life as a Salvationist, as a writer, editor, and arranger of SA music. His thoughts range widely, discussing function via the design of festivals, mission in terms of whether a message was getting across, and a change that took place in his approach to writing SA music. Versatility–adaptability–flexibility like Himes' outline!

> *When I lived in Scotland there was a kind of 'macho' culture prevalent – the band wasn't rated unless it tackled the latest 'pseudo test-piece' Festival number. I suspect we pummelled many audiences into submission...*
>
> *In 1983 I moved to New York, joined the Staff Band and anticipated more of the same, at a higher level. After all, Staff Bands had the technique to play anything, didn't they? The programming was a revelation. Here was a band who actually thought about their audiences. A major work was placed in the programme only in*

context. Sydney Congress Hall Band visited and took programming even further with their 'Brass Encounters' show. The Holy War *became a multi-media event, and far from demoting the music to the role of accompaniment, it enhanced and clarified the programmatic element.*

The NYSB toured England in 1985, utilising many of these ideas and others, including Harold Burgmayer's 'Sight and Sound' concept. The majority of audiences were knocked out—we even got a couple of standing ovations which amazed the ex-patriate Brits in the band (standing ovations go against the British reserve). A number of letters followed in the Musician *along the lines of 'why can't our UK Bands get their act together and communicate like these guys?'*

I returned to the UK in 1986 and was appointed BM at Regent Hall soon after. I wanted the band's presentations to have relevance to everyone, not just band enthusiasts. Using the NY and Sydney models we designed themed programmes—Past, Present and Future—utilising ideas from old-time music hall, audio-visual and vocal presentations. We thought carefully about our Annual Band Weekend Celebrations—to attract as wide-ranging an audience as possible we involved TV-celebrity guests, choirs, and, very daring this, contest band soloists! We ran out of seats for the festival, introduced many non-Salvationists to the Army, made a terrific contact in Roy Castle (who later appeared with the band on a number of occasions) and raised over £1,000 for a Children's Hospital (though I got a formal reprimand from the Music Council for allowing the band to accompany the euphonium virtuosi Childs Brothers. Those were the days...)

All credit to the band, who worked extremely hard and went along with this crazy young Scotsman, though some in the corps felt that I was 'dumbing-down' the repertoire. We no longer played, what to me were interminable devotional selections, on Sunday evening, preferring simple hymn arrangements. I thought I was right, they thought they were...

The whole experience shaped my thinking about the type of music I should write for SA bands. My lengthiest

Festival piece will now be around 8 minutes and the technical demands 'realistic'.[13]

In *Shine as the Light* Graham proved that he could write an excellent piece in the 8-minute range that still 'advanced' SA music forward (modern style and compositional technique) while providing a fine example of 'music with a message'. In doing so, perhaps he is, in the words of his colleague Derek Scott, *regaining a cultural consensus*.[14] The work, analysed in Volume II, links up-to-date song literature of the SA within a 'hipper' musical language that is also symphonic in the way it unfolds. This allows it to be admired for its wide audience appeal as well as for its artistic merits.

Because Army music is highly referential, SA composers, generally speaking, never made the great modernist mistake of becoming so complex that only a handful of aesthetes would listen—or even care to listen. SA music came close to this in the 1960s and 1970s but it never leapt into the abyss.

Certain works of Steadman-Allen, Brenton Broadstock, or Bruce Broughton, to name but three, may have taken SA music to the edge! Certainly it has never lost its tonal moorings and its broad connection or commonality with common practice period (c. 1600–1900) musical style, form, and syntax. It would not surprise me if SA musicians in the next few decades embrace many of the postmodern techniques of art music from the last two decades of the 20th century. This would parallel the way so many aspects of American jazz, and pop-styles that developed from it, have been integrated into SA scores since the mid-1970s. That might make it all the more interesting and effective.

But let us consider that a work like, *Shine as the Light*, as effective as it is, is playable only by more advanced corps sections, staff bands, or the occasional music camp top band or regional ensemble. It is a piece that the majority of band members will only reach occasionally in their lives (having that goal achieved is no small matter, nor should the work towards it be easily dismissed). If the average SA band worldwide is now like that in the UK or the USA, they can rarely handle much more than the *American Instrumental Ensembles Series*, or the *Triumph Series*. A look at two recent efforts in both of these journals gains us some insight into future trends in SA music from a variety of angles. I have chosen one graded set of the *AIES*, Grade 3 for 1999, and the July 1999 issue of the *TS*, for this brief case study. The technical levels required are generally equal (*AEIS* is released in four levels, level 1 'easy' to level 4 'advanced'), levels chosen as ideal for a majority of corps senior and junior bands.

The four separately-published Grade 3 pieces for *AIES* 1999 are as follows:

> Song Arrangement: *In My Heart There Rings a Melody*
>   (James Anderson)
> Song Arrangement: *Soon and Very Soon*
>   (Andrae Crouch/Stephen Bulla)
> Hymn Meditation: *Beneath the Cross of Jesus*
>   (James Curnow)
> E Flat or F Instrument Solo: *Amen* (Stephen Bulla)

In each case the arranger was commissioned this specific piece within certain stylistic and technical parameters, having received the assignment and deadline for submission from the USA South Music Department (James Curnow, Editor; Dr. Richard Holz, TMS). All three men are professional musicians,

Peter Graham conducts Black Dyke Band during its visit supporting Portsmouth Salvation Army celebrations, 2005.

two making their full-time employment as composers and arrangers. The most traditional of the tunes is the short (1 minute and 25 seconds; 1:25), march-like, rhythmically animated setting of the 6/8 chorus, *In My Heart;* the arranger suggests this piece is suited to a 'Praise Meeting' context. James Curnow's meditation-like setting of, *Beneath the Cross* is set in a light-rock ballad style, thus bringing an old favourite up-to-date in a tasteful fashion; it is the longest of the set, at 3:34, and suited well to a serious worship service. (See Volume II, *Scoring and Instrumentation*, for first page of score). Each grade of the *AIES* contains a solo, and this solo is a setting of the familiar spiritual *Amen*; the ABA-form work contains the spiritual in the middle 'pastorale' section, the outer portions in a more upbeat, festive praise mood in a mildly contemporary style. The final item, *Soon and Very Soon*, is to be played in a relaxed African-American gospel style, the music very carefully marked in order to assist the players achieving the correct approach to this Christian rock classic (and they can get the demo CD, as well). All four tunes are very well known within the Christian community, two from older hymn repertoire, one of more recent CCM origin, and the one probably known by anyone in America (*Amen*), Christian or not. Festival, praise, and worship meeting repertoires are all provided for with attractive, contemporary arrangements of short duration.

The July 1999 issue of the *Triumph Series* is as follows:

1073 *Intrada on 'Austria'* (David Ayma)
1074 Festival Arrangement: *Dance Before the Lord*
   (Peter Graham)
1075 Hymn Tune Arrangement: *Churchbury*
   (Richard Phillips)
1076 March: *Kinshasa* IV (Kapela Ntoya)

On first glance, it plays out as a typical issue, four items in a set, which a band on the subscription scheme must take whether they like every piece or not. The compositional categories are as might be expected, a march, two hymn tune arrangements (one called an *Intrada*), and a festival arrangement. Two of the arrangers are familiar names, proven professional talents perhaps a guarantee for the issue, Graham and Phillips. Two are not so well known. David Ayma, hailing from Chile, South America, has had five other works published thus far in the SA band journals. (See Volume II, *Scoring and Instrumentation* for the first page of the Ayma score.) Kapela Ntoya, from Congo–Kinshasa Territory, makes his first appearance in the time worn way via a march, this one written in tribute to his comrades at a corps celebrating its 50th anniversary.

The SA is making great strides in countries like Chile and the Congo, so it is not unexpected that we will see more and more talent emerging from these 'non-traditional' countries; more and more music will be aimed at or earmarked for them. This points to a dilemma for the editor at the time, Richard Phillips, who had to first think of his 70% UK market, while also paying homage to the fact that his office does have an international image, if not, technically speaking, international responsibility. Peter Graham's offering is a witty 'crowd pleaser' in a Hungarian-dance, or gypsy style, a setting of a recent song by Graham Kendrick, *Jesus put this Song into our Hearts*. The arrangement ends with the band shouting, *Hoi!* like a bunch of Russian Cossacks in an operetta! Most likely, and hopefully, designed for the festival or praise meeting stage! Phillips' arrangement is intended for multiple use, either as a separate musical offering, or as a congregational song accompaniment to the recommended associated text 'Fairest Lord Jesus', the tune being from a recent *Sing to the Lord* songster selection. The piece from Chile has a pleasantly modern sound to it, though there is nothing Chilean about it, and the march from Africa is not 'African', but is quite in the expected, almost predictable mould. Both of the latter tunes have the great merit of being very playable. No doubt Ayma and Ntoya, if encouraged and mentored, will continue to develop distinct individual voices that will enrich SA music.[15]

Thus, this issue of the *Triumph Series* is very practical in terms of the usefulness of the music and in terms of playing level, the Graham piece being one that might prove to be a 'stretch' for some. Worship, festival, and outreach functions are addressed. The musical style in all four is of a tasteful, conservative nature, at least in this issue (Not even a hint of light-rock or swing!).

The remaining questions in evaluating such a journal relate

to the relevancy of the music depending on the context chosen for 'performance', or, in terms of the old evaluation form criteria, its appeal to the 'man on the street'. On what street, you might ask? Well, David Ayma in Chile might choose *Austria*, Haydn's beautiful old tribute to his Emperor – with a nasty usurpation by the Germans into, *Deutschland, Deutschland über alles* – without worrying about any cultural baggage. In many countries this tune has multiple hymn texts associated with it, including the grand jingoistic SA 'Bless our Army'. As a prelude of 'praise' or 'call to worship' it could see good use. In fact, the score notes tell us that the intent is that the piece is to be approached, understood, and used as a processional on a theme by Haydn, no text association required.

Graham's frolic will amuse, get the toes tapping, and might even pass off as cartoon music, especially when the vast majority of listeners will have no idea at all of the song. Maybe the corps sacred dance troupe will join the band on it for a real dance before the Lord? The march is, well, another simple march like thousands of others, but stirring and appealing to me, and perhaps to others, *emotionally*, if not aesthetically, at least when we consider its origins. Phillips' arrangement could be the most widely used and might have the most impact in terms of reaching the hearts of the hearers, especially if referred to the text or, even better, if they sing it with the band.

Both journals, *AIES* and *TS*, seem to be delivering the goods, so to speak, for the typical small corps band, each issue providing appealing music for a variety of functions. All the pieces share the desirable quality of short length. Editorial policy and management are quite a contrast, the UK effort following, not unexpectedly, the more traditional path, and also continuing an opportunity for developing writers. The tunes chosen for the American set have a much broader appeal, not restricted to the SA. At least two of the *TS* set (depending on your view of how audiences will hear *Austria*) are drawn from recent SA vocal literature, and will benefit by first being heard and used within the SA environment (but not restricted to that).

That use of the shouted, *Hoi!* in the above-mentioned Graham festival arrangement might be an entertainment

Major Ntoya Kapela, brass band composer, is seen here conducting the All-Africa Congress band and choir.

The Congress Band, composed of South African and Zimbabwe bandsmen is conducted by Lieut. Col. Robert Ward at the All-Africa Congress, Harare, 2005.

The Zambian Territorial Band on the march, 1999.

Korea Children's Home
Band in Seoul. The
'ancestor' of this band
was the Seoul Boys'
Band which was forced
to march into North
Korea in 1952 and was
never seen again.

The only band in
Myanmar (Burma).

ploy, but it underscores some forward thinking on the part of recent SA arrangers. For example, William Himes', *To the Chief Musician* (FS 438; Sept. 1983) one of the most popular works of the last 25 years, uses choric speaking of psalm texts in a very effective, dramatic way. The decision to have Evangeline Booth's, *I Bring Thee All,* sung in movement two, rather than just playing it, makes the listening experience complete for any audience, as even most Salvationists do not know this 'old' song anymore. It is, indeed, all about communication, for SA music is never music for music's sake.[16]

In 1996 Richard Phillips shared in an interview with *Brass Band World* a guiding philosophy behind how he chose music. He had recently assumed the duties of music editor in the MMU, an historic appointment as the first non-officer in the job taken at approximately the same time as the first non-officer bandmaster of the ISB, Stephen Cobb. He stated he must constantly question the validity of a SA score in light of the SA mission, regardless of whether it would be stimulating, or a 'show-stopper' for bands. *Today, I believe we are looking at what music says like we have never looked before. The message of what we are about is more important than ever and for us to get that across to people more effectively is essential* (*BBW*, October 1996, p7).

It may have been unfair to zero in on those two journals, neither seen in the context of the issues that came before or have since succeeded them. All in all, these releases come off as a success for the average SA band. The greater issue is how that average SA band will use this music – why, where and how they would use one of these short arrangements. Our best composers will be sought out for those special commissions for big festivals-tours-congresses, and even have an inspiration themselves from time to time without having to provide 'occasional' music. I have no fear for the continued production of advanced-style, large-scale, and advanced level music for SA brass bands. The single greatest concern I have for the future of SA musical composition will be that the usefulness and quality of standard fare in the journals below the *Judd Street Collection* level (now that the *Festival Series* no longer continues) be kept high, and remain useful for everyday, week-in, week-out banding service. That is the greatest need. Most SA band pieces, the vast majority of them, have a life span of no more than 20–25 years. Some exceptional pieces last up to 40–50. Only the very finest transcend generations, styles and preferences and become, therefore, truly classic works. Change is always to be expected, anticipated, and embraced. Networking on a global scale will help our editors meet the immediate needs of our far-flung family of bands in the best way possible, despite the seemingly insurmountable complexities of our now multicultural Army. One thing is sure, change is what they can count on, especially changes in fashionable styles of music. In light of all that, our short sample, or case study, is an encouraging one.

Summary and Vision

The cold-water brigades who attempt to drench the fire of SA bands, the doom sayers who prophesy the end of bands continue to do so by imperilling the existence of the SA as a denomination.[17] If the SA resembles a church, a denomination, it does so in many places simply because it has a congregation tied together through the activities of its music sections. That may be unbalanced practice, but it is a reality. Most Salvationists are proud of their past, but unsure about the future, worried about the quality of worship, worried about maintaining relevance in a complex, increasingly secular, or even pagan society. Yet the authors of this book have shown what a marvellous heritage SA musicians have, what great achievements precede them than can speak of something significant in terms of human and divine achievement well beyond the confines of the parochial boundaries of the SA's immediate sphere of influence.[18]

Perhaps key to the future, for establishing a balanced mission, can be found in the past, or at least at key moments in that story. My personal view is that the SA faces as drastic a change in the first decades of the 21st century as it faced in the first 20 years of the 20th, when the SA went from radical 'sect' or movement, to settled denomination or church. All this started to happen just as William Booth began to loosen the reins on the music bands could play and as he began to allow choirs to form. When the Army was most dynamic, issues of the excellence achieved in SA musical composition were irrelevant (there was no band composition, as such) and in performance mattered little. What counted was militant

The euphonium soloist of the Leopoldville Band, playing at Clapton Congress Hall in 1965.

soul winning. Just as SA bands became respectable, denominational, its first great revival spirit flamed out and it became like any other Christian movement going into its second generation. In these days there are attempts to rid the SA of its true distinctive identity, to make it more like a non-denominational community church, with officers free to pursue whatever means, styles, and methods they feel will work. Wally Court wondered to me if we might soon be called the Salvation Fellowship! Dr. Roger Green has pointed out the SA had its greatest success when it was *clearest about its identity and mission, which was largely sectarian and counter-cultural*. He goes on to assert that an attempt to make the SA like every other denomination only diminishes the impact the Army can have upon a given culture.

> *Accommodation to the broader culture signalled a decrease in impact upon the culture, not because people liked quaint sectarian groups with bonnets and tambourines, but because ultimately people respect intentional communities who are faithful to their own traditions, heritage and way of life. So it is with the*

Church; the point of greatest influence will come not as the Army becomes more like the local community church, but as the Army identifies and embraces what most marks the Army as an intentional community – the military metaphor by which Salvationists live and die, the emphasis upon social and personal holiness, the commitment to women and men in ministry, a vision of the sacramental life, and a unique form of worship, including a unique contribution to the use of brass bands in worship.[19]

The International Music Council, before its cancellation, was currently reviewing a draft for an *International Orders, Regulations, and Guidelines for Music Sections and Groups.*[20] Within the document the mission statement of the SA remained unchanged, but the complex nature of SA music is recognised by embracing the concept of Territorial Mandate, what used to be labelled as Territorial Discretion. Issues like the performance of non-Army music by SA bands, uniform wearing, and guidelines for other SA music groups falling under local management in recognition that each region has its own distinct needs, concerns, and culture. The overriding value system and Kingdom-building world view are what are important, those which have been proven to enhance the soul-saving work of the SA, those that throughout SA history have helped it steer the proper course, regardless of method or media chosen, or type of musical style used.

SA musicians should rejoice in what has been achieved within our bands' history. But they should not rest on their laurels! The danger of idolatry is always present worshipping a culture, traditions, past leaders, great music rather than the true source of Grace and Redemption, the reason SA music exists. It does come down to inward motivation, why SA musicians do what they do. Bill Himes, in an article entitled 'The Direction of Salvation Army Music in the USA', cut to the heart of the matter:

...That which was originally implemented to attract and aid in our worship can indeed become its centre. Our musical heritage comes from the likes of Fred Fry and family, who happened to be musicians. We need to

continually examine our motives so that we do not become simply proficient, sophisticated musicians who may just happen to be Christians. There can be a danger of maintaining musical traditions without spiritual impetus, of adding those to our number almost automatically because of their acceptable age and proficiency, rather than their qualifications of personal faith and witness

In our quest for excellence, it is easy to latch on to the notes, the increasing complex rhythms and harmonies, and in our pursuit, lose sight of the One we came to glorify... The direction of Salvation Army music will be shaped by our motives – by who or what we worship. (*AWC*, March 13, 1982, p9).

In this new century when nothing stops a Salvationist musician from involvement in many different kinds of musical activity, the reasons chosen for playing in a SA band must be different from those which motivate involvement in simply musical endeavours, as noble and enriching as those can be. When General of the SA, John Gowans, was interviewed for, *Christianity Today*, he declared his own mandate to restate and revitalise the original Army vision, and calling: *The*

Composer Kenneth Downie relaxes with grandaughter Niamh. In recent years Downie's music has been much in demand with both SA and contesting bands.

Salvation Army was created to achieve three aims: to save souls, to cultivate saints, and to serve suffering humanity. My intention is to remind Salvationists not to be diverted from those three aims and not to allow any attractive side paths to divert them from those highways. (June 14, 1999 p30)

The degree to which SA bands and their members allow their activities to become 'side paths' rather than mainline 'Warfare' will determine the real future of this remarkable part of the Christian church and its music. Perhaps we need to have a global Commission of Inquiry to help them regain their fighting trim. Ray Steadman-Allen shared with me that all renewal within SA banding must come and will only come through a return to careful Bible study and prayer on the part of groups and individuals within SA band structures. Having bands study to know *why* they exist and *why* they are doing what they are doing from a scriptural and theologically sound base is crucial. Unscriptural regulations both from above and from within can no longer be the motivators for changing behaviour or for deciding function within mission. Correct motivation is the key. This is why scriptures give us so little about styles and types of worship – the how and what we use – but tell us so much about who and why we serve.

There are, of course, many concerns that must be addressed and quickly, especially the training of more competent, committed music leaders by which both the adult and youth band programmes of the SA can be maintained. How easily bands are sidetracked by other 'stuff' – most of it reviewed or highlighted in this and previous chapters – without thinking and praying clearly about the 'main things'. SA bands may not be able to be all things to all peoples, but they can remain loyal to their mission, to strive for 'Salvation worked out in Sound'. In the face of many changes in societies, cultures, music and worship styles, SA bands have proven resilient over the past 128 years when they did not give up the fight they were called to carry out in Salvation warfare. They were, after all, **Salvation** Army Brass Bands. Whether the adjective still holds true in the future is all that will ultimately matter.

Notes

1. Provided by Brindley Boon from his unpublished Chapter 16 of

CHAPTER 463

ISB, 'Harry Appleby', p8.

2. Each summer this group functioned primarily as an outreach ministry of the Asbury Park, NJ, Corps, especially at the seaside resort's Boardwalk. Each year the band had a different name: Salt Water Soul, Peacemeal, Redemption, The Salvation Army Band.

3. The label 'radical' does not come from Phil, but he probably would not dispute it. He has an international ministry, especially through SA youth gatherings like, *Extreme*, or *On the Edge*. To get a flavour of some of the ongoing dialogue in the UK SA press about 'radical' Salvationism, see the series 'Beyond the Pale', starting with Duncan Park's 'Radical Salvationism', *The Salvationist* (UK), January 23, 1999. An example of the official embracing of *Roots* would be the USA South's *Roots* in June 2004, held concurrent with the annual Commissioning Weekend.

4. Interview with Phil Wall, November 3, 1999. See also Phil Wall, 'A New Rhythm for a New Day', *The Officer*, August 1998, pp16–19.

5. 'International Spiritual Life Commission Report'. *AWC*, May 16, 1998, pp16–20.

6. 'Confronting the Issues: A Report on the 1994 Salvation Army National Forum'. SA NHQ, June 3, 1994.

7. Concerning the matter of flexibility, Geoffrey and Violet Brand, both former Salvationists and both with family members still active in the SA, shared in an interview with me, April 1995, that flexibility would be a key factor for the future of SA bands in the UK. They wondered how William Booth would approach the problem of relevance, and would he embrace TV and other media, without falling into the shallow entertainment trap of so much televangelism? Can SA bands find a meaningful way to connect now that so many of the old venues don't hold? No doubt SA bands and their leaders cannot be all things to all people, but perhaps a new kind of multiculturalism might be needed in light of the complexities of British or American society, for example. Such ideas have been echoed by many across the globe.

8. The following SA bands have been featured at NABBA Gala Concerts, several on multiple occasions: New York Staff, Canadian Staff, National Capitol, Chicago Staff, Southern Territorial. Salvationist adjudicators have included James Anderson, Charles Baker, Stephen Bulla, Brian Burditt, James Curnow Bram Gregson, Richard Holz, Kenneth Moore, Kevin Norbury, Ronald Waiksnoris, and Keith Wilkinson. NABBA officers have included Ronald Holz (President, Contest Controller, Editor of *Bridge*), Thomas Scheibner (Contest

Controller), and Anita Cocker Hunt (current President). The God & Country Concert that the SA and the Brass Band of Columbus offer each year is another notable example of this mutual cooperation.

9. I dare not open the can of worms concerning the possible 'misuse', or at least, poor stewardship, of vital financial resources spent on some tours.

10. The Central Territory's *Hallelujah Choruses* series now contains two side-by-side versions of each song. There is the up-to full brass band, with rhythm section version, and now a parallel version for smaller Praise Band, using rhythm section, vocals, and three *soli* brass. The two versions are complementary, but not designed to be played at the same time. The P&W debate is widespread, the SA but one among many struggling with the issue. Two recent articles summarise many of the issues: Michael S. Hamilton, 'The Triumph of Praise Songs: How Guitars Beat Out the Organ In the Worship Wars', *Christianity Today*, July 12, 1999, pp229–32,34–35; Mark A. Noll, 'We Are What We Sing: Our Classic Hymns Reveal Evangelicalism At Its Best', *Christianity Today*, July 12, 1999, pp37–41. The designation 'Praise and Worship' is most unfortunate because, though it originally meant the blending of two types of contemporary songs or choruses – lively and upbeat with quiet and meditative – it now becomes a category of the worship service itself. It is as if the structure of the service only contains praise and worship during that narrow portion. Therefore, any other congregational singing, or any other musical activity, is not part of praise and worship. The distinction is not a subtle one, though hardly intentional. Thus the problem with the title Praise Band, as well. In most SA meetings where this is now included, a so-called balance is attempted, unfortunately the 'older' songs and hymns usually getting the short end of it, as their verses are not repeated multiple times in an almost mantra-like manner, as can be the case with 'praise and worship' choruses.

11. Interview with Len Ballantine, May 4, 1995; August 3, 1999.

12. Philip Wilby's test pieces with a clear sacred connection, several listing scripture passages in the score notes, include *The New Jerusalem, Revelation: Symphony for Brass Band*, and *The Dove Descending*. Certainly these pieces are as worthy of examination by SA bands as *Isaiah 40, Odyssey*, or *Resurgam*.

13. See also Peter Graham, 'Fulfilling the Needs of the People', *British Bandsman*, June 25, 1988, pp7,10.

14. Derek Scott also teaches at Salford University. The following article, written from a post-modern position, contains food for thought for the SA brass band scene. Derek Scott, "Regaining Musical Consensus,"*Brass Band World*, June, 1999, pp12–14.

CHAPTER 465

15. Peter Ayling's recent visit to the Congo as a guest conductor provided him with an interesting twist to the issue of multiculturalism *ala* the SA: *Needless to say, the emulation of the Western world is now inherent in the African continent and this is reflected in The Salvation Army. So while we would wish to encourage the development of their own musical forms the current generation of African youth want very much to identify with their image of SA musical culture in the West.* Peter Ayling, 'Congo Experience', *Salvationist* (UK), November 6, 13, 1999. Quote from 11/6/99, p18.

16. One of Bill Himes' great gifts to SA music has been a return to the effective use of humour, and joy, in SA music and musical festivals. Two of his popular works, still in manuscript, come immediately to mind: *Solo Secondo – A Major Work for Second Horn and Brass Band; Jericho Revisited.* The latter tells the story of Joshua using a rap-style narration. The former defies description here!

17. The phrase cold-watering was one I heard frequently when talking to music leaders in the UK in both 1995 and 1999.

18. One measure of this was apparent in a symbolic way in the September 12, 1999, Concert of the Century at Symphony Hall, Birmingham. Organiser Bram Gay shaped the highly successful, several-hours-long concert to revisit over 100 years of brass band music. Despite all the groups being top contesting bands, the SA was well represented, including Heaton's *Praise* (Tredegar Town Band), Downie's *In Perfect Peace* and Graham's *Shine as the Light* (Marple Band), Gregson's *Laudate Dominum* (Fodens Courtois), and Ball's *Star Lake* (Williams Fairey). Several of Eric Ball's works with spiritual underpinnings were also played: *Resurgam* and *Journey Into Freedom.* Notice that it was not just the big test-piece work which was chosen; the Army spirit and Army mission were not ignored, although certainly the conductors might not have been thinking of advancing the Christian faith when they selected their tunes! Another measure from that parallel sub-culture came in the final selections for the *Brass Band World Hall of Fame* (August 1999 issue). The list of nominations ranged over more than 150 years of brass band history. Of the 50 finalist names selected, the criterion being that the person had to be either dead or retired from involvement in any aspect of the brass band scene, just over 10% were Salvationists: Eric Ball, Sir Dean Goffin, Wilfred Heaton, Erik Leidzén, Roland Cobb, George Marshall.

19. Quotes from paper by Dr. Roger Green presented at Asbury College, the Andrew S. Miller Lecture Series, April 2002, *The Salvation Army and the Evangelical Tradition*, p19. In another article, Roger Green has sent forth a call for an international conference dealing with the SA's evolving identity from a sect

into a Church. Could this be an adjunct to a new Commission of Inquiry? Roger Green, 'Facing History: Our Way Ahead for a Salvationist Theology', *Word and Deed*, May, 1999, pp23–40. In this same article Green wrestles with issues like uniform wearing, placing it in theological perspective. It is interesting to compare the development of the SA's brass band history and music literature to other Protestant denominations that used brass instruments. The Moravians, for instance, who still use brass music in their services, use a brass music locked centuries in the past, a calculated decision. The SA has fostered constant change and growth.

20. I am grateful to Dr. Richard Holz, chair of the International Music Council at that time, for sharing the November 1999 rough draft of this document, which was, at the time of writing this book, only in the early formative stages.

Epilogue

REFLECTIONS ON THE INTERNATIONAL MILLENNIAL CONGRESS (2000) AND SA BAND MUSIC

Ronald W. Holz

From June 28 to July 2, 2000 the SA held its *International Millennial Congress [IMC]* in Atlanta, GA. Subtitled *The Army Next: Carrying the Flame Into the Future*, the impressive event drew nearly 20,000 delegates from the 107 countries where the SA maintains a ministry. This epilogue reflects on my own personal experience as a delegate, done in the light of writing this book and, in particular, Chapter 10, the initial draft of which was completed just a few months prior to this event. I must honestly say I went with a skeptical frame of mind, yet came away heartened and encouraged for the worldwide work, and music, of The Salvation Army. These thoughts should not be considered definitive. They may help the on-going thought that must be given to the role of brass bands in this denomination by both its members and by disinterested parties.

Brass Bands and a Multi-cultural Army

Music played a crucial role in the Congress. The kinds of musical ensembles featured and the music used reflected the complex, multi-cultural riches of Salvationist worship. What styles of music and musical groups were chosen during these five days would stand as 'endorsed and approved' for SA worship and practice and, as a result, such examples would have far reaching consequences for the future of the SA. Brass bands were but a part of this critical, representative sampling, although a vital and important part. Five bands were chosen as official participants: Canadian Staff Band (BM Brian Burditt), Chicago Staff Band (BM William Himes), Hendon Corps Band, UK (BM Stephen Cobb), New York Staff Band (BM Ronald Waiksnoris), Southern Territorial Band, USA South (BM Dr. Richard Holz). All five bands demonstrated a high standard of musical performance and their directors made musical choices that greatly contributed to the overwhelming success of the Congress.[1]

In Chapter 2 of this study the International Congress of 1904 provided a key position from which to assess the progress of SA bands as they entered the 20th century. What took place at this 2000 Congress, as unique and specialized as such gatherings can be, provided me with a chance to test certain observations made in Chapter 10 about current and future functions for SA bands in denominational practice with the 21st century. In addition, these bands shared new brass band music, much of it confirming compositional and stylistic trends discussed in Volume II. The quality and power of that new music stood out to me as the most significant aspect of Salvationist culture, perhaps unmatched by any other art form seen or heard in Atlanta in those five jammed packed days. Indeed, from great public demonstrations and parades to beautifully planned worship, I could not imagine the IMC without brass bands, though they by no means dominated. The Congress planners had come up with a wonderfully diverse, balanced program.

Brass bands were certainly not the only types of SA music making showcased. The other traditional 'sections' included songster brigades (choirs) from Australia, Korea, New Zealand, and Zimbabwe, though each of these groups offered music unique to their own region of the world as well as much new non-Army music. Timbrel brigades from Australia and the Congo ran a similar gamut of styles and music chosen, from SA marches to native dances. In

Snapshots from the International Millennial Congress, held in Atlanta, 2000.

The Canadian Staff Band (Bandmaster Brian Burditt) in enthusiastic mood!

Bandmaster Richard Holz conducts the USA Southern Territorial Band.

Guest soloist Robert Childs, is congratulated by Bandmaster Stephen Cobb and Hendon Band (UK), following an outstanding performance at the Congress.

This picture of the New York Staff Band (Bandmaster Ronald Waiksnoris)
performing in the CNN Building lobby captures some of the
atmosphere of the International Millennial Congress.

Guests from the UK, Hendon Band,
with Bandmaster Stephen Cobb.

addition, a wide range of vocal, instrumental, and keyboard soloists were featured at various venues. Among the more recent 'gospel art' forms that use music, mimo, dramatic sketches, and sacred dance also added powerful new examples, although the concerns raised in Chapter 10 about how little SA musical sources are used for these demonstrations, and how heavily commercial Contemporary Christian Music is embraced were confirmed.

That trend continued in all the official Youth sessions where NO brass band, to my knowledge, saw the light of day. Instead, "praise and worship" bands, gospel choirs, steel drum bands, several excellent chamber-size all-male vocal groups, and assorted 'contemporary' ensembles were the order of the day. The decision to exclude brass bands from youth programs must be viewed as a calculated, symbolic decision, and in my opinion, a misguided one.

On a more positive, inclusive note, some of the more colourful indigenous ensembles like the Indonesia Bamboo Band, Papua New Guinea Cultural Dancers, and Pakistan Folk Dance Group were on display at various meetings.[2] Throughout the Congress the 'broadway' style musical of choice was not, as one would have expected, a revival of a Gowans and Larsson hit, but the late-60's American rock show, *Godspell*. The IMC did have something for everyone and for every musical taste.

Here I must interject my own studied, and know doubt biased opinion, about the successful use of brass bands throughout the Congress. In the united sessions each 'duty' band became the glue that held the diverse services together. The best congregational singing was that undertaken with brass band accompaniment, whether on traditional songs and hymns or with new praise-and-worship anthems and choruses. This proved again what a great tool brass band accompaniment is in SA worship. Their back-up accompaniments of vocal soloists, timbrel drills, or even a few dramatic mime or dance offerings were so much more compelling than much of the canned music used for some presentations.

In fairness to the latter, that still seems an unavoidable aspect of their practice until such time as more is done to work out cooperative efforts. Above all, ministry through well-chosen music, music of rich design and thought-provoking content, was a hallmark of the contributions made by these five brass bands. The objective musical observer would no doubt have noticed the relatively high level of musical sophistication evident in the 'traditional' brass band offerings. Yet within those pieces the arrangers and composers had blended much of the new in worship material with 'classic' processes.

New Music for Brass Bands

A representative sample is given below of new (by which I mean written within 2—4 years preceeding the IMC) brass band scores featured at the IMC either in a united session or at one of the many small-scale musical festivals held throughout the five days:

> *An American Journey* (Jim Cheyne); Southern Territorial Band
> *Ad Optimum* (Peter Graham); New York Staff Band
> *Caprice for Cornet* (William Himes); Chicago Staff Band
> Cornet Trombone Duet: *Freedom* (Dorothy Gates); Southern Territorial Band
> *Parakletos* (Robert Redhead); Canadian Staff Band
> *Renaissance* (Peter Graham); Hendon Corps Band
> *Truth Aflame* (Kevin Norbury); New York Staff Band

While there are several large-scale works here that exceed ten minutes in length (for example, Cheyne's symphonic suite, *An American Journey*, based on "How Firm a Foundation"), the majority did not exceed eight minutes. This reinforces Peter Graham's comments shared earlier in this study in which he now keeps the length of his new SA pieces to just under eight minutes, a wise choice when confronting the average person's attention span. Several of the bands added video shows to these works as a further enticement, some of which were a successful enhancement, some of which were a distraction.

Two works, both presented at the IMC by the New York Staff Band with the aid of videos, clearly represent some of

*From the Bengal,
Bands of the Army
take on many guises!*

The Ladies' Flute Band from Andra Pradesh, India.

Congo-Brazzaville Territorial Band was created in 1960 by Major Besson (a French missionary officer). It now has 35 members and proves very effective for worship and evangelism, as well as ecumenical and government events. The present bandmaster is André Sensa Malanda.

The Brass Band at Kerala, India accompanies the congregational singing.

the most recent trends in SA composition and arranging: *Truth Aflame* and *Ad Optimum*. Both works may be described as symphonic overtures of dramatic scope and power. Each articulate large-scale ABA forms in which the middle, or B portion, moves at a slower pace and takes a more reflective stance. The musical language chosen is that of eclectic 20th-century neoclassicism—everything from neotonal sonata process to jazz and rock stylistic inflections. The musical—semantic arguments are easily followed, the emotional—expressive aspects, captivate and engage the listener throughout.

In, *Truth Aflame,* Kevin Norbury takes the late 19th-century SA song (words by William Booth) "Thou Christ of Burning, Cleansing Flame, Send the Fire!" as the central idea, a song of spiritual empowerment and renewal. He chose to develop two contrasting settings of this Holiness anthem. The first is a recent "praise-and-worship" style rock setting (music by Lex Loizides) that appears as the secondary subject of the initial exposition. The second, the slower moving, more lyrical congregational tune used by Salvationists for nearly 100 years, called, *Tucker* after the author of the music (Frederick Booth-Tucker), appears in the developmental B section.[3] Fragments of both tunes provide, along with some original music, the basis of the symphonic argument. The composer portrays in sound a central doctrine of the church, the power of the Holy Spirit to inspire and guide the believer into all Truth.

Peter Graham selected three songs for *Ad Optimum* ("To the Highest"), a work in which he pays tribute to the 'high' purposes, motivations, and intentions of SA music and its bands: to glorify God and proclaim the Christian gospel.[4] The opening notes of his own vocal piece, *In the Name of Jesus,* serve as the uniting motive, the energetic rising line heard at the onset. The entire song appears in the softer, subdued middle of the work. This is surrounded in the faster sections by the hymn tunes, *Laudes Domini* ("When Morning Guilds the Skies ... May Jesus Christ be Praised!") and *Richmond* ("O For a Thousand Tongues to Sing My Great Redeemer's Praise"). The latter sounds out in augmentation in the concluding bars, accompanied by swirling reiterations of the unifying motive from, *In the*

Name of Jesus.

In both the Graham and Norbury compositions the programmatic content and emotional zeal are intentional. They are compositions following William Booth's injunction to go beyond mere performance. Their authors speak with fervor to the heart of the listener messages of hope, joy, and love. These are readily accessible works, though their structure reveals polish and depth of musical thought. Such musical craft harnessed to the fundamental mission of SA brass music portends well for the future of SA music.

A Leadership Crisis

Another positive element of the IMC showed that there was some support at high administrative levels for the SA's traditional music program as well as the emerging 'gospel arts'. This came in the form of a series of Music Leadership Training Seminars held over two days during the period of the Congress. It has been clearly recognized that the greatest need at present in SA music worldwide is for trained, dedicated lay leaders. Most of the seminars were supported by one of the official congress musical ensembles that served as demonstration groups for the lectures given. The following list cites all the instrumental, vocal/choral and gospel arts seminars offered.

Brass Band Seminars

Teaching Beginners *(Richard Holz)*
Youth Band and Ensemble Rehearsal Techniques
    (Brian Burditt)
Brass Ensemble Scoring/Introduction to Band
    Scoring *(Ronald Holz)*
Advanced Instrumental Rehearsal Technique
    (Stephen Cobb)
Advanced Orchestration *(William Himes)*

Choral Vocal Seminars

Children's Chorus/Youth Chorus Resources and
    Techniques *(Graeme Press)*
Basic Song Writing: Lyrics and Music
    (William Himes)

Advanced Choral Rehearsal Techniques
(Beatrice Holz)
Advanced Choral Composition *(Peter Ayling)*

Gospel Arts and Combined Effort Seminars

Developing a Worship Team *(Donna Peterson)*
Don't Forget the Children *(Brad Bonner)*
Basic Acting *(Chad Schnaar)*
Music and Worship Resources for Today's Corps
(John Mathias)
Worship Evangelism *(Peggy Thomas)*

Some of these sessions were quite technical in nature and therefore only appealed to a smaller audience. Several, however, drew larger crowds of interested delegates. The main point to make here is that these sessions helped set up or reinforced already existing, international contacts, relationships, and networking that is enabling excellent materials the SA has produced for its musicians to not only be distributed, but also to be understood and used wisely. The pool of trained music leaders must be increased if the SA music program is to survive into the next few decades. These sessions were certainly a step in the right direction.

Finding the Common Ground

The SA has relied for more than a century on the spiritual, emotional, and intellectual renewal that comes from gatherings of this sort. This particular congress departed from all other international congresses, by far, in the degree to which non-Army elements played major roles in program content. There is no question that the more open, less isolationist stance of the SA in recent years has been of great benefit, the brass band scene being just one example of where the removal of long-standing barriers is bearing positive fruit. Yet the all-persuasive presence of non-Army music in most of the new gospel arts presentations should sound alarm bells for anyone concerned about the SA music continuing to be unique and distinctive.

Throughout the IMC General John Gowans led his troops with rare humor, wit, and with a vulnerable, open demeanor. He joked about uniform styles and yet it is a divisive issue for some. He joked about musical styles and yet is as an issue that also divides. He knows that a complex organization like the SA needs its diversity, needs to exult in its regional and national differences, as well as personal, social, and aesthetic preferences. He also knows that the SA faces its greatest challenge in maintaining its identity as a unique part of the church universal.

Perhaps an understanding of the history of the collaborative efforts of Gowans and his right hand man, then Chief of the Staff Commissioner John Larsson [later General of the SA], point a way towards common ground in the SA's diverse musical culture. Their pace setting musicals caused controversy at first, but are now an accepted part of Army practice.

Why is this so? One explanation is that what they wrote included a careful blend of the traditional and the untraditional musically, dramatically, and poetically speaking. The shows were intended or had the effect, at least in part, to unite a certain alienated element with the mainstream Army youth, both as participants and as members of the intended audience.

In the matter of a generation their musical songs had become popular SA congregational hymns. They became accepted by a wide consensus. One of the most powerful moments at the IMC was the time when the five combined brass bands joined together Sunday morning at the conclusion of the prelude music with what is now an SA anthem, "For Thine is the Kingdom", from the first musical, *Take-Over Bid*. Gowans and Larsson songs have been used in all manner of SA brass band arrangements: overtures, suites, festival arrangements, even in tone poems. Therefore, new efforts in all the gospel arts, including the brass band, should be done in the context of ongoing SA practice, the new side by side with the traditional.

The Congress did provide, at times, a model for this blend. Above all, the SA must avoid a polarization of its musical forces. Handled correctly, what has been achieved in SA brass bands and their music over the past century and a quarter can become a guidepost for the basis by which all music endeavors may similarly flourish.

In this context, I saw the awarding of the Order of the Founder to Staff Bandmaster William Himes during the final Sunday morning service of the Congress, as a welcome, symbolic act and for two primary reasons. In recognizing someone who has given his life and considerable creative talent to Christian service within the ranks of the SA, it broke new ground in the selection of a relatively young, professional-employee soldier (when compared with the bulk of recipients of this highest order given to a Salvationist). William Himes is precisely the kind of versatile musician the SA needs; he sees the merits of all kinds of good music, musical styles and combinations; he then masters them for effective ministry.

In Bill's song, *All That I Am*, the humble submission of skill and talent to Divine Will is emphasized as the heart of any undertaking in Christian mission. As I recall the many thousands of delegates singing this song all these reflections and speculations about SA bands, in fact all SA ensembles and their music get set in the right context: *Accept and use, Lord, as You would choose Lord, right now today.*

Bandmaster William Himes of the Chicago Staff Band receives the Order of the Founder from General John Gowans and Commissioner Giselle Gowans, July 2nd 2000.

Notes

1 Bands were chosen by an IMC committee from recommendations received from various territories around the world. These territories had to commit to the complete funding of any participating band. Many territories in the more affluent nations gave substantial funds to assist in the expenses of many of the musical groups from poorer nations. Whether the five bands chosen were the most representative ones could, of course, be the subject of endless, and perhaps pointless, debate.

2 Interestingly, all these types of groups participated in the united sessions, as well, though unfortunately, I must stress that no brass band played at the youth programs.

3 *Tucker* stands for Commissioner Frederick Booth-Tucker, son-in-law to General William Booth. Curiously, this music first appeared as a piece of "Funeral Music" arranged for mixed instrumental ensemble in the *Musical Salvationist* before it became wedded to the text!

4 *Ad Optimum* is the motto of the Enfield Citadel (UK) Band and Graham in his score notes pays tribute to the legacy of Bandmaster James Williams and that band, models of excellence with the right focus. Williams recently received the MBE award at the Queen's Birthday Honours List for services to the brass band movement and to the Salvation Army. A performance under Williams' baton of Leidzén's, *None Other Name,* at Star Lake Musicamp, 1985, provided the initial inspiration. Graham also shares that the spirit of Eric Ball also pervades the work. Quite a symbolic package: two of the greatest SA composers, one of the finest bandmasters.

Index of Bands and Personalities

Photograph Acknowledgements

Page i. SA International Heritage Centre; p.*iii*. SA Heritage Centre; p.*iv* Holz Collection; p.*xi* Robin Bryant; p.*xv* Holz Collection; p.33 (top) Robin Bryant; p.33 (bottom) Robin Bryant; p.34 (top) Canadian Staff Band; p.34 (bottom) Chicago Staff Band; p.35 (top) Robin Bryant; p.35 (bottom) Emily Coles; p.36 (top) Holz Collection; p.36 (bottom) Robin Bryant; p.42 Goldspink Collection; p.45 Robin Bryant; p.53 Robin Bryant; p.64 SA Heritage Centre; p.66 David Wooton; p.80 Music Ministries, London; p.83 American *War Cry*; p.90 Reading Citadel Band; p.92 Music Ministries; p.98 and p.99 Music Ministries; p.101 Holz Collection; p.103 Steadman-Allen Collection; p.112 and p.113 Richard Holz; p.130 SA Heritage Centre; p.134 Steadman-Allen Collection; p.140 and p.141 Music Ministries and Robin Bryant; p.146 Salvation Army Collectables; p.153 Mrs Norman Asher; p.158 Steadman-Allen Collection; p.159 Holz Collection; p.161 Heritage Centre; p.177 Robin Bryant; p.181 Cardiff Canton Band; p.183 Enfield Citadel Band; p.184 Robin Bryant; p.186 Brass Band World; p.197 Bristol Easton Band; p.200 Norwich Citadel Band; p.201 Polyphonic; p.203 Derby Central Band; p.205 Stotfold Band; p.206 Gloucester Band; p.209 Chelmsford Band (John Farrar); p.210 (top) Croydon Citadel Band; p.210 (centre) Robin Bryant; p.210 (bottom) Sunderland Millfield Band; p.221 Canadian *War Cry*; p.224 Wally L Court; p.226 Canadian *War Cry*; p.227 and 228 SA Collectables; 229, 232 and 233 Canadian *War Cry*; p.235 SA Collectables; p.237 Holz Collection; p.238 Robin Bryant; p.240 Canadian *War Cry*; p.246 (top) Canadian *War Cry*; p.246 (bottom) Wally L Court; p.248 London Citadel Band; p.250 Robin Bryant: p.251 Wally L Court; p.257 (top and bottom) Torgny Hanson; p.258 Wally L Court; p. 260 and 261 Svensk Festmusik; p.262, 263, 264, 266, 267, 268 and 271 Torgny Hanson; p.336 Barrie Gott; p.337 John Cleary; p.346, 351, 363 and 374 Warren Baas; p.378 USA Central Museum; p.381 Michael Orfitelli; p.384 (top) American *War Cry*; p.384 (bottom) Heritage Centre; p.385, 386, 387, 388 and 393 Holz Collection; p.394 W Bearchell; p.395, 397, 399, 400, 401, 404 and 406 Holz Collection; p.409 Manchester Citadel Band, USA; p.410 Holz Collection; p.413 Bill Gordon; p.417 Norridge Citadel Band, USA; p.420 (bottom) Holz Collection; p.421 Chicago Staff Band; p.434 Robin Bryant; p.441 Japan Staff Band; p.446 Richard Holz; p.455, 456 and 459 The Salvation Army IHQ; p.461 Kenneth Downie; p.469 Richard Holz; p.470 (top) Emily Coles; p.470 (bottom) Richard Holz; p.473 and 474 The Salvation Army IHQ; p.479 Richard Holz.

Whilst every effort has been made to credit the copyright owners of photographs printed in *Brass Bands of The Salvation Army*, the publisher wishes to apologise for material that may have, inadvertently, not been acknowledged. The publisher would also like to thank the many people who submitted illustrations and photographs for reproduction in this book and would like to acknowledge the kind help and assistance received from The Salvation Army and SA Collectables.